Rob van Driesum

Rob grew up in several Asian and African countries before moving to the Netherlands, where he finished school in The Hague and studied modern history at the University of Amsterdam. He lived in a canal house on Reguliersgracht for 11 years, studying and working as a history teacher, bartender and freelance journalist to finance his motorcycle travels. A motorcycle journey around the world was cut short in Australia, where he worked as a labourer, flower salesman, truck driver and motorcycle magazine editor before joining Lonely Planet to help set up its range of Europe titles. He is now Lonely Planet's publisher in charge of books on Europe, the former Soviet Union, Australasia and bits of the Americas. Though firmly ensconced in Melbourne, which he considers an ideal place to live, he still thinks of Amsterdam as 'home' and an ideal place to visit.

From the Author

It's very difficult to research and write this sort of book while holding down a full-time job, and I don't think it can be done without help from others. I wish to thank the following people: David Stanley, for laying the groundwork with lists of worthwhile establishments; Doekes Lulofs, for hospitality, many tips and last-minute checking; Reinier van den Hout, for tips and advice; the good folk at Unica, for enthusiastic support and invaluable advice; Jules Marshall, for information on digital media and last-minute checking; the COC's media officer, Sjoerd Beumer, for information on gay & lesbian Amsterdam; Robbert Tilli, for information about the Amsterdam music scene; Els Wamsteeker from the NBT, for help beyond the call of duty; Charlotte van Beurden and Ans Schrijer from the Amsterdams Historisch Museum, for help with illustrations; Dani Valent, for last-minute checking; Georgina Perry from LP's UK office, for transport details from the UK; and Sacha Pearson from LP's US office, for flight details from the USA.

Some of the information in this book was adapted from the Netherlands chapter in *Western Europe on a shoestring*, written by Leanne Logan & Geert Cole.

I'm also indebted to my colleagues at Lonely Planet's Melbourne office, who covered for me while I was away in Amsterdam and tolerated the frequent days and afternoons I spent writing; and in particular to my editor, Suzi Petkovski, and cartographer, Rachel Black, who accepted my delays and disordered material with tact and good humour. Last but certainly not least, a heartfelt thanks to Liesbeth Blomberg for putting up with my physical and mental absence.

From the Publisher

This 1st edition of *Amsterdam* was edited at the Lonely Planet head office in Melbourne by Suzi Petkovski, with help from Paul Harding. Rachel Black navigated her way through countless canals in producing the maps, with assistance from Anthony Phelan, and then steered the project through layout. Tamsin Wilson lent her flair to the illustrations, as did Louise Klep, who also contibuted to the mapping. Steve Womersley and Matt King were the eagle-eyed checkers. Sharon Benson produced the index and the

Uranus unit added the crowning touch with the cover.

Warning & Request

Things change – prices go up, schedules change, good places go bad and bad places go bankrupt. Nothing stays the same. So, if you find things better or worse, recently opened or long since closed, please tell us and help make the next edition even more accurate and useful.

We value all of the feedback we receive from travellers. Julie Young coordinates a small team who read and acknowledge every letter, postcard and e-mail, and ensure that every morsel of information finds its way to the appropriate authors, publishers and editors.

Everyone who writes to us will find their name in the next edition of the appropriate guide and will also receive a free subscription to our quarterly newsletter, *Planet Talk*. The very best contributions will be rewarded with a free Lonely Planet guide.

Excerpts from your correspondence may appear in new editions of this guide; in our newsletter, *Planet Talk*; or in the Postcards section of our Web site – so please let us know if you don't want your letter published or your name acknowledged.

Contents

Introduction

Amsterdam is a work of art, a living monument with some of Europe's finest 17th and 18th century architecture. It's also at the cutting edge of social, cultural and economic developments thanks to its famed tolerance, which brings together people, ideas and products and allows them to flourish.

There's a lively arts scene, fantastic pubs and unrivalled nightlife. Gays and lesbians find the city a breath of fresh air. Affordable restaurants serve food from all corners of the globe. Street artists – musicians, acrobats, fire-eaters – provide ready entertainment. Open-air markets sell anything from food and flowers to funky clothes, disused furniture and 78rpm records, and myriad shops full of quirky items line side streets and alleyways.

Despite the ready availability of sex and drugs there's surprisingly little violent crime. Whoever made this whole affair work has done a great job.

Amsterdam has often been called the Venice of the north, and in many respects the comparison is apt. Venice occupies a lagoon, Amsterdam a marshland on the margin of sea and river, and both have had to struggle with water in order to survive (Venice has 117 islands, 150 canals and 400 bridges; Amsterdam has 90 islands, 160 canals and 1281 bridges). Both were city-states that built far-flung maritime trading empires and had a ruling class with strongly republican sentiments, whose wealth rested not on inherited property but on money created through commerce and finance. Both left a world-class legacy in visual arts.

There are marked differences too: Venice has no road traffic – only pedestrians and a large fleet of busy water craft; Amsterdam has 550,000 bicycles, too much road traffic and, apart from tourist boats, no water transport to speak of. Venice is an architectural marvel full of tourists, but in the off season

AMSTERDAMS HISTORISCH MUSEUM

The Herengracht on the corner with Leidsegracht, painted in 1783 by Isaak Ouwater.

the place seems dead; Amsterdam is equally attractive and full of tourists, but in the off season it keeps powering along. In short, Amsterdam is a thriving city that's alive in all respects; Venice is a museum with relatively little to sustain itself in the modern age.

The phrase 'cosmopolitan melting-pot' is often used carelessly for cities around the world but it is particularly appropriate for Amsterdam, which has traditionally enticed migrants and nonconformists. Despite (or because of) this transient mix, people accept each other as they are and strive to be *gezellig*, a nigh-untranslatable term that means something like 'companionable', 'chummy' or 'convivial', a mood often experienced by people warmly chatting over a drink or two in a cosy 'brown' café.

The whole city is *gezellig* – buildings are intimate, attractive (very rarely imposing), and pleasantly balanced by tree-lined canals and scattered parks (Amsterdam is Europe's greenest capital city). Everything seems designed on a human scale.

The city is also compact and easily explored on foot, with frequent and efficient public transport to get you to and from the central canal belt.

The rest of the country is compact too, and is serviced by an efficient train network. Within an hour you can walk along the beach or through magnificent dunes; explore old fishing villages along the IJsselmeer; visit small but proud cities such as Haarlem, Leiden or Delft; admire Europe's most beautiful sculpture garden in the forested Hoge Veluwe national park; shop along the refined streets of The Hague; tour the largest harbour in the world at Rotterdam; or cycle through endless, brightly coloured fields of blossoming bulbs.

On trips such as these you'll realise that Amsterdam is unique even within the Netherlands, with a mix of old and new, moral rectitude and sleaze, and traditional and alternative cultures that visitors both Dutch and foreign find baffling and delightful.

This book provides background reading, advice and tips, but a lot of things happen in Amsterdam that guidebook researchers can't always know about. Go out and discover the place for yourself: in this regard few cities are more rewarding.

Facts about Amsterdam

HISTORY
Birth of the City

The oldest archaeological finds in Amsterdam date from Roman times, when the IJ (pronounced as the 'ey' in 'they'), an arm of the shallow Zuiderzee or 'Southern Sea', formed part of the northern borders of the Roman Empire. Coins and a few artefacts betray human presence but there is no evidence of settlement.

This is not surprising because most of the region that later became known as Holland (in the west of the present-day Netherlands) was a soggy land of constantly shifting lakes, swamps and spongy peat lying at or below sea level. Its contours kept changing with fierce autumn storms and floods. This was certainly the case where the Amstel river emptied into the IJ – the site of what was to become Amsterdam.

Isolated farming communities gradually tamed the marshlands with ditches and dykes. Between 1150 and 1300 the south bank of the IJ was dyked all the way to the north of Haarlem. Dams were built across the rivers flowing into the IJ, with locks to let water out and boats in. Around 1200 there was a fishing community known as 'Aemstelredamme' – the dam built across the Amstel, at what is now Dam square.

The distant feudal authorities (the bishop of Utrecht and later the Holy Roman Emperor) cared little for these massive water-engineering feats and the ever-present threat of dyke-bursts. So the local inhabitants, under the tutelage of the count of Holland, set up a network of work-and-maintenance groups and pooled their resources against the common foe. This tradition of local democracy and pioneering self-help fostered notions of local autonomy and regard for individual opinions and contributions.

On 27 October 1275 the count of Holland granted toll freedom to those who lived around the Amstel dam, which meant they didn't have to pay tolls to sail through the locks and bridges of Holland. This event stands as the official founding of Amsterdam. The town had obviously become important in the count's power struggle with the bishop of Utrecht, and soon it received city rights – the right to self-government and taxation. Shortly after 1300, the count incorporated the surrounding areas into Holland, severing Amsterdam's ties with the bishopric of Utrecht for good.

Early Trade

The city grew rapidly. Agriculture in this marshland was difficult at the best of times so fishing remained important, but trade provided new opportunities for growth. Powerful cities of the day, such as Dordrecht, Utrecht, Haarlem, Delft and Leiden, concentrated on overland trade to and from the burgeoning economies of Flanders and northern Italy. Amsterdam, however, focused on maritime trade in the North and Baltic seas, which was dominated by the Hanseatic League.

Using cheap timber from Germany and the Baltic regions, Amsterdam's wharves churned out cogs – broad-beamed merchant ships with a capacity of 100 tonnes, five times that of their predecessors. They revolutionised maritime trade and enabled the city to play a key role in the transit trade between Hanseatic cities and southern Europe. The toll freedom helped, too.

Instead of joining the League, Amsterdam's freebooters bypassed prominent Hanseatic cities such as Hamburg and Lübeck and sailed straight to the Baltic themselves, with cargoes of cloth and salt in return for grain and timber. Their efficient transport and acute business sense outclassed the intricate contracts and transport agreements of the Hanseatic merchants.

The Amsterdammers cooperated as their forebears had done when they fought the sea, pooling resources into firms that financed

St Andrew's Crosses & the Cog

Amsterdam's coat of arms consists of three St Andrew's crosses arranged vertically – a wonderfully simple design that is found on anything from VVV tourist brochures to the thousands of brown 'penises' (so-called *Amsterdammertjes*) that keep cars from parking on sidewalks. Its origins are unclear, though the St Andrew's Cross itself was a popular symbol in this part of the world before Amsterdam existed.

According to legend, a Norwegian prince on the run with a Frisian fisherman and his dog drifted around for days in their damaged boat before being blown into the reeds along the IJ, where they founded Amsterdam. When the city began to engage in Baltic trade it did so with cogs, ships of a late-medieval design known around Europe. The clinker-built (or lapstrake) vessels had a single mast, a rounded bow

and stern, fore and after castles and were very broad in the beam. They reduced the cost of transport to a fraction of what it had been with the smaller and less seaworthy ships used previously.

AHM

St Andrew's crosses, topped by the crown of Holy Roman Emperor Maximilian I.

AHM

The city authorities gave thanks to the cog by promoting a coat of arms (see left) that consisted of a cog with two men (a soldier and a merchant) and a dog (symbolising loyalty). This survived for several centuries, often depicted together with the St Andrew's crosses, but the crosses proved more durable. ∎

ships and spread risk by dividing large and valuable cargoes among several ships, thus enabling them to undertake audacious ventures without fear of losing everything in a single shipwreck. This novel form of cooperation was spectacularly successful: by the end of the 15th century, 60% of ships sailing to and from the Baltic Sea were from Holland, and the vast majority of these had Amsterdam as their base.

The original harbour in the Damrak and Rokin had been extended into the IJ along what is now Centraal Station. To cater for growing numbers of merchant warehouses, canals had been cut – in the 1380s the Oudezijds Voorburgwal and Oudezijds Achterburgwal, as well as the Nieuwezijds Voorburgwal and Nieuwezijds Achterburgwal (the present Spuistraat), then the Geldersekade and Kloveniersburgwal, and around 1500 the Singel. By then the population numbered 10,000. A great fire in 1452 destroyed three-quarters of the city, including most of the wooden buildings, but it was soon rebuilt, with regulations stipulating the use of brick.

Amsterdam started life as a 'modern' city, a place where skippers, sailors, merchants, artisans and opportunists from the Low Countries (roughly the present-day Netherlands, Belgium and Luxembourg) gained their livelihood through contacts with the outside world. There was no tradition of stable feudal relationships sanctioned by the Church, no distinction between nobility and serfs, and little if any taxation by some faraway monarch. In time, of course, class distinctions did develop based on wealth, with the so-called patricians at the top of the pyramid, but it's fair to say that Amsterdam society was more individualistic and protocapitalist than others in Europe.

Ironically, Amsterdam was also a city of religious pilgrimage, a 'Canterbury of the Low Countries' thanks to a banal but profitable religious miracle: in 1345 a dying man regurgitated the Host, which was thrown in the fire where it refused to burn. As a consequence, the city crammed no less than 20 monasteries into its confined space, and Holy Roman emperors such as Maximilian I and Charles V visited to pay their religious respects. In 1489 Maximilian recovered from an illness here and showed his gratitude by allowing the city to use the imperial crown on its documents, buildings and ships. The Reformation put an end to all this but Amsterdam never became as staunchly Protestant as the other cities of Holland – after all, diversity and tolerance were good for trade.

The Independent Republic

The northern European Protestant reform movement known as the Reformation was more than just a religious affair: it was a struggle for power between the emerging class of merchants and artisans in the cities on the one hand, and the aristocratic order sanctioned by the established – the 'universal', or 'Catholic' – Church on the other; between 'new money' earned through trade and manufacturing, and 'old money' rooted in land ownership.

The form of Protestantism that took hold in the Low Countries was Calvinism, the most radically moralistic stream. It stressed the might of God as revealed in the Bible and treated humans as sinful creatures whose duty in life was sobriety and hard work. It scorned Church hierarchy and based religious experience on local communities led by lay elders, similar to Presbyterianism in Scotland.

The Anabaptists

The city authorities promoted tolerance and diversity in the name of trade but ruthlessly persecuted the Anabaptists, a revolutionary Protestant sect of the early 16th century that was strong in Germany and the Low Countries. Anabaptists, influenced by the teachings of Ulrich Zwingli in Zürich, believed that people shouldn't be baptised until they knew the difference between right and wrong; they also believed in a form of communism that included polygamy, and sometimes walked around naked because everyone was equal that way. Martin Luther was appalled and advised his followers to join even with Catholics to suppress the movement.

Many Anabaptists fled from Germany to Amsterdam, where their ideas appealed to the city's artisans in a time of rising prices and stagnating incomes. Their political agenda – a communist state, ruled by the faithful – was fleetingly carried out in the German town of Münster in 1534-35 under the dictatorship of a Dutch tailor, John of Leyden, but the expected world revolution failed to materialise. In Amsterdam a group of naked Anabaptists occupied the city hall but were defeated by the city watch in a fierce battle. The survivors had their hearts ripped out and thrown in their faces – uncharacteristically harsh treatment in a city that punished other heretics, such as Lutherans, by making them take part in Catholic processions. Anabaptists, however, advocated the abolition of property and called for the overthrow of the state, and this was too much even for the tolerant Amsterdam authorities.

John of Leyden

An Anabaptist was last burned at the stake on Dam square in 1576, the symbolic end of Protestantism's radical fringe. The more moderate Baptists retained the principle of mature baptism but dropped the Anabaptists' revolutionary politics. ∎

Merchants & Burgomasters

The city government during Amsterdam's Golden Age was headed by four burgomasters, or mayors, who were elected for a one-year period on 1 February. Their power was almost unlimited, although judicial matters were handled by a *schout* (sheriff) and nine *schepenen* (magistrates) who were also elected for one-year periods. The electing was done by a *vroedschap* (council) of 36 *burgers* (citizens) who had to be consulted on important matters.

These officials and 'citizens' almost always came from the wealthiest merchant families, the so-called patrician class, who made sure they stayed in control through co-optation and nepotism and so cultivated a new aristocracy in all but name. Nevertheless, the division of power and the annual elections meant that a lot of politicking went on, with constantly shifting coalitions and factions, and government was probably as democratic as it could get in those days. It was also remarkably efficient and competent, at least until about 1700 when self-serving lethargy took over.

Order was upheld by several *schutterijen* (citizen militias) that were also dominated by patricians. Rembrandt's famous *Nightwatch* (a name later given to the painting because it had become so dirty) shows one of these militias in full regalia. ∎

Calvinism was integral to the struggle for independence from the fanatically Catholic Philip II of Spain, who, thanks to the inheritance politics of the day, had acquired the 17 provinces that made up the Low Countries and ruled them as if they were a South American colony. The trouble began in 1566 when a coalition of Catholic and Calvinist nobles petitioned Philip not to introduce the Spanish Inquisition in the Low Countries. Philip refused and the resulting war of independence lasted for more than 80 years.

Fanatical Calvinist brigands, who wore the disparaging nickname *geuzen* ('beggars') as a badge of honour, roamed from city to city, murdering priests, nuns and Catholic sympathisers and smashing 'papist idolatry' in the churches. Some took to the water as *watergeuzen* and harassed Spanish and other Catholic ships. Amsterdam was caught in the middle: its ruling merchants were pragmatic Catholics, but the merchants who weren't in power adopted Calvinism along with most of the population, who resented the heavy Spanish taxation imposed from Brussels. In 1578 the geuzen captured Amsterdam in a bloodless coup, the so-called Alteration.

With mighty Amsterdam now on their side, the seven northern provinces, led by Holland and Zeeland, formed the Union of Utrecht the following year and declared themselves an independent republic. The union was led by a stadholder (chief magistrate), a role played by William the Silent of the House of Orange, the forefather of today's royal family (dubbed 'the Silent' because he refused to enter into religious debate). The provinces were represented in a parliament, the Estates General, that sat in The Hague. The Seven United Provinces (the republic's official name) became known to the outside world as the Dutch Republic – or simply 'Holland', in view of that province's dominance. Within Holland, Amsterdam towered over the other cities put together.

The Golden Age (1580-1700)

Amsterdam's fortunes continued to rise when its major trading rival in the Low Countries, the Protestant city of Antwerp, was retaken by the Spaniards. In retaliation, watergeuzen from Zeeland closed off the Scheldt, which was Antwerp's access to the sea and its trade lifeline. Half the population fled, including the merchants, skippers and artisans who flocked to Amsterdam with trade contacts and silk and printing industries – the world's first regular newspaper, full of trade news from around Europe, was printed in Amsterdam in 1618.

Amsterdam also welcomed Jews from Portugal and Spain (some via Antwerp) who knew about trade routes to the West and East Indies. They also introduced the diamond

The Bank of Amsterdam

European money in the 16th century was in a mess. There were hundreds of different coins minted by states, cities and even individuals who sometimes tampered with the silver or gold content. The Amsterdam authorities realised that a stable, reliable currency was vital if trade was to flourish, and founded the Bank of Amsterdam in the cellars of the city hall in 1609.

The bank accepted coins in any currency from anyone, assessed their gold or silver content, and allowed the depositor to withdraw the equivalent amount in gold florins minted by the bank. A *gulden florijn* – hence, *gulden*, or guilder, and the abbreviation *f* or *fl* – was of fixed weight and purity, and was soon sought as 'real' money throughout Europe and beyond.

Depositors could also draw cheques against their accounts, which were guaranteed by the government, and take out loans at regulated interest rates. Amsterdam thus attracted capital far and wide, and remained the financial centre of Europe until the Napoleonic occupation, when London took over. ■

The *gulden florijn*, or gold florin, was a coin that meant something in Europe and beyond.

industry (fed by Brazilian diamonds) and made Amsterdam a tobacco centre. In later years there were Germans who provided a ready source of sailors and labourers; a new wave of Jews from Central and Eastern Europe; and a large influx of persecuted Calvinists from France, the enterprising Huguenots. Amsterdam had become a cosmopolitan city where money and pragmatism combined to pioneer new developments in the world economy.

Money reigned supreme and Amsterdam was not averse to trading with the enemy. Spanish armies were paid with money borrowed from Amsterdam banks and fed on Baltic grain imported through Amsterdam; wrecked Spanish fleets (such as the Armada) were rebuilt with timber supplied by Amsterdam merchants. Amsterdam shrewdly avoided land battles and was never raided by Spanish troops like so many other Dutch cities.

Meanwhile the city kept growing – in 1600 the population numbered 50,000, by 1650 it was 150,000 and from 1700 it stabilised at around 220,000. In the 1580s land was reclaimed from the IJ and Amstel to the east (the current Nieuwmarkt neighbourhood). Two decades later, work began on the famous canal belt that more than tripled the area of the city.

By 1600, Dutch ships dominated seaborne trade between (and often along) England, France, Spain and the Baltic, and had a virtual monopoly on North Sea fishing and Arctic whaling.

Meanwhile, Portugal and Spain built trading empires beyond Europe. Some of this trade flowed to Amsterdam through the port of Lisbon until Spain conquered Portugal in 1580 and closed Lisbon to Dutch ships. Thanks to Jewish refugees, however, Dutch mariners learned something about distant trade routes and soon they plied the world's oceans, acquiring navigational intelligence of their own.

They searched in vain for an Arctic route to the Pacific and rounded the tip of South America instead, naming it Cape Horn after the city of Hoorn north of Amsterdam. In 1619, Dutch traders expelled the Portuguese from the Moluccas (the so-called Spice Islands) in what is now Indonesia, and established the town of Batavia (Latin for Holland, now Jakarta), the administrative centre for what was to become the Dutch East Indies. Five years later they founded a trading post on Manhattan Island called New Amsterdam, the future New York. They set up posts along the west coast of Africa, established plantations in South America and the Caribbean, and took a keen interest in the slave trade.

The Dutch competed with the Spaniards for control of Formosa (Taiwan) and gained the upper hand there in 1641. That year Japan expelled all foreigners except the Dutch, who received sole trading rights on an island at Nagasaki, perhaps because their ambitions were more clearly mercantile than territorial. In 1652 they captured the Cape of Good Hope from the Portuguese, a crucial staging post in trade with the East Indies, and established one of the few colonies to attract Dutch settlers in significant numbers (the only colony where Dutch language and culture persist to this day). They booted the Portuguese out of Ceylon (Sri Lanka) soon after. They also explored the coastlines of New Zealand (named after the province of Zeeland) and New Holland (known as Australia since the 1850s) but found nothing of value there.

The Dutch were traders first and foremost and didn't have the population reserves for the settler-type colonisation pursued by other European powers. Their arrival was often welcomed by local rulers who had suffered the missionary and imperial zeal of earlier colonists. Dutch traders consolidated their settlements with divide-and-rule tactics, bribery, gunship diplomacy and, where necessary, mercenary forces recruited locally. They also engaged in piracy, especially against the Spaniards, with whom they were theoretically at war until the Peace of Münster, one of the treaties comprising the Peace of Westphalia in 1648.

These overseas ventures were financed by merchants and other investors who pooled their resources in trading companies: the United East India Company (Vereenigde Oostindische Compagnie, or VOC), founded in 1602, which pursued trade in India and the Far East; and the West India Company (WIC, 1621), which ran plantations in the Americas and soon controlled half the world's slave trade.

AMSTERDAMS HISTORISCH MUSEUM

Procession of the Lepers, Dam Square, painted by Adriaen van Nieulandt in 1633. Pictured from left to right are the old city hall, the Nieuwe Kerk, the Weigh House (demolished by Napoleon's brother king), and the Damrak with small freighters drying their sails. The procession, an annual event to gather donations, was last held in 1603.

The First Multinationals

The United East India Company (VOC) and West India Company (WIC) were the world's first multinationals. Their trading posts around the globe operated with a great degree of autonomy. They were authorised to negotiate with local rulers on behalf of the Dutch Republic, to pursue trade opportunities as they saw fit, to build forts and to raise local militias. More than 1000 shareholders back home – not only merchants but also artisans, clergy, shopkeepers and even servants – contributed capital for ships and trade ventures, thus spreading risk and reaping rewards through generous annual dividends when risks paid off.

The VOC was founded to coordinate the often competing trade efforts of cities in Holland and Zeeland. It consisted of six 'chambers' representing Amsterdam, Middelburg, Delft, Rotterdam, Hoorn and Enkhuizen, and was supervised by 17 directors (the Heeren XVII, or '17 Gentlemen') on behalf of the shareholders. Because of the high degree of risk and long turnaround times in trade with India and the Far East, the VOC's shareholders

Logo of the United East India Company.

tended to be people with capital to spare – usually wealthy merchants based in Amsterdam, who owned more than half the VOC's capital.

The WIC consisted of five 'chambers' supervised by 19 directors. Trade in the Atlantic was less risky and had shorter turnaround times, but offered a lower rate of return. The WIC attracted small investors, particularly in Zeeland. Competition from Spain and Portugal (and later Britain and France) was fierce, and the WIC's expenditures often outstripped income. The company relied on state subsidies to conquer and defend its sugar plantations and slave ports, and was thus more truly colonial than the VOC. As with the VOC, more than half the WIC's capital was owned in Amsterdam, but there was more internal bickering and jealousy between Holland and Zeeland.

Wealthy merchants preferred the comforts of home to the dangers of tropical trading posts, so VOC and WIC employees came mainly from the poorer strata of society and were almost always underpaid. Left to their own devices and with minimal supervision (there was no colonial ministry to oversee and coordinate them), they were easily tempted to pursue personal gain. Penalties were harsh but rarely enforced, and shrewd operators amassed great personal fortunes in the course of glittering careers. ■

Despite the glamour of these expeditions and the exotic products that became commodities back home (coffee, tea, spices, tobacco, cotton, silk, porcelain), most of Amsterdam's wealth was still generated by the mundane fishing industry and European trade. In the 1590s Amsterdam's shipwrights introduced the flûte (from the Dutch *fluyt*), a small supply vessel that could be sailed by 10 people instead of the 30 required for ships of similar size – perfect for coastal freight. Around 1650 the Dutch had more seagoing merchant vessels than England and France combined, and half of all ships sailing between Europe and Asia were Dutch.

It still seems a bit of a mystery why tiny Amsterdam played such a prominent role on the world stage (Venice at the height of its power was merely a dress rehearsal by comparison) but several factors helped. Both England and France were embroiled in internal troubles, and Spain was far too busy managing its overstretched colonial empire. Meanwhile, Dutch freight was unrivalled in terms of cost and efficiency thanks to a combination of cheap Baltic hemp and timber, Europe's largest shipbuilding industry, abundant investment capital supplied by thousands of shareholders, and low wages for sailors, many of whom had small farming plots north of Amsterdam.

England, however, began to flex its muscle and in 1651 passed the first of several Navigation Acts: goods shipped to England and its colonies had to be carried in English ships, or ships of the country where the goods originated. This posed a serious threat to the Dutch transit trade, and the two countries fought

Republicans & Monarchists

Contrary to the European trend, the Netherlands started life as a republic and became a monarchy less than 200 years ago. The Dutch Republic was a loose federation of autonomous provinces dominated by cities, with almighty Amsterdam determining foreign policy and influencing most other things the weak central government did.

Amsterdam's role was similar to that played by Athens among the ancient Greek city-states, except that there was no 'Sparta' to act as a counter-balance. There was, however, the stadholder, the chief magistrate of the Republic and the military leader of the revolt against Spain. After William the Silent's assassination the mantle passed to his son, who in turn passed it on to his, thus laying the foundations for a monarchy under the House of Orange. This was not to the liking of the patricians of Amsterdam who had established their own oligarchy based on trade wealth and were not about to have this taxed by some monarch.

William the Silent

Dutch politics between 1580 and 1800 see-sawed between the republican (and 'pacifist', pro-business) sentiments of Amsterdam's ruling elite and the monarchistic, militaristic aspirations of the House of Orange. The latter faction was often supported by the poorest classes of society and the many cities who were keen to keep 'arrogant' Amsterdam in its place. In 1673, in the midst of war against France, the provinces (with the sole exception of Holland) voted to make the office of stadholder hereditary in the House of Orange, but Amsterdam's influence was strong enough to keep the state a republic until Napoleon installed his brother as king in 1806.

Under French occupation the provinces became a unitary state with Amsterdam as its capital. In 1813 the French left, and in 1814 William VI of Orange was proclaimed King William I of The Netherlands in Amsterdam's Nieuwe Kerk. ∎

several naval wars that were generally inconclusive, though the Dutch lost New Amsterdam. Louis XIV of France took the opportunity to march into the Low Countries, where he occupied the Spanish provinces in the south and three of the seven republican provinces in the north during what was known as the 'Disaster Year' of 1672.

The Dutch rallied behind their stadholder, William III of Orange, who repelled the French with the help of Austria, Spain and Brandenburg (Prussia). A consummate politician, William then supported the Protestant factions in England against their Catholic King James II, who was to all intents and purposes in Louis XIV's employ. In 1688 William invaded England, where he and his wife, Mary Stuart (James II's Protestant daughter – the plot thickens), were proclaimed king and queen. From then on, England played a key role in checking France's expansion on the Continent. It is ironic that the military leader of the Dutch Republic, denied a throne at home because of Amsterdam's opposition, became king of a foreign country and thus ensured the Republic's survival.

Wealthy Decline (1700-1814)

The dramatic events in the second half of the 17th century stretched the Republic's resources to the limit, and its naval heroism made way for peace at all costs – a combination of neutrality and bribery. The Republic didn't have the human resources to keep meeting France and England head-on but at least it had Amsterdam's money to keep them at bay and ensure freedom of the seas. Money became more important than trade as merchants began to invest their fortunes more securely, often in the form of loans to foreign governments.

MAP 1

Dutch Republic c. 1610

0   25   50km

1635 - Year of land creation (polder)

Leeuwarden   Groningen

FRIESLAND

DRENTE

Afsluitdijk (1932)

1847

1930

1599

Enkhuizen

Alkmaar   Hoorn

1631

1635

Zuolle

1612

Zuiderzee

OVERIJSSEL

IJ

Haarlem   Amsterdam

1852

GELDERLAND

NORTH

Leiden

SEA

The Hague

Utrecht

Delft

UTRECHT

Rotterdam

ZEELAND

Middelburg

Breda

BRABANT

Antwerp

Ghent

SPANISH

FLANDERS   NETHERLANDS

Maastricht   Cologne

Brussels

HOLLAND

RICHARD NEBESKY

Amsterdam's coat of arms

ROB VAN DRIESUM

Stained-glass windows in the Oude Kerk

MAP 2

Western Islands

Volewyck

IJ

Amsterdam in the 17th Century

0   0.5   1 km

Western Canal Belt

Medieval City

Dam

Rokin

Damrak

Eastern Islands

Southern Canal Belt

Amstel

City around 1500
additions to 1520
additions to 1613
additions 1613-25
additions 1625-1700

RICHARD NEBESKY

The replica of the *Amsterdam* moored alongside the Scheepvaartmuseum

The result in the 18th century was stagnation. Gone were the heady days of daring sea voyages to unknown lands, of new trading posts and naval expeditions against the Spaniards, of monumental achievements in art, science and technology, of pioneering forms of government and finance. The cosmopolitan melting-pot of Amsterdam, where everything was possible if it turned a profit, became a lethargic place where wealth creation was a matter of interest rates. It was still the wealthiest city in Europe and Dutch freight was still the cheapest, but the 17th century eagerness to conquer the world was gone. Harbours such as London and Hamburg became powerful rivals.

The decline in trade brought poverty to those without money in the bank, among them many Jews who had escaped pogroms in Germany and Poland – between 1700 and 1800, the proportion of Jews in Amsterdam's population increased from 3% to 10%. To compound matters, the 18th century brought a mini ice age over Europe, with exceptionally cold winters that made for colourful paintings of skating scenes but also hampered transport and led to serious food shortages. The winters of 1740 and 1763 were so severe that some Amsterdam residents froze to death and many suffered thirst – the canals doubled as sewers and clean water supplies from elsewhere had come to a halt.

The ruling patrician class became ever more corrupt and self-centred, and there was intense political bickering between patricians, Orangists (monarchists) and a new-generation middle class with enlightened ideals, the so-called Patriots.

Amsterdam's rulers naively supported the American War of Independence, resulting in a British blockade of the Dutch coast followed by British conquests of Dutch trading posts around the world. The West India Company folded in 1791, and the mighty East India Company, which once controlled European trade with Asia, went bankrupt in 1800.

Amsterdam's patricians eventually allied themselves with Orangists against the Patriots, who had become emboldened by the American example and were ever more vocal in their democratic demands. A Patriot coup in Amsterdam in 1787 was put down by Prussian troops who had come to the aid of William V of Orange. By now, Amsterdam's leadership of the Dutch Republic was over.

In 1794, French revolutionary troops invaded the Low Countries and marched straight across the frozen rivers that should have formed a natural barrier. They were accompanied by exiled Patriots who helped the French install a Batavian Republic, transforming the fragmented 'united provinces' into a centralised state with Amsterdam as its capital.

In 1806 this republic became a monarchy when Napoleon nominated his brother Louis Napoleon as king. In 1808, the city donated the grand city hall on Dam square, symbol of the wealth and power of the merchant Republic, as a palace to the new king. Two years later Napoleon dismissed his uncooperative brother and annexed the Netherlands into the French Empire.

Britain responded to Napoleon's conquests by blockading the Continent and occupying the Dutch colonies on behalf of William V. Napoleon in turn prohibited all trade with Britain and tried to make the Continent self-sufficient with France as its hub – the so-called Continental System. Amsterdam's trade, already in decline, came to a complete halt along with its important fishing industry. Dutch society turned to agriculture and Amsterdam became a local market town.

After Napoleon's defeat at Leipzig in 1813, the French troops left Amsterdam peacefully. William V had died in exile, but his son returned to Holland and was crowned King of the Netherlands in the Nieuwe Kerk in 1814. The city hall became the new king's palace and has remained with the House of Orange ever since. The Britons returned the Dutch East Indies but kept the Cape of Good Hope and Ceylon. Amsterdam's seaborne economy recovered only slowly from Napoleon's disastrous Continental System and Britain now dominated the seas.

New Infrastructure (1814-1918)

The new kingdom included present-day Belgium which fought for its independence in 1831. Apart from this incident, Amsterdam in the first half of the 19th century was a sleepy place. Its harbour had been neglected, and the sand banks in the IJ, which were always an obstacle in the past, proved too great a barrier for modern ships; Rotterdam was set to become the country's premier port.

Things began to look up again as the rail system took shape – the country's first railway, between Amsterdam and Haarlem, opened in 1839. Major infrastructure projects were funded by the notorious 'culture system' in the East Indies – forced, large-scale production of tropical crops for export, overseen by the VOC and WIC's successor, the Netherlands Trading Society. Trade with the East Indies was now the backbone of Amsterdam's economy, although the North Sea Canal between Amsterdam and IJmuiden, built between 1865 and 1876, and later the Merwede Canal to the Rhine (expanded into the Amsterdam-Rhine Canal after WWII) also allowed the city to benefit from the industrial revolution at home and in Germany.

The harbour was expanded to the east. The diamond industry boomed after the discovery of diamonds in South Africa. Amsterdam again attracted immigrants and its population, which had declined in the Napoleonic era, doubled in the second half of the 19th century, passing the half-million mark by 1900. Speculators hastily erected new housing estates beyond the canal belt – dreary tenement blocks, shoddily built and with minimal facilities.

In 1889 the city was literally cut off from its harbour by the massive Centraal Station, built on a series of artificial islands in the IJ. Commentators at the time saw this as the symbolic severing of Amsterdam's ties with the sea. An open waterfront was no longer considered vital to the city's survival, and in the closing years of the 19th century some of its major waterways (Damrak, Rokin, Nieuwezijds Voorburgwal) and smaller canals were filled in, both for hygienic reasons (after several cholera epidemics) and to allow for increased road traffic. Plans to fill in more canals were shelved amid mounting criticism of 'ostentatious boulevards'.

The Netherlands remained neutral in WWI but Amsterdam's trade with the East Indies suffered from naval blockades. There were riots over food shortages, exacerbated by refugees from Belgium, but on the whole things could have been worse. Some soldiers, impatient to be decommissioned, mutinied in November 1918. There was even an attempt to extend the socialist revolutions in Russia and Germany to the Netherlands but this was quickly put down by loyalist troops.

Boom & Depression (1918-1940)

After the war Amsterdam remained the country's industrial centre, with a wide range of enterprises that fed each other. Its shipbuilding industry was no longer the world leader, but the Dutch Shipbuilding Company still operated the world's second-largest wharf and helped carry an extensive steel and diesel-motor industry.

The harbour handled tropical produce that was finished locally (tobacco into cigars, copra into margarine, cocoa into chocolate – Amsterdam is still the world's main distribution centre for cocoa).

In 1920 the KLM (Koninklijke Luchtvaart Maatschappij – Royal Aviation Company) began the world's first regular air service, between Amsterdam and London, from an airstrip south of the city and bought many of its planes from Anthony Fokker's aircraft factory north of the IJ. There were two huge breweries, a sizable clothing industry, and even a local car factory that produced the venerable Spijker. The 1920s were boom years for Amsterdam, crowned by the Olympic Games hosted in 1928.

The population kept growing until it reached 700,000 in the mid-1920s, still the figure today. The city had already begun expanding north of the IJ, with housing projects for harbour workers and dockers in the new suburb of Amsterdam Noord. Now it also expanded southwards, filling in the area between the Amstel and what was to become the Olympic Stadium.

Unfortunately the world depression in the 1930s hit Amsterdam hard. Unemployment rose to 25% and would have risen further if the East Indies hadn't borne the brunt of the misery. Labour party members, who dominated the city council, resigned in protest at public-service salary cuts, and the conservative, spend-nothing national government of Hendrik Colijn (the Herbert Hoover of the Netherlands) had free reign.

Public-works projects such as the Amsterdamse Bos (a recreational area south-west of the city) did little to defuse mounting tensions between socialists, communists and the small but vocal party of Dutch fascists. The fascists' influence on national politics was negligible, though they gained a few seats in the Amsterdam council elections of 1939 and had strong support among colonists in the East Indies. Amsterdam received some 25,000 Jewish refugees from Germany, although a shamefully large number was turned back at the border because of the Netherlands' neutrality policies.

WWII (1940-1945)
The Netherlands tried to stay neutral in WWII but Germany had other plans and invaded in May 1940. For the first time in almost 400 years the population of Amsterdam experienced the grim realities of war first-hand. Few could believe that things would turn nasty, and when the German occupiers began to introduce anti-Jewish measures they did so in a series of carefully staged small steps. Local police and public servants cooperated. In February 1941 Amsterdam's working class finally came out in force to support their Jewish compatriots in a general strike led by dockworkers, but the strike was soon put down and by then it was already too late.

Only one in seven Jews in the country survived the war; in Amsterdam, however,

only one in 16. It was the highest proportion of Jews murdered anywhere in Western Europe, though this sad fact was effectively whitewashed after the war by Anne Frank's diary which created the impression that Amsterdam hid its Jews. Anti-Semitic feeling was not particularly strong among the Dutch and they never cared much for fascism; but the ingrained – some would say 'Calvinist' – ethos of order and propriety told them to shun the futile grand gesture, to retreat within the privacy of their homes and mind their own business in order to survive.

The Germans cultivated such compliance by treating the country relatively leniently at first, strengthening people's hopes that things would be all right if they avoided trouble – and if they ignored the plight of the Jews. The resistance movement, set up by an unlikely alliance of Calvinists and Communists, only became large-scale when the increasingly desperate Germans began to round up able-bodied men to work in Germany, thus shattering the sanctity of home and family.

The severe winter of 1944-45 became known as the winter of hunger. The Allies had liberated the south of the country but were checked at Arnhem and decided to concentrate on their push into Germany, thus isolating the north-west and Amsterdam. Coal shipments from the south ceased, men aged between 17 and 50 had gone into hiding or worked in Germany if they had no dispensation, public utilities ground to a halt, and the Germans began to plunder anything that could help their war effort. Dark, freezing Amsterdam suffered severe famine and thousands died. In May 1945, at the very end of the war in Europe, Canadian troops finally liberated the city.

Postwar Growth (1945-1962)
The city's growth resumed after the war, with US aid (through the Marshall Plan) and newly discovered fields of natural gas compensating for the loss of the East Indies, which became independent Indonesia after a four-year fight. The focus of the harbour moved westwards, towards the widened

North Sea Canal that had provided access to the sea since the 1932 completion of the Afsluitdijk – the 30-km-long barrier dam between North Holland and Friesland that closed off the Zuiderzee and turned it into the IJsselmeer (IJssel Lake). The long-awaited Amsterdam-Rhine Canal opened in 1952.

Massive apartment blocks arose in areas annexed to the west of the city – Bos en Lommer, Osdorp, Geuzenveld, Slotermeer and Slotervaart – to meet the continued demand for housing, made ever more acute by the demographic shift away from extended families. The massive Bijlmermeer housing project (now called the Bijlmer) to the south-east of the city, begun in the mid-1960s and finished in the early 1970s, was built in a similar vein.

The Cultural Revolution (1962-1982)
In the early 1960s Amsterdam began to undergo a cultural revolution that would last for 20 years and would often serve as a beacon for similar developments abroad. It was fuelled by the interaction between a conservative established order and tolerance (but not necessarily love) of alternative views, and the tradition of incorporating such views into the structure of society.

Over the past 80 years Dutch society had become characterised by *verzuiling* ('pillarisation'), a social order sanctioned by the 1917 'Pacification' compromise in which each religion and/or political persuasion achieved the right to do its own thing, with its own schools, political parties, trade unions, cultural institutions, sports clubs etc. Each of these groupings represented a separate pillar that supported the status quo in a general 'agreement to disagree'. What seemed like an elegant solution to a divided society in the 19th and early 20th centuries became stifling in a modern society where the old divisions were increasingly irrelevant. In the 1960s people began to question the status quo and the pillars came tumbling down.

Provos & the 'Magic Centre' The first group to rattle the structure were the Provos, whose playful 'happenings' elicited sense-

less police reprisals that polarised public opinion and led even the older generation to wonder whether this was what they had stood for during the war.

Provos were at the centre of public protests against the wedding on 10 March 1966 of Princess Beatrix and the congenial German diplomat Claus von Amsberg, who had served in Hitler's army. The princess insisted on getting married in Amsterdam, against the advice of the mayor. In spite of massive security precautions a live chicken was hurled at the royal coach, smoke bombs ignited as the procession made its way along Raadhuisstraat, and bystanders chanted 'my bicycle back' – a reference to the many bikes commandeered by German soldiers in the final months of the war. Scuffles and police charges were beamed out live on TV.

The following June, Provos supported construction workers in a violent strike in which one of the workers died of a heart attack. The resulting political fallout led to the dismissal by the national government in The Hague of Amsterdam's chief of police and later the mayor himself.

As society broke out of its prewar framework, Amsterdam became the 'Magic Centre' of Europe, an exciting place where anything was possible. The late 1960s saw an influx of hippies smoking dope at the National Monument on Dam square, unrolling sleeping bags in the Vondelpark, and tripping in the nightlife hot spots of Paradiso, Fantasia and the Melkweg.

It was also a time of upheaval in the universities, with students demanding a greater say and, in 1969, occupying the Maagdenhuis on Spui square, the administrative centre of the University of Amsterdam. The women's movement took hold: the Dolle Minas ('Mad Minas', after the radical, late 19th century Dutch feminist Wilhelmina Drucker) began a *Baas in eigen Buik* ('Boss in own Belly') campaign that fuelled the abortion debate throughout the 1970s.

Kabouters The Provos disbanded in 1967, but their representative in the city council,

Provos

The Provos, successors to the beatniks, awoke Dutch society from its slumber in the 1960s. Their core consisted of a small group of anarchic individuals who staged street 'happenings', or creative, playful provocations (hence the name). Misguided and disproportionately harsh police reprisals made the general public uneasy about the established order.

In 1962 a self-professed window cleaner and sorcerer, Robert Jasper Grootveld, began to deface cigarette billboards with a huge letter 'K' (for *kanker*, cancer) in order to expose the role of advertising in addictive consumerism by the *klootjesvolk* ('narrow-minded populace'). He held get-togethers in his garage – dressed as a medicine man and chanting anti-smoking mantras under the influence of pot – which attracted other bizarre types, such as the poet Johnny van Doorn, aka Johnny the Selfkicker, who bombarded his audience with frenzied, stream-of-consciousness recitals; Bart Huges, who drilled a hole in his forehead – a so-called 'third eye' – to relieve pressure on his brain and attain permanently 'expanded' consciousness; and Rob Stolk, a rebellious, working-class printer, whose streetwise tactics came to the fore when the get-togethers moved to the streets.

In the summer of 1965 the venue of choice was the rather appropriate *Lieverdje* ('Little Darling') on Spui square, the endearing statuette of an Amsterdam street-brat that had been donated to the city by a cigarette company. The police, unsure of how to deal with 'public obstructions' by excited youngsters chanting unintelligible (and indeed often meaningless) slogans around 'medicine man' Grootveld, responded the only way they knew: with the baton and arbitrary arrests.

The pub terraces lining the square were a favourite haunt of journalists, resulting in eyewitness accounts of senseless police brutality against kids having fun. Soon it seemed the whole country was engaged in heated debate for and against the authorities. The generation gap was only part of it: many of the older generation, uneasy about how little had changed after the war, came out in favour of the Provos and could not understand why the authorities had so completely lost the plot.

Throughout 1965 and 1966 the Provos maintained the initiative with a series of White Plans to protect the environment, including the famous White Bicycle Plan to tackle the city's traffic congestion with a fleet of free white bicycles. They symbolically donated a white bicycle that was promptly confiscated by the police. But the creative anarchists at the heart of Provo were horrified to admit that their movement showed all the signs of becoming a political party (to their surprise they even won a seat in the municipal elections of 1966), and with a ceremony involving a coffin they buried Provo in the Vondelpark in the summer of 1967. ■

The *Lieverdje* (Little Darling) on Spui square, an appropriate focus for campaigns by the Provos against addictive consumerism.

Roel van Duijn, kept alive their concerns about urban congestion and pollution.

The Provos' successors called themselves *kabouters* (gnomes), after the helpful, bearded gnomes of Dutch folklore. In 1970 they proclaimed an Orange Free State on Dam square, an alternative city populated by caring people preoccupied with the environment. In the elections that year they won five seats in the Amsterdam city council and

several more in other cities. Kabouter idealism soon fell victim to the grim realities of urban politics, but many of their ideas – such as banning cars from the city centre and the desirability of an inner city where people could live, work and shop – became widely accepted.

In the early 1970s, while city planners were still preoccupied with vast apartment blocks in the suburbs populated by commuters who worked in offices and banks in the city centre, the public mood was shifting. A projected motorway from Centraal Station via the IJ-Tunnel to the south-east – the wide Weesperstraat and Wibautstraat are ugly reminders – was stopped by public protests from intruding any further into the city.

Metro & Nieuwmarkt The fiercest conflict between arrogant planners and disaffected Amsterdammers involved the metro line through the Nieuwmarkt neighbourhood. The original plans for the huge Bijlmermeer housing project south-east of the city called for a four-line metro network, though this was eventually whittled down to a single line between the Bijlmermeer and Centraal Station. The available technology did not yet allow tunnelling through swampy ground, and a large portion of the derelict Nieuwmarkt had to be razed so caissons could be lowered. The inhabitants, many of them former Provos and kabouters who had settled there as *krakers* (squatters), refused to leave and turned the area into a fortress. The Nieuwmarkt was eventually cleared with much violence on 'Blue Monday', 24 March 1975. Some 30 people were injured, most of them policemen, and it was surprising that no-one was killed.

The Nieuwmarkt episode was a watershed: in the following years the council set about renovating inner-city neighbourhoods and providing new housing in the heart of the city. Nieuwmarkt itself was rebuilt, not with the planned office complexes and luxury apartments but with affordable council houses. The metro opened in 1980, with wall paintings in Nieuwmarkt station commemorating the events five years earlier.

Squatters Meanwhile families still deserted the city and the demographic balance continued to shift towards the elderly and the young – small households with modest incomes whose housing needs outstripped the council's efforts to meet them. The housing shortage fuelled a speculative trend, particularly within the desirable canal belt, which pushed free-market rents – let alone

the cost of buying a house – out of reach of the average citizen. The waiting period for a council apartment was anything up to five years.

Many young people saw squatting as the only solution, and buildings left empty by speculators (or assumed speculators) provided an appropriate target. Existing legislation made eviction difficult, giving rise to the phenomenon of *knokploegen*, or 'fighting groups' of tracksuited heavies sent by owners to evict squatters by force. The squatters of the late 1970s, however, represented a new generation, less ideologically or politically motivated than their predecessors and more prepared to defend their personal needs with barricades and a well-organised support network.

In February 1980 police evicted squatters from an empty office at Vondelstraat 72. Hundreds of squatters re-took the building and erected street barricades that were eventually cleared by tanks fitted with bulldozer blades. A few months later, on 30 April, Queen Beatrix was crowned in the Nieuwe Kerk and the squatting movement vented its anger with a large demonstration that soon got out of hand. Literally everyone who was out on the streets that day had tears in their eyes – not for joy over the coronation but from tear gas that hung thick in the air. The term 'proletarian shopping', a euphemism for looting, entered the national lexicon. Never before or since has Amsterdam experienced rioting on such a scale.

In the following months and years several famous squats made world headlines, but the movement was weakened by internal power struggles and became more and more isolated. 'Ordinary' Amsterdammers, initially sympathetic towards exposure of the housing shortage, became fed up with violent riots, such as the three-day rampage (complete with burning tram) that followed the clearing of the 'Lucky Luyk' villa in the Jan Luyckenstraat in October 1982. Law-abiding citizens who had waited years for council accommodation watched squatters jump the queue and grab choice apartments. Such squatters often reached rental agreements with the owners or were bribed to leave peacefully; sometimes the council bought the building so the squatters could stay with subsidised rents. By the mid-1980s the movement had little or no outside support and was all but dead. Squatting still takes place now, but the rules of the game are clear and the mood is less confrontational.

New Consensus

Twenty years after the first Provo 'happenings' on Spui square, Amsterdam's cultural revolution had run its course. Gone were the days of unbridled growth for growth's sake, of autocratic government, of arrogant planners and grandiose housing schemes in distant suburbs, of motorways and parking garages in the heart of the city, of demolition of old neighbourhoods. A new consensus had arrived, epitomised by the labour party mayor, Ed van Thijn. The ideals were decentralised government through neighbourhood councils; a livable city with work, schools and shops within walking distance; a city no longer strangled by cars; renovation rather than demolition; friendly neighbourhood police on hybrid bikes; a practical, non-moralistic approach towards drugs; and legal recognition of homosexual couples.

Thanks to this new consensus, the opening of the combined city hall and opera house in 1986 passed relatively peacefully, although opposition had been all but peaceful when it was planned and built. This monstrosity, dominating the Amstel waterfront at what used to be the heart of the Jewish quarter on Waterlooplein, had attracted much criticism for its size and hybrid design. Opponents dubbed it the Stopera – pronounced 'stowpera', a contraction of *stadhuis* (city hall) and opera, and of 'Stop the Opera' – and the name has stuck.

As the city entered the calm 1990s it had changed beyond recognition. Families and small manufacturing industries, which dominated city neighbourhoods in the early 1960s, had been replaced by tertiary-sector professionals and a service industry of pubs, 'coffee shops', restaurants and hotels. The ethnic make-up had changed too: Surinam-ese, Moroccans, Turks and Antillians, once a small minority, now comprise 25% of the population.

The harbour, fifth-largest in Europe, has a new lease of life with petrochemical industries and container transhipment. Schiphol airport is booming and running out of space to expand. The eastern harbour areas are being transformed into much-hyped and overpriced housing estates, and new office towers are rising to the south-east and west of the city beyond the completed ring freeway. Even the metro network is back on the agenda, with new technology allowing tunnelling through swampy ground (at this stage just a line from Noord through the city to the south).

Tourists keep flocking to the city – only London, Paris and Rome attract more of them in Europe. But the lack of affordable tourist accommodation shows that the city's most pressing problem remains its housing shortage.

GEOGRAPHY

Much of the land around Amsterdam is *polder*, land that used to be at the bottom of lakes or the sea. It was reclaimed by building dykes across sea inlets or across rivers feeding lakes, and pumping the water out with windmills, and later with steam and diesel pumps. Polders were created on a massive scale: in this century for instance, huge portions of the former Zuiderzee (now the IJsselmeer) were surrounded by dykes and the water was pumped out to create vast swathes of flat and fertile agricultural land – the complete province of Flevoland, north-east of Amsterdam, was reclaimed from the sea.

For more on water management, see Cleaning the Canals in the following Ecology & Environment section.

Sea Level & NAP

It is said that most of Amsterdam (and indeed more than half the country) lies a couple of metres below sea level, but what is sea level? This varies around the globe, and even the average level of the former Zuiderzee, in the lee of Holland, was slightly lower than that of the North Sea along Holland's exposed west coast. A display in the Stopera, in the arcade between the Muziektheater and City Hall (near the Waterlooplein metro exit), shows the ins and outs of NAP (Normaal Amsterdams Peil – 'Normal Amsterdam Level' or Amsterdam Ordnance Datum), established in the 17th century as the average high-water mark of the Zuiderzee. This still forms the zero reference for elevation anywhere in the country and is also used in Germany and several other European countries.

Water in the canals is kept at 40 cm below NAP and many parts of the city lie lower still. Touch the bronze knob as you walk down the stairs and you'll realise the importance of all those dykes. Three water columns represent the sea levels at IJmuiden and Flushing (Vlissingen), and the highest level reached in the disastrous floods in 1953 that led to the extensive Delta Works in the province of Zeeland. Pamphlets in Dutch, English, French, German and Spanish explain the details.

The water in the canals is about three metres deep but residents reckon you can deduct a metre for mud and another metre for discarded bicycles. People have indeed received nasty cuts from falling into the water.

Peat & Piles

Amsterdam, that big city, is built on piles/And if that city were to fall over, who would pay for it? – Dutch nursery rhyme

Amsterdam sits on a mixture of spongy peat and clay resting on a stable layer of sand more than 12 metres down. The first wooden houses were simply placed on top of the peat and occasionally had to be raised as they sank. When heavier brick and stone replaced wood, engineers perfected the art of driving wooden piles down to the sand layer, sawing off the protruding ends to equal height and erecting buildings on top of the stable foundation – there are 13,659 piles under the palace on Dam square alone!

So long as the piles were completely submerged in ground water and air couldn't get to them, they wouldn't rot, but ground-water levels varied a bit and problems were unavoidable. Also, less scrupulous builders didn't always use enough piles, drive them deep enough or worry about piles that snapped in the process, and many old buildings show signs of unequal subsidence – very expensive to fix. Since WWII, concrete piles have been used: they cannot rot and can be driven deeper – 20 metres into the second sand layer, or even 60 metres into the third.

CLIMATE

Amsterdam has a temperate maritime climate with cool winters and mild summers. Precipitation is spread pretty evenly over the year, often in the form of endless drizzle, though it tends to fall in short, sharp bursts in the spring months of March to May. May is a pleasant time to visit: the elms along the canals are in full bloom and everything is nice and fresh.

The sunniest months are May to August, and the warmest are June to September. Indian summers are common in September, which can be an excellent time to visit, though some people find the summer months uncomfortable due to the high relative humidity. Blustery autumn storms occur in October and November.

December to February are the coldest months with occasional slushy snow and temperatures around freezing point. Frosts usually aren't severe enough to allow skating on the canals, but when they are, the city comes alive with colourfully clad skaters. If there's a decent cloak of snow to add a serene

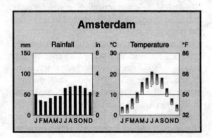

white setting, you couldn't wish for better photo material.

ECOLOGY & ENVIRONMENT

Foreign visitors in the past commented on residents obsessively scrubbing stoops and cleaning windows. The spotless houses stood in stark contrast to smelly, filthy canal water and foul air thick with smoke from coal and peat fires.

Today's young residents are less obsessed with cleaning their houses and some catering establishments can seem a bit shabby – dirty even. The canals are a lot cleaner though (see the following section), and environmentally friendly natural gas has cleared the air. Industrial pollution is kept firmly in check with some of the strictest regulations in the world. Even the visual pollution of thousands of TV antennas has disappeared now that almost all households are hooked up to cable TV.

The inner city has also become a much more pleasant place for pedestrians thanks to the council's *autoluw* ('car-abatement') policies. Until the mid-1980s the canal belt was choked by traffic jams and cars parked on pavements, but the number of parking spaces is strongly curtailed now and cars are actively discouraged. A slim majority of residents supported these policies in a landmark referendum (with a disappointing 28% turnout) in 1992.

One environmental problem persists, however: Amsterdam is still the dog-shit capital of the world, even though owners are compelled to steer pooch to the gutter and have to carry a spade and bag on their daily walk. Amsterdammers love dogs, which is nothing new: Japanese artists used to depict Dutchmen with dogs. They keep them in great numbers, cooped up in 3rd-floor apartments, and will stand up for their mutt's right to do whatever it damn well likes on its daily sniff around the block.

Greenpeace supporters will be interested to know that the international head office (☎ 523 62 22) is at Keizersgracht 176; the Dutch branch (☎ 626 18 77, information on

☎ 422 33 44) is in the same complex at Keizersgracht 174.

Cleaning the Canals

Until the 1980s the canals doubled as sewers and had to be flushed daily. Before the 17th century the water level in the canals was regulated by locks leading into the IJ, and sea water was allowed into the canals at rising tide and back out again as the tide dropped. This made the canal water brackish and led to a backup of filth in the Amstel. From 1674 the Amstelsluizen in front of today's Carré Theatre allowed flushing to occur with fresh water from the Amstel, a vast improvement. Maids protested that they would lose their jobs, since they wouldn't have to clean windows and stoops as often.

With the opening of the North Sea Canal in the 19th century and the completion of locks at Schellingwoude at the mouth of the IJ, the IJ was cut off from tidal influences. The solution, used to this day, was to pump water from the Zuiderzee (later IJsselmeer) into the canals, since WWII by means of a huge pumping station on the artificial island of Zeeburg opposite Schellingwoude. Locks on the west side of the city were left open so water could flow out into the North Sea Canal, taking canal filth with it. This was released into the North Sea at low tide (or pumped out if necessary), completing the hydraulic system.

Until the mid-1980s the Zeeburg station pumped 600,000 cubic metres of water each night, the equivalent of 300 swimming pools. Now that all households are connected to sewerage pipes (except for 2500 house boats), the pumps are turned on twice a week in winter and four times a week in summer. When the Amstel is in flood, or westerly storms increase water levels in the North Sea Canal, the pumps at Zeeburg are reversed and water is pumped out of the canals into the IJsselmeer.

The canal water is relatively clean these days, despite its dirty appearance and occasional algal blooms. Oxygen levels are healthy and many fish species have returned, though you still wouldn't want to drink it.

The council employs seven boats to collect flotsam – anything from old fridges, dolls, handbags and bits of driftwood to discarded bicycles (about 10,000 a year). Three dredges slowly work their way around the 100 km of canals, completing the circuit every 10 years. The polluted sludge they dredge up is processed in special facilities in the Jan van Riebeeckhaven.

FLORA

An aerial photo of Amsterdam in summer creates the impression of a huge park. Indeed, if you include the gardens that one rarely sees from the street, the centre of Amsterdam has more trees per sq km than any other capital city in Europe. The canals used to be lined with linden trees but they were replaced by elms in the 18th century, chosen for their light leaf cover that allows daylight to filter into the houses. The Dutch elm disease is so named because local arborists have done much research into this beetle-induced fungus that first entered the country in the 1920s.

The city has many pleasant parks with an amazing variety of species. The Hortus Botanicus at Plantage Middenlaan is justly famous, but the Vondelpark, Artis zoo and the Amsterdamse Bos also hold much of interest, as do smaller local parks such as the Sarphatipark and Oosterpark. And when it comes to flowers, where do you start? Try March or April, when bulbs (tulips, hyacinths and daffodils) burst into bloom everywhere, from parks to narrow nature strips along busy roads.

FAUNA

There are some 35 mammal species in the city. The mole and wood mouse are the most common park inhabitants, along with rabbits and hares a bit further from the city centre. Rats are fairly common too, especially the water vole and brown rat. At dusk you might spot the occasional bat, especially the dwarf bat that inhabits city buildings. The most common indoor mammal is of course the house mouse. The black rat and otter, which used to be common in and around Amsterdam, are now presumed to have disappeared from the city.

Sparrows, thrushes, swifts and crows are common birds here as elsewhere in Europe, and in some parts of the city you might wonder whether any other birds exist besides feral pigeons. The canals are favoured by mallards, coots and the occasional heron, swan or grebe, and in water areas around the city you'll see herons, cormorants and coots. Black-headed gulls (with white heads in winter) seem to be everywhere, supremely adapted to this windswept, coastal habitat.

The only two reptile species known to exist in Amsterdam are the harmless grass snake, which is becoming rare, and the sand lizard, which is on the verge of extinction. You might spot an occasional red-cheeked turtle but it will always be a released pet – the North American import can't reproduce in this climate. Prevalent amphibians are the common newt, the common toad, the brown frog and various species of green frog.

There are about 60 fish species in Amsterdam waters. The habitat varies from fresh (the canals) to salt (the deeper parts of the North Sea Canal, the western harbour area and parts of the IJ), with transitional, brackish zones. Many sea fish enter the North Sea Canal through the huge sluices at IJmuiden. One of the most interesting species is the eel, which survives in both fresh and salt water and is common in the city's canals, yet it would have been born from one of 20 million eggs laid by its mother at a depth of 250 metres in the Sargasso Sea off Bermuda! Bream is even more common in the canals, where it is outnumbered only by the roach. White bream, rudd, pike, perch, stickleback and carp also enjoy the canal environment.

There are 12 crustacean species in the waters in and around Amsterdam, of which the common shrimp and the epidemic import, the Chinese mitten crab, are the most common.

GOVERNMENT & POLITICS

The Greater Amsterdam area (population 1.3

million) consists of the City of Amsterdam (population 720,000), Almere, Amstelveen, Haarlemmermeer (Schiphol), Purmerend and Zaanstad. These municipalities established formal administrative cooperation in 1992, with integration under a single council scheduled for 1998, though the timing seems overly ambitious and will probably be modified by experiences with a similar setup in Rotterdam.

In the meantime, the City of Amsterdam's city council and municipal executive (consisting of the mayor and aldermen) oversee the city's 16 districts – each with their own district council and executive committee – and run the central city within the canal belt and the western harbour area. The 45 members of the council are elected every four years by all residents over 18 years of age, including foreigners who have been resident for at least five years. Council members elect the aldermen (currently seven) from their midst, but the mayor is appointed by the Crown (the queen plus the national government) for a period of six years. Mayor and aldermen divide the portfolios; the mayor is at least chief of police.

District councils and executive committees differ in size depending on the number of residents. They are elected in the same way as the city council, except that the chairman of each district is not appointed but elected by the district council. Districts serve residents in their daily lives, within guidelines laid down by the city council and municipal executive. Electricity, gas, water, sewerage, water management, health and public transport are handled by the central city administration.

Amsterdam has been a left-wing city ever since its residents achieved the vote. At the last council elections in 1994 the labour party (PvdA) won 14 seats, followed by the progressive liberals (D66) and conservative liberals (VVD) with eight each, environmental socialists (Green Left) with six, the anti-immigrant Centre Democrats with four, Christian Democrats with three, and finally the radical socialists (SP) and Greens (represented by the eternal Roel van Duijn) with one each. The

current municipal executive, which includes the appointed mayor (traditionally labour), is a coalition of four labour, two progressive liberal and two conservative liberal.

City politics are lively, with plenty of media coverage. Amsterdammers have strong opinions about their city and aren't reluctant to voice them. Burning issues include IJburg, a scheme that would see 15,000 residences on artificial islands in the shallows of the eastern IJ, which would wipe out wildlife in this ecologically sensitive area; and the persistent housing shortage with 50,000 house-hunters.

Land & Housing Policies

About 80% of land in the city is government-owned and is leased to private owners under 50-year leasehold arrangements (also 100-year leaseholds since 1991). Most land within the canal belt, however, is freehold (ie owned privately in perpetuity), though any freehold land acquired by the government is converted to leasehold. A leasehold is only granted when a property developer has an end user lined up, which keeps speculation in check and ensures that supply meets demand.

A whopping 40% of city real estate is government-owned, and is either rented out or used for government purposes; of the remaining 60% in private hands, only one-tenth is owner-occupied and the rest is rented out. Rents are strictly controlled, unless the property is so up-market that it jumps the hurdle into the free-market category. There are also strict controls on the number of rooms a household can occupy, regardless of whether the dwelling is rented or privately owned.

There are about 2500 house boats with 6000 people moored along the canals. These converted barges began proliferating with the first acute housing shortage in the 1950s, but rules have been tightened and the only way you can live on a boat these days is to buy an existing one. An average boat in the older parts of Amsterdam costs up to f200,000, which includes f50,000 for the spot (a similar two-bedroom apartment costs f250,000-plus). Owners pay f500-1000 a year in tax, for which they receive garbage service and connections to gas, electricity and water. It might seem romantic to live on a boat, but it can get cold and damp in winter and maintenance bills are high.

ECONOMY

Until about 25 years ago Amsterdam was the industrial centre of the Netherlands, a role it had played since the industrial revolution of the mid-19th century. In the 1960s and 1970s, however, the city's worsening congestion and environmental constraints forced many industries to move to parts of the country where industrial conditions were more relaxed. This caused great hardship among employees who were too old to reskill or relocate, but the city bounced back as it reinvented its historical role as a centre of trade, finance and services.

The main economic activities in the Greater Amsterdam area can now be divided into four categories employing roughly equal numbers of people: manufacturing and crafts; commerce, tourism and finance; administration; and science and arts. Tourism generates a turnover of f2 billion a year and employs 6% of the workforce.

The harbour is still the fifth-largest in Europe and Schiphol airport is the fastest growing – the third-largest in terms of freight and fourth-largest in terms of passengers. Less well known is the fact that the Dutch control about 40% of European road freight and many of these trucking companies are based in Amsterdam. The government has devoted massive subsidies to office complexes to the west, south and south-east of the city. This, coupled with a highly skilled, multilingual workforce and easy-going tax laws, has prompted many multinationals to establish their European headquarters here in time for the single European market.

The city remains the undisputed financial capital of the country and a major money centre in Europe. It holds the headquarters of the mighty ABN-AMRO banking group, the ING (Postbank) and the Nederlandsche Bank (the central bank), along with several other private banks and the offices of some 30 foreign banks. The European Options Exchange and the national stock exchange (the fourth-largest in Europe) add to the city's financial clout – 15% of the working population is employed in finance and related sectors.

Industry remains important in the corridor between Amsterdam and IJmuiden, particularly chemicals, petrochemicals and steel. Other important industries include aviation, cars and trucks, engine-building, clothing, paper and of course diamonds (industrial-grade). The country's major printers, including the national newspapers, are based south-east of the city. Amsterdam is also one of the world centres for the development of electronic media.

In spite of a strong base in the service economies of the future and a rock-solid currency, Amsterdam's economy is under continual strain from generous social security provisions. These include the blanket public pension scheme in a greying population, and welfare cheques of just over f1000 a month (after tax) guaranteed to every resident of working age who cannot find employment (a sum, by the way, that hasn't changed in 15 years). This problem exists in the national economy too, but Amsterdam is particularly hard hit because the majority of its population is either young or old. The proportion of welfare recipients is around 10%, down from 20% in the mid-1980s but still twice the national average.

POPULATION & PEOPLE

Amsterdam has an official population of 722,000 plus an estimated 20,000 unregistered ('illegal') residents. About 40% of the population is aged between 20 and 35; the proportion of elderly (60 years-plus) inhabitants is also relatively high. Children and middle-aged people are underrepresented compared with other Dutch cities.

Ethnic minorities make up about 30% of the population. In the mid-1970s, the granting of independence to the Dutch colony of Suriname in South America saw a large influx of Surinamese, who now number 68,000 and form the majority of the city's black population. In the 1960s, 'guest labourers' from Morocco and Turkey performed jobs spurned by the Dutch; they and their descendants now number 46,000 and 30,000 respectively. There are about 24,000 people from Indonesia, 19,000 Germans and 11,000 migrants from the Netherlands Antilles. Next in line are the Brits, with 7500. About 3700 Americans and 1000 Aussies also call Amsterdam home.

ARTS

Amsterdam has always been an international centre of the arts thanks to its tolerant and cosmopolitan spirit. It lacked a powerful court and wealthy Church – the usual art patrons elsewhere in Europe – but more than compensated for this with a large middle class that didn't mind spending a bit of money on art. Amsterdam achieved international renown in painting and architecture, and the current music scene is second to none. Unfortunately its impressive literary and theatrical traditions are less accessible to foreigners.

Painting

The distinction between Dutch and Flemish painting dates from the late 16th century, when the newly Protestant northern provinces of the Low Countries kicked out the Spaniards but couldn't dislodge them from the provinces in the south. Until then, most paintings in the Low Countries originated in the southern, 'Flemish' centres of Ghent, Bruges and Antwerp, and dealt with biblical and allegorical subject matter that was popular with the patrons of the day – the Church, the court and to a lesser extent the nobility.

Famous names include Jan van Eyck (died 1441), the founder of the Flemish School who perfected the technique of oil painting; Rogier van der Weyden (1400-64), whose religious portraits showed the personalities of his subjects; Hieronymus (or Jeroen) Bosch (1450-1516), with macabre allegorical paintings full of religious topics; and Pieter Breugel the Elder (1525-69), who used Flemish landscapes and peasant life in his allegorical scenes.

In the northern Low Countries, meanwhile, artists began to develop a style of their own. In Haarlem, painters were using freer, more dynamic arrangements in which people came to life. Jan Mostaert (1475-1555), Lucas van Leyden (1494-1533) and Jan van Scorel (1494-1562) brought realism into their works, modifying the mannerist ideal of exaggerated beauty. Around 1600 the art teacher Karel van Mander claimed that Haarlem was creating a distinctively Dutch style of painting.

In Utrecht, however, followers of the Italian master Caravaggio, such as Hendrick ter Bruggen (1588-1629) and Gerrit van Honthorst (1590-1656), made a much more fundamental break with mannerism. They opted for realism altogether and played with light and shadow, with night scenes where a single source of light created dramatic contrasts – the *chiaroscuro* ('clear-obscure') approach used to such dramatic effect by Caravaggio in Rome.

Golden Age (17th Century) Both these schools influenced the golden age of Dutch painting in the 17th century with its stars like Rembrandt, Vermeer and Frans Hals. Unlike earlier painters or some contemporaries, none of this trio made the almost obligatory pilgrimage to Italy to study the masters. Their work showed that they no longer followed but led – much like the young Republic that seemed to burst out of nowhere.

Artists suddenly had to survive in a free market. Gone was the patronage of Church and court. In its place was a new, bourgeois society of merchants, artisans and shopkeepers who didn't mind spending 'reasonable' money to brighten up their houses and workplaces with pictures they could understand. Painters rose to the occasion by becoming entrepreneurs themselves, churning out banal works, copies and masterpieces in studios run like factories. Paintings became mass products that were sold at markets among the furniture and chickens. Soon the wealthiest households were covered in paintings from top to bottom like wallpaper – carefully composed snapshots of a world that had ceased to be a mysterious place. Foreign visitors commented that everyone seemed to have a painting or two on the wall, even bakeries and butcher shops.

Artists specialised in different categories. There was still a market for religious art though this had to be 'historically correct' rather than mannerist, in line with the Calvinist emphasis on true events as described in the Bible. Greek or Roman historical scenes were an extension of this category. Portraiture, in which Flemish and Dutch painters had already begun to excel, was a smash hit in a society of middle-class upstarts brimming with confidence, though group portraits cost less per head and suited a republic run by committees and clubs. Maritime scenes and cityscapes sold well to the government, and landscapes, winter scenes and still lifes (especially of priceless, exotic flowers and delicious meals) were found in many living rooms. Another favourite in households was genre painting, which depicted domestic life or daily life outside.

These different categories may help visitors to the Rijksmuseum understand what they're looking at, but some painters defy such easy classification. **Rembrandt van Rijn** (1606-69), the greatest and most versatile of 17th century artists, excelled in all these categories and pioneered new directions in each. Sometimes he was centuries ahead of his time, as with the emotive brush strokes of his later works.

He grew up in Leiden as the son of a miller and was already an accomplished chiaroscuro painter when he came to Amsterdam in 1631 to run Hendrick van Uylenburgh's painting studio. Portraits were the most profitable line and Rembrandt and his staff (or 'pupils') churned out scores of them, including group portraits such as *The Anatomy Lesson of Dr Tulp* (1632). In 1634 he married Van Uylenburgh's Frisian niece, Saskia, who often modelled for him.

Rembrandt fell out with his boss, but his wife's capital helped him buy the sumptuous

Rembrandt van Rijn

house next door (the current Rembrandthuis) where he set up his own studio, with staff who worked in a warehouse in the Jordaan. These were happy years: his paintings were a success and his studio became the largest in Holland, though his gruff manners and open agnosticism didn't win him dinner-party invitations from the elite.

Rembrandt became one of the city's main art collectors and often sketched and painted for himself, urging staff to do likewise. Residents of the surrounding Jewish quarter provided perfect material for his dramatic biblical scenes.

In 1642, a year after the birth of their son Titus, Saskia died and business went downhill. Rembrandt's majestic group portrait, *The Nightwatch* (1642), was considered innovative by the art critics of the day (it's now the Rijksmuseum's prize exhibit), but the people in the painting had each paid f100 and some were unhappy that they were pushed to the background. Rembrandt told them where to push the painting and suddenly he received far fewer orders. He began an affair with his son's governess but kicked her out a few years later when he fell for the new maid, Hendrickje Stoffels, who bore him a daughter, Cornelia. The public didn't take kindly to the man's lifestyle and his spiralling debts, and in 1656 he was bankrupt. His house and rich art collection were sold and he moved to the Rozengracht in the Jordaan.

No longer the darling of the wealthy set, he continued to paint, draw and etch – his etchings on display in the Rembrandthuis are some of the best ever produced in this medium – and received the occasional commission. His pupil Govert Flinck was asked to decorate the new city hall, and when Flinck died Rembrandt scored part of the job and painted the monumental *Conspiracy of Claudius Civilis* (1661). The authorities disiked it and had it removed within a year. In 1662 he completed the *Staalmeesters* (the 'Syndics') for the drapers' guild and ensured that everybody remained clearly visible, but it was the last group portrait he did.

The works of his later period show that Rembrandt lost none of his touch. No longer constrained by the wishes of wealthy clients, he enjoyed a new-found freedom and his works became more unconventional while showing an even stronger empathy with their subject matter, for instance in *A Couple: the Jewish Bride* (1665). The many portraits of Titus and Hendrickje, and his ever gloomier self-portraits, are among the most stirring in the history of art.

A pest epidemic in 1663-64 killed one in seven Amsterdammers, among them his faithful companion Hendrickje. Titus died in 1668, aged 27 and just married, and Rembrandt died a year later, a broken man.

Another great painter of this period, **Frans Hals** (1581/85-1666), was born in Antwerp but lived in Haarlem. He devoted most of his career to portraits, dabbling in occasional genre scenes with dramatic chiaroscuro. His ability to render the expressions of his subjects was equal to that of Rembrandt though he didn't explore their characters as much. Both masters used the same expressive, unpolished brush strokes, and seemed to develop from a bright exuberance in their early careers to a darker, more solemn approach later on.

A good example of Hals' 'unpolished' technique is *The Merry Drinker* (1630) in the Rijksmuseum, which almost seems as if it was painted by one of the 19th century impressionists who so admired his work. His famous children's portraits are similar. Hals was also an expert of beautiful group portraits in which the groups almost looked natural, unlike the rigid lineups produced by lesser contemporaries, though he wasn't as tactless as Rembrandt in subordinating faces to the composition. A particularly good example is the pair of paintings known collectively as *The Regents & the Regentesses of the Old Men's Alms House* (1664) in the Frans Hals Museum in Haarlem, which he painted near the end of his long life.

The grand trio of 17th century masters is completed by **Jan Vermeer** (1632-75) of Delft. He produced only 35 meticulously crafted paintings in his career and died a poor man with 10 children – his baker accepted two paintings from his wife as payment for a debt of more than f600. His work is devoted almost entirely to genre painting which he mastered like no other. Exceptions are a few historical/biblical scenes in his earlier career, his famous *View of Delft* (1661) in the Mauritshuis in The Hague, and some tender portraits of unknown women, such as the stunningly beautiful *Girl with a Pearl Earring* (1666), also in the Mauritshuis. His Catholicism and lingering mannerism might help explain the emphasis on beauty rather than the personalities of the people he portrayed, also in his genre paintings.

The Little Street (1658) in the Rijksmuseum is Vermeer's only street scene; the others are set indoors, bathed in serene light pouring through tall windows. The calm, spiritual effect is enhanced by dark blues, deep reds and warm yellows, and by supremely balanced compositions that adhere to the rules of perspective. Good examples include the Rijksmuseum's *The Kitchen Maid* (also known as *The Milkmaid*, 1658) and *Woman in Blue Reading a Letter* (1664), or, for his use of perspective, *The Love Letter* (1670). In Woman in Blue, note the map on the wall, a backdrop he used in several other works, as did many other artists of the period. Maps were appreciated as valuable works of art in 17th century Dutch society just like paintings, which might say something about Dutch appreciation for spatial relationships (something to do with the flat country and ongoing land reclamation perhaps?).

Around the middle of the century the atmospheric unity in Dutch paintings, with their stern focus on mood and the subtle play of light, began to make way for the splendour of the baroque. **Jacob van Ruysdael** went for dramatic skies and **Albert Cuyp** for Italianate landscapes, while Ruysdael's pupil **Meindert Hobbema** preferred less heroic and more playful bucolic scenes full of pretty detail.

This almost frivolous aspect of baroque also announces itself in the genre paintings of **Jan Steen** (1626-79), the tavern-keeper whose depictions of domestic chaos led to the Dutch expression 'a Jan Steen household' for a disorderly household. A good example is the animated revelry of *The Merry Family* (1668) in the Rijksmuseum. It shows adults having a good time around the dinner table, oblivious to the children in the foreground pouring themselves a drink. There's a lot going on in this painting and it all comes together well, but it's also very busy as baroque art so often is.

18th & 19th Centuries The golden age of Dutch painting ended almost as suddenly as it began, when the French invaded the Low Countries in the 'Disaster Year' of 1672. The economy collapsed and with it the market for paintings. A mood of caution replaced the carefree optimism of the years when the world lay at the Republic's feet. Painters who stayed in business did so with 'safe' works that repeated earlier successes, and in the 18th century they copied French styles, pandering to the awe for anything French.

They produced many competent works but nothing ground-breaking. **Cornelis Troost** (1697-1750) was one of the best genre painters, sometimes compared with Hogarth for introducing quite un-Calvinistic

humour into his pastels of domestic revelry reminiscent of Jan Steen.

Gerard de Lairesse (1640-1711) and **Jacob de Wit** (1695-1754) specialised in decorating the walls and ceilings of buildings – De Wit's *trompe l'oeuil* decorations in the current Theatermuseum and Bijbels Museum are worth seeing.

The late 18th century and most of the 19th century produced little of note, though the landscapes and seascapes of **Johan Barthold Jongkind** (1819-91) and the gritty, almost photographic Amsterdam scenes of **George Hendrik Breitner** (1857-1923) were a bit of an exception. They appear to have inspired French impressionists, many of whom visited Amsterdam at the time. The work of these two painters also reinvented 17th century realism and influenced the Hague School in the last decades of the 19th century, with painters such as **Hendrik Mesdag** (1831-1915), **Jozef Israels** (1824-1911) and the three **Maris brothers** (Jacob, Matthijs and Willem). The landscapes, seascapes and genre works of this school are on display in the Mesdag Museum in The Hague, where the star attraction is the recently restored *Panorama Mesdag* (1881), a gigantic, 360° painting by the artist of the seaside town of Scheveningen viewed from a dune. It's quite impressive.

Without a doubt the greatest 19th century Dutch painter was **Vincent van Gogh** (1853-1890), whose convulsive patterns and furious colours were in a world of their own and still defy comfortable categorisation. A post-impressionist? A forerunner of expressionism? For more about his life and works, see the description of the Van Gogh Museum in the Things to See & Do chapter.

20th Century In his early career, **Piet Mondriaan** (1872-1944) painted in the Hague School tradition but he soon developed a style of his own that reduced form and colour to their essentials. After flirting with Cubism he began painting in bold rectangular patterns, using only the three primary colours of yellow, blue and red set against the three neutrals (white, grey and black), a

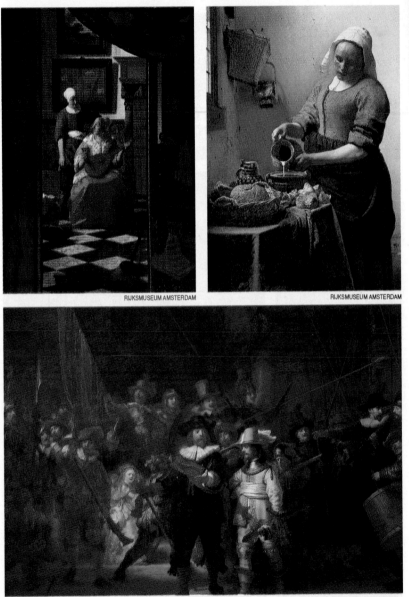

RIJKSMUSEUM AMSTERDAM

RIJKSMUSEUM AMSTERDAM

RIJKSMUSEUM AMSTERDAM

Left: Vermeer's *The Love Letter*
Right: Vermeer's *The Kitchen Maid*
Bottom: Rembrandt's *The Nightwatch*

Wall tablets, or cartouches, helped to identify houses before the introduction of house numbers

ALL PHOTOS: TONY WHEELER

style known as 'neo-plasticism' – an undistorted expression of reality in pure form and pure colour. His *Composition in Red, Black, Blue, Yellow & Grey* (1920) in the Stedelijk Museum is an elaborate example of this; his later works were starker (or 'more pure') and became dynamic again when he moved to New York in 1940. The world's largest collection of his paintings resides in the Gemeentemuseum (Municipal Museum) of his native The Hague.

Mondriaan was one of the leading exponents of De Stijl (The Style), a Dutch design movement that aimed to harmonise all the arts by bringing artistic expressions back to their essence. Its advocate was the magazine of the same name, first published in 1917 by **Theo van Doesburg** (1883-1931). Van Doesburg produced works similar to Mondriaan's, though he dispensed with the thick, black lines and later tilted his rectangles at 45°, departures serious enough for Mondriaan to call off the friendship.

Throughout the 1920s and 1930s, De Stijl attracted not just painters but also sculptors, poets, architects and designers. One of these was **Gerrit Rietveld** (1888-1964), who designed the Van Gogh Museum and several other buildings but is best known internationally for his furniture, such as the Mondriaanesque *Red Blue Chair* (1918) on display in the Stedelijk Museum, and his range of uncomfortable zigzag chairs that, viewed side-on, are simply a 'Z' with a backrest.

Other schools of the prewar period included the Bergen School, with the expressive realism of **Annie 'Charley' Toorop** (1891-1955), daughter of the symbolist painter Jan Toorop; and De Ploeg (The Plough), headed by **Jan Wiegers** (1893-1959) in Groningen, who were influenced by the works of Van Gogh and German expressionists. In her later works Charley Toorop also became one of the exponents of Dutch surrealism, more correctly known as Magic Realism, which expressed the magical interaction between humans and their environment. Leading Magic Realists included Carel Willink (1900-83) and the almost naive autodidact Pyke Koch (1901-91).

One of the most remarkable graphic artists of this century was **Maurits Cornelis Escher** (1902-1972). His drawings, lithos and woodcuts of blatantly impossible images continue to fascinate mathematicians. Many works contain strange loops that defy the laws of Euclidian geometry (not to mention nature): a waterfall feeding itself, people going up or down a staircase that ends where it starts, a pair of hands drawing each other etc. He also possessed an uncanny knack for tessellation, or 'tiling' – the art of making complex, preferably 'organic' shapes fit into one another in recurring but subtly changing patterns. Though often dismissed as novelties that belong in poster shops, his meticulously crafted works betray a highly talented artist who deserves credit for challenging our view of reality.

After WWII, artists rebelled against artistic conventions and vented their rage in abstract expressionism, the more furious the better. In Amsterdam, **Karel Appel** (1921-) and **Constant** (Constant Nieuwenhuis) drew on styles pioneered by Paul Klee and Joan Miró, and exploited bright colours and 'uncorrupted' children's art to produce incredibly lively works that leapt off the canvas. In Paris in 1945, they met up with the Dane Asger Jorn (1914-73) and the Belgian Corneille (Cornelis van Beverloo), and together with several other artists and writers formed a group known as CoBrA (Copenhagen, Brussels, Amsterdam).

Their first major exhibition, in the Stedelijk Museum in 1949, aroused a storm of protest with predictable comments along the lines of 'My child paints like that too'. Though they disbanded in 1951, the CoBrA artists continued to exert a strong influence in their respective countries. The Stedelijk Museum has a good collection of their works but the CoBrA Museum in Amstelveen displays the more complete range.

It is probably too early to say much about the significance of Dutch art from the 1960s onwards – form your own opinions in the

Stedelijk Museum. Works include the op art of Jan Schoonhoven, influenced by the Zero movement in Germany; the abstracts of Ad Dekkers and Edgar Fernhout; and the photographic collages of Jan Dibbets.

Architecture

Amsterdam is an architectural marvel, though there are no grand monuments and only a few buildings that impress with size. Its beauty, especially within the canal belt, lies in the countless private buildings with distinguishing features that make each one stand out in its own particular way. No other city in Europe has such a wealth of residential architecture. It was built by citizens and businesses, not by some central authority.

Middle Ages The oldest surviving building is the Gothic Oude Kerk (Old Church), which dates from the early 14th century. The second-oldest is the late-Gothic Nieuwe Kerk from the early 15th century. In both these churches, note the timber vaulting (the marshy ground precluded the use of heavy stone) and the use of brick rather than stone in the walls. Stone was not only heavy but also scarce, and there was plenty of clay and sand to produce bricks. Also note how the interior focus has shifted from the (Catholic) choir and altar to the (Protestant) pulpit. The pulpit takes centre stage in churches built after the Protestant takeover in 1578; a good example is the Noorderkerk in the Jordaan.

The earliest houses were made of timber and clay with thatched roofs. In the 15th century, timber side walls made way for brick in a process of natural selection brought about by fires, and in the 16th century the thatched roofs were replaced by tiles. Timber was still used for façades and gables into the 17th century but eventually brick and sandstone triumphed here too. Only two houses have survived with timber façades: Begijnhof 34 (mid-15th century) and Zeedijk 1 (mid-16th century). Timber, however, remained an essential building material for floor beams and roof frames.

Dutch Renaissance From about the middle of the 16th century the Italian Renaissance began to filter through to the Netherlands, where architects developed a unique style with rich ornamentation that merged classical and traditional elements. In the façades they used mock columns, so-called pilasters, and they replaced the traditional spout gables with step gables richly decorated with sculptures, columns and obelisks. The playful interaction of red (or rather, orange) brick and horizontal bands of white or yellow sandstone was based on strict mathematical formulas that pleased the eye.

The city carpenter Hendrick Staets (who planned the canal belt), the city bricklayer Cornelis Danckerts and the city sculptor **Hendrick de Keyser** (1565-1621) were jointly responsible for municipal buildings. Utrecht-born De Keyser's artistic contributions were the most visible and it was he who perfected Dutch-Renaissance architecture. His Bartolotti House at Herengracht 170-172 is one of the finest examples of his work. He also designed the Zuiderkerk and the Westerkerk in which he retained Gothic elements, but he set a new direction in Dutch Protestant church-building with the Noorderkerk, laid out like a Greek cross with the pulpit in the centre.

Dutch Classicism During the Golden Age of the 17th century, architects such as **Jacob van Campen** (1595-1657) and **Philips Vingboons** (1607-78) and his brother Justus adhered more strictly to Greek and Roman classical design and dropped many of De Keyser's playful decorations. Influenced by Italian architects such as Palladio and Scamozzi, they made façades resemble temples. The pilasters looked more like columns, with pedestals and pediments. In order to accentuate the vertical lines, the step gable changed to a neck gable with decorative scrolls, topped by a triangular or rounded fronton to imitate a temple roof. Soft red brick was made more durable with brown paint.

Van Campen's city hall (now Royal Palace) on Dam square is the most impress-

Gables & Hoists

A gable not only hid the roof from public view but also helped to identify the house until the French-led government introduced house numbers in 1795 (the current system of odd and even numbers dates from 1875). The more ornate the gable, the easier it was to recognise. Other distinguishing features included façade decorations, signs or wall tablets (cartouches).

There are four main types of gables. The simple **spout gable** with semicircular windows or shutters, a copy of the earliest wooden gables, was used mainly for warehouses from the 1580s to the early 18th century. The **step gable** was a late-Gothic design favoured by Dutch-Renaissance architects from 1580 to 1660. The **neck gable,** also known as bottle gable, was introduced in the 1640s and proved most durable, featuring occasionally in designs of the early 19th century. Some neck gables incorporated a step. The **bell gable** first appeared in the 1660s and became popular in the 18th century.

Many houses built from the 18th century onwards no longer had gables but straight, horizontal cornices that were richly decorated, often with pseudo-balustrades.

Many canal houses have a slight forward lean. This has nothing to do with subsidence but everything to do with hoisting goods into the attic and furniture into the (removable) windows without them bumping into the house. A few houses have huge hoist-wheels in the attic with a rope and hook that run through the hoist beam. Almost all other houses, even those built today, have a beam with hook for a hoist block. The forward lean also allows the façade and gable to be admired from the street – a fortunate coincidence. ■

| spout gable | step gable | neck gable | neck gable with step | bell gable | cornice with 'balustrade' | cornice with bulge |

ive example of this style. The Vingboons brothers specialised in residential architecture and their work can be found throughout the western canal belt, such as the current Bijbels Museum at Herengracht 364-370 and the White House (now Theatermuseum) next to the Bartolotti House, or the fine example at Keizersgracht 319.

Classical elements became more restrained later in the 17th century. Make-believe columns became less ornamental or disappeared altogether as external decorations made way for sumptuous interiors. This was the period of the southern canal belt, when wealthy Amsterdammers often bought two adjoining plots and built houses five windows wide instead of the usual three. Justus Vingboons' Trippenhuis at Kloveniersburgwal 29 is a good example.

This austere classicism is best seen, however, in the works of **Adriaan Dortsman** (1625-82), whose designs include the Round Lutheran Church and the current Museum Van Loon at Keizersgracht 672-674. A mathematician by training, he favoured a stark, geometrical simplicity – preferably with flat, sandstone façades – that enhanced the grandeur of his buildings.

18th Century 'Louis Styles' The wealthy class now began to enjoy the fortunes amassed by their predecessors. Many turned to banking and finance and conducted their business from the comfort of opulent homes. Those who still engaged actively in trade no longer stored goods in the attic but in warehouses elsewhere.

The preoccupation with all things French provided fertile ground for Huguenot refugees, such as **Daniel Marot** (1661-1752) and his assistants **Jean & Anthony Coulon**, who introduced French interior design with matching exteriors. Interiors were bathed in light thanks to stuccoed ceilings and tall sash windows (a French innovation), and everything from staircases to furniture was designed in harmony. Elegant bell gables, introduced around 1660, became commonplace, though many architects did away with gables altogether in favour of richly decorated horizontal cornices.

The Louis XIV style dominated until about 1750, with its dignified symmetry and façades decorated with statuary and leaves. Around 1740 the Louis XV style brought asymmetrical rococo shapes resembling rocks and waves. Pilasters or pillars made a comeback around 1770 with Louis XVI designs that showed a renewed interest in classical motifs. An extreme example of this is the Felix Meritis building at Keizersgracht 324 designed by **Jacob Otten Husly** (1738-97), with enormous Corinthian half-columns that seem to carry the structure. The Maagdenhuis on Spui square, designed by city architect **Abraham van der Hart** (1747-1820), is a much more sober interpretation of the new classicism.

19th Century Neo-Styles Architecture stagnated in the first half of the 19th century as Amsterdam struggled to recover from the economic disasters of the Napoleonic era. Safe neoclassicism held sway until the 1860s when architects here and elsewhere in Europe began to rediscover other styles of the past.

The main Amsterdam styles in the latter half of the century were neo-Gothic, which harked back to the grand Gothic cathedrals in which no design element was superfluous; and neo-Renaissance, which brought De

Keyser's Dutch Renaissance architecture back into the limelight. The former suited the boom in Catholic church-building now that Catholics were free to build new churches in Protestant parts of the country; the latter appealed to local architects because houses in this style were being demolished at a rapid rate.

One of the leading architects of this period was **Pierre Cuypers** (1827-1921), who built several neo-Gothic churches but often merged the two styles, as can be seen in his Centraal Station and Rijksmuseum which have Gothic structures and Dutch Renaissance brickwork. Another fine example of this mixture is CH Peters' general post office (now Magna Plaza) at Nieuwezijds Voorburgwal 182. Alfred Tepe's Krijtberg church at Singel 448 is more clearly Gothic (but note the use of brick), while the milk factory at Prinsengracht 739-741 designed by Eduard Cuypers (Pierre's nephew) sits firmly in the Dutch Renaissance tradition.

Other architects were more eclectic and also incorporated medieval Dutch and German designs in a very personal way. Good examples are Isaac Gosschalk's houses at Reguliersgracht 57-59 and 63, and AC Bleijs' PC Hooft store on the corner of Keizersgracht and Leidsestraat. AL van Gendt's Concertgebouw is obviously neoclassical but its interplay of red brick and white sandstone is Dutch Renaissance.

A popular European style around the turn of the century was Art Nouveau. In Amsterdam, Art Nouveau's abundant use of steel and glass with curvilinear designs resembling plants showed up mainly in shop fronts but in little else. There are, however, a handful of fine examples, such as the current Greenpeace headquarters at Keizersgracht 174-176, the American Hotel at Leidseplein, and the riotous Tuschinskitheater at Reguliersbreestraat 26-28.

Berlage & the Amsterdam School The neo-styles and their reliance on the past were strongly criticised by **Hendrik Petrus Berlage** (1856-1934), the father of modern Dutch architecture. Instead of expensive construction and excessive decoration, he favoured simplicity and a rational use of materials. His Beurs (Bourse, or Stock Exchange) on Damrak displayed his ideals to the full. He cooperated with sculptors, painters and tilers to ensure that ornamentation was integrated into the overall design in a supportive role, rather than being tacked on as an embellishment to hide the structure.

Berlage's residential architecture approached a block of buildings as a whole, not as a collection of individual houses. In this he influenced the young architects of what became known as the Amsterdam School, though they rejected his stark rationalism and preferred more creative designs. Leading exponents were **Michel de Klerk** (1884-1923), **Piet Kramer** (1881-1961) and **Johan van der Mey** (1878-1949). The latter heralded the Amsterdam School in his Scheepvaarthuis at Prins Hendrikkade.

These architects built in brick and treated housing blocks as sculptures, with curved corners, oddly placed windows and ornamental, rocket-shaped towers. Their housing estates, such as De Klerk's 'Ship' in the Oostzaanstraat and Kramer's Cooperatiehof in the Pijp neighbourhood, have been described as fairy-tale fortresses rendered in a Dutch version of Art Deco. Their preference for form over function meant that their expressionistic designs were interesting to look at but not always fantastic to live in, with small windows and inefficient use of space.

Many architects of this school worked for the city council and designed the buildings of the ambitious 'Plan South'. This was a large-scale expansion of good-quality housing, wide boulevards and cosy squares between the Amstel and what was to become the Olympic Stadium. It was mapped out by Berlage and instigated by the labour party alderman FM Wibaut, though Berlage didn't get much of a chance to design the buildings, with council architects pushing their own designs. Subsidised housing corporations provided the funding here and elsewhere in the 1920s, a period of frantic residential building activity beyond the canal belt.

Functionalism While Amsterdam School-type buildings were being erected all over the city, a new generation of architects began to rebel against the school's impractical (not to mention expensive) structures. Influenced by the Bauhaus School in Germany, Frank Lloyd Wright in the USA and Le Corbusier in France, they formed a group called *de 8* (the 8) in 1927.

Architects such as B Merkelbach and Gerrit Rietveld believed that form should follow function and sang the praises of steel, glass and concrete. They believed that buildings should be spacious, practical structures with plenty of sunlight, not inert masses of brick treated as works of art for the glory of individual architects.

The all-important Committee of Aesthetics Control didn't agree with this, however, and kept the functionalists out of the canal belt, relegating them to the new housing estates on the outskirts of the city – although Rietveld did build his glass gallery on top of the Metz department store at Keizersgracht 455.

Functionalism finally came to the fore after WWII and put its stamp on new suburbs west and south of the city, thanks to the General Extension Plan that had been adopted in 1935 but interrupted by the war. The acute housing shortage meant that these high-rise suburbs were built on a larger scale than originally planned, yet they still weren't sufficient and the Bijlmermeer south-east of the city was added in the 1960s. By this time, however, there was increasing resistance to such high-rise monstrosities.

Suburbs have been built on a more human scale since the 1960s, with low and medium-rise apartments integrated with shops, schools and offices. The KNSM Eiland in the eastern harbour is a good example of one that's developing now. Strict functionalism has made way for more imaginative designs, such as A Alberts and M van Huut's ING Bank (1987) in the Bijlmermeer; built to anthroposophical principles, this S-shaped complex of linked towers has few right angles.

In the inner city, the emphasis has been on

urban renewal with innovative designs on a scale appropriate to their surroundings. In this, architects follow the examples set by Aldo van Eyck (1918-) and his student Theo Bosch (1940-). Van Eyck's designs include the Moederhuis at Plantage Middenlaan 33; Bosch's include the Pentagon housing complex on the corner of St Anthoniesbreestraat and Zwanenburgwal. Opinions are mixed, however, with critics dismissing such designs as 'parasite architecture' – modern housing projects that look a bit out of place, with huge windows so residents can stare out of their aquarium onto wonderful 17th and 18th century surroundings.

The many aspects of urban planning are displayed in an excellent permanent exhibition in the Zuiderkerk (see Zuiderkerk in the Things to See & Do chapter). The Architectuur Centrum Amsterdam (ARCAM, ☎ 620 48 78), Waterlooplein 213, organises temporary exhibitions about architectural themes.

Music

The dour church elders of the past dismissed music as frivolous and only began to allow organ music in churches in the 17th century because it kept people out of pubs. Amsterdam therefore contributed relatively little to the world's music heritage, which makes its vivid music scene today all the more remarkable.

The world's top acts are now billed matter-of-factly, and local musicians excel in (modern) classical music, jazz and techno/dance. In July and August, free jazz, classical and world-music performances are staged in the Vondelpark, and free lunch-time concerts are held at various venues throughout the year. The Uitmarkt festival at the end of August (see Public Holidays & Special Events in the Facts for the Visitor chapter) also provides lots of free music. For more about music venues, see the Music section in the Entertainment chapter, and check the free entertainment paper *Uitkrant* for details.

Classical The country's best symphony orchestras and classical musicians perform

in the Concertgebouw. You can't go wrong with tickets for the world-renowned, Riccardo Chailly-conducted Concertgebouw Orkest, which plays music by 'big' composers.

If the pianist Ronald Brautigam is on the bill you'll be guaranteed a top-flight performance. He often collaborates with violinist Isabelle van Keulen. Other great violinists include Quirine Viersen and Jaap van Zweden. The latter is a national celebrity who often gets a solo spot or appears as guest conductor of the Concertgebouw Orkest. His appearances with the Amsterdam Saxophone Quartet mark just one of his many musical sidesteps. Teenager Wibi Soerjadi is an upcoming piano talent taking Amsterdam by storm. Soprano Charlotte Margiono and mezzo-soprano Jard van Nes are worth catching too.

In 'old music', you can't go past the Combattimento Consort Amsterdam (Bach, Vivaldi and Händel), or the Amsterdam Baroque Orchestra conducted by Ton Koopman. He also heads the Radio Chamber Orchestra, along with Frans Bruggen, best known for his work with The 18th Century Orchestra. Performances by the Radio Philharmonic Orchestra, conducted by the Sydney Symphony Orchestra's Edo de Waart (usually in the Concertgebouw), are often recorded for radio and TV.

The Nederlandse Opera is based in the Stopera (officially the Muziektheater), where it stages world-class performances though not everyone will appreciate the sometimes experimental approach.

Modern Classical & Experimental Paradiso and De IJsbreker are the usual venues for this type of music, which seems to thrive in Amsterdam. Dutch modern composers of note (so to speak) include Louis Andriessen, Theo Loevendie, Klaas de Vries and the late Ton de Leeuw. Worthwhile performers include The Trio, Gaudeamus, Asko Ensemble, Nieuw Ensemble and last but not least the Reinbert de Leeuw-conducted Schönberg Ensemble. The latter two ensembles also do an annual stint with the Argentinian-

How to Murder Music: Street Organs & Carillons

Street organs and carillons are to the Dutch what bagpipes are to the Scots: they seem to elicit the same mixed feelings.

The elaborate street organs *(draaiorgels*, literally barrel organs) developed out of the hand-held barrel organs that were once popular throughout Europe but have now all but disappeared. Their atrocious tuning and repetitive repertoire contributed to their demise: people tended to pay organ grinders to stop rather than continue.

One of the factors that ensured their survival in the Netherlands was the leasing system established in Amsterdam in 1875: grinders leased their organs from owners who were responsible for maintenance and tuning, which ensured reasonable standards upheld by strict licensing laws. Even today, grinders are assigned limited hours in particular areas of the city so they are evenly distributed, and they can spend five minutes on the same spot before having to move on.

The repertoire is varied and includes anything from *Tulips from Amsterdam* and *The Blue Danube* to wacky renditions of the latest Top 40 hits. Fluctuations in temperature and humidity still play havoc with tuning, especially in the critical bourdon register where each tone is represented by two pipes tuned a few hertz apart for the desired vibrato, sometimes resulting in a cat's-wail effect. Is it music? Who knows, but most will agree that a street organ at full tilt is a pretty impressive bit of machinery. They used to be operated by hand but now little generator motors do the hard work.

The Dutch infatuation with mechanical instruments extends to the out-of-tune carillons that adorn many public buildings, especially church towers. They're usually operated by machines though a select group of carillonneurs pounds the keys during occasional concerts. These live interpretations of the works of classical and modern composers are often played with a surprising amount of feeling if you consider the natural limitations of the instrument.

Carillons are wonderfully quaint and attractive in passing, but if your accommodation is in the shadow of a church that has one, the repetitive time chimes every 15 minutes can drive you up the wall. Thank God they fall silent at night. ■

ROB VAN DRIESUM

Street organ

German composer Maricio Kagel to celebrate his birthday.

Jazz Quite often the distinction between modern classical and improvised music can be vague. Jazz band leaders such as Willem Breuker and Willem van Manen of the Contraband have a reputation for straddling the two genres.

More recently, the Dutch jazz scene has become more mainstream with gifted young chanteuses such as Fleurine and Surinameborn Denise Jannah. The latter is the first singer from Suriname to be signed to the legendary Blue Note label, which in 1996 released her outstanding album *Different*

Colours. The former has an album out on Blue Music titled *Meant to Be*, which refers to her collaboration with jazz luminaries such as producer Don Sickler, drummer Billy Drummond and tenor saxophonist Christian McBride.

Astrid Seriese and Carmen Gomez operate in the crossover field, where jazz verges on, or blends with, pop. Father and daughter Hans & Candy Dulfer, both tenor saxophonists, are a bit more daring. Dad in particular constantly extends his musical boundaries by experimenting with sampling techniques drawn from the hip-hop genre. In instrumental jazz, you can't go past pianist Michiel Borstlap and his soul and label-mate, bass player Hein van de Geyn. Borstlap recently picked up the prestigious Thelonious Monk award.

The city's most important jazz venue is the Bimhuis on Oude Schans; others come and go but the Bimhuis remains an institution.

Pop & Dance In the mid-1980s Amsterdam was a centre for guitar-driven rock bands but since then it has evolved into the capital of the dance genre, from techno to R&B. Perhaps the best known Dutch dance variant internationally is the so-called 'gabber', a style in which the number of beats per minute and the noise of buzzing synthesizers goes beyond belief. Amsterdam also boasts a vital hip-hop scene, spearheaded by De Osdorp Posse, who rap in their mother tongue.

Rave parties are organised in the Amsterdam dance clubs, such as Mazzo, Seymour Likely and iT. Worthwhile DJs who do the club rounds include the Belgian grandmaster and Amsterdam resident, Eddy de Clerq, as well as DJ Dimitri and DJ 100% Isis. Quazar is the excellent dance project set up by Gert van Veen, music critic with the daily newspaper *De Volkskrant*.

Alternative rockers Claw Boys Claw, 1960s pop legend Wally Tax and the Dutch-language rockers The Scene, De Dijk and Trockener Kecks have survived everything new, but rock bands are making a comeback and promising new bands are surfacing – check the bills at Paradiso, Melkweg and Arena. The newly launched Excelsior Records label is home to Daryll Ann and upstarts such as Caesar, Johan, Benjamin B and Scram C Baby. Other newcomers are popsters The Bartales, based at music café De Koe, which appears to be fertile ground for Amsterdam rock. Pop outfits such as Shine and Rex, both fronted by ex-Fatal Flowers mainstay Richard Janssen, have recruited their members here. Other bands hanging around here are country rockers Goldrush and The Cornfields.

Experimental pop's heyday is over and has gone underground again. However, with the music of Det Whiel being used by top international choreographers for modern dance performances in the Muziektheater, the future for 'difficult music' is looking brighter.

New Age music is gaining territory – Coen Bais is one of the household names and Oibibio is the happening place. Human Alert represents the reborn punk movement, while .nuClarity provides a mix of jazz, funk, hip-hop, ragga, and kaseko from Suriname.

World Music Cosmopolitan Amsterdam offers a wealth of world music. Suriname-born Ronald Snijders, a top jazz flautist, often participates in world-music projects. Another jazz flautist heading towards 'world' is Chris Hinze, for instance with his album *Tibet Impressions*.

African-influenced music is provided by Fra-Fra-Sound, but the bulk of world repertoire from Amsterdam is Latin, ranging from Cuban salsa to Dominican merengue and Argentinian tango. Try the following bands to get a taste of the local world scene: Nueva Manteca (salsa), Sexteto Canyengue (tango), Eric Vaarzon Morel (flamenco) and Na'f Mi'Wong (various styles).

For more information about these artists and gigs at Paradiso, Melkweg, Akhnaton and Latin bars, see the excellent monthly salsa magazine *Oye Listen*. It's published in Dutch and Spanish, costs f5, and is available in specialist world-music shops such as Tjin Record Shop (☎ 685 09 27), Nassaukade 334, and South Miami Plaza (☎ 662 28 17), Albert Cuypstraat 182. Look for CDs by the above-mentioned bands on the Lucho, Munich and M&W labels. In hotels with cable radio, tune in to roots music station Radio London, a Dutch station named after the 1960s English pirate station, on 90.4 FM.

Theatre
The city has a rich theatrical tradition dating back to medieval times. In the Golden Age, when Dutch was the language of trade, local companies toured the theatres of Europe with Vondel's tragedies, Bredero's comedies and Hooft's verses. They're still performed locally in more modern renditions.

Theatre was immensely popular with all

levels of society, perhaps because the city lacked a decent theatre building and plays were often performed outdoors. Gradually, however, the patrician class and their preoccupation with French culture turned theatre into a more elitist affair, and towards the end of the 19th century it had become snobbish, with little room for development.

This attitude persisted until the late 1960s, when disgruntled actors began to throw tomatoes at their older colleagues and engaged the audience in discussion about the essence of theatre. Avant-garde theatre companies such as Mickery and Shaffy made Amsterdam a centre for experimental theatre, and many smaller companies sprang up in the 1970s and 1980s.

Most of these have now merged or disappeared as a result of cutbacks in government subsidies, while musicals and cabaret are enjoying a revival. But survivors and newcomers are still forging ahead with excellent productions – visual feasts with striking sets and lighting, creative costumes etc. The language barrier is of course an issue with Dutch productions, though with some of them it plays a very minor role.

English-language companies often visit Amsterdam, especially in summer – check the *Uitkrant* or ask at the AUB Uitburo. For more about theatre venues, see Theatre in the Entertainment chapter. The Holland Festival in June and the Uitmarkt on the last weekend in August are big theatre events (see Public Holidays & Special Events in the Facts for the Visitor chapter); also worth catching is the International Theatre School Festival at the end of June, held in the theatres around the Nes (Frascati, Brakke Grond etc).

Film

Dutch films haven't exactly set the world on fire, though this has more to do with the language barrier and funding problems in a modest distribution area than with lack of talent.

One of the most 'important' Dutch directors of all time was Joris Ivens (1898-1989), who was influenced by Russian film-makers but added his own impressionistic lyricism.

He made award-winning documentaries about social and political issues – the Spanish Civil War, impoverished Belgian miners, Vietnam – but was also an accomplished visual artist in his own right; for instance in *Rain* (1929), a 15 minute impression of a rain shower in Amsterdam that took four months to shoot.

Directors, actors and camera operators who made the jump to English have done quite well for themselves. Paul Verhoeven *(Robocop, Total Recall, Basic Instinct)* is perhaps the best known director abroad, though his reputation has suffered from his disastrous *Showgirls*. George Sluizer *(The Vanishing)*, Dick Maas *(Flodder in Amerika, Amsterdamned)*, Fons Rademakers *(The Assault)* and Marleen Gorris *(Antonia's Line*, which won the Oscar for best foreign film in 1996) have also made a name internationally, if not always among the general public. Ms Gorris' follow-up is an English-language film adaptation of Virginia Woolf's *Mrs Dalloway* starring Vanessa Redgrave. Jan de Bont, who won accolades for his camera work in *Jewel of the Nile* and *Black Rain*, directed the box-office hit *Speed*.

Rutger Hauer began his acting career at home as the lead in Paul Verhoeven's *Turks Fruit* (Turkish Delight, an Oscar nominee for best foreign film in the early 1970s), but has since gone on to glory in Hollywood with convincing bad-guy performances in disturbing films such as *The Hitcher* and *Blade Runner*. Jeroen Krabbé has also become a well-paid Hollywood actor *(The Fugitive, The Living Daylights, Prince of Tides)*.

The Filmmuseum in the Vondelpark is the national museum on this subject and is well worth a visit. See Cinemas in the Entertainment chapter for more about films.

Literature

Dutch literature has been neglected by the English-speaking world, which is a shame. The lack of English translations is partly to blame. Interestingly, Flemish authorities are happy to subsidise translations of their authors but Dutch authorities are less inclined to do so.

The Dutch Shakespeare, Joost van den Vondel, is heavy going in his tragedy *Gijsbrecht van Aemstel* (1637), which is available in translation. It recounts the agony of the local count who had to go into exile after losing out to the count of Holland and his toll privileges. Vondel's best tragedy, *Lucifer* (1654), which describes the rebellion of the archangel against God, has also been translated. Other big authors of this period, Bredero (comedies) and Hooft (poems, plays, history, philosophy), have yet to appear in English.

The most interesting 19th century author was Eduard Douwes Dekker, a colonial administrator and Amsterdam native who wrote under the pseudonym Multatuli (Latin for 'I have suffered greatly'). His *Max Havelaar: or the Coffee Auctions of the Dutch Trading Company* (1860) exposed colonial narrow-mindedness in the dealings of a self-righteous coffee merchant. It shocked Dutch society and led to a review of the 'culture system' in the East Indies (the forced production of tropical crops for export). The Hague author Louis Couperus *(The Hidden Force*, 1900) explored the mystery of the East Indies from the colonialist's perspective.

The WWII occupation was a traumatic period that spawned many insightful works. *The Diary of Anne Frank* is a moving account of a Jewish girl's thoughts and yearnings while hiding in an annexe to avoid deportation by the Germans. The poignancy is enhanced by the knowledge that she was killed in the end. Etty Hillesum's *Etty: An Interrupted Life* is in a similar vein but more mature. Marga Minco *(The Fall, An Empty House, Bitter Herbs)* explores the war years from the perspective of a Jewish woman who survived.

Amsterdam author Harry Mulisch focuses on Dutch apathy during WWII *(The Last Call* and *The Assault,* which was made into an Oscar-winning film), but he has written much else that doesn't involve the war. His works have their ups and downs but he is one of the Great Authors of Dutch literature.

Jan Wolkers shocked Dutch readers in the 1960s with his provocatively misogynist but powerful *Turkish Delight,* which was made into a (Dutch) film by Paul Verhoeven starring Rutger Hauer. Xaviera Hollander (Vera de Vries) shocked the USA with an account of her call-girl experiences in *The Happy Hooker.*

Simon Carmiggelt *(A Dutchman's Slight Adventures, I'm Just Kidding)* wrote amusing vignettes of Pijp neighbourhood life in his column in the newspaper *Het Parool.* Nicolas Freeling *(A Long Silence, Love in Amsterdam, Because of the Cats)* created the BBC's Van der Valk detective series. Jan-Willem van der Wetering *(Hard Rain)* is another author of off-beat detective stories.

Cees Nooteboom *(A Song of Truth and Semblance, In the Dutch Mountains)* is accessible and amusing. Lieve Joris, a Flemish author who lives in Amsterdam, writes about cultures in transition in Africa, the Middle East and Eastern Europe; her *Gates of Damascus,* about daily life in Syria, has been published in the Lonely Planet Journeys series. Another book in this series is *The Rainbird: a Central African Journey* by Jan Brokken, a highly regarded novelist, travel narrator and literary journalist. It's a fascinating account of white explorers, missionaries, slavers and adventurers who traipsed through the jungles of Gabon.

For more about books and where to buy them, see the Bookshops and Markets sections in the Shopping chapter. The third week in March is the national Boekenweek, when buyers who spend more than a certain amount in a bookshop receive a free (Dutch) book.

SOCIETY & CONDUCT
Stereotypes
The Netherlands in general and Amsterdam in particular seem to be 15 years ahead of the rest of the world on some moral and social issues (drugs policy, abortion, euthanasia, homosexuality). On others they're 15 years behind, for instance with media policy, where every religious and ideological affiliation can broadcast but commercial motivation is frowned

upon. Sometimes they step 15 years sideways, for instance in preaching to the rest of the world about right and wrong – perhaps the only other preachers with similar drive are the Americans.

Critics attribute this to the 'minister's mentality' of moral rectitude epitomised by the Calvinist minister scowling from the pulpit. An acute sense of moral right and wrong is manifest in the earnest insistence that it hardly matters *how* you say something, it's *what* you say that counts, which gives the Dutch a bit of a reputation for bluntness.

It also gives them a reputation for lack of humour, yet they have an unusual ability to laugh at themselves and will cut down people who take themselves too seriously. For well over 30 years the TV icons *van Kooten & de Bie* have been doing the same types of sketches as the British *Smith & Jones* and *Fry & Laurie*, though their tendency towards 'meaningful' social and cultural commentary again betrays a minister's mentality.

There's little nationalist pride except on the soccer field. Amsterdammers love to complain about their city and their 'irrelevant' country, and are keen to learn new things foreign. English words in daily speech and print are not meant to accommodate tourists: they seem part of a national inferiority complex.

You won't find many monumental buildings or projects in the city. Most attempts have traditionally been criticised, ridiculed and sabotaged, though Calvinist frugality has played a role too. It's almost as if Amsterdammers are proud of not being proud, but when they compare Amsterdam with other Dutch cities they agree there's nothing like it.

It is said that the Calvinist Dutch, like the Presbyterian Scots, are careful with money, and they certainly have proven to be astute traders. It's worth remembering that the Netherlands and especially Amsterdam have always had a money culture; there was little or no traditional aristocracy with large landholdings. The people who dominated society built their own wealth and it all rested on money – if they squandered it, there was nothing to fall back on.

The earlier History section discussed the phenomenon of 'pillarisation' (verzuiling), which allowed different ideologies their place in society so long as they maintained the status quo by compromise – important in an overpopulated country where freedom of expression is taken so seriously. Although verzuiling's social and cultural segmentation is considered outdated now, it has led to a culture of tolerance with few strict conventions, and nowhere is this more evident than in Amsterdam. If there is one convention it is probably 'reasonableness', allowing others to have their say, live and let live. Everyone is expected to have an opinion and to voice it, but meddling in others' affairs is definitely 'not done'.

Do's & Don'ts

The accepted greeting is a handshake – make it firm but not bone-crushing. Cheek-kissing (two or three pecks) is common between men and women (and between women but not men) who know one another socially.

The typically pragmatic convention for queuing is to take a numbered ticket from a dispenser and await your turn. Always check whether there's a dispenser if you find yourself in a post office, government office, bakery, or at a delicatessen counter in a supermarket etc.

If you're invited home for dinner, bring something for the host: a bunch of flowers or a plant, a bottle of wine, or some good cake or pastries. It's polite to arrive five to 15 minutes late (never early), but business meetings always start on time.

Dress standards are casual (most concerts, most restaurants) or smart casual (theatre, opera, up-market restaurants and some business dealings); and slightly formal (most business dealings) or quite formal (bankers).

RELIGION

Amsterdam started out as a Catholic city without being fervently anti-Protestant; after all, the money machine dictated tolerance. Even after the Alteration of 1578, when

Amsterdam went over to the Protestant camp and Calvinism became the leading faith in the northern Netherlands, the city authorities still promoted religious tolerance (though not freedom), even towards those who didn't belong to any church. Civil marriages (sanctioned by public officials rather than clergy) were legally recognised as early as the 17th century, which was a first in Europe.

The Protestant Hervormde Kerk (Dutch Reformed Church) was also fairly tolerant of dissenting views among its members, but in the late 19th century a growing minority of low-income strugglers disagreed and broke off to form the Gereformeerde Kerk ('Rereformed' Church) in pursuit of orthodox-Calvinist doctrine. The schism persists to this day though it affects an ever smaller number of people.

Agnosticism and atheism reign supreme: almost 60% of Amsterdammers have no religious affiliation. Catholics are the largest religious grouping with 19% of the population against a national average of 32% – the term 'Catholic' should be used in preference to 'Roman Catholic' because many Catholics locally and nationally disagree with the pope on issues such as church hierarchy, contraception and abortion. The next largest religious grouping is Muslim at 8.3% (the national average is 3.7%), followed by Hervormd at 5.5% (national average 15%), Gereformeerd at 3% (national average 7%) and other religions (mainly Hindu and Buddhist) at 5.2% (national average 3%).

LANGUAGE

Almost every Amsterdammer from age eight onwards seems to speak English, often very well and always better than you'll ever learn Dutch, so why bother? That's a good question because you'll rarely get the opportunity to practise: your Dutch acquaintances will immediately launch into English, maybe to show off but more likely to ease communication. However, a few words in Dutch show goodwill which is always appreciated, and you might begin to understand a bit more of what's going on around you. For more extensive coverage of Dutch, see Lonely Planet's *Western Europe phrasebook*.

Most English speakers use the term 'Dutch' to describe the language spoken in the Netherlands and 'Flemish' for that spoken in the northern half of Belgium and a tiny north-western corner of France. Both are in fact the same language, called Netherlandic *(Nederlands)*. The differences between Dutch and Flemish *(Vlaams)* are similar to those between British and North American English.

Dutch gives its nouns genders like many languages do. There are three: masculine, feminine (both with *de* for 'the') and neuter (with *het*). Where English uses 'a' or 'an', Netherlandic uses *een* ('ern') regardless of gender.

There's also a formal and an informal version of the English 'you'. The formal is *U* (pronounced like the German 'ü'), the informal is *je* ('yer'). As a general rule, people who are older than you should be addressed as *U*.

Dutch, like German, strings words together, which can baffle a foreigner trying to decipher (let alone remember) street names, eg Eerste Goudsbloemdwarsstraat – 'First Marigold Transverse Street'. Chopping a seemingly endless name into its separate components might help a bit. The following are some terms that frequently appear in the names of streets and sights:

baan – path, way
binnen – inside, inner
bloem – flower
brug – bridge
buiten – outside, outer
dijk – dyke
dwars – transverse
eiland – island
gracht – canal
groot – great, large
hoek – corner
huis – house
kade – quay
kapel – chapel
kerk – church
klein – minor, small
laan – avenue
markt – market
molen – (wind)mill

nieuw – new
noord – north
oost – east
oud – old
plein – square
poort – city gate
sloot – ditch
sluis – sluice, lock
steeg – alley
straat – street
toren – tower
veld – field
(burg)wal – (fortified) embankment
weg – road
west – west
zuid – south

Pronunciation

Vowels Single vowels are pretty straightforward as Continental languages go, with long and short sounds for each. Combined vowels are more unusual:

a	short, as the 'u' in 'cut'
a, aa	long, like the 'a' in 'father'
au, ou	both pronounced somewhere between the 'ow' in 'how' and the 'ow' in 'glow'
e	short, like the 'e' in 'bet', or the 'er' in 'fern'
e, ee	long, like the 'ay' in 'day'
ei	like the 'ey' in 'they'
eu	like the German 'ö', or Queen Elizabeth's pronunciation of 'o' in 'over'
i	short, as in 'in'
i, ie	long, like the 'ee' in 'meet', but clipped
ij	like the 'ey' in 'they'
o	short, as in 'pot'
o, oo	long, as in 'note'
oe	like the 'oo' in 'zoo'
u	short, similar to the 'u' in 'urn'
u, uu	long, like the 'u' in the German *über*, or Queen Elizabeth's pronunciation of 'o' in 'who'
ui	no equivalent sound in English; in French, the 'eui' in *fauteuil* is close (if you leave out the slide towards the 'l')
ÿ	**ij**, but less common

Consonants These are also pretty straightforward, except for the **ch** and **g** that give (northern) Netherlandic its characteristic harshness:

ch,g	in the north (and commonly in Amsterdam), a guttural 'kh' sound as in the Scottish loch, really hard as if you're bringing up phlegm; in the south, a softer, lisping sound
j	like the 'y' in 'yes'; sometimes like the 'j' or 'zh' sound in 'jam' or 'pleasure'
r	in the south (and commonly in Amsterdam), a trilled sound made with the tip of the tongue; in the north it varies, often guttural
s	like the 's' in 'sample'; sometimes like a 'z'
sch	at the end of a word, like the 's' in 'sample'; otherwise, an 's' followed by 'ch'
w	at the beginning of a word, a clipped sound almost like a 'v'; at the end of a word, like the English 'w'

Basics

Hello	*Dag/ Hallo*
Goodbye	*Dag/ De mazzel*
Yes/No	*Ja/Nee*
Please	*Alstublieft/alsjeblieft*
Thank you	*Dank U/je (wel)/ Bedankt*
Excuse me	*Pardon*

Small Talk

How are you?
Hoe gaat het (met U/jou)?
I'm fine, thanks.
Goed, bedankt.
What's your name?
Hoe heet U/je?
My name is ...
Ik heet ...
Where are you from?
Waar komt U/kom je vandaan?
I am from ...
Ik kom uit ...

Language Difficulties

I don't understand.
Ik begrijp het niet.
Do you speak English?
Spreekt U/Spreek je Engels?
Please write it down.
Schrijf het alstublieft/alsjeblieft op.

Getting Around

What time does the ... leave/arrive?
Hoe laat vertrekt/arriveert de ...?

bus	*bus*
train	*trein*
tram	*tram*

Where is the ... ?
Waar is de/het ... ?

bus stop	*de bushalte*
metro station	*het metrostation*
train station	*het (trein) station*
tram stop	*de tramhalte*

I'd like a one-way/return ticket.
Ik wil graag een enkele reis/een retour.
I'd like to hire a car/bicycle.
Ik wil graag een auto/fiets huren.

Directions

What street/road is this?
Welke straat/weg is dit?
How do I get to ...?
Hoe kom ik bij ...?

(Go) straight ahead.	*(Ga) rechtdoor.*
(Turn) left.	*(Ga naar) links.*
(Turn) right.	*(Ga naar) rechts.*
at the traffic lights	*bij het stoplicht*
at the next corner	*bij de volgende hoek*

Around Town

Where is the ...?
Waar is de/het ...?

bank	*de bank*
embassy	*de ambassade*
exchange office	*het wisselkantoor*
post office	*het postkantoor*

public toilet	*het openbaar toilet*
telephone centre	*het telefoonkantoor*
tourist information office	*de VVV*

What time does it open/close?
Hoe laat opent/sluit het?

Useful Signs

CAMPING GROUND	*CAMPING*
ENTRANCE/EXIT	*INGANG/UITGANG*
INFORMATION	*INFORMATIE/ INLICHTINGEN*
OPEN/CLOSED	*OPEN/GESLOTEN*
POLICE	*POLITIE*
PROHIBITED	*VERBODEN*
ROOMS AVAILABLE	*KAMERS VRIJ*
TOILETS	*WC'S/ TOILETTEN*

Accommodation

Do you have a room?
Heeft U een kamer?
How much is it per night/per person?
Hoeveel is het per nacht/per persoon?
Is breakfast included?
Is ontbijt inbegrepen?
Can I see the room?
Kan ik de kamer zien?

youth hostel	*jeugdherberg*
camping ground	*camping*
hotel	*hotel*
guesthouse	*pension*

Food

breakfast	*ontbijt*
lunch	*lunch/middageten*
dinner	*diner/avondeten*
restaurant	*restaurant*

I'm vegetarian.
Ik ben vegetarisch.

Shopping

How much is it?	*Hoeveel is het?*
Can I look at it?	*Kan ik het zien?*

It's too expensive for me.
Het is mij te duur.

bookshop	*boekwinkel*	9	*negen*
chemist/pharmacy	*drogist/apotheek*	10	*tien*
clothing store	*kledingzaak*	100	*honderd*
laundry	*wasserette*	1000	*duizend*
market	*markt*	10,000	*tienduizend*
supermarket	*supermarkt*		
newsagency	*krantenwinkel*		
stationers	*kantoorboekhandel*	one million	*een miljoen*

Time & Dates

What time is it?	*Hoe laat is het?*
When?	*Wanneer?*
today	*vandaag*
tonight	*vanavond*
tomorrow	*morgen*
yesterday	*gisteren*
Monday	*maandag*
Tuesday	*dinsdag*
Wednesday	*woensdag*
Thursday	*donderdag*
Friday	*vrijdag*
Saturday	*zaterdag*
Sunday	*zondag*

Numbers

1	*een*
2	*twee*
3	*drie*
4	*vier*
5	*vijf*
6	*zes*
7	*zeven*
8	*acht*

Health/Emergencies

I need a doctor.
 Ik heb een dokter nodig.
Where is the hospital?
 Waar is het ziekenhuis?
Call the police!
 Haal de politie!
Call an ambulance!
 Haal een ziekenauto!
Help!
 Help!
I'm lost.
 Ik ben de weg kwijt.
I'm diabetic/epileptic/asthmatic.
 Ik ben suikerziek/epileptisch/astmatisch.

antiseptic	*ontsmettingsmiddel*
aspirin	*aspirine*
condoms	*condooms*
constipation	*verstopping*
diarrhoea	*diarree*
nausea	*misselijkheid*
sunblock cream	*zonnebrandolie*
tampons	*tampons*

Facts for the Visitor

WHEN TO GO

Any time can be the best time to visit. The summer months are wonderful as the whole city seems to live outdoors and there are things going on everywhere. It's also the peak tourist season, when accommodation is hard to find and prices are high. Many Amsterdammers go on holidays in summer and some businesses close down or adapt their activities (eg museums, orchestras).

From mid-October to mid-March the climate is miserable but there are less tourists. Accommodation is relatively cheap (except around New Year) though some hotels might be closed. You'll mingle with 'real' Amsterdammers in cosy pubs and be able to enjoy the city's cultural life at its most authentic. The shoulder seasons, roughly from mid-March to late May and late August to mid-October, can offer the best of both worlds, though you might want to avoid Easter if you hate hordes of tourists or expensive hotels.

A festival or special event can enhance your visit – see Public Holidays & Special Events later in this chapter – but it won't be a secret and you might have trouble finding accommodation. If weather is your main concern, see Climate in the previous chapter.

ORIENTATION

Most of Amsterdam lies south of the IJ, an arm of what was once the Zuiderzee (an extension of the North Sea) but is now a vast lake, the IJsselmeer. The modern city sprawls in all directions and is several times larger than it was even 80 years ago.

The old city is contained within the ring of concentric canals *(grachten)* dating from the 17th century that form the crescent-shaped canal belt *(grachtengordel)* bordered by the Singelgracht. Most areas beyond this tidy structure have been added since the second half of the 19th century.

The Amstel river cuts through the old city, which arose around Dam square. East of this is the Oude Zijde (Old Side) and west is the Nieuwe Zijde. This medieval *binnenstad* (inner city) is enclosed by the Singel ('moat', not to be confused with the Singelgracht) to the west and south, and the Kloveniersburgwal/Geldersekade to the east.

Centraal Station, the central train and bus station, lies on the south bank of the IJ at what used to be the mouth of the Amstel river, though the 'centre of town' would have to be Dam square a little to the south. It's the city's largest square and major road arteries radiate out from it, but there are several other 'centres' where everything seems to happen: Leidseplein, with much of the city's cultural life and nightlife; Rembrandtplein (nightlife); Spui ('intellectual' life); Munt (the city's busiest intersection); Stationsplein in front of Centraal Station (the main transport hub); Nieuwmarkt square (daily life in general); Waterlooplein with the Stopera (market life behind a landmark on the Amstel); the large, windswept Museumplein (culture); and other, smaller focal points that make the city such a joy to explore.

Finding your way around the canal belt can be confusing, though it's a breeze compared with Venice. Think of it as half a bicycle wheel: the medieval city is the hub, and several main roads and minor canals (and the Amstel itself) function as spokes. Orientation becomes easier once you know the sequence of the main canals (from the centre outwards: Singel, Herengracht, Keizersgracht, Prinsengracht and Singelgracht) and the names of some of the major 'spokes' (anti-clockwise: Haarlemmerstraat/Haarlemmerdijk, Brouwersgracht, Raadhuisstraat/Rozengracht, Leidsestraat, Vijzelstraat, Utrechtsestraat, Amstel, Weesperstraat and Plantage Middenlaan).

House numbers along the main canals start at the north-western end, at Brouwersgracht, with odd numbers along the inner quays (the 'city-centre' sides). Elsewhere, numbers start at the end of the street closest to the city centre.

MAPS

The maps in this book will probably suffice in most cases, though you'll need something a bit more dedicated for the (outer) suburbs and for looking up streets. The VVV tourist offices sell a cheap map showing most of Amsterdam and listing many streets (with a blow-up of the medieval inner city).

Newsagencies and many other outlets sell the Dutch-produced Cito Plan or the German Falkplan. They're both good but the Cito is probably the clearest, in either the ring-bound booklet or large sheet version, though it has to be tilted clockwise a bit to get true north facing up. The Swiss Hallwag sheet map is also good and very clear but the smallest streets aren't labelled.

A beautiful souvenir map to hang on the wall when you get home is the lovingly drawn bird's-eye view produced by Bollmann, a German map publisher specialising in this type of product. The map shows the city centre in 1971 and every house is recognisable. It can be hard to find, but geographical bookshop Jacob van Wijngaarden at Overtoom 97 should have it.

TOURIST OFFICES
Local Tourist Offices

Within the Netherlands, tourist information is supplied by the VVV (Vereniging voor Vreemdelingenverkeer – Society for Foreigner Traffic), which has four offices in Amsterdam and a fifth, called Holland Tourist Promotion, at the airport. All its publications cost money and it charges high commissions for services (f5 per person to find a room, f2.50 each on theatre tickets etc). The offices are often very busy but it's worth queuing to get an Amsterdam Culture & Leisure Pass (see Useful Cards in the following Documents section).

The GWK office (official exchange, see Changing Money in the following Money section) inside Centraal Station also books rooms for a f5 commission (plus the full hotel fee) at a separate counter that's usually much quieter than the VVV counters.

The VVV information number (☎ 0900-340 340 66) operates Monday to Friday from 9 am to 5 pm and costs a hefty f1 a minute. The VVV fax number is 625 28 69 and the mailing address is Postbus 3901, 1001 AS Amsterdam. Office details are as follows:

VVV, Stationsplein 10 in front of Centraal Station (Map 2) – the main VVV office, open Monday to Saturday from 9 am to 5 pm; expect long queues and variable service

VVV, inside Centraal Station, next to the international railway reservations office – Monday to Saturday from 8 am to 7.30 pm, Sunday from 9 am to 4.30 pm; always busy

VVV, Leidseplein 1 on the corner of Leidsestraat (Map 15) – Monday to Saturday from 8.30 am to 8 pm, Sunday to 5 pm; shares premises with a GWK-affiliated exchange office that offers reasonable rates

VVV, Van Tuyll van Serooskerkenweg 125 at Stadionplein (Map 8) – Monday to Saturday from 9 am to 5 pm, Sunday to noon; useful if you're arriving by car from the south and usually much quieter than the other offices

Holland Tourist Promotion (VVV), Schiphol Plaza in the airport – open seven days a week from 7 am to 10 pm

Tourist Offices Abroad

The Nederlands Bureau voor Toerisme (NBT) handles tourism outside the country:

Belgium (plus Luxembourg)
    NBT, Louizalaan 89, Postbus 136, Brussels 5 (☎ 02-534 23 26)
Canada
    Netherlands Board of Tourism, 25 Adelaide St East, Suite 710, Toronto, Ont, M5C 1Y2 (☎ 416-363 15 77)
France
    Office Néerlandais du Tourisme, 9 rue Scribe, 75009 Paris (☎ 01-43 12 34 20)
Germany
    Niederländisches Büro für Tourismus, Friesenplatz 1, Postfach 270580, 50511 Cologne (☎ 0221-92 57 17) – information Monday to Friday from 10 am to noon and 2 to 4 pm on ☎ 0221-25 70 383
Japan
    Netherlands Board of Tourism, NK Shinwa Building 5f 5-1, Koijmachi, Chiyoda-ku, Tokyo 102 (☎ 03-32 22 11 12)
Sweden (plus Denmark, Norway & Finland)
    Holländska Turistbyrån, Högbergsgatan 50, 1118 26 Stockholm (☎ 08-714 82 50)
UK (plus Ireland)
    Netherlands Board of Tourism, 18 Buckingham Gate, London SW1E 6LB (☎ 0171-828 79 00)

USA
> Netherlands Board of Tourism, 355 Lexington Ave, 21st Floor, New York, NY 10017 (☎ 212-370 73 60)
>
> 9841 Airport Blvd, Suite 103, Los Angeles, CA 90045 (☎ 310-348 93 39)
>
> 225 N Michigan Ave, Suite 1854, Chicago, IL 60601 (☎ 312-819 16 36)

The NBT office in Sydney, Australia, has closed down – the embassy in Canberra, consulates in the major cities or the KLM office in Sydney might be able to help.

Other Information Offices

The VVV is all right for mainstream tourist information but there are other places where you might be served better. If you're interested in the arts (theatres, concerts, films, museums etc), the Amsterdam Uitburo, or AUB (Map 15; ☎ 621 12 11), Leidseplein 26, has lots of free magazines and brochures, and sells tickets for a f3 markup. The staff are friendlier and more helpful than at the VVV. The office is open Monday to Saturday from 10 am to 6 pm, Thursday to 9 pm. The telephone number operates seven days a week from 9 am to 9 pm for information and ticket reservations. Information is also available on the Uitweb at www.aub.nl; for specific queries and reactions, e-mail: aub@aub.nl.

The Dutch automobile association ANWB (Map 15; ☎ 673 08 44), Museumplein 5, has free or heavily discounted maps and brochures and provides a wide range of useful information and assistance if you're travelling with any type of vehicle (car, bicycle, motorcycle, yacht etc). The material on Amsterdam itself is limited but there's more than enough about the country and Europe. You'll probably have to show proof of membership of your automobile club (see Useful Cards in the following section).

If you plan to stay in Amsterdam for a while, the city hall information centre (☎ 624 11 11), Amstel 1 (Waterlooplein entrance), has pamphlets and booklets on almost every aspect of living in the city, some of them in English. It's open Monday to Friday from 9 am to 5 pm. The staff are quite helpful and, as almost everywhere else, speak English. They use their computerised database to track down addresses and phone numbers of relevant organisations.

DOCUMENTS

Visas

Tourists from Australia, Canada, Israel, Japan, Korea (south), New Zealand, Singapore, the USA and most of Europe need only a valid passport – no visa – for a stay of up to three months. EU nationals can enter for three months with just their national identity card or a passport expired less than five years.

Nationals of most other countries need a so-called Schengen Visa, named after the Schengen Agreement that abolished passport controls between the Netherlands, Belgium, Luxembourg, Germany, France, Spain and Portugal. A visa for any of these countries should in theory be valid throughout the area, but it pays to double-check with the embassy or consulate of each country you intend to visit (the French in particular may be difficult). Residency status in any of the Schengen countries negates the need for a visa, regardless of your nationality.

Three-month tourist visas are issued by Dutch embassies or consulates and can take a while to process (up to three months, if you're unlucky), so don't leave it till the last moment. You'll need a valid passport and 'sufficient' funds to finance your stay. Fees vary depending on the country – the embassy or consulate can tell you more.

Visas for study purposes are complicated – check with the Dutch embassy or consulate. For work visas, see Work later in this chapter.

Visa Extensions

The Netherlands are the most densely populated country in Europe and voters seem to support the government crackdown on people who don't 'belong'. Tourist visas can be extended for another three months maximum, but you'll need a good reason and the extension will only be valid for the Netherlands, not the Schengen area.

Visa extensions and residence permits are handled by the Vreemdelingenpolitie (Aliens' Police, ☎ 559 63 00), Bijlmerdreef 90, Bijlmer, Monday to Friday from 8 am to 5 pm. Bring something to read – you'll probably have to wait a couple of hours.

Photocopies

All important documents (passport data page and visa page, credit cards, travel insurance policy, air/bus/train ticket, driving licence etc) should be photocopied before you leave home. Leave one copy with someone at home and keep another one with you, separate from the originals.

Travel Insurance

Medical or dental costs might already be covered through reciprocal health-care arrangements (see Health later in this chapter) but you'll still need cover for theft or loss, and for unexpected changes to travel arrangements (ticket cancellation etc). Check what's already covered by your local insurance policies or credit card: you might not need separate travel insurance. In most cases, though, this secondary type of cover is very limited with lots of tricky small print. For peace of mind, nothing beats straight travel insurance at the highest level you can afford.

Driving Licence & Permits

Of course you'll need to show a valid driving licence when hiring a car. Visitors from outside the EU should also consider an international driving permit (IDP). Car-rental firms will rarely ask for one but the police might do so if they pull you up. An IDP can be obtained for a small fee from your local automobile association – bring along a valid licence and a passport photo – and is only valid (for a year) together with your original licence.

Useful Cards

A Hostelling International card is useful at the official youth hostels – nonmembers are welcome but pay f5 more per night. Other hostels may give small discounts. If you don't pick up a HI card before leaving home you can buy one at youth hostels in the Netherlands.

An International Student Identity Card (ISIC) won't give admission discounts but it might pay for itself through discounted air and ferry tickets, and the GWK exchange offices will waive their commission when exchanging cash. The same applies to hostel cards, as well as the GO 25 card for people aged under 26 who aren't students, issued by the Federation of International Youth Travel Organisations (FIYTO) through student unions or student travel agencies.

The Cultureel Jongeren Paspoort (CJP, Cultural Youth Passport) is a national institution that gives people aged under 26 whopping discounts to museums and cultural events around the country – any young person with a particular interest in the arts is well advised to get one. It costs f20 a year and is available at VVV offices or the Amsterdam Uitburo (see Other Information Offices in the previous section). You don't have to be Dutch but you do need decent ID.

The Museumjaarkaart (Museum Year Card) gives free admission to most of the city's museums – see Museums later in this chapter.

Teachers, professional artists, museum conservators and certain categories of students may get discounts at a few museums or even be admitted free – it seems to depend on the person behind the counter. Bring along proof of affiliation, eg an International Teacher Identity Card (ITIC).

The VVV offices and some large hotels sell the Amsterdam Culture & Leisure Pass. This contains 28 vouchers that give free entry or substantial discounts to the most important museums, a free canal cruise, and discounts on land and water transport and some restaurants. The pass represents a total value of f140 and sells for f29.90 – a good investment.

If you're travelling with any type of vehicle, the Dutch automobile association ANWB (see Other Information Offices in the previous section) will provide a wide range of services free of charge if you can show proof of membership of the equivalent association at home, preferably in the form of a letter of introduction such as the yellow Entraide Touring Internationale document. Your automobile club should be able to provide this; if the staff have never heard of it, ask for someone who knows their stuff.

CONSULATES & EMBASSIES

Amsterdam is the country's capital but the government and ministries are based in The Hague, so that's where all the embassies are. There are, however, 46 consulates in Amsterdam, listed under 'Consulaat' in the phone book. These include:

Denmark
 Radarweg 503 (☎ 682 99 91)
France
 Vijzelgracht 2 (☎ 625 79 58) – open weekdays from 9 to 11 am
Germany
 De Lairessestraat 172 (☎ 673 62 45)
Italy
 Herengracht 609 (☎ 624 00 43)
Japan
 Vijzelgracht 50 (☎ 691 69 21)
Luxembourg
 Reimersbeek 2 (☎ 301 56 22)
Norway
 Keizersgracht 534-I (☎ 624 23 31)
Spain
 Frederiksplein 34 (☎ 620 38 11) – open weekdays from 9 to 11 am
Sweden
 Radarweg 501 (☎ 682 21 11)
Thailand
 Emmastraat 40 (☎ 679 99 16)
UK
 Koningslaan 44 near the Vondelpark (☎ 676-4343) – open weekdays from 9 am to noon and 2 to 3.30 pm
USA
 Museumplein 19 near the Concertgebouw (☎ 575 53 09) – open weekdays from 8.30 am to noon and 1.30 to 3.30 pm (note the elaborate security precautions)

Embassies in The Hague, a 40-minute (f16) train ride away, include:

Australia
 Carnegielaan 10-14 (☎ 070-310 82 00)
Belgium
 Lange Vijverberg 12 (☎ 070-364 49 10)

Canada
 Sophialaan 7 (☎ 070-361 41 11)
Finland
 Groot Hertoginnelaan 16 (☎ 070-346 97 54)
Ireland
 Dr Kuyperstraat 9 (☎ 070-363 09 93)
Korea (south)
 Verlengde Tolweg 8 (☎ 070-352 06 21)
New Zealand
 Carnegielaan 10 (☎ 070-346 93 24)
South Africa
 Wassenaarseweg 40 (☎ 070-392 45 01)

CUSTOMS

Visitors from EU countries can bring virtually anything they like, provided they bought it in an EU country where the appropriate local tax was levied, but tax-free allowances (for instance when flying) are less than those applying to visitors from outside the EU. The staff at tax-free shops will ask to see your ticket and will tell you in no uncertain terms how much (or rather, little) they're willing to sell you. Unless the EU's finance and economy ministers have a change of heart, tax-free allowances between EU countries will be abolished altogether in July 1999.

Visitors from a European country outside the EU and not resident in the EU can import goods and gifts valued up to f125 (bought tax-free) as well as 200 cigarettes (or 50 cigars or 250g of tobacco), one litre of liquor more than 22% by volume or two litres less than 22% by volume, plus two litres of wine and eight litres of non-sparkling Luxembourg wine, 60g of perfume and 0.25 litre of eau de toilette.

Visitors from outside Europe and resident outside Europe can bring in 400 cigarettes (or 100 cigars or 500g of tobacco) plus other goods, spirits, wines and perfumes as for non-EU Europeans.

Tobacco and alcohol may only be brought in by people aged 17 and over.

MONEY
Currency

The unit of currency is the guilder (*gulden*, abbreviated f, fl, Hfl or Dfl), divided into 100 cents. There are f1000, f250, f100, f50, f25 and f10 bank notes, and f5, f2.50, f1, f0.25, f0.10 and f0.05 coins. One-cent coins no longer exist – prices in supermarkets are still indicated in cents (eg f5.99) but the bill is rounded off to the nearest five cents when paid in cash.

The Dutch flair for graphic design shows in the eye-catching bank notes (the bland coins are widely considered a flop), in particular the f100 note with its Escher-type 'building blocks', or the f250 'lighthouse'. If you're on the sort of budget where you would receive a f1000 note from the bank, ask to have it broken down into f250 and preferably f100 and f50 notes because many places refuse the largest denominations.

Cash

This is still very much a cash-based society and nothing beats cash for convenience (or risk of theft/loss). Plan to pay cash for most daily expenses, though staff at up-market hotels might cast a furtive glance if you pay a huge bill with small-denomination notes rather than a credit card, and car-rental agencies may refuse to do business if you only have cash. Keep the equivalent of about US$50 separate from the rest of your money as an emergency stash.

Travellers' & Euro Cheques

Banks charge a commission to cash travellers' cheques (with ID such as a passport). American Express and Thomas Cook don't charge commission on their own cheques but their rates might be less favourable. Shops, restaurants and hotels always prefer cash; a few might accept travellers' cheques but their rates will be anybody's guess. Eurocheques (with guarantee card) are much more widely accepted, and because you write the amount in guilders there's no confusion about exchange rates; they will be charged to your account at the more favourable interbank rate.

ATMs

Automatic teller machines can be found outside most banks, though in some cases you might have to swipe your card through a slot to gain entry to a secure area. There are ATMs around the airport halls as well, and a couple in the main hall of Centraal Station (slightly to the left as you enter through the main entrance). Visa and MasterCard/Eurocard are widely accepted, as are cash cards that can access the Cirrus network. Logos on ATMs show what they accept.

Credit Cards

All the major international cards are recognised, but Amsterdam is still quite strongly cash-based and many restaurants and hotels (even some of the more up-market ones) may refuse payment by card. Check first. Shops might levy a cheeky 5% surcharge (sometimes more) on credit-card purchases to offset the commissions charged by card providers.

To withdraw money at a bank counter instead of through an ATM, go to a VSB Bank or GWK branch (see the following Changing Money section). You'll need to show your passport.

Report lost or stolen cards to the following 24-hour numbers:

American Express – ☎ 504 80 00 (Monday to Friday from 9 am to 6 pm), ☎ 504 86 66 (other times)
Diners Club – ☎ 557 34 07
Eurocard and MasterCard have a number in Utrecht (☎ 030-283 55 55) but foreigners are advised to ring the emergency number in their home country to speed things up.
Visa – ☎ 660 06 11

International Transfers

Transferring money from your home bank will be easier if you've authorised somebody back home to access your account. In Amsterdam, find a large bank and ask for the international division. A commission is charged on telegraphic transfers, which can take up to a week but usually less if you're well prepared; by mail, allow two weeks.

The GWK (see the following Changing Money section) is an agent for Western Union and money is transferred within 15 minutes of lodgment at the other end. The person lodging the transfer pays a commission that varies from country to country – a transfer *from* the Netherlands costs f24.

Money can also be transferred via American Express and Thomas Cook (see the Changing Money section for addresses).

Exchange Rates

Exchange rates at the time of going to press were:

Australia	A$1	=	f1.50
Canada	C$1	=	f1.38
Belgium	Bf1	=	f0.055
Denmark	Dkr1	=	f0.30
France	1FF	=	f0.33
Germany	DM1	=	f1.12
Italy	L1000	=	f1.12
Japan	¥100	=	f1.55
Switzerland	Sfr1	=	f1.30
United Kingdom	UK£	=	f3.044
United States	US$1	=	f1.90

Changing Money

Avoid the many private exchange booths dotted around the tourist areas: they're convenient and open late hours but rates and/or commissions are lousy, though competition is fierce and you may do reasonably well with a bit of hunting around. Banks and post offices stick to official exchange rates and charge a maximum of f5 commission, as do the Grenswisselkantoren (GWK, Border Exchange Offices, ☎ 0800-566 free information service). Reliable exchange centres include:

GWK, Centraal Station at the west end of the station hall (☎ 627 27 31) – open 24 hours; commission f5 on cash and travellers' cheques (with a student card there's no commission on cash). Usually very busy (though its separate hotel-booking counter for bookings only, open from 7.45 am to 10 pm seven days a week, is usually quieter than the VVV ones). There's a GWK-affiliated office with slightly worse rates next to the VVV office in Leidsestraat, on the corner of Leidseplein.
GWK, Schiphol airport (☎ 653 51 21) – open 24 hours
American Express, Damrak 66 (Map 13; ☎ 520 77 77) – open Monday to Saturday from 9 am to 5 pm; no commission on Amex cheques
Thomas Cook, Dam 23-25 (Map 13; ☎ 625 09 22), with other offices at the beginning of Damrak opposite Centraal Station and at Leidseplein 31A – open weekdays from 9 am to 7 pm, Saturday to 6 pm, Sunday from 10 am to 4.30 pm; no commission on Thomas Cook cheques

VSB Bank, Singel 548 at the Flower Market near Vijzelstraat (Map 13; ☎ 624 93 40) – just one of several branches of this bank, where you can withdraw money over the counter with a credit card; 24-hour exchange machine (and of course the usual ATMs) outside

Costs

The sky's the limit in Amsterdam: you can easily throw hundreds of guilders down the drain each day with little to show for it. At the bottom end, if you stay at a camp site or hostel and eat cheaply, you'll probably spend f50 a day. A (very) cheap hotel, pub meals and the occasional beer and sundries will set you back f100. Things start to become quite comfortable at f150 a day, depending on your point of view.

Tipping & Bargaining

Tipping is not compulsory, but if you're pleased with the service by all means 'round up' the bill by 5-10% – many people do so in taxis and restaurants. A tip of 10% is considered generous. In pubs with pavement or table service it's common practice (but not compulsory) to leave the small change. Service is usually efficient but hardly ever formal and sometimes quite indifferent: shouting or 'talking down' to staff will ensure they ignore you. Toilet attendants should be tipped between 25 and 50 cents.

Ironically for a city with such a rich trading history, there's very little bargaining – it's definitely not done in shops. People do bargain at flea markets, though you'll have to be pretty good at this if your Dutch isn't fluent. Prices at food markets are generally set but become more negotiable later in the day.

The so-called Dutch auction, where the auctioneer keeps lowering the (high) starting price until somebody buys the item, is still practised at flower and plant auctions such as the huge flower market in Aalsmeer and the Monday plant market on Amstelveld.

Discounts

Students or those aged under 26 won't get a lot of discounts with their ISIC or GO 25 cards, but a CJP card (see the earlier Useful Cards section) can pay for itself many times over. Seniors get discounts on a wide range of services (see Senior Travellers later in this chapter).

If you plan to visit several of Amsterdam's excellent museums, invest in a Museumjaarkaart (Museum Year Card) – see Museums later in this chapter.

Taxes & Refunds

Value-added tax (Belasting Toegevoegde Waarde, or BTW) is calculated at 17.5% for most goods except consumer items like food, which attract 6%. The usual high excise *(accijns)* is levied on petrol, cigarettes and alcohol – petrol here is among the most expensive in Europe. The price for a packet of cigarettes is indicated on an excise sticker, and it will cost the same whether you buy it in the Amstel Hotel or the corner tobacco shop, separately or by the carton.

Hotel accommodation is subject to a 'tourist tax' which is always included in the price and varies from town to town and year to year; in Amsterdam at the time of writing it was f1 per night.

Travellers from non-EU countries can have the BTW refunded on goods over f300 if they're bought from one shop on one day and are exported within three months. To claim the tax back, ask the shop owner to provide an export certificate when you make the purchase. When you leave for a non-EU country, get the form endorsed by a Dutch customs official, who will send the certificate to the supplier, who in turn refunds you the tax by cheque or money order. If you want the tax before you leave the country, it's best to buy from shops displaying the 'Tax Free For Tourists' sign, though you'll lose about 5% of the refund because of red tape. In this case the shopkeeper gives you a stamped cheque that can be cashed when you leave.

Buying with a credit card is the best system as you won't pay tax so long as you get customs to stamp the receipt the shop owner gave you and you send the receipt back to the shop.

DOING BUSINESS

Amsterdam's authorities make much of the city's function as the gateway to Europe with its busy airport and harbour, its multilingual, highly educated and productive workforce, its easy-going tax laws, and its vast expertise in trade, transport, finance and communication services that make it an appropriate centre for international business. IBM, Xerox, Sony and Nissan are just a few of the growing number of companies who have set up their European headquarters in Amsterdam.

The trade office at the Dutch embassy in your home country can probably provide initial information and help establish the necessary contacts, as can your embassy's trade office in The Hague. Also in The Hague, the Netherlands Foreign Investment Agency (fax 070-379 63 22) offers similar support. Once you have a better idea of what you want, get in touch with the Amsterdam Chamber of Commerce & Industry (Map 11; ☎ 523 66 00; fax 523 66 77), De Ruijterkade 5, 1013 AA Amsterdam, who can help with the logistics.

Businesswomen might find the Women's International Network useful, an association that offers business contacts, advice and support for professional women aged over 25 and employed for at least five years. Membership (f150 a year) is open to foreign women working in the Netherlands and Dutch women working for international companies or with experience of working abroad. Contact the WIN (☎ 662 00 84) at Postbus 15692, 1001 ND Amsterdam.

Business Services

The luxury hotels (and Schiphol airport) all offer business services. Some have fully serviced business centres but they can be quite expensive. A cheaper option might be the Mini Office (Map 12; ☎ 625 84 55; fax 638 78 94; e-mail: moffice@xs4all.nl), Singel 417, with services for the short-term business visitor including hardware and software that can be rented by the hour (if you need to fix a document or two), bindings and mailings, e-mail and fax service (send and receive), personal answering service, private office, and even an office address.

The first European branch of the US Kinko's chain (minus the helpful and knowledgeable staff) offers the same services as the Mini Office but is open 24 hours a day. It's at Overtoom 62 near Leidseplein and can be contacted on ☎ 589 09 10, fax 589 09 20. By the time you read this it will probably do video-conferencing too.

If you're a bit more committed and want to start operating straight away without the headaches of establishing a base from scratch, the Euro Business Center (Map 12; ☎ 520 75 00; fax 520 75 10), Keizersgracht 62, can help with the paperwork and will supply an office with furniture, phone, computer etc for f1250 to f5000 a month. Secretarial help and a range of other services are also available.

For difficult translations, contact Berlitz Translation Services (☎ 639 14 06; fax 620 39 59), Rokin 87, though they're not cheap.

Exhibitions & Conferences

Amsterdam has become a popular place for trade fairs and conferences – it hosts more than 100 international and many hundreds of national conventions each year.

The major luxury hotels, such as Grand Hotel Krasnapolsky on Dam square (see Places to Stay), are often used for modest meetings and shows, and have the facilities to handle international gatherings from 25 to 2000 people.

Amsterdam RAI (Map 9; ☎ 549 12 12; fax 646 44 69), Europaplein 8, is the largest exhibition centre in the country (see the Things to See & Do chapter). It's also a conference centre with 21 conference rooms and a main auditorium that seats 1750. If necessary, one of the 11 exhibition halls can be converted for that spectacular gathering. Nearby is the World Trade Center (Map 9; ☎ 575 91 11; fax 662 72 55), Strawinskylaan 1, with conference rooms seating four to 200 people, and a full range of facilities and support services including a branch office of the Chamber of Commerce & Industry.

POST & COMMUNICATIONS
Post

Post offices are open weekdays from 9 am to 5 pm. The main post office at Singel 250 (Map 12) is open weekdays from 8.30 am to 6 pm (Thursday to 8 pm) and Saturday from 10 am to 1.30 pm. The poste restante section is to the left of the main entrance as you face the building, downstairs in the postbox area; the staff there can be a bit rude – not a good advertisement for the Dutch postal service. The district post office at Centraal Station, Oosterdokskade 3 (Map 14; a few hundred metres east of the station, alongside the huge boat hotel), is open on weekdays from 8.30 am to 9 pm and on Saturday from 9 am to noon. For queries about postal services, ring ☎ 0800-417 (free) – wait for the messages to finish and you'll eventually be helped by a human.

Mail is delivered locally six days a week (ie also Saturday). Unless you're sending mail within the Amsterdam region, the slot to use in the rectangular, red letterboxes is *Overige Bestemmingen* (Other Destinations).

Rates Letters within Europe (only air mail) cost f1 up to 20g; beyond Europe they cost f1.60 (air mail) or f1.20 (surface mail). Postcards (only air mail) cost f1 to anywhere outside the country. Aerogrammes cost f1.30. Within the country, letters (up to 20g) or postcards cost f0.80.

Addresses The postal code (four numbers followed by two letters) comes in front of the city or town name, eg 1017 LS Amsterdam. The codes are complicated and there's no apparent logic to them, but they pinpoint an address to within 100 metres. The telephone book provides the appropriate postal code for each entry, or you can pick up a free booklet at a post office (not always in stock). Amsterdam postal codes start with 10. No two streets in the city have the same name, so if you don't know the code but you've got the address right your mail should still arrive albeit after a few days' delay.

There are a few peculiarities with street

numbers. Sometimes they're followed by a letter or number (often in Roman numerals). Letters (eg No 34A or 34a) usually indicate the appropriate front door when two or more share the same number, whereas numbers (34-2, 34^2 or 34-II) indicate the appropriate floor. In modern dwellings, letters often indicate the appropriate apartment irrespective of the floor. The suffix 'hs' (34hs) stands for *huis* (house) and means the dwelling is on the ground floor, which may be half a floor above street level (in which case it's sometimes called *beletage*, the floor behind the door bell). The suffix 'bg' (34bg) stands for *begane grond* (ground floor). The suffix 'sous' (34sous) stands for *souterrain* and means the dwelling is in the basement (or rather, a basement that's half under street level: it can't be much deeper because of groundwater levels).

Telephone

This is one of the more expensive countries in Europe for phone calls but at least the network is efficient. Prices might come down a bit as the new phenomenon of competition begins to bite. Unfortunately there's no longer an official telephone centre but there are plenty of public telephones and you can always call from a post office. There are a few phone centres run by the (privatised) telephone company but they seem more interested in selling mobile phones and answering machines. Dozens of 'international call centres' seem to pop up all over the place, run by shady-looking characters who charge funny rates. Some might be all right but many are fly-by-nights (if not fronts for something else). As always, using a hotel phone is much more expensive than any other type of phone (OK, shore-to-ship might cost more but you get the point).

To place a collect call *(collect gesprek)*, person-to-person or other operator-assisted calls, ring ☎ 0800-04 10 (free call). International directory enquiries can be reached on ☎ 0900-84 18 (f1.05, free from a public phone). For local directory information, call ☎ 0900-80 08 (f0.66, free from a public phone).

Dialling Tones Tones are similar to those used throughout most of Continental Europe: an even dialling tone at fairly lengthy intervals means the number is ringing; a similar tone at shorter intervals means the number is engaged; a three-step tone means the number isn't in use or has been disconnected.

Costs Calls within the metropolitan area are time-based, and on weekdays the 'pulse' beats at f0.165 every 2½ minutes (or part thereof) from a private phone or f0.25 every two minutes from a public phone. Between 6 pm and 8 am and all Saturday and Sunday it's cheaper from private phones, with a pulse every five minutes, but public phones aren't discounted. For calls beyond Amsterdam private/public phones beat at f0.165/0.25 every 47 seconds at expensive times and every 94 seconds at cheap times.

The cost of international calls varies with the destination and is often lower on weekends (the front of the phone book provides details – look at prices marked *incl BTW*, including value-added tax): Britain costs f0.82-1.05 a minute, the USA f1.37-1.87 and Australia f3.30-3.85.

Phone Cards Most public telephones are card phones; there may be queues at the few remaining coin phones. Cards are available at post offices, train station counters, VVV and GWK offices and tobacco shops for f5 (f0.27 per phone pulse), f10 (f0.25 per pulse) and f25 (f0.24 per pulse). Public phones cost a minimum of 50 cents, though the occasional old coin phone in a pub might let you have a go for 25 cents.

When calling abroad to some countries, it's cheaper to buy a PTT Telecom Country Card which gives a 15-20% discount over an ordinary phone card. Country cards are available for the USA and Canada (f25, gives 15% discount), Australia, New Zealand and South Africa (f50, 20% discount), and Morocco, Turkey, Suriname and the Netherlands Antilles – all countries with which the Netherlands have strong ties through migration. These cards look like a normal phone card and can be used from both private and public phones but they must not be inserted into a card phone: you dial ☎ 0800-04 03 and a voice computer (in English or several other languages) does the rest as you enter a code. Ask at any post office how they work.

0800, 0900 & 06 Numbers Many information services, either recorded or live, use phone numbers beginning with ☎ 0800 (free) or ☎ 0900 (which cost between f0.20 and f1 a minute depending on the number). Until January 1997 the prefix for these sorts of calls was 06, and some numbers might still be quoted this way till 1998 when the 06 prefix becomes reserved for mobile telephones. (Note: old information numbers beginning with 06-0, 06-4, 06-3000 or 06-3009 are free, the others are charged). To avoid running up big phone bills, care should be taken whenever dialling ☎ 0900. Businesses that quote an 0900 number are required by law to state what it costs, but costs can vary depending on where you ring from so this isn't always clear.

Numbers beginning with ☎ 0909 are for paid amusement (radio and TV games, for instance); ☎ 0906 numbers are for sex and chat lines.

The emergency number, ☎ 112 (formerly 06-11), costs the same as a call beyond Amsterdam from a home phone but is free from a public phone.

Using Phone Books Similar surnames are listed alphabetically by address, not by initials, because people recall an address more readily than someone's initials. Confusingly, Dutch dictionaries and most other listings put the contracted vowel 'ij' after the 'i' but phone books treat it as a 'y'. Note that surnames beginning with 'van', 'de' etc are listed under the root name, eg 'V van Gogh' would be under the 'G' as 'Gogh, V van'. For married women and widows who use their husbands' names, the maiden name traditionally comes after the name of the husband.

The phone book lists postal codes for each entry and fax numbers where relevant.

Phone Codes To ring abroad, dial ☎ 00 followed by the country code for your target country, the area code (drop the leading 0 if there is one) and the subscriber number. The country code for the Netherlands is ☎ 31 and the area code for Greater Amsterdam is ☎ 020 (drop the leading 0 if ringing from another country). Other area codes include:

Alkmaar	☎ 072
Delft	☎ 015
Haarlem	☎ 023
IJmuiden	☎ 0255
Leiden	☎ 071
The Hague	☎ 070
Rotterdam	☎ 010
Utrecht	☎ 030
Zaandam	☎ 075

The area code for Schiphol is the same as for Amsterdam but numbers are listed separately at the end of part 2 of the phone book (just before the pink business pages that are copied in both parts). The southern suburb of Amstelveen (area codes ☎ 020 or ☎ 0297) is not included in the Amsterdam phone book, nor is the eastern suburb of Diemen (☎ 020 or 0294).

Home Country Direct Instead of placing a collect call through the local operator you could dial directly to your home country operator and then reverse charges, charge the call to a phone company credit card or perform other credit feats. This is possible to many (not all) countries and costs a fair bit – check with your home phone company before you leave though you might not get the full cost story. The following is a selection (with the relevant country codes in brackets for reference); ring international directory enquiries if your country isn't listed:

(61) Australia	☎ 0800-022 00 61 (Telstra),
	☎ 0800-022 55 61 (Optus)
(32) Belgium	☎ 0800-022 11 32
(1) Canada	☎ 0800-022 91 16
(358) Finland	☎ 0800-022 03 58
(33) France	☎ 0800-022 20 33
(49) Germany	☎ 0800-022 00 49
(852) Hong Kong	☎ 0800-022 08 52

(353) Ireland	☎ 0800-022 03 53
(39) Italy	☎ 0800-022 60 39
(81) Japan	☎ 0800-022 00 81
(82) Korea (south)	☎ 0800-022 00 82
(352) Luxembourg	☎ 0800-022 03 52
(64) New Zealand	☎ 0800-022 44 64
(47) Norway	☎ 0800-022 00 47
(65) Singapore	☎ 0800-022 88 65
(27) South Africa	☎ 0800-022 02 27
(34) Spain	☎ 0800-022 00 34
(46) Sweden	☎ 0800-022 00 46
(886) Taiwan	☎ 0800-022 08 86
(66) Thailand	☎ 0800-022 01 66
(44) UK	☎ 0800-022 99 44
(1) USA	☎ 0800-022 91 11 (AT&T),
	☎ 0800-022 91 22 (MCI),
	☎ 0800-022 91 19 (Sprint)

Fax, Telegraph & E-mail

It's difficult to send or receive faxes as a visitor. Some of the more up-market hotels are happy to help if you announce your requirements in advance, and most hotels with fax (quite a few of the cheaper hotels don't have one) will at least let you receive the occasional message. (Business travellers take note: this might convince the boss that you need to stay at something a bit more up-market.) Copy shops and call centres send faxes, but in order to receive one you have to be on good terms with the proprietor. Kinko's (☎ 589 09 10; fax 589 09 20), Overtoom 62 near Leidseplein, offers 24-hour office support and will send faxes for f4.50 a page and receive them for f1 a page.

You can send (but not receive) faxes from large post offices but it's not cheap. If you're sending to a private machine, the basic charge is f20 plus f2.50/5 a page within/outside Europe – for a small number of pages it's cheaper to use a copy shop or telecommunication centre. If the fax is going to a post office and has to be hand delivered, the costs per page are the same but the basic charge is f33.50.

Telegrams can be sent from post offices for a basic charge of f23.50 plus f0.85/1.35 per word (maximum 10 characters, otherwise it's two words) within/outside Europe, including address and signature. It doesn't take much for a telegram to cost considerably more than a hand-delivered fax. The only advantage of a telegram is that it might be quicker because a hand-delivered fax goes by regular mail delivery at the other end. For more information, including lodgment by telephone (billed to the phone account), ring ☎ 0800-409.

Internet data transfer is doubling every two months, the number of users every three. See the Digital Media section later in this chapter for details.

BOOKS

Guidebooks

There are more guidebooks to Amsterdam than you can shake a bicycle spoke at. Women might wish to consult Catherine Stebbings' *Amsterdam – the Woman's Travel Guide* published by Virago. The *Best Guide to Amsterdam & the Benelux* is the definitive gay guide.

If you plan to settle in Amsterdam for a while, get hold of *Live & Work in Belgium, The Netherlands and Luxembourg* from Vacation Work Publications, with detailed explanations of the necessary paperwork and more.

History

CR Boxer's *The Dutch Seaborne Empire 1600-1800*, first published in 1965, remains one of the most readable academic textbooks on how this small corner of Europe dominated world trade. Simon Schama's *The Embarrassment of Riches: an Interpretation of Dutch Culture in the Golden Age* (1987) deals with the tensions between vast wealth and Calvinist sobriety, and much more. Peter Burke's *Venice and Amsterdam* (1994) discusses the obvious similarities and less obvious differences between these trading empires.

Amsterdam, A Short History (1994) by Dr Richter Roegholt provides a good, concise summary but few insights. Serious students should track down Pieter Geyl's *The Revolt of the Netherlands, 1555-1609* (1958) and *The Netherlands in the 17th Century, 1609-1648* (1961/64). Johan Huizinga's *The Waning of the Middle Ages: A Study of the Forms of Life, Thought, and Art in France and the Netherlands in the 14th and 15th Centuries* (1924) is world-famous (among historians at least) and is as much a literary work as a study.

If you read Dutch, Geert Mak's *Een Kleine Geschiedenis van Amsterdam* (1994) offers revelations and potted dramas, and a perceptive analysis of the cultural revolution that swept the city from the mid-1960s to mid-1980s – Mak calls it the '20-year city war'.

The famous *Diary of Anne Frank*, an autobiography written by a Jewish teenager, movingly describes life in hiding in Nazi-occupied Amsterdam.

General

For practical architecture and engineering, see *Building Amsterdam* by Herman Janse (De Brink, 1994), with clear drawings showing how it was done, from houses and churches to bridges and locks. The most beautifully produced book about canal-belt architecture is *Het Grachtenboek* (1993) by Paul Spies and others, which catalogues every building along the canals with a wealth of historical photos and illustrations. Part 1 (also available in English) deals with the major canals and Part 2 (only in Dutch) with the medieval city. They're all out of print, but a few bookshops still have them if you hunt around.

Dutch Painting (1978) by RH Fuchs is a good introduction. *The UnDutchables* (1989) by Colin White & Laurie Boucke takes a humorous look at Dutch life; sometimes it's spot-on and sometimes so wide of the mark it becomes slapstick. Henry James described the Amsterdam canals as 'perfect prose' and 'perfect bourgeois' in *Transatlantic Sketches* (1875).

For literature by Amsterdam authors, see the Arts section in the Facts about Amsterdam chapter.

NEWSPAPERS & MAGAZINES

The European editions of *The Economist* and *Time* are printed here, and most of the major international newspapers and magazines (and many of the more obscure ones) are readily available. Newsagents at the airport and Centraal Station stock a wide selection, as do the Athenaeum newsagency on Spui square and WH Smith in the Kalverstraat.

By far the largest national newspaper is the Amsterdam-based *De Telegraaf*, a right-wing daily that was 'wrong' during the war (ie collaborated with the Germans). Its Wednesday edition is worth perusing for rental accommodation but you'll need help from a Dutch speaker. Also based in Amsterdam are *De Volkskrant*, a one-time Catholic daily with leftist leanings, and *Het Parool*, an evening paper full of Amsterdam politics. The highly regarded *NRC Handelsblad*, a merger of two elitist papers from Rotterdam and Amsterdam, sets the country's journalistic standards. *Het Financieële Dagblad* focuses on business and finance.

Useful Publications

The free *Uitkrant* is the definitive publication for art and entertainment – if it's not listed in here it's not happening. It's published 11 times a year, unfortunately only in Dutch though you can usually decipher enough to make a phone call to the relevant establishment for more information. Pick up a copy at the Amsterdam Uitburo or anywhere with free publications, such as Centraal Station, the Stopera and many museums.

The VVV's English-language *What's On in Amsterdam* is published every three weeks and costs f3.50. It has entertainment schedules and an address listing but is far less comprehensive than the *Uitkrant*. It's available from the VVV, large book and magazine outlets, and many hotels.

Via Via, a paper with reams of classified ads, is published Thursdays (in Dutch) and lists everything from apartments to starter motors.

RADIO & TV

The BBC broadcasts on 648 kHz medium wave, clearly receivable on any AM radio. Most of the programmes are in English and the German broadcasts seldom last longer than 30 minutes.

Dutch TV is a godsend for insomniacs,

though the large proportion of ad-free, English-language sitcoms and films with Dutch subtitles is a plus. Fortunately the Netherlands have the highest density cable-TV network in the world, and in Amsterdam the percentage of households hooked up to cable is approaching 100%. Cable means access not just to Dutch and Belgian channels but many channels from Britain, France, Germany and Italy, and all sorts of other so-called Euro-channels with sport and music clips, as well as Turkish and Moroccan stuff and, of course, CNN.

Hundreds of pages of up-to-date information – international news, the weather in Cairo, tonight's concert performances, aircraft departures and arrivals at Schiphol, you name it – is available through Teletext, a wonderful information service that hides behind many TV channels. On TVs equipped with Teletext you simply hit the Teletext button to switch from the channel you're watching to the information pages lurking behind it; the screen menu tells which page to scroll to. English-language versions are available on BBC and CNN.

DIGITAL MEDIA

Amsterdam's role as a central node for incoming phone traffic to Europe (something the government is trying to exploit by inviting call centres to set up shop) has had a large impact on its cyber-development. Encouraged by the city's famed liberal tolerance, a large and skilled community of hackers and phone phreaks flourished in the late 1980s, based around Hacktic – one of Europe's most (in)famous bunch of techno-anarchists, along with Germany's Chaos Computer Club – which co-hosted legendary global hacker conferences in 1989 and 1994. The city remains a popular venue for 'flesh meets' and has close ties with the San Francisco digerati. The late Tim Leary, JP Barlow, Howard Rheingold and RU Sirius have been frequent visitors. *Wired* magazine began life as an Amsterdam-based bimonthly called *Electric Word*.

Add one of the most progressive and efficient state-owned telecommunications companies in Europe (recently privatised), and a strong international reputation for graphic design and typography, and all the ingredients were in place by the early 1990s for the development of a small but creative local multimedia industry. This received a further boost when Hacktic developed into a legitimate provider of cheap Internet access called xs4all ('access for all'), and its members dispersed to work in multimedia, computer security and Web authoring.

Internet & E-mail

In a unique collaboration with the city council and arts community, xs4all established the widely copied DDS (De Digitale Stad – The Digital City, one of Europe's most effective freenets) as a new 'electronic suburb' of the city. For any virtual visitor to Amsterdam, DDS (www.dds.nl) remains the essential first stop, with hundreds of information resources (many in English), interaction opportunities, 'residential' home pages and links.

Visitors who need to get on-line here should note that the Netherlands use a four-pin phone plug which accommodates a US-style jack; otherwise adapters are cheaply picked up at the airport and the usual retail outlets in town.

Cybercafés include *Freeworld* (☎ 620 09 02) at Nieuwendijk 30 ('smoking'), the *Cyber Café* (☎ 623 51 46) at Nieuwendijk 19 ('straight'), *Coffeeshop Internet* (☎ 638 41 08) at Prinsengracht 480 ('smoking'), and *Mystère 2000* (☎ 620 29 70) at Lijnbaansgracht 92 – the latter is more of a 'New Edge' centre with lectures and workshops, open Tuesday to Friday from 11 am to 5 pm, Thursday to 9 pm. Typically, such places are open from 10 am to 1 am and offer Net access at f2.50 per 20 minutes.

These are fine for checking e-mail but not quite hip enough to attract the local netheadz. There are rumours that *Wired* magazine plans to open a cool websurfing joint, but until then the place to be seen is the *Society for Old & New Media* (☎ 557 98 98; fax 557 98 80; e-mail: society@waag.org) in the refurbished Waag building in the middle of Nieuwmarkt square.

The cavernous, medieval bar-restaurant is a good place to meet up with cyber-friends you may have met before arrival. There are regular lectures, cyberarts installations and seminars, and the society recently opened a public reading room with a custom-designed Web interface. This is proving very popular and is set to receive a boost with a council-backed network of 40 public terminals around the city, perhaps incorporating one of the digital cash-card schemes being trialled. Details of this and other society projects can be found at www.waag.nl.

Another key nexus of wired Amsterdam is the Dutch Design Institute, organiser of the influential Doors of Perception conferences on interaction design. Its well-designed pages (www.design-inst.nl/) are filled with information about the conferences and its other digital activities.

Checking what's going down prior to a visit is one of the great boons of online media. Time Out maintains weekly updated listings and schedules at www.timeout.co.uk. CliX (www.clix.net/) and Channels (www.stad.com/) are both well-supported sites with information of use to the tourist, the former being more youth-oriented, the latter a city-backed promotion. Also good for a look is www.channels.nl.

These sites, along with DDS, include a plethora of links to the various Amsterdam museums, clubs, institutes, galleries and arts centres that have either their own web site or at least a home page.

CD-ROM & Disk

DiscOver Amsterdam, published by Quince Intermedia (☎ 618 16 61; fax 689 88 52; e-mail: discover@quince.nl), is a CD-ROM available from bookshops, computer shops and several hotels, that brings the city to life in 240 full-colour panoramic photos that can be scanned 360 degrees. It allows you to wander from point to point and provides copious amounts of information (English or Dutch installation option) about monuments, sights, nightlife, events, hotels, restaurants and tourist services. The information can be kept up to date through links with the Internet sites maintained by the VVV, Amsterdam Uitburo (AUB) and Netherlands Tourist Board (NBT). DiscOver insists on Windows 95 and requires a fast CD drive and plenty of RAM to run properly, but it's pretty convincing and makes a great souvenir. At f19.95 you can't go wrong.

Another CD-ROM worth considering, for novelty value if nothing else, is *Fotoview Amsterdam* (f49.50), published by CityDisc in The Hague (☎ 070-324 05 40; fax 070-324 51 39) and available from many bookshops and tourist outlets. It's a photographic aerial view of the city that can be magnified to the point where you see individual cars, though the image does get fuzzy at this level of detail.

The index function for streets, sights and landmarks is useful, but not as useful as it is on another product put out by CityDisc on 3.5-inch floppy (about 670 Kb-worth), the *CityDisc Amsterdam*. This digital city map, based on the Falkplan map, allows you to look up streets, points of interest, map locations of businesses (with details such as address and phone number) and distances between A and B – print out the map sections you want and carry them for reference. It costs f29.50, or f119 for Amsterdam and 20 other Dutch cities on CD-ROM. As with the aerial photo CD, the instructions are in Dutch; the commands are straightforward but you won't be able to look up businesses by category if you don't know Dutch.

PHOTOGRAPHY & VIDEO

Film is widely available but fairly expensive by European standards – a Kodak 64 (36-exposure) slide film costs about f22 – so it's best to stock up tax-free on your way over. High-speed film (eg 200 ASA or higher) is sensible because the sky is often overcast, and even if it's not, buildings and trees tend to cast unwanted shadows. If there's a blanket of snow with sunshine (a rare combination but a fantastic photo opportunity) you might want slower film. Film developing is easy and quick, and costs f5.50 plus f1 per print. Cassettes for video cameras cost about f7.50/24 for 30/90 minutes.

Living-room video cassette recorders use the PAL image-registration system, the same as most of Europe and Australia, which is incompatible with the NTSC system used in North America and Japan or the SECAM system used in France. This means that if you buy a pre-recorded video tape here (as opposed to a video-camera cassette) you might not be able to play it at home – check your unit's requirements before leaving home. Shops might stock NTSC versions but very few have tapes in SECAM.

TIME
The Netherlands are on Central European time, GMT/UTC plus one hour. Noon is 11 am in London, 6 am in New York, 3 am in San Francisco, 6 am in Toronto, 9 pm in Sydney and 11 pm in Auckland, and then there's daylight-saving time. Clocks are put forward one hour at 2 am on the last Sunday in March and back again at 3 am on the last Sunday in October. They used to be put back in September which gave an even six months, but this was changed in 1996 as an EU concession to the wayward Brits and Irish.

When telling the time, beware that Dutch uses *half* to indicate 'half before' the hour. If you say 'half eight' (8.30 in many forms of English), a Dutch person will take this to mean 7.30. Dutch also uses constructions like *tien voor half acht* (7.20) and *tien over half acht* (7.40), and less surprisingly, *kwart voor acht* (7.45) and *kwart over acht* (8.15).

ELECTRICITY
Electricity is 220V, 50 Hz and plugs are of the Continental two-round-pin variety. If you need an adapter, get it before you leave home because most of the ones in the Netherlands are for locals going abroad.

LAUNDRY
A self-service laundry is called a *wasserette* or a *wassalon* and Amsterdam could do with more of them. They normally cost about f8 to wash five kg; add a few f1 coins for the

dryer. You can also get the staff to wash, dry and fold a load (a full garbage bag) for f15 or less – drop it off in the morning, pick it up in the afternoon. Up-market hotels will of course do your laundry too, but at a price.

Happy Inn, Warmoesstraat 30 near Centraal Station (Map 13; ☎ 624 84 64) – f12.50 to wash, dry and fold up to six kg; open Monday to Saturday from 9 am to 6 pm

Aquarette Self-Service, Oudebrugsteeg 24 off Damrak at the Beurs van Berlage (Map 13; ☎ 638 13 97) – f7 to wash six kg yourself, plus f1 per eight minutes in the dryer; open daily from 8 am to 10 pm (last wash 9.30 pm)

Wasserette Van den Broek, Oude Doelenstraat 12, the eastern extension of Damstraat (Map 13; ☎ 624 17 00) – full service (f15 wash, dry and fold) or self service, open Monday to Friday from 8.30 am to 7 pm, Saturday from 10 am to 5 pm

Wasserette, Haarlemmerstraat 45 (Map 13) – open Monday to Saturday from 9 am to 7 pm, Sunday from 10 am to 5 pm

The Clean Brothers, Kerkstraat 56 off Leidsestraat (Map 15; ☎ 622 02 73) – f8 to wash up to five kg plus f1.25 to dry, or leave it with them for f12.50; open daily from 7 am to 9 pm

WEIGHTS & MEASURES
Napoleon introduced the metric system which has been used ever since (before then it was feet, inches and pounds). In shops, 100g is an *ons* and 500g is a *pond*. EU directives have prohibited the use of *ons* in pricing and labelling but the term is so ingrained it will take a while to disappear. Like other Continental Europeans, the Dutch indicate decimals with commas and thousands with points.

HEALTH
The Netherlands have reciprocal health arrangements with other EU countries and Australia – check with your public health insurer which form to include in your luggage (E111 for British and Irish residents, available at post offices). You still might have to pay on the spot but you'll be able to claim back home. Citizens of other countries are well advised to take out travel insurance – medical or dental treatment is less expensive than in North America but still costs enough.

There are no compulsory vaccinations but if you've just travelled through a yellow fever area you could be asked for proof that you're covered. Up-to-date tetanus, polio and diphtheria immunisations are always recommended whether you're visiting Amsterdam or not.

For minor health concerns, pop into a local *drogist* (chemist) or *apotheek* (pharmacy, to fill prescriptions). For more serious problems, go to the casualty ward of a *ziekenhuis* (hospital) or ring the Centrale Doktersdienst (☎ 0900-503 20 42), the 24-hour central medical service that will refer you to an appropriate doctor, dentist or pharmacy. In a life-threatening emergency, the national telephone number for police, ambulance and fire brigade is ☎ 112.

Forget about buying flu tablets and antacids at supermarkets: for anything more medical than toothpaste you'll have to go to a drogist or apotheek, of which there are far too few because it's a protected profession.

Hospitals include the following:

Onze Lieve Vrouwe Gasthuis, Eerste Oosterparkstraat 1 at Oosterpark near the Tropenmuseum (Map 17; ☎ 599 91 11) – the closest public hospital to the centre of town; emergencies 24 hours a day
Andreas-Ziekenhuis, Theophile de Bockstraat 8 west of the Vondelpark (Map 8; ☎ 511 11 15) – handles emergencies 24 hours a day
Sint Lucas Ziekenhuis, Jan Tooropstraat 164, north of Andreas-Ziekenhuis (Map 5; ☎ 510 89 11) – emergencies 24 hours a day
Slotervaart Ziekenhuis, Louwesweg 6 south-west of Andreas-Ziekenhuis (☎ 512 45 12)
Academisch Ziekenhuis der VU, De Boelelaan 1117, Amsterdam Buitenveldert (Map 8; ☎ 444 44 44) – emergencies 24 hours a day; traditionally the VU (Vrije Universiteit, Free University) was orthodox Calvinist but its hospital has established a name for itself in sex-change operations
Academisch Medisch Centrum, Meibergdreef 9, Bijlmer (☎ 566 91 11) – hospital of the Universiteit van Amsterdam; emergencies 24 hours a day; regular outpatient clinics weekdays from 8.30 am to 5 pm; famous for its AIDS research
Boven-IJ Ziekenhuis, Statenjachtstraat 1, Amsterdam Noord (bus No 34 from Centraal Station; ☎ 634 63 46) – emergencies 24 hours a day

STDs & HIV/AIDS

Free testing for sexually transmitted diseases is available at the Municipal Medical & Health Service, GG&GD (Map 13; ☎ 555 58 22), Groenburgwal 44 in the old town. You must arrive on a weekday between 8 and 10.30 am to be tested that day. Bring along a book or magazine as you'll probably have to wait a couple of hours. If a problem is diagnosed they'll provide free treatment immediately, but the results of blood tests are only available after a week (they'll give you the results over the phone if you aren't returning to Amsterdam). This excellent service is available to everyone and it's not necessary to give an address or show identification (English is spoken). There's also a gay STD and HIV clinic (tests etc) on Friday from 7 to 9 pm.

HIV/AIDS is a problem in the Netherlands but the spread has been contained to some extent by active, practical education campaigns and free needle-exchange programmes. Telephone help lines include:

AIDS Information Line (☎ 0800-022 22 20, free call) – questions about HIV and AIDS answered from 2 to 10 pm; discretion guaranteed
HIV-plus-lijn (☎ 685 00 55) – telephone help line for people with HIV, or their friends and relatives; Monday, Wednesday and Friday from 1 to 4 pm, Tuesday and Thursday from 8 to 10.30 pm

TOILETS

Public toilets are scarce but there are plenty of bars or other establishments you can duck into. These toilets aren't always the cleanest – public facilities in department stores are more hygienic. Toilet attendants (there are a lot of them) should be tipped 25 to 50 cents.

Dutch toilets are usually of the 'hospital' variety with a platform in the bowl; lay down some toilet paper to avoid leaving skid marks.

WOMEN TRAVELLERS

Dutch women attained the right to vote in 1919, and in the late 1960s and 1970s the Dolle Minas ('Mad Minas' – see the History section) made sure that abortion on demand was more or less accepted and paid for by the

TONY WHEELER

ROB VAN DRIESUM

RICHARD NEBESKY

Top: Scene in the Western Canal Belt
Middle: The Rokin
Bottom: Water craft in front of Centraal Station

ROB VAN DRIESUM

RICHARD NEBESKY

ROB VAN DRIESUM

Left: The Magere Brug across the Amstel, with the Stopera in the background
Right: Canal tour boats provide a different perspective of the city
Bottom: The picturesque intersection of Reguliersgracht and Keizersgracht; on a good
        day you can see 15 bridges from here

national health service. Though there is some way to go before it can be said that women are fully emancipated (their participation rate in the labour force, for instance, is one of the lowest in Europe with the highest proportion of part-time work), Dutch women on the whole are a rather confident lot. On a social level, equality of the sexes is taken for granted and women are almost as likely as men to initiate contact with the opposite sex. There's very little street harassment and Amsterdam is probably as safe as it gets in the major cities of Europe. Just take care in the red-light district, where it's best to walk with a friend to minimise unwelcome attention.

The feminist movement is less politicised than elsewhere, more laid-back and focused on practical solutions such as cultural centres and archives, bicycle repair shops run by and for women, or support systems to help women set up businesses. For more about feminism, or a full rundown of the many women's groups, contact the following organisations:

Het Vrouwenhuis (The Women's House), Nieuwe Herengracht 95 near the Botanical Garden (☎ 625 20 66) – a centre for several women's organisations and magazines, with workshops, exhibitions and parties; there's also a bar and a library

IIAV (International Information Centre & Archives of the Women's Movement), Obiplein 4 east of Muiderpoortstation (☎ 665 08 20) – centre for feminist studies; extensive collection of clippings, magazines and books

Support & Health

The following organisations may prove useful in times of crisis:

De Eerste Lijn (The First Line, ☎ 612 75 76) – for victims of sexual violence

Vrouwen Bellen Vrouwen (Women Call Women, ☎ 625 01 50) – advice and support

Aletta Jacobshuis, Overtoom 323 (☎ 616 62 22) – clinic named after the country's first female doctor, a feminist and tireless campaigner for birth control; information and help with sexual problems and birth control, including morning-after pills

Vrouwengezondheidscentrum Isis, Obiplein 4 (Women's Health Centre; ☎ 693 43 58) – advice, support and self-help groups

Rechtshulp voor Vrouwen, Willemsstraat 24B (Legal Aid for Women; ☎ 624 03 23)

GAY & LESBIAN TRAVELLERS

Partisan estimates put the proportion of gay and lesbian people in Amsterdam at 20-30%. There's no doubt that Amsterdam is the gay and lesbian capital of Europe, although the lesbian scene, as always, is less developed than the gay one. Mainstream attitudes have always been reasonably tolerant but it wasn't until the early 1970s that the age of consent for gay sex was lowered to 16, in line with hetero sex, and only in 1993 did it become illegal to discriminate against job-seekers (for instance, teachers) on the basis of sexual orientation.

The fact that Christian parties are in opposition for the first time since 1917 has finally made it possible to tackle issues relating to family law. Hot topics at the moment are same-sex marriage (on the verge of being recognised by law) and the attendant right to adopt children (which could take a bit longer to be recognised), and the ongoing struggle to provide gays and lesbians the social respect they need to function freely. The government has long subsidised the national organisation COC – one of the world's largest organisations for gay and lesbian rights – but now trade unions are busy researching the lot of homosexual employees, the police advertise in the gay media for new applicants, and there's even a foundation called Homosexuality & Army.

One attractive feature of gay and lesbian venues in the city is their openness: no covered windows or locked doors, but an open, welcoming attitude to anyone who wants to come in (and 'out'). There's no lack of places to go to, with more than 60 bars and discos, gay hotels, bookshops, sport clubs, choirs, theatres, archives etc, and a wide range of organisations that help gays and lesbians who have questions or problems. Almost all these places are within walking distance in the centre of town or are easily accessible by public transport. See the listings below and the Places to Stay, Shopping and Entertainment chapters for further details.

Amsterdam also has its Homomonument, the first such monument in the world, designed by Karin Daan and unveiled under the shadow of the Westerkerk in 1987. It consists of three triangles of pink granite: one points to the Amsterdam office of the COC, the second to the Anne Frankhuis and the third to the water. It commemorates those who were persecuted for their homosexuality by the Nazis.

Information & Support

One of the best guidebooks is the *Best Guide to Amsterdam & the Benelux*, which, as the title indicates, focuses mainly on Amsterdam. Catherine Stebbings' *Amsterdam – the Woman's Travel Guide* published by Virago is aimed at women in general but lesbians might find it useful. The SAD-Schorerstichting (see list below) publishes *Gay Tourist Information*, covering Amsterdam and safe sex, and a *Gay Tourist Map*, both available free of charge at gay venues.

Dutch-language publications include the gay tabloid *Gaykrant*, the more up-market COC magazine *XL* for men and women, and the highbrow *Homologie*. For those aged under 27 there's *Expreszo*, and for lesbians, *Zij aan Zij* and *Madam*. Gay and lesbian bookshops (see the Shopping chapter) sell most of the major foreign publications, and many newsagencies also have reasonably extensive selections.

The home page of the Dutch gay and lesbian body is at www.xs4all.nl/~nvihcoc – it's in Dutch and deals with political issues but there's also an English section.

Gay Games 98 has an interesting site at www.dds.nl/gaygames. Another good site is www.xs4all.nl:80/~heinv/dqrd/index.html, one of Europe's QRDs, the network of 'queer resources directories'. Gay information on Teletext is available on TV3, page 447. The local gay radio station MVS broadcasts from 6 to 9 pm daily on 106.8 FM (cable 103.8 FM), with an English programme on Sunday.

The following organisations may prove useful:

Gay & Lesbian Switchboard (☎ 623 65 65) – the best first source for gay and lesbian information, addresses, what's on etc, daily 10 am to 10 pm

COC, Rozenstraat 14 (Map 12; ☎ 623 40 79) – Amsterdam branch of the national gay & lesbian organisation. The phone number is that of the CO2 Info Coffeeshop, which you can ring or visit Monday to Saturday from 1 to 5 pm, and Sunday (only for those aged under 27) from 2 to 6 pm. There's a mixed disco Friday and women's disco Saturday, both from 10 pm to 4 am – the women's disco is the only one in Amsterdam to have survived for years. The CO2 Info Coffeeshop also organises seniors' meetings and theme parties (check the bimonthly schedule), and HIV meetings. The COC head office (Map 13; ☎ 623 45 96) is at Nieuwezijds Voorburgwal 68-70, open weekdays from 9 am to 5 pm, but it's not equipped to deal with general enquiries from the public.

SAD-Schorerstichting, PC Hooftstraat 5 (Map 15; ☎ 662 42 06) – gay counselling, HIV prevention and homo buddy project (HIV support), weekdays from 9 am to 5 pm; gay STD and HIV clinic (tests etc) at Groenburgwal 44, Friday 7 to 9 pm

HIV Vereniging, Eerste Helmersstraat 17 (Map 15; ☎ 616 01 60) – national organisation for those who are HIV positive; runs the Internet service HIVNET and provides personal assistance; also operates the HIV-plus-lijn (see the earlier Health section)

AIDS Information Line – see Health

Homodok, Oudezijds Achterburgwal 185 (Map 13; ☎ 525 26 01) – extensive documentation centre for gay and lesbian studies, open Wednesday to Friday from 10.30 am to 4.30 pm; telephone enquiries weekdays from 9 am to 5 pm; e-mail: homodok@sara.nl

Lesbisch Archief, Eerste Helmersstraat 17 (Map 15; ☎ 618 58 79) – lesbian documentation centre; organises lectures and other events; open weekdays from 1 to 4.30 pm (phone enquiries from 9 am)

Safe Sex

The Dutch government and organisations such as the COC, SAD-Schorerstichting and HIV Vereniging all do their bit to prevent the spread of STDs and HIV. Virtually all bars, bookshops and saunas that cater for gays provide safe-sex leaflets. Many also sell condoms suitable for anal sex, eg the Hot Rubber or DUO brands; cosmetics chains such as the Body Shop also sell them.

Special Events

The last Saturday in June is *Roze Zaterdag* (Pink Saturday), the gay pride celebration commemorating the gay-rights riots at the Stonewall Inn in New York in June 1969. It's held in a different city each year, with a big parade, information stands and theme parties. The COC or the Gay & Lesbian Switchboard can tell you more.

Amsterdam will host the Gay Games from 1 to 8 August 1998 (the last were held in New York in 1994), which will attract tens of thousands of gay and lesbian participants. Apart from the sporting events, the organising committee is planning a cultural festival, a gay and lesbian film festival and a huge choir festival.

The biggest party in Amsterdam each year is *Koninginnedag* (Queen's Day) which celebrates the Queen Mother's birthday on 30 April. Ex-queen Juliana and her daughter Queen Beatrix are very popular among the gay community and this day is celebrated with great enthusiasm, causing some confusion among foreign gays about the 'queen' everyone is so happy about. On this day a big gay and lesbian party called the *Roze Wester* (Pink Wester) is held at the Homomonument, with bands and street dancing; the Reguliersdwarsstraat and Amstel also get very lively. It helps if you like beer, because you can hardly get anything else.

Dangers & Annoyances

Although gays and lesbians can generally move freely in Amsterdam, violent crime is a distinct possibility when cruising – don't carry too much money and certainly no cards or passport; an emergency whistle is also worth considering.

There are many popular cruising places in and around the city: the Vondelpark, the nude beach at Zandvoort and the dunes behind it, or Landschapspark De Oeverlanden by the Nieuwe Meer bordering the Amsterdamse Bos, though the latter can be outright dangerous. (A joke among gays is that the best place for cruising is an Albert Heijn supermarket between 5 and 6 pm, particularly the one in Westerstraat in the Jordaan.)

Always report anti-gay or anti-lesbian violence to the police. Most police stations have staff members who are trained to treat your case with respect.

DISABLED TRAVELLERS

Travellers with a mobility problem will find Amsterdam fairly well equipped to meet their needs, certainly considering the natural limitations of some of the older buildings. A large number of government offices and museums have lifts and/or ramps. Many hotels, however, are in old buildings with steep stairs and no lifts; restaurants tend to be on ground floors, though 'ground' sometimes includes a few steps. The metro stations have lifts, many trains and some taxis have wheelchair access, and most train stations and public buildings have toilets for the disabled. People with a disability get discounts on public transport and can park in the city free of charge (see the sections on Public Transport and Car & Motorcycle in the Getting Around chapter). Train timetables are published in braille and bank notes have raised shapes on the corners for identification.

The *stadsmobiel* ('citymobile') is a special taxi service for people with mobility, sight or hearing impairments. There's a cloud hanging over the future of this scheme – an extension of the public transport system – but with luck it will pass. The service operates from 8 am to 10 pm all week and is surprisingly cheap: trips within one 'region' (roughly equivalent to a zone with public transport) cost a mere f1.50 (f0.80 for those aged over 65); for two or more regions you'll never pay more than f5. It's a shared service, so there might be other passengers and the trip might take a bit longer than with a normal taxi. To order a stadsmobiel, ring ☎ 411 00 55. You have to become a member first, which can happen over the phone, though you'll need a local address – perhaps your hotel, relative or friend can enrol on your behalf.

See also Car Rental in the Getting Around chapter for an excellent deal on a rental car specially adapted for wheelchairs.

Many Dutch organisations work with and for people with disabilities but unfortunately there's no central information service. However, the helpful Nederlands Instituut voor Zorg & Welzijn NIZW (☎ 030-230 66 03; fax 030-231 96 41), Postbus 19152, 3501 DD Utrecht, has extensive information on accessible places to stay throughout the country and can refer you to other organisations if your request is more specific. The Amsterdam Uitburo (see Other Information Offices under the earlier Tourist Offices section) has information about accessible entertainment venues.

In Great Britain, the Royal Association for Disability & Rehabilitation (RADAR; ☎ 0171-250 3222), 12 City Forum, 250 City Rd, London EC1V 8AF, may be able to help plan your trip. Its guide, *Holidays & Travel Abroad: A Guide for Disabled People*, gives a good overview of facilities in Europe (published in even-numbered years).

In the USA, the Society for the Advancement of Travel for the Handicapped (SATH; ☎ 212-447 7284), 347 Fifth Ave No 610, New York, NY 10016, has information sheets on a wide range of destinations or will research your specific requirements. Membership is $45 a year ($25 for seniors and students); the information charge for non-members is $5, which covers costs. Mobility International (☎ 541-343 1284), PO Box 10767, Eugene, OR 97440, offers international educational exchanges but will also answer questions and help travellers with special needs. Finally, it might be worth browsing through www.access-able.com, a Web page for travellers with disabilities.

SENIOR TRAVELLERS

The minimum age for senior discounts is 65 (60 for the male or female partner) and they apply to public transport, museum entry fees, theatres, concerts and more. You could try flashing your home-country senior card but you may have to show your passport to be eligible.

Senior travellers who are concerned about their personal safety can perhaps take heart from the fact that people up to 24 years of age are six times more likely to become a victim of crime than those aged over 65. If you have difficulty walking, see the previous Disabled Travellers section: the stadsmobiel service also caters for seniors.

An organisation worth knowing about is Gilde Amsterdam (Map 12; ☎ 625 13 90, Monday to Friday from 1 to 4 pm), Hartenstraat 18, a group of volunteers aged 50 and over who offer their experience in a variety of ways. Gilde members with a keen knowledge of Amsterdam organise walks for small groups of locals and visitors (maximum of eight people) – a wonderful way to discover the city with mature-aged people and to see and learn things that professional tours ignore. It helps if you're reasonably mobile because the walks last an hour or two. It's all very informal; every guide does it differently and you might even take the tram. There are three walks to choose from – city centre, the Jordaan and 'roving' – and the cost per person is a f4 contribution, in return for which you get 50% off entry fees to the Amsterdams Historisch Museum (city history) and the Joods Historisch Museum (Jewish history), as well as a 25% discount on pancakes at the end of the walk. Recommended.

Stichting Wijzer (☎ 560 03 25), Rijnspoorplein 1, organises a range of activities – film nights, music programmes, summer excursions etc – aimed at Amsterdammers aged over 50 but foreigners are welcome too.

AMSTERDAM FOR CHILDREN

Lonely Planet's *Travel with Children* by Maureen Wheeler is worth reading if you're unsure about travelling with kids. Much of her advice is valid in Amsterdam, where there is much to attract the attention of kids. Unfortunately the city also has a lot of open water (Dutch children learn to swim at school).

Attitudes to children are very positive, apart from some hotels with a no-children policy – check when you book. Most restaurants have high chairs and children's menus. Facilities for changing nappies (diapers), however, are limited to the big department stores and Centraal Station and you'll pay 50 cents to use them.

Amsterdam's children are surprisingly spontaneous and confident, a reflection of the relaxed approach to parenting. They're allowed in pubs (but aren't supposed to buy beer till they're 16) and the age of consent is 12, though parents can intervene if the partner is over 16. There's a Kindertelefoon (☎ 0800-432) where children can report cases of abuse daily between 2 and 8 pm, and a Kinderrechtswinkel (Children's Rights Shop, ☎ 626 00 67), Staalstraat 19, where youngsters aged under 18 can enquire about their rights towards teachers, parents and employers.

Some hotels offer a baby-sitting service and others may be able to advise. Baby-sitters charge between f5 and f12.50 an hour depending on the time of day, sometimes with weekend and/or hotel supplements, and you may have to pay for their taxi home if it gets late. Agencies use male and female students and you may not always be able to specify which sex; they get busy on weekends so book ahead. Try Oppas-Centrale Kriterion (☎ 624 58 48 daily between 5.30 and 7 pm), Roetersstraat 170hs, which has been in business for a long time and seems to be consistently reliable. Oppascentrale De Peuterette (☎ 679 67 93), Hectorstraat 20, also receives good reports. There are one or two other agencies (look in the phone book under *Oppascentrale*).

Many special events and activities aimed at children take place throughout the year. Check the *Uitkrant* (under 'Agenda Jeugd') or contact the Amsterdam Uitburo. Or try the following options, most of which are described in more detail elsewhere in this book:

- The Vondelpark (Maps 5, 8 & 15) – for picnics, children's playground, ducks etc
- Amsterdamse Bos (Map 8) – huge recreational area with animal enclosure, children's farm etc
- Tram Museum Amsterdam (Map 8) – ride in a historic tram past the Amsterdamse Bos
- Tropenmuseum (Maps 7 & 17) – separate children's section with activities focusing on exotic locations

- climb up a church tower – if that doesn't exhaust them, nothing will
- Artis zoo (Maps 14 & 17)
- the beach at Zandvoort – only a short train ride away
- hire a canal bike
- harbour cruise
- swimming pool – especially the high-tech Mirandabad (Map 9)
- disco – discotheque Richter (Map 16; ☎ 626 15 73), Reguliersdwarsstraat 36, has a children's disco every first Sunday of the month from 2 to 5 pm
- circus – in Theater Carré (Map 16) from mid-December to early January
- Koninginnedag on 30 April – a wonderful party for kids as much as grown-ups
- Impuls Dutch Science Center (Map 14)
- hire a bike for a day out in the country

Kids love the **Madame Tussaud Scenerama** (☎ 622 99 49, recorded message), Dam 20 on the corner of Dam square and Rokin, open from 10 am to 5.30 pm (in July and August from 9.30 am to 7.30 pm). Admission costs a hefty f17.50 but children up to 14 years pay f12.50 and family and group rates are available. Some of the characters on display won't mean much to foreigners.

The national aviation museum, **Aviodome Schiphol** (☎ 604 15 21), at the airport (Schipholweg 1; take the train, or bus Nos 68, 173 or 174), is also a hit with kids, who can play in old planes and sit in a cockpit. Adults will also enjoy the displays, which consist of 25 aeroplanes including the Wright Flyer (the plane with which the Wright brothers made the first motorised flight in 1903), several Fokker aircraft including a 1911 Fokker Spin ('Spider') and Baron von Richthofen's WWI triplane, a Spitfire and a Dakota. There's a large section devoted to space flight. The museum is open daily from 10 am to 5 pm and costs f7.50 (children aged between four and 12 pay f5).

LIBRARIES

Many museums and institutes have private libraries, mentioned throughout this book. To borrow books from a public library *(openbare bibliotheek)* you need to be a resident, show ID and pay f34 a year (cheaper for young adults and seniors, free for under-18s), but nobody will stop you browsing or reading there.

The main public library, the Centrale Bibliotheek (Map 12; ☎ 523 09 00), is at Prinsengracht 587 and is open Monday from 1 to 9 pm, Tuesday to Thursday from 10 am to 9 pm, Friday and Saturday from 10 am to 5 pm, and Sunday (only from October to March) from 1 to 5 pm. It has a wide range of English-language newspapers and magazines, a coffee bar and an extremely useful notice board. For other public libraries, look in the phone book under *Bibliotheken, Openbare*.

UNIVERSITIES

Amsterdam has two universities and over 40,000 students. About 27,000 attend the Universiteit van Amsterdam (UvA), which has existed in various guises since 1632. Its buildings are spread throughout the city. The main UvA faculties are Arts (with 6000 students), Social Sciences (4400), Law (3500) and Economics (2700).

Another 13,500 students attend the orthodox-Calvinist Vrije Universiteit (VU, Free University) established in 1880. Initially its buildings were also spread throughout the city but in the 1960s almost the entire VU moved to a large campus along De Boelelaan in the southern suburb of Buitenveldert. Philosophy is a compulsory subject so students think about the role of science in society. The VU specialises in Economics (3500 students), 'Social-Cultural' Sciences (1700) and Medicine (1600).

For information about international education programmes in English offered by the University of Amsterdam, contact Universiteit van Amsterdam, Service & Informatiecentrum, Binnengasthuisstraat 9, 1012 ZA Amsterdam (☎ 525 33 33; fax 525 29 21; e-mail: uva-info@bdu.uva.nl). Tuition fees are approximately f10,000 per academic year; fees for regular study programmes in Dutch are approximately f2300 per academic year.

The Free University (Map 8) can be contacted at Onderwijsvoorlichting Vrije

Universiteit, De Boelelaan 1105, 1081 HV Amsterdam (☎ 444 50 00, Monday to Friday from 9 am to 4 pm).

The Foreign Student Service (☎ 671 59 15), Oranje Nassaulaan 5, 1017 AH Amsterdam, is a support agency for foreign students. It provides information about study programmes and intensive language courses, and helps with accommodation, insurance and personal problems. It's open weekdays from 9 am to 5.30 pm.

CULTURAL CENTRES

There are many cultural centres and institutes besides the city's museums and theatres. These include:

British Council, Keizersgracht 343 (☎ 622 36 44) – educational and cultural exchanges; information centre open Wednesday and Thursday from 1 to 4 pm

Cedla, Keizersgracht 395-397 (☎ 525 34 98, library ☎ 525 32 48) – centre for Latin American studies and documentation

De Balie, Kleine Gartmanplantsoen 10 on Leidseplein (☎ 623 29 04, recording in Dutch) – café, restaurant, theatre, seminars, political debates, lectures etc; hangout of trendy intellectuals

Goethe Institut, Herengracht 470 (☎ 623 04 21) – German cultural centre with lectures, films (some with English subtitles), plays and discussions, plus German language courses at all levels and Dutch courses for Germans; office hours 9 am to 5 pm weekdays (to 4.30 pm Friday); library open Tuesday to Thursday from 1 to 6 pm, Friday to 4 pm

Italian Cultural Institute, Keizersgracht 564 (☎ 626 53 14)

Jewish Cultural Centre, Van der Boechorststraat 26 (☎ 644 01 80)

John Adams Institute, Herenmarkt 97 in the former West Indisch Huis (☎ 624 72 80) – Dutch-US friendship society that organises lectures, readings and discussions on US culture and history led by heavyweights such as Saul Bellow, John Kenneth Galbraith, Gore Vidal and Jay McInnery; the lectures (once a month or more frequently) are often interesting and surprisingly affordable, and provide a focus for the US and British expat community; definitely worth checking

Maison Descartes, Vijzelgracht 2A (☎ 622 49 36) – French cultural centre named after the philosopher who in Amsterdam found the intellectual freedom denied him at home; includes an excellent restaurant (see Places to Eat). Many

activities are organised by the Alliance Française
(☎ 625 65 06) at Keizersgracht 708

South Africa Institute, Keizersgracht 141 (☎ 624 93
18) – library

Vlaams Cultureel Centrum de Brakke Grond, Nes 43
(☎ 626 00 44) – Flemish cultural centre; very
active (readings, plays, lectures, films); includes
a theatre, café and restaurant

MUSEUMS

Everyone should find something to enjoy in
Amsterdam's wide range of museums.
Weekends tend to be the busiest times, along
with Wednesday afternoons when many
primary schools have the afternoon off and
children are herded into museums. Many
museums are closed on Monday.

Display captions may be in Dutch only –
ask for an English-language brochure (often
free) when you buy your ticket. Even so,
captions are often short and you may wish to
buy one of the guidebooks in the museum
shop that explain things in more detail. Many
museums have pleasant coffee shops (sometimes even restaurants) with gardens or
courtyards, good places to relax and read up
on the items on display.

A handful of museums are free but most
charge admission (usually less than f10) and
you might have to pay extra for special exhibitions. Discounts are frequently available
for those aged over 65 or under 18, for students (rare), CJP Pass holders (see Useful
Cards earlier in this chapter) and holders of
several other passes.

The Museumjaarkaart (Museum Year
Card) gives free entry to 400 museums
around the country for a year at f45 (f15 for
those aged 18 and under). It's valid for most
museums in Amsterdam including the major
ones (Rijksmuseum, Van Gogh Museum,
Stedelijk Museum, Joods Historisch
Museum, Scheepvaartmuseum) but not the
Anne Frankhuis; at the others you'll usually
get a discount, though special exhibitions
might be an exception. After five or six
museums the card will have paid for itself.
Enquire at participating museums or the
VVV (one photo required).

The Museum Boat is also worth considering for the discounts offered with its day card

(see Boat in the Getting Around chapter),
though if you want the discounts to work it's
probably better to visit the Rijksmuseum
separately because this can take a large
chunk out of your day.

For details of the museums themselves,
see the individual entries elsewhere in this
book.

DANGERS & ANNOYANCES

The national emergency number (police,
ambulance, fire brigade) is ☎ 112; the
Amsterdam police can also be contacted
direct on ☎ 622 22 22.

Amsterdam is a small city by world standards but requires big-city street sense,
though it's positively tame if you're used to
New York or Johannesburg. Violent crime is
unusual but theft, especially pickpocketing,
is a real problem. Don't carry more money
onto the streets than you intend to spend –
use a secondary wallet or purse and keep
your main one safe. Don't walk around con-
spicuously with valuables, or give away that
you're a tourist with map, camera or video.
Walking purposefully helps.

A car with foreign registration is a popular
target, and if it's parked along a canal it will
probably get broken into. Don't leave things
in the car: definitely remove registration and
ID papers, and if possible the radio.

If something is stolen, by all means get a
police report for insurance purposes but
don't expect the police to retrieve your property or to apprehend the thief – put the matter
down to experience. This might seem weak
but it's not a police state and usually there's
very little they can do.

The people you see walking around in
blue-and-red jackets carrying mobile phones
aren't police but members of the 600-strong
Stadswacht (City Watch), a make-work
project for long-term unemployed. They
keep an eye on things, help if you're lost or
have a problem, and call for assistance if the
matter is serious. The operation will soon be
merged with the parking police and the sani-
tation police (who see to it that people don't
put out garbage too early). Only 'real' police
carry guns.

If you have trouble on the train to Amsterdam or at Centraal Station itself, contact the railway police at the west end of track 2A. You can report violence or missing/stolen property here, and the staff can put you in touch with your consulate or other relevant support agencies. They'll also put through a station announcement if you're only looking for someone.

The red-light district is full of shady characters. They seem harmless enough, but if you're accosted, simply say *Nee dank* (No thanks) and keep walking. Don't take photos of the prostitutes.

The mosquitoes in summer can be another nuisance. They breed in stagnant parts of the canals and in water under houses. In some parts of the city they're no problem, but the author of this book used to live in a canal house where the tenants slept under mosquito nets six months of the year.

Amsterdam is still the dog-shit capital of the world (see the earlier Ecology & Environment section) and you soon learn to look where you're going. Also, North Americans and Australians should accept that non-smokers have few rights here: tobacco smoke in pubs can be thick enough to deter all but the most committed smokers, and the Dutch seem allergic to open windows.

DRUGS

Contrary to what you may have heard, cannabis products are illegal. The confusion arises because the authorities have had the sense to distinguish between 'soft' drugs (cannabis) and addictive 'hard' drugs (heroin, crack, pills) when deciding where to focus their resources. Soft drugs for personal use (defined as up to five grams, down from 30 grams after table-thumping from France) are unofficially tolerated, but larger amounts put you in the persecuted 'dealer' category.

The key phrase is *gedogen* (sometimes translated as 'tolerating'), a wonderful Dutch term that means official condemnation coupled with looking the other way when common sense dictates it. Hard drugs (including LSD) are treated just as seriously as anywhere else and can land you in big trouble, although the authorities tend to treat genuine, registered addicts as medical cases rather than as serial killers – Amsterdam pioneered methadone and needle-exchange programmes.

Neighbouring countries take a dim view of such tolerance now that border controls have been abolished in theory, and the government is under EU pressure to clamp down – never mind that most hashish reaches the Netherlands through France and Belgium and most heroin through Germany. In typical Dutch fashion this has led to some tightening of rules and regulations without losing sight of the common-sense approach.

One of the positive results of this approach has been to move cannabis off the streets and into registered 'coffee shops', driving a wedge between cannabis users and predatory street dealers who would rather sell the more profitable hard stuff. Since the late 1980s the number of heroin addicts in the Netherlands has stabilised at around 1.6 per 1000 inhabitants, slightly more than in Germany, Norway, Austria or Ireland; but in hard-line France the proportion is 2.6 per 1000, and in Greece, Spain and Italy it's higher still. Dutch addicts have the best average survival rate in Europe and the lowest incidence of HIV infection.

These tolerant policies attract many drug tourists – drugs are cheaper and more readily available here than elsewhere, and generally of better quality. The country has become a major exporter of high-grade marihuana (grown locally) and is the European centre for the production of 'xtc' (ecstasy). Much of Europe's cocaine passes through Rotterdam harbour.

For more about (soft) drugs, see 'Coffee Shops' in the Entertainment chapter.

Warning

Never, *ever* buy drugs on the street: you'll get ripped off or mugged. And *don't* light up in view of the police, or in an establishment without checking that it's OK to do so.

LEGAL MATTERS

The Amsterdam police *(politie)* are a pretty relaxed and helpful lot, which is quite remarkable considering their workload. If you do something wrong, they can hold you up to six hours for questioning (another six hours if they can't establish your identity, or 24 hours if they consider the matter serious) and do not have to grant a phone call, though they'll ring your consulate.

Since 1994 there's a 'limited' requirement for anyone over 12 years of age to carry ID (eg in public transport without a valid ticket, at soccer stadiums, in the work place and when opening a bank account). Typically, theory doesn't always match practice and everyone is confused, but it seems that foreigners should carry their passport. Then again, a photocopy of the relevant data pages should be OK unless there's a reason to suspect you're an illegal immigrant. Logical, isn't it? A driving licence is not OK because it doesn't show your nationality.

The Bureau voor Rechtshulp (Office for Legal Help, ☎ 626 44 77), Spuistraat 10 and three other places around the city, is a nonprofit organisation of qualified lawyers who give free legal advice during business hours to those who can't afford it. They deal with a wide range of issues, including immigration and residency, and will refer you if they can't deal with the matter themselves or if they think you're wealthy enough.

BUSINESS HOURS

As a general rule, banks are open from 9 am to 4 pm Monday to Friday, offices from 8.30 am to 5 pm Monday to Friday, and shops from 9 am to 5.30 pm Monday to Saturday. Now for the exceptions:

On Monday many shops don't open till noon but they stay open until 8 or 9 pm on Thursday night. Department stores and supermarkets generally close around 6 pm weekdays and at 5 pm on Saturday but most supermarkets near the city centre stay open till 8 pm. Most regular non-tourist shops outside the canal belt close at 5 or 6 pm weekdays and at midday Saturday, depending on their line of trade, and almost all are closed on Sunday. Within the canal belt, however, most shops are open from 9 am (noon on Monday) to 5 pm (9 pm on Thurs-

day) throughout the week including Saturday, and many are open from noon to 5 pm Sunday.

Government offices, private institutions, monuments and even museums follow erratic and sometimes very limited opening hours to suit themselves; they're mentioned in this book where possible. Many museums are closed Monday.

PUBLIC HOLIDAYS & SPECIAL EVENTS

Public holidays are New Year's Day *(Nieuwjaarsdag)*, Good Friday *(Goede Vrijdag)*, Easter Sunday and Easter Monday *(Eerste* and *Tweede Paasdag)*, Queen's Day *(Koninginnedag)* on 30 April, Ascension Day *(Hemelvaartsdag)*, Whit Sunday (Pentecost) and Monday *(Eerste* and *Tweede Pinksterdag)*, Christmas Day and Boxing Day *(Eerste* and *Tweede Kerstdag)*. People take public holidays seriously – you won't get much done.

There are many festivals and special events throughout the year. Summer is a time of open-air concerts, theatre and other events around the city, often free; favoured venues include the Vondelpark and the Amsterdamse Bos. The queen mother's birthday on 30 April is celebrated with the biggest street party in the country, an unforgettable experience. Culture-lovers might aim for the Holland Festival in June or the Uitmarkt at the end of August. A few of the following events aren't in Amsterdam but are definitely worth a day trip:

January

A 'dead', seemingly never-ending month, with cold, dull, dark days. Skating on the canals (frost permitting) is the only excitement. If it has been freezing hard enough for long enough, people go into a frenzy as they prepare for the *Elfstedentocht* (Eleven Cities' Journey), a gruelling skating marathon through the countryside of Friesland that attracts thousands of participants and stops the entire nation. It was last held early in 1997 but years may pass before conditions are right.

February

Carnaval – a southern (Catholic) tradition best enjoyed in Breda, Den Bosch or (especially) Maastricht, but Amsterdammers also know how to don silly costumes and party; information: Stichting Carnaval in Mokum (☎ 623 25 68), Herengracht 513, 1017 BV Amsterdam

Commemoration of the February Strike – 25 February, in memory of the anti-Nazi general strike in 1941; wreath-laying at the Dockworker monument in the former Jewish quarter

March

Stille Omgang – Silent Procession, Sunday closest to 15 March; Catholics walk along the Holy Way (the current Heiligeweg is a remnant) to St Nicolaaskerk to commemorate the Miracle of Amsterdam

HISWA boat show – the latest pleasure craft in the RAI exhibition grounds (☎ 549 12 12; fax 646 44 69)

Blues Festival – at the Meervaart Theatre (☎ 610 74 98), Osdorpplein 205, 1068 SW Amsterdam

April

National Museum Weekend – usually the third weekend; free entry to all museums (extremely crowded); information at Amsterdam Uitburo or Stichting Museumjaarkaart (☎ 670 11 12)

World Press Photo exhibition – from mid or late April in the Nieuwe Kerk (☎ 626 81 68)

Koninginnedag – Queen's Day, 30 April, actually Queen Mother Juliana's birthday (Queen Beatrix's birthday is in January, far too cold for *the* party of the year). If you could visit Amsterdam at any time, this is it. There's a free market throughout the city (anyone can sell anything they like, kids love it), street parties, live music, dense crowds and lots of beer – a collective madhouse. The whole country under the age of 30 visits Amsterdam, while all of Amsterdam over the age of 30 escapes. The next morning everything has been cleaned up.

May

Remembrance Day – 4 May, for the victims of WWII; Queen Beatrix lays a wreath at the Nationaal Monument on Dam square and the city observes two minutes silence at 8 pm; making noise then is thoughtless in the extreme (Germans in particular should take care)

Liberation Day – 5 May, end of German occupation in 1945; street parties, free market, live music; the Vondelpark is a good place to be

Luilak – 'Lazy-Bones', Saturday before Whit Sunday; children go around in the early hours ringing door bells, making noise and waking people up; remnant of pre-Christian festival celebrating the awakening of spring

National Cycling Day – second Saturday; family cycling trips along special routes; information: AVN (☎ 071-560 59 72), VVV, ANWB or NBT.

National Windmill Day – second Saturday; windmills unfurl their sails and are open to the public; information: Vereniging De Hollandsche Molen (☎ 623 87 03), Sarphatistraat 634, 1018 AV Amsterdam

Drum Rhythm Festival – mid-month; world music, jazz and blues in the Westergasfabriek; information: Amsterdam Uitburo

Open Garden Days – mid-month; see some of the beautiful private gardens behind canal houses; information: VVV

June

RAI Arts Fair – first week; exhibition of all facets of contemporary art in RAI exhibition grounds (☎ 549 12 12; fax 646 44 69)

Holland Festival – all month; the country's biggest music, drama and dance extravaganza, mainly in Amsterdam and The Hague; world premieres etc, often highbrow and pretentious but also many fringe events; information: VVV, Amsterdam Uitburo, or Stichting Holland Festival (☎ 627 65 66), Kleine Gartmanplantsoen 21, 1017 RP Amsterdam

Canal Run – usually second weekend but dates vary; Amsterdam's marathon consisting of five, nine and 18-km runs along the canals, organised by *De Echo*, a local weekly paper; information: VVV or Echo Grachtenloop (☎ 585 92 22), Basisweg 30, 1043 AP Amsterdam

Dutch TT Assen – last Saturday; Dutch round of the world series motorcycle grands prix, held since 1925 near the town of Assen in the north-east of the country; many European championship events during 'Speedweek' leading up to the main event that attracts crowds in excess of 150,000; a unique experience even if you're not particularly interested in motorcycles; just turn up at the gate

International Theatre School Festival – end of the month; Dutch and international theatre schools strut their stuff; information: Amsterdam Uitburo or VVV

July

North Sea Jazz Festival – mid-month; world's largest jazz festival, in the Congresgebouw in The Hague; many musicians take the opportunity to visit Amsterdam at this time; information: Amsterdam Uitburo or VVV

August

Uitmarkt – end of the month; local troupes and orchestras present their coming repertoires free of charge throughout the city; a bit like Koninginnedag but much more easy-going; information: Amsterdam Uitburo or VVV

Prinsengracht Concert – end of the month (usually last Friday); free classical concert from boats in front of the Pulitzer Hotel; information: Amsterdam Uitburo, VVV or Pulitzer Hotel (☎ 523 52 35), Prinsengracht 315-331, 1016 GZ Amsterdam

September

Bloemencorso – Flower Parade, first Saturday; spectacular procession of floats wends its way from Aalsmeer in the morning to Dam square and back again at night (illuminated); information: VVV

Jordaan Festival – second week; street festival with much merriment and entertainment in 'typically Amsterdam' neighbourhood; information: VVV

Monumentendag – second Saturday; listed buildings and monuments have an open day; information: VVV or Bureau Monumentenzorg (☎ 626 39 47; fax 620 37 66), Keizersgracht 123, 1015 CJ Amsterdam

Prinsjesdag – third Tuesday; opening of parliament in The Hague; Queen Beatrix arrives in Golden Coach and presents budget

October

Jumping Amsterdam – international indoor show-jumping at RAI exhibition grounds (☎ 549 12 12; fax 646 44 69)

November

Sinterklaas arrives – mid-month; the children's saint arrives by ship 'from Spain' (see December); the mayor presents the keys to the city on Dam square; information: VVV

Cannabis Cup – third week; marihuana festival hosted by *High Times* magazine; the cup itself goes to the best grass, other awards to the biggest spliff etc; also hemp expo and fashion show; information: any 'coffee shop'

December

Sinterklaas – officially 6 December but the main focus is gift-giving on the evening of the 5th, in honour of St Nicholas, the patron saint of children (historically the bishop of Myra in western Turkey around 345 AD). The white-bearded saint, dressed as a bishop with mitre and staff, arrives by ship 'from Spain' a few weeks beforehand and enters the city on a grey or white horse. He is accompanied by a host of mischievous black servants called Black Peters *(Zwarte Pieten)*, who throw sweets around and carry sacks in which to take naughty children away (politically correct Blue and Green Peters proliferate these days). On the evening of 5 December people give one another anonymous and creatively wrapped gifts *(surprises)* accompanied by funny/perceptive poems about the recipient written by Sinterklaas. The commercialisation of Christmas has weakened the impact of this charming festival. The name Santa Claus comes from Sinterklaas (Klaas is a nickname for Nicolaas).

Christmas – 25 & 26 December, but religious families traditionally celebrate Christmas Eve on the 24th instead, with Bible-readings and carols around the Christmas tree

New Year's Eve – wild parties everywhere; drunken revelry with fireworks, sometimes burning tires or even overturned cars on the streets etc; hundreds of injuries each year

WORK

Nationals from EU countries (as well as Iceland, Norway and Liechtenstein) may work in the Netherlands, but they require a renewable residence permit, a tedious formality. However, there are few legal openings for non-EU nationals and the government tries to keep immigrants out of this already overpopulated country. You may be eligible if you are filling a job that no Dutch or EU national has the (trainable) skill to do, are aged between 18 and 45, and have suitable accommodation, but there will be a mound of red tape.

As a rule, you need to apply for temporary residence before an employer can apply for a work permit in your name; if all goes well, you will be issued a residence permit for work purposes. The whole rigmarole should take about five weeks. For more information, contact the Dutch embassy or consulate in your home country. Alternatively, for residence permits you can contact the Immigratie- en Naturalisatiedienst (☎ 070-370 31 24, fax 370 31 34), Postbus 30125, 2500 GC The Hague. For work permits and details of the Aliens Employment Act, contact the Landelijk Bureau Arbeidsvoorziening, Postbus 415, 2280 AK Rijswijk.

Au pair work is easier to organise, provided you are aged between 18 and 25, hold medical insurance and your host family earns at least f3000 a month after tax. The maximum period is one year. Nationals of the EU, Australia, Canada, Japan, Monaco, New Zealand, Switzerland and the USA can organise the necessary residence permit with the Vreemdelingenpolitie (Aliens' Police –

see Visa Extensions in the earlier Documents section) after arrival in the Netherlands; others must organise this with the Dutch embassy or consulate in their home country.

Illegal jobs (working 'black') are pretty rare these days, with increased crackdowns on illegal immigrants working in restaurants, pubs and bulb fields (traditional employers of 'black' labour). Some travellers' hotels in Amsterdam still employ touts to drum up guests by pouncing on newly arrived back-packers; the pay isn't much but you may get free lodging.

If you're fortunate enough to find legal work, the minimum wage is about f1700 a month after tax.

Getting There & Away

Amsterdam is an easy city to get to, and many travellers pass through. If you're looking for cheap deals, advice, shared rides or whatever, you're likely to be successful.

AIR

Many of the world's airlines fly directly to/from Amsterdam's Schiphol airport. As always, it pays to shop around but keep in mind that the best quote might not always be the cheapest: a package deal that includes hotel accommodation, for instance, could save you a small fortune on Amsterdam's notoriously expensive hotels.

Also consider the option of flying to other airports in the region, such as London which is one of the cheapest destinations from outside Europe, or Frankfurt, Luxembourg, Brussels or Paris. It doesn't cost much to take a train or bus from these cities to Amsterdam. If you're flying from outside Europe, many airlines offer a free return flight within Europe (KLM even offers two) – definitely worth including in your calculations.

Amsterdam is a major European centre for discounted tickets to many destinations – see Travel Agents later in this chapter. For special deals, also check the Saturday editions of the *Volkskrant, Parool, Trouw* or *Telegraaf* newspapers, probably in that order.

On weekdays there are five daily return flight connections between Schiphol and four other airports in the Netherlands (reduced services on weekends): Eindhoven (KLM Cityhopper), Enschede and Groningen (Fairlines), and Maastricht/Aachen (Air Excel Commuter).

For information about the airport itself and transport to/from the city, see Schiphol Airport in the Getting Around chapter.

The UK

Even during the high season, roughly from March to September, you should be able to fly London-Schiphol return for less than UK£100. However, if you front up at the airline counter and buy a regular ticket on the spot you could be paying UK£140 one way! The flight takes just under an hour and then it's another 20 minutes by train into the centre of the city; by bus, train or car you'll spend at least 10 hours, usually more.

Campus Travel and STA Travel have worthwhile deals (STA seems to be a couple of pounds cheaper) but these change all the time and the flights mentioned below are just an indication. Also check the Sunday papers, or the listings magazine *Time Out* or the *Evening Standard* for good-value benchmarks. In general, the cheapest fares must be booked at least 21 days in advance and carry a minimum stay of one week and a maximum of a month.

KLM flies Heathrow-Schiphol return for UK£78 plus UK£14.50 airport tax any time of the year under condition that you stay at least one Saturday and return within a month; a ticket for three months costs UK£84 plus tax. Transavia flies from Gatwick for UK£81 plus tax any time of the year. BA and British Midland seem to be slightly dearer.

Students or those aged under 26 should be able to fly for about UK£10 less. For instance, STA Travel can put you on Transavia from Gatwick or British Midland from Heathrow for UK£69 return plus tax, but the British Midland fare goes up to UK£84 in the high season whereas the Transavia fare stays put (the ticket is valid for a year, so this seems to be the best option).

The USA

Tickets in the high season can cost almost twice as much as those in the low season. The high season lasts roughly from mid-June to mid or late September; low is roughly from October to March. The few months on either side are the shoulder seasons, with prices gradually rising or falling. It's like a bell curve, with August at the peak.

Many US airlines fly direct to Amsterdam. National, Delta and Northwest offer decent fares but KLM offers the most frequent flights in conjunction with its partner, Northwest. Approximate fares are US$575/1035 return in the low/high season from San Francisco or US$460/805 from New York. Many flights from the west coast stop in one other US city along the way. Check with a travel agent or in your local Sunday newspaper for the best deals.

Travellers aged under 27 may get a 15% discount on these fares from Council Travel (☎ 800-226 8624) or STA Travel (☎ 800-777 0112), agencies that specialise in cheap travel even for those who are older. They have offices in most major cities. Discount Travel International in New York (☎ 212-362 3636; fax 212-362 3236) might be able to put you on a courier flight from New York for US$400-500 return.

Airhitch (☎ 800-326 2009 or ☎ 212-864 2000, e-mail: airhitch@netcom.com), 2641 Broadway, 3rd Floor, New York, NY 10025, offers flights on stand-by basis. You must be able to leave any time within a set period (usually five to seven days). You may have to wait a bit longer to get a direct flight to Amsterdam; less if you are willing to fly to another major city nearby. A one-way flight costs US$169 from New York, and US$269 from San Francisco or Los Angeles.

Icelandair operates a flight between JFK airport (New York) and Amsterdam for US$540/748 return in the low/high season (don't make the mistake of buying the high-season one-way ticket for US$1092!). Flights also leave from Baltimore, Boston, Fort Lauderdale and Orlando. The flights go via Reykjavík, where you could stop over and visit Iceland (not many people can say they've done that). There's no extra charge, but you must either buy one of Icelandair's special package deals or make your own arrangements for accommodation. Icelandair also flies between JFK and Luxembourg for US$616 return or US$308 one way regardless of the season. The train and/or bus to Amsterdam is not included.

Canada

Travel CUTS is a chain of budget travel agents with offices throughout Canada. The main office is in Toronto (☎ 416-977 3703), but you can consult their web page at www.travelcuts.com. Flights to Amsterdam start at C$599/750 return in the low/high season for students (or rather, those aged under 27). Once again, KLM offers the most frequent flights.

For courier flights, contact FB On Board Courier Services (☎ 514-631 7925 in Montreal or ☎ 604-278 1266 in Vancouver).

Australia & New Zealand

There's a big difference between low and high-season fares, and unlike trans-Atlantic flights, where prices rise and fall gradually on either side of the high season, the increases and decreases are more sudden. Book well ahead if you intend to fly close to the crossover dates around April/May and September. One-way flights cost about two-thirds of return flights.

Discounted return fares on mainstream airlines through a reputable budget agency like STA Travel or Flight Centres International cost around A$1500/2500 in the low/high season. Airlines such as Garuda and Philippine Airlines can be slightly cheaper but you might spend 36 hours or more getting to Amsterdam from Sydney, rather than the already gruelling 22 hours with KLM.

KLM flies between Amsterdam and Sydney three times a week, with a one-hour stop in Singapore, for A$1650/2459 return in the low/high season (Ansett connecting flight to/from Melbourne included) – the most hassle-free option if you can afford it.

From November to March, no-frills Britannia Airways flies between Sydney/Melbourne and Maastricht/London/Manchester for A$1175-1700 return depending on the date, and also between Brisbane/Adelaide and London/Manchester, or between Cairns and Maastricht. One-way fares are half the return fare. Contact Britannia Airways (☎ 02-9251 1299), 6th Floor, 210 George St, Sydney 2000.

The cheapest return fares from New Zealand are routed through the USA but a round-the-world ticket could be cheaper still. This is sometimes the case from Australia too.

Airline Offices

Airline offices in Amsterdam, listed under *Luchtvaartmaatschappijen* (Aviation Companies) in the pink pages of the phone book, include:

Aer Lingus
    Heiligeweg 14 (☎ 623 86 20)
Aeroflot
    Weteringschans 26-III (☎ 627 05 61)
Air France
    Evert van der Beekstraat 7, Schiphol (☎ 446 88 00)
Air India
    Papenbroeksteeg 2 (☎ 624 81 09)
Air UK
    Wallaardt Sacrestraat 250, Schiphol (☎ 601 06 33)
Alitalia
    Paulus Potterstraat 18 (☎ 577 74 44)
British Airways
    Neptunusstraat 33, Hoofddorp (☎ 565 00 66)
British Midland
    Strawinskylaan 721 (☎ 662 22 11)
Cathay Pacific
    Evert van der Beekstraat 18, Schiphol (☎ 653 52 25)
China Airlines
    De Boelelaan 7 (☎ 646 10 01)
Delta Air Lines
    De Boelelaan 7 (☎ 661 00 51)
El Al
    De Boelelaan 7-VI (☎ 644 01 01)
Garuda Indonesia
    Singel 540 (☎ 627 26 26)
Icelandair
    Muntplein 2-3 (☎ 627 01 36)
Japan Airlines
    Jozef Israelskade 48E (☎ 675 98 79)
KLM
    Gabriel Metsustraat 2-6 (☎ 474 77 47)
Lufthansa
    Wibautstraat 129 (☎ 668 58 51)
Malaysia Airlines
    Weteringschans 24A (☎ 626 24 20)
Northwest Airlines
    Weteringschans 85C (☎ 627 71 41)
Philippine Airlines
    Nijenburg 2 (☎ 646 43 46)
Qantas
    Stadhouderskade 6 (☎ 683 80 81)

Singapore Airlines
    De Boelelaan 1067 (☎ 646 60 46)
South African Airways
    Polarisavenue 49, Hoofddorp (☎ 568 54 44)
Thai Airways
    Singel 466-468 (☎ 622 18 77)
Transavia
    Westelijke Randweg 3 (☎ 601 56 66)
United Airlines
    Strawinskylaan 831-B8 (☎ 662 32 36)

BUS

Amsterdam is well connected to the rest of Europe by long-distance bus. Eurolines has regular bus services between Amsterdam and many Western, Eastern, Mediterranean and Central European destinations as well as Scandinavia and North Africa. Hoverspeed Citysprint buses run mainly between London, Belgium and the Netherlands. Depending on the service, there are stops in Breda, Rotterdam, The Hague and Utrecht as well as Antwerp and Brussels in Belgium. Some Eurolines buses and all Citysprint buses cross the Channel via Calais in France. Travellers using either service should check whether they'll require a French visa (Australians do, for instance).

Eurolines offices include Eurolines (☎ 0171 – 730 8235), 52 Grosvenor Gardens, London SW1W 0AU; Deutsche Touring (☎ 089-54 58 70 15) at the train station in Munich; Lazzi Express (☎ 06-88 40 840), Via Tagliamento 27R in Rome; and Eurolines (☎ 01-43 54 11 99), 55 Rue Saint Jacques in Paris. In Amsterdam, tickets can be bought at most travel agencies as well as at the Netherlands Railways (NS) Reisburo (Travel Bureau) in Centraal Station. There are reduced fares for those aged under 26.

The Eurolines Amsterdam office (Map 13; ☎ 627 51 51) is at Rokin 10 near Dam square. Free timetables with fare information are cheerfully supplied; fares are consistently lower than the train. Buses leave from the bus station (☎ 694 56 31) next to Amstel-station (Map 10), easily accessible by metro. The only problem with these buses is heavy cigarette-smoking on some services (enquire when booking). Cities like Bruges, Paris, London, Berlin, Copenhagen and Budapest are easily accessible by Eurolines bus. The buses to Paris and London travel overnight, allowing you to save a night's hotel bill coming and going. A one-way ticket to London costs f100/90 for those aged over/under 26 and the journey takes 10 to 12 hours.

Hoverspeed Citysprint (☎ 664 66 26), Pieter de Hoochstraat 55 near Museumplein, has three daily buses to London in summer, one daily in winter. A one-way ticket costs f90/80 for those aged over/under 26. There are also buses to Berlin and several other European destinations. Bookings are handled by the VVV (Map 8) at Stadionplein, the departure point for the buses (tram No 24 from Centraal Station); arrivals from London are dropped more centrally at Leidseplein.

From London's Victoria Coach Station, Hoverspeed (☎ 0171-730 3499) charges UK£39/37 for a return ticket in winter for those aged over/under 26 and about UK£10 more in summer. Eurolines (☎ 0171-730 8235, or through National Express ☎ 0990-808 080) charges UK£36/49 one way/return in summer. Fares may rise or fall considerably depending on cutthroat competition among cross-Channel services.

For information about regional buses in the Netherlands, for instance to places not serviced by the extensive train network, call ☎ 0900-92 92 (f0.50-0.75 a minute).

TRAIN

Amsterdam's main train station is Centraal Station (commonly known as CS), which has regular and efficient train connections throughout the country and to all neighbouring countries. Eurail, Inter-Rail, Europass and Flexipass tickets are valid on Dutch trains, which are run by the Nederlandse Spoorwegen (NS).

Information

For international train information and reservations, head for the NS international reservations office (☎ 620 22 66) inside the station, open daily from 6.30 am to 10 pm. In peak periods it's wise to reserve seats in advance. For trains within the country, ring

the public-transport information number on ☎ 0900-92 92 (f0.50-0.75 a minute) or simply turn up at the station: you'll rarely have to wait more than an hour for a train to anywhere.

A book with complete train timetables is available at the station counters and at newsagencies for f9.75. It includes a brief user's guide in English, German, French, Turkish and Arabic on pages 14-23. Timetables are also available on diskette (with a useful tripplanning function) for f12.75 (DOS) or f19.75 (Windows), and free on Teletext pages 751-755 (Dutch TV channels). See the Excursions chapter for more about trains within the country.

Main Lines

There are two main lines south from Amsterdam. One passes through The Hague and Rotterdam and on to Antwerp (f46, 2¼ hours, hourly trains) and Brussels (f56, three hours, hourly trains) and then on to either Paris (f123 plus an f8 EuroCity supplement, six hours, 10 a day) or Luxembourg City (f102, six hours). The other line south goes via Utrecht and Maastricht to Luxembourg City (f98, six hours) and on to France and Switzerland, or branches at Utrecht and heads east via Arnhem to Cologne (f69 plus an f8 EuroCity supplement, 2½ hours, every two hours) and further into Germany.

The main line east eventually branches off to the north-east of the country or continues east to Berlin, with a branch north to Hamburg. There's also a line north from Amsterdam to Den Helder in the tip of Holland. All these fares are one way in 2nd class; people aged under 26 get a 25% discount. The new high-speed train, the *Thalys*, runs four times a day between Amsterdam and Antwerp (f55, two hours), Brussels (f63, 2½ hours) and Paris (f132, 4¾ hours). Those aged under 26 get a 45% discount and seniors with a Rail Europe Senior (RES) card are entitled to 30% off.

The UK

British Rail International (☎ 0171-834 2345) has a train-boat-train combo with

RICHARD NEBESKY

RICHARD NEBESKY

TONY WHEELER

Top: The gilded façade of Centraal Station
Middle: Amsterdam tram - efficient and relatively cheap transport
Bottom: Bikes chained to a bridge and then to each other, but even that is no
guarantee against theft

TONY WHEELER

RICHARD NEBESKY

TONY WHEELER

ROB VAN DRIESUM

Top Left: Biking it: *the* way to get around
Top Right: Bike that's seen better days
Bottom Left: Even a fool should understand this
Bottom Right: This fool didn't

Stena Sealink from Liverpool St Station which uses the ferry between Harwich and Hook of Holland (Hoek van Holland) west of Rotterdam. The normal adult return fare is UK£71 with a validity of two months and there are supplements for a reclining chair on the ferry or a range of cabins. The daytime run takes 10½ hours; the overnight service takes 13 hours and costs a bit more. There's an advance-purchase special of UK£49 which must be booked seven days in advance and has a validity of one month, with both outward and inward dates confirmed on booking; it applies to the daytime run only, the night run costs more. Those aged under 26 can get discounts down to as low as UK£39 for the advance-purchase special.

Another service, from Victoria Station this time, uses the ferry between Ramsgate and Ostend in Belgium. This costs roughly the same as the above trip and is of similar duration, though for a supplement there's also the option of a jetfoil crossing which shaves two to three hours off the total time.

Alternatively, you can take the highly civilised Eurostar passenger train service from Waterloo Station through the Channel Tunnel to Brussels and proceed from there to Amsterdam. This takes about five hours in total and costs UK£175 return in 2nd class, flexible and refundable. There are specials all the time (eg UK£77 inflexible, non-refundable and staying away a Saturday night) and passengers aged under 26 get the usual discounts. Eurostar tickets are available from some travel agents, at Waterloo Station, from Victoria Station's International Rail Centre and the international ticket offices at many of the UK's mainline train stations, or you can book by phone on ☎ 0990-300 003.

CAR & MOTORCYCLE

Freeways link Amsterdam to The Hague (A4/E19 and A44), Rotterdam (A4/E19) and Utrecht (A2/E35) in the south, and Amersfoort (A1/E231) and points further east and north-east. The A10/E22 ring freeway encircles the city, with tunnel sections under the IJ. Amsterdam is about 480km (six hours'

drive) from Paris, 840km from Munich, 680km from Berlin, and 730km from Copenhagen. The ferry port at Hook of Holland is about 80km away, the one at IJmuiden is just up the road along the North Sea Canal (see the following Boat section for ferry details). Coming from the UK it's a fair bit cheaper to take the ferry rather than the shuttle through the Tunnel, though the latter might save a few hours travelling time from London if you're desperate.

Vehicles obviously have to be roadworthy, registered and insured. The standard European road rules and traffic signs apply. Trams always have the right of way unless you're on a right-of-way road. Speed limits are 50 km/h in built-up areas, 80 km/h in the country, 100 km/h on major through roads and 120 km/h on freeways (sometimes 100 km/h, clearly indicated). The blood-alcohol limit when driving is 0.05%. Petrol is very expensive.

For more about driving (or rather, not driving) in Amsterdam and about rental cars, see Car & Motorcycle in the Getting Around chapter.

Documents

Anyone driving a car or riding a motorcycle in the Netherlands must be able to show a valid licence as well as the vehicle's registration papers on the spot. With rental cars the registration papers usually live in the dashboard compartment; take them with you whenever you park to avoid theft. Foreign-registered vehicles must have proof of third-party insurance in the form of a Green Card.

The Dutch automobile association ANWB (Map 15; see under Tourist Offices in the Facts for the Visitor chapter) provides a wide range of information and services if you can show a letter of introduction from your own association.

BICYCLE

The Netherlands are extremely bike-friendly; once you're in the country you can pedal most of the way to/from Amsterdam on dedicated bicycle paths. Everything is wonderfully flat, but powerful winds have free reign and they always seem to come from ahead. Beware that mopeds use bike paths too and might be travelling well in excess of their 40 km/h speed limit! Bikes (or mopeds) are not allowed on freeways at all. Bicycle helmets are only used by the occasional competition cyclist or poser.

If you want to bring your own bike, consider the high risk of it being stolen in Amsterdam. You can bring it along on the train for a nominal charge and (most) ferries charge nothing. Airlines usually treat it as normal accompanied luggage – enquire in advance, and also ask what to do if bike and luggage exceed your weight allowance or you could be charged a fortune for the excess.

For organisations offering local advice and support, see Bicycle in the Getting Around chapter.

HITCHING

Hitching is never entirely safe in any country in the world and we don't recommend it. Travellers who decide to hitch should understand that they are taking a small but potentially serious risk.

Many Dutch students have a government-issued pass allowing free public transport (though this is under review). Consequently the number of hitchhikers in the country has dropped dramatically and car drivers are no longer used to the phenomenon. Hitchers have reported long waits.

On Channel crossings from the UK, the car fares on the Harwich-Hook of Holland ferry as well as the shuttle through the Channel Tunnel include passengers, so you can hitch to the Continent for nothing at no cost to the driver (though the driver will still be responsible if you do something illegal).

The International Lift Center (Map 13; ☎ 622 43 42), Oudezijds Achterburgwal 169, arranges lifts in private cars to points around Europe (Madrid f115 per person, London f45, Munich f51, Copenhagen f60). The agency collects an annual membership fee of f10 plus f10 to f20 commission per

ride. It's open weekdays from 1 to 6 pm, Saturday from 11 am to 3 pm.

BOAT

Several companies operate car/passenger ferries between the Netherlands and England, and one company has a ferry to Norway. For information on train-ferry-train services, see the earlier Train section. Most travel agents have information on the following services but might not always know the finer points – it's easier to catch eels with your bare hands than to pin down who's doing what exactly when it comes to ferries. Once again, expect prices and deals to fluctuate madly depending on cross-Channel competition. Reservations are essential for motorists, especially in the high season, though motorcycles can often be squeezed in at the last moment.

Stena Sealink (☎ 0990-707 070) sails between Harwich and Hook of Holland and has both a day (6½-hour) and night (nine-hour) service. Foot passengers pay upwards of UK£36 return (five-day limit). Fares for a car with up to five people range from UK£80 to UK£156 depending on the season (extra passengers pay the foot-passenger fare). Options such as reclining chairs and cabins cost extra and are compulsory on night crossings. The same company also does Dover-Calais, but this isn't really cheaper and once you've added travel expenses on the Continent you've spent much more.

P&O Lines (☎ 0990-980 980) operates an overnight ferry (14 hours) between Hull and Europoort (near Rotterdam). Return fares are UK£64/80 for a foot passenger in the low/high season, and UK£126 for a car or UK£55 for a motorcycle plus UK£64/80 per person low/high (with discounts for three or more people).

Scandinavian Seaways sails between Newcastle and IJmuiden, the closest port to Amsterdam, with two or three departures a week at each end depending on the season. The journey takes 14 hours. Low-season fares operate from October to 26 March, high season from 14 July to 18 August, and mid season at other times. Foot passengers pay upwards of UK£30/58/84 low/mid/high for a one-way trip (bicycles are transported free of charge). Cars are UK£69/99/119 Apex return (ie booked in advance, with limitations) plus the foot-passenger rate for each person; motorcycles are UK£42/52/62 Apex return plus the foot-passenger rate per person. Cabins cost extra.

From May to August, the same company also sails three times a week between IJmuiden and Kristiansand (Norway). From IJmuiden, fares for the 20-hour voyage start at f130/200 for a car in the low/high season. Passengers must be paid for separately, and rates start at f190/230, or f210/250 in a cabin. Future Line Travel (Map 17; see Travel Agents later in this chapter) has information and discount tickets for official hostel members.

TRAVEL AGENTS

Many travel agents specialise in discounted fares; many more don't but still manage to be competitive with interesting packages. The best advice is to shop around, beginning with the following agents:

Budget Air, associated with the Dutch post office, with offices in the main post office at Singel 250 (Map 12; ☎ 556 33 33) and a larger office at Rokin 34 (Map 13; ☎ 627 12 51) – free brochure published every two months with 700 exact fares for cheap flights to cities around the world; pick up a copy for comparison

NBBS, Rokin 38, (Map 13; ☎ 624 09 89) and several branches around town, including Leidsestraat 53 (☎ 638 17 26) and Haarlemmerstraat 115 (Map 11; ☎ 626 25 57) – the official student travel agency; prices are not the best, so compare the discount travel agencies along Rokin before booking anything here

Amber Reisbureau, Da Costastraat 77 (Map 12; ☎ 685 11 55) – open weekdays from 10 am to 5 pm, Saturday to 3 pm; has a great travel book-store and good prices on tickets to Asia

Flyworld/Grand Travel, Wallaardt Sacrestraat 262, Schiphol (☎ 657 00 00; fax 648 04 77) – cheap long-haul flights; all bookings by phone or fax

Future Line Travel, Professor Tulpstraat 2 (Map 17; ☎ 551 31 33; fax 639 01 99) – run by the Youth Hostel Association; open weekdays from 9 am to 5 pm

Ashraf, Haarlemmerstraat 140, 1013 EZ Amsterdam (Map 11; ☎ 623 24 50; fax 622 90 28) – runs overland adventure tours to Africa and Asia for young people

DEPARTURE TAXES

There are none.

WARNING

The information in this chapter is particularly vulnerable to change: prices for international travel are volatile, routes are introduced and cancelled, schedules change, special deals come and go, and rules and visa requirements are amended. Airlines and governments seem to take a perverse pleasure in making price structures and regulations as complicated as possible. You should check directly with the airline or a travel agent to make sure you understand how a fare (and ticket you may buy) works. In addition, the travel industry is highly competitive and there are many packages and bonuses.

The upshot of this is that you should get opinions, quotes and advice from as many airlines and travel agents as possible before you part with your hard-earned cash. The details given in this chapter should be regarded as pointers and are not a substitute for your own careful, up-to-date research.

Getting Around

SCHIPHOL AIRPORT

The airport at Schiphol is 18km south-west of the city centre. It lies five metres below sea level on the bottom of a former lake, the Haarlemmermeer, drained in 1852. The spacious yet surprisingly compact one-terminal design ensures that everything is within easy reach, and the signposting couldn't be much clearer.

The arrivals hall, built around a V-shaped concourse with shops called Schiphol Plaza, is on the ground floor, with the Holland Tourist Promotion office (for tourist information daily from 7 am to 10 pm) in the far left corner as you emerge from the passenger area. The departures hall is upstairs. Passengers travelling to/from Schengen countries (see Visas in the Facts for the Visitor chapter) are kept separate from other passengers and do not go through passport control, regardless of their nationality, though they should carry their passport as a means of identification and to transfer from Schengen to non-Schengen lounges.

On arrival, yellow signs and transfer information monitors direct you to the transfer gates or desks (if you don't already have a boarding pass for your onward flight), green signs to the various amenities. It's worth paying a quick visit to the city if you need to kill a few hours in transit. Holland Tours, at the Transport Desk in the left corner near the central exits of Schiphol Plaza, offers short guided tours to various spots in this part of the country, but it's just as easy to take the train into Amsterdam for a bit of a stroll.

Schiphol is world-renowned for its tax-free shopping; the scale and variety of goods are second to none and many prices are beaten only by airports such as Dubai and Abu Dhabi. In addition there's every facility you'd expect (and even some you wouldn't) of one of the world's leading international airports – it consistently rates near or at the top of business travel surveys. There's an interesting aviation museum nearby (see

Amsterdam for Children in the Facts for the Visitor chapter) and even a casino, open from 6 am to 8 pm in the passenger-only section of the non-Schengen departure lounge, accessible to passengers aged over 18 with a valid boarding pass and passport.

For airport and flight information, ring ☎ 0900-503 40 50 (f0.75 per minute).

Left Luggage

Luggage up to 30kg can be left at the staffed counter (☎ 601 24 43) in the basement under the plaza for a minimum of a day and a maximum of a month. This costs f7 for the first day, then f6 per day up to 15 days and f5 per day up to 30 days. The counter is open from 6 am to 10.45 pm but staff may be called through the intercom at other times. Lockers in the same area (f6 per day for small items, f10 for large ones) are available for a maximum of 72 hours.

To/From the Airport

A taxi into the city takes 20-45 minutes (maybe longer in peak-hour traffic) and costs f50-60. Trains to Centraal Station leave every 15 minutes, take 15-20 minutes and cost f6 (f10.25 return). Train-ticket counters are in the central court of Schiphol Plaza – buy your ticket before taking the escalator down to the subterranean platforms (you might want to buy a *strippenkaart* for public transport while you're at it – see the following Public Transport section). If your hotel is some way out of the city centre, it could be worth taking a train to one of the other stations around the city (see Train in the following section) and transferring to a taxi from there. Trains also connect Schiphol to 75% of train stations in the country either direct or with one change, and to major cities in Belgium, France and Germany.

Free shuttle buses travel to the Bastion, Hilton, Ibis, Golden Tulip, Holiday Inn, Dorint and Mercure airport hotels. A KLM shuttle bus runs between the airport and about 15 major hotels in the city every 20 minutes from the early morning to mid-evening at a cost of f17.50 one way, f30 return. For information, contact the Transport Desk (open from 7.30 am to 11.30 pm), the Holland Tourist Promotion desk, or ring NZH Travel on ☎ 649 56 51. Bus No 172 maintains a regular service between the airport and Centraal Station but there are many other bus services that could better suit your purposes – ring ☎ 0900-92 92. There are also buses to other parts of the country.

One of the country's main road arteries, the A4 freeway linking Amsterdam, The Hague and Rotterdam, tunnels under one of the airport runways. Just north of the airport is the A9 to/from Haarlem in the west, which runs south of the city and connects with the A2 to Utrecht and the south-east of the country. A bit further north of the A9 is the intersection with the A10 ring road around Amsterdam. Car-rental offices at the airport are in the right corner near the central exits of Schiphol Plaza.

Parking The P1 and P2 short-term parking garages (under cover) charge f3 per half hour for the first three hours, then f3 per hour. The maximum charge is f45 a day for the first two days, f22.50 a day thereafter. Pay at the machines before going to your car. The P3 long-term parking area (open air) is a fair distance from the terminal but is connected by 24-hour shuttle bus. The parking charge is f85 for up to three days and f7.50 for each day thereafter – a worthwhile alternative to parking in the city.

PUBLIC TRANSPORT

Amsterdam is compact and you can get to a lot of places on foot, but public transport (tram, *sneltram*, bus and metro), run by the GVB (Gemeentevervoerbedrijf – Municipal Transport Company), is comprehensive and efficient. The only problem is within the canal belt: trams and buses stick to the 'spoke' roads, so if you want to cover distance along a canal you'll have to take a tram or bus into the centre and another back out again.

The hub of the transport system is Centraal Station (CS), where most tram and bus lines and the metro converge. The GVB information office (Map 13) in front of the station is open weekdays from 6 am to midnight, weekends from 7 am, and sells all types of tickets and passes. Pick up a free map of central-area public transport; a transport map covering all of Amsterdam, including lines of night buses, costs f1.50.

For transport information, call ☎ 0900-92 92 weekdays from 6 am to midnight, weekends from 7 am. This costs f0.50-0.75 a minute, which can add up quickly if your query is complicated. Expect to be put on hold for a couple of minutes as other calls are answered ahead of you.

Tickets & Passes

Ticketing is based on zones. Most of Amsterdam proper (the canal belt and surrounding districts) is one zone; travel to the older suburbs is two, and to the newer, outer suburbs is three.

The strip ticket *(strippenkaart)* is valid on all buses, trams and metros in the country, as well as trains within municipal areas (though in Amsterdam's case Schiphol is *not* included). Fold the ticket to the relevant strip and stick it into the yellow machine to cancel two strips for the first zone and an additional strip for each additional zone – always one strip more than the number of zones. Any number of people can travel on the one ticket, so long as you cancel the appropriate number of strips for each person. When you get to the bottom of the ticket, cancel the last strip and proceed with the next ticket. The validity for one, two or three zones is one hour, during which time you can transfer as often as you like.

Strip tickets (f11 for 15 strips, f32.25 for 45) are available at tobacco shops, post offices, train-station counters, many bookshops and newsagencies, and special outlets such as the GVB offices (Map 13) in front of Centraal Station and in Amstelstation (Map 10). Drivers and conductors only sell two/three/eight-strip tickets for f3/4.50/12, or an Amsterdam day pass for f12 (actually an eight-strip ticket stamped vertically). Children, pensioners and people with disabilities pay f6 for a 15-strip ticket that has to be bought in advance. Travelling without a valid ticket (frequent spot checks) incurs a fine of f60 plus the ticket price, and playing the ignorant foreigner won't work.

The GVB offices also sell day passes valid for all zones from f12 for one day, f16 for two and then in f3.75 increments up to f42.25 for nine days; those eligible for a discount pay f6 for one day, rising in f2 increments up to f22 for nine days. Passes valid for one zone cost f16 a week or f54 a month (f9.50 or f33 with discount). The GVB offices can advise of several other options.

Night buses take over when regular transport stops running shortly after midnight. They cost three strips for one or two zones, four strips for three zones etc. Passes, however, are valid during the night following the day(s) indicated on the pass.

Tram

Most trams can be entered or exited through any of the doors, where there are yellow machines to stamp strip tickets. If you need to buy a ticket, enter at the front by the driver. Some trams have a separate conductor in the back and can only be entered through the rear doors (there are one-way bars at the others); in that case, show your ticket to the conductor. When getting in or out, the bottom step locks the door in the open position and prevents the tram from leaving.

There are also a few *sneltram* (fast tram) lines in the southern and south-eastern suburbs – ordinary trams that travel a bit faster along dedicated tracks with elevated platforms. Tickets are cancelled the same way as in ordinary trams except where the sneltram shares the metro line, in which case you use the yellow machines at the stairways to the platforms.

Always assume that pickpockets are active on busy trams.

Circle Tram The GVB expects to put a circle tram into operation in the summer of 1997. Starting and ending at Centraal Station, it will do a wide loop through the city along all the major tourist sights in either direction every 10 minutes from 9 am to 6 pm. The tram will accept normal strip tickets and passes, and will sell a special 'Circle-tram-ticket' valid on all public transport at f10/15/19/23 for one/two/three/four days. At least, that's the idea.

Bus

Trams don't venture to Amsterdam Noord and only a few go to the outer suburbs, so you're likely to need a bus there. Buses should be boarded through the front door; show your ticket to (or buy it from) the driver.

Metro

The metro is useful mostly for getting to the international bus station at Amstelstation (one zone) or to the Bijlmer (three zones). In the city there's only one line but after Amstelstation it branches into three lines – one to the southern suburbs of Buitenveldert and Amstelveen and two to the south-eastern suburb of Bijlmer. Cancel your strip ticket at the machines near the stairways to the platforms.

Anyone interested in seeing another side of Amsterdam should hang around Weesperplein metro station during the morning or afternoon rush hours when people from the Bijlmer change from the metro to trams at this station. It's just like a little New York!

Train

You're most likely to use the train in Amsterdam when travelling to/from Schiphol airport. The options are Centraal Station, at the hub of the public transport system; Lelylaan, De Vlugtlaan and Sloterdijk in the western suburbs; Zuid WTC and RAI exhibition centre in the southern suburbs; or Duivendrecht and Diemen-Zuid in the south-eastern suburbs. A sneltram connects RAI station to Amstelstation for trains to/from Utrecht and the east of the country, though such trains also call at Centraal Station.

You can use strip tickets to travel on trains in the Amsterdam region – cancel your ticket at the machines near the stairways to the platforms. Muiderpoort and Amstelstation are two strips to/from Centraal Station; Diemen, Diemen-Zuid, Duivendrecht, RAI, Zuid WTC, Lelylaan, De Vlugtlaan and Sloterdijk are three strips; and Bijlmer is four strips. Strip tickets are *not* valid to/from Schiphol, which requires a normal train ticket.

CAR & MOTORCYCLE

See Car & Motorcycle in the previous chapter for general information about road rules, documents etc.

Central Amsterdam's narrow canalside streets were not built for heavy vehicular traffic, and driving into the city is actively discouraged by the authorities with their so-called *autoluw* ('car-sheltered') policy. Of course, the most effective way to reduce the number of cars is by limiting parking space. There's absolutely no free parking in the canal belt or surrounding areas, and even if it looks like the parking is free because no warning signs are posted, there's a hungry automatic ticketing machine in the vicinity. You'll receive a receipt which you should place on the dashboard inside the car (check that it stays there when you slam the door shut). Parking charges are payable Monday to Saturday from 9 am to 11 pm, Sunday from noon to 11 pm, and cost f4.25 per hour Monday to Saturday from 9 am to 7 pm, f2.25 per hour at other times (check the notice on the machine: conditions are likely to become stricter).

The ticketing machine may not be visible immediately but do find it, otherwise a bright yellow *wielklem* (wheel clamp) will be attached to your car and it will cost f122 to have it removed. Don't expect to talk your way out of this: they've heard it all before. The infringement ticket on your windshield will give the location of the parking management *(parkeerbeheer)* office closest to wherever you happen to be and you must go there personally – telephoned requests for service are not accepted.

Alternatively, instead of hunting around for the specific office, for a fee of f29 (cash)

© HEIN DE KORT 1997

or f37.50 (credit card) on top of the f122 fine, you can use the services of a wheel-clamp agent such as Klem-Hulp City Service (☎ 620 37 50), which ensures you'll be able to drive off within 45 minutes (if they answer the phone!). Klem-Hulp will also deliver a day or week permit (see below) to your car or address for f10 on top of the permit fee.

There are five parking-management offices that can remove wheel clamps. The ones at Bakkersstraat 13 (off Rembrandtplein) and Ceintuurbaan 159 (between the Sarphatipark and Van Woustraat) are open from 8 am to 8 pm Monday to Saturday. The ones at Korte Leidsedwarsstraat 2 (off Leidseplein) and Nieuwezijds Kolk (off Nieuwezijds Voorburgwal) are open Monday to Saturday from 7.30 am to 11 pm. The only office open 24 hours a day seven days a week is at Cruquiuskade 25 in the east of the city beyond the Scheepvaartmuseum, behind the windmill (bus No 22 or 32 or night bus No 71). The head office (☎ 553 03 00) at Weesperstraat 105A (between Weesperplein and Waterlooplein, on the corner of

Nieuwe Prinsengracht) is open from 8.30 am to 4.30 pm weekdays but doesn't service wheel clamps.

If you don't report to one of these five offices within 24 hours your car will be towed away and a f300 towing charge plus f83.60 per day garage fee will be collected in addition to the parking fine. Towed cars are taken to the Cruquiuskade 25 office, so before jumping to the conclusion that your vehicle has been stolen, call this office on ☎ 555 98 00.

You can easily avoid these potential problems by parking your car outside the centre and entering the city by tram or metro. For instance, the 'transferium' parking garage (☎ 563 29 90) under the Arena stadium in the Bijlmer charges f2.50 per hour or f12.50 per day, including transfers to the metro and two return tickets to Centraal Station – an excellent deal.

It's also possible to buy a city parking permit at any of the above offices for f24/120/432 a day/week/month (half-price for areas outside the canal belt or museum quarter). Some hotels also issue special three-day passes for f60, and a few luxury hotels have their own arrangements that aren't cheap. Parking garages in the city centre (eg on Damrak, near Leidseplein and under the Stopera) are often full and cost more than a parking permit, though they do provide shelter and some security against theft and vandalism. Alternatively, you could book into your hotel and then leave the car in the long-term parking area at Schiphol airport for the duration of your stay, which is probably the wisest option (see the earlier Schiphol Airport section).

Drivers with a disability and the appropriate windscreen marker may park free of charge in designated parking spots, or the above-mentioned offices can issue day passes that allow free parking in any parking spot.

Motorcyclists don't face parking problems: they can park on the pavement (sidewalk) free of charge provided they don't obstruct anybody. Security is a big problem with any parked vehicle, however, irrespective of the time of day, so don't leave luggage on the bike and don't rely on the steering lock.

Car Rental

There's no point renting a car to tour the city but it's a good way to make excursions into the countryside. The car-rental market is fluid, and prices and deals change by the week. The following list represents a snapshot of what was available at the time of research, but it pays to ring around to find the deal that suits you best. Bring a credit card. Local companies are usually cheaper than the multinationals (Avis, Budget, Hertz, Europcar etc) but don't offer as much backup or flexibility (eg one-way rentals within or outside the Netherlands). Rentals at Schiphol airport cost about f60 extra because of airport company tax.

Avis, Nassaukade 380 not far from Leidseplein (☎ 683 60 61), President Kennedylaan 783 (☎ 644 36 84), Klokkenbergweg 15 (☎ 564 15 11), international reservations ☎ 564 16 11 – f163 a day for the cheapest car with unlimited km, insurance and tax included; otherwise it's f118 a day plus f0.40 per km (the first 100 km are free), tax and insurance included

Budget, Overtoom 121 (☎ 612 60 66), Schiphol Plaza (☎ 604 13 49), international reservations ☎ 023-567 12 22 – f222 a day for the cheapest car unlimited km, insurance and tax included; this is expensive but Budget also offers one of the cheapest deals in the country through the post office – see below

Europcar Interrent, Overtoom 51-53 (☎ 683 21 23) – a Renault Twingo for f60 a day plus f0.29 a km (the first 100 km are free); add f60 if you rent it at Schiphol Plaza

Hertz, Overtoom 333 (☎ 612 24 41), Stromarkt 5 (☎ 623 61 23), Prof Tulpplein 2C (☎ 520 32 00), international reservations ☎ 023-562 00 28 – f139 a day with unlimited km for an Opel Corsa; the branch at Schiphol Plaza has cars from f209 a day with unlimited km

Kaspers en Lotte, Van Ostadestraat 232 south of the Sarphatipark (☎ 671 70 66) – f114 a day for the cheapest car, unlimited km, tax and insurance included

Kuperus BV, Middenweg 175 (☎ 693 87 90; fax 665 98 78) on the south-eastern side of town (tram No 9) – cheapest car is f65 a day including insurance, tax and 100 km (extra kms f0.20 each); cars with unlimited km begin at f185 for three days, all inclusive

Safety Rent-a-Car, Papaverweg 3b near the Galaxy Hotel, Amsterdam Noord (☎ 636 63 63) – cheapest car is f73 a day plus f0.22 per km (after the first 100 km), tax and insurance included; unlimited km rentals also available, depending on where you want to go

Siem Faas Autoverhuur, Grasweg 3, behind the Shell Oil facilities across the IJ from Centraal Station, Amsterdam Noord (☎ 637 18 26) – cheapest car is f56 a day plus f0.25 per km (the first 100 km are free), tax and insurance included; unlimited km rentals available at f70 a day for a minimum of three days

The cheapest arrangement of all involves a main post office, where you buy a voucher that gets you the smallest Budget car for only f55 a day including insurance, tax and unlimited km. The vouchers are valid for six months and you must book your car directly at a Budget office no less than 24 hours in advance. A Renault Cariole specially adapted for a wheelchair in the back costs f85 a day but must be booked at least a week in advance. Call the postal information service on ☎ 0800-417 (free number) for the address of the nearest post office offering this service.

Camper Van Purchase

Braitman & Woudenberg (☎ 622 11 68), Droogbak 3-4 at Singel diagonally opposite Hotel Ibis, sells camper vans to travellers with a guaranteed repurchase agreement. A good VW Westfalia costs f10,000, and if you return it in good condition within three months you'll get 75% back, within six months 65%, and within a year 60%; longer periods are negotiable. Occasionally there are cheaper vans at around f5000.

Motorcycle Rental

You can rent a car more cheaply than a motorcycle but sometimes a car just won't do, will it? For instance, you might want to visit the Dutch TT at Assen on the last weekend in June. Ring around:

KAV Autoverhuur, Johan Huizingalaan 91 in the south-west of the city (☎ 614 14 35) – 36 different types of motorcycles ranging in price from f85 a day plus f0.25 per km (first 100 km free) to f195 a day and f0.42 per km (after the first 100 km), tax included; insurance f25 a day; credit card and international driving permit required

Kuperus BV, Van der Madeweg 1 (☎ 668 33 11) – Yamaha Virago at f99 a day including insurance, tax and 100 km (extra kms f0.20 each); three-day, unlimited-km hire is f425 all inclusive; international driving permit required

Motorsport Selling, Amsteldijk 161 (☎ 644 83 69) – Honda CB750 at f105 a day plus f0.25 per km (the first 125 km are free), tax and insurance included; on a weekly basis it's f605 with 875 km free; f1000 deposit required

TAXI

Amsterdam taxis are among the most expensive in Europe and the drivers are rude – you'd be rude too if you had to put up with such frequent traffic delays and road closures. To call a taxi anywhere in the city, dial ☎ 677 77 77, which is no more expensive than walking to a taxi stand. Taxis aren't supposed to be hailed on the street but nobody seems to care much; the taxi is available if the sign on the roof is illuminated.

BICYCLE & MOPED

See Bicycle in the previous chapter for general information about road rules etc.

Amsterdam has 550,000 bicycles, an ideal way to get around. Most carry a couple of locks that are worth more than the bike itself, indicative of the fact that 200,000 bicycles are stolen each year.

An alternative to renting a bike (see below) is to buy one, which is worth considering if you're going to spend more than a month or so in town. Bicycle shops sell second-hand bikes for f140-200; add f60-100 for one or two good locks to attach the frame and front wheel (not just the front wheel) to a bridge railing or something solid. Drug addicts might offer bikes for considerably less – as little as f25 if they're desperate enough – but Amsterdam residents boycott such activity and detest tourists who 'acquire' their vehicle this way. It's also highly illegal and can land you in big trouble.

If you arrive with your own bicycle, the Dutch automobile association ANWB (Map 15; see under Tourist Offices in the Facts for the Visitor chapter) provides information and services if you can show a letter of introduction from your automobile association (or your cycling association, but that seems to depend on the person behind the counter). The letters ANWB stand for General Netherlands Cyclists' Federation – that's how it started and cyclists haven't been forgotten completely. However, serious cyclists will get more joy out of the local cyclists' association, the ENFB (☎ 685 47 94), Wilhelmina Gasthuisplein 84, 1054 BC Amsterdam (advice on activities, rental, purchase, tours, train transport etc).

Bicycle Rental

Many visitors rent a bike towards the end of their stay and wish they had done so sooner. The chaotic traffic can be challenging. Amsterdam cyclists have been weaving through this mess all their lives, and believe with justification that the embarrassingly obvious rental bikes spell trouble. Take care, and watch those tram tracks: if they catch a wheel you'll go down and it will hurt.

All the companies listed below require ID plus a credit-card imprint or a cash deposit. The NS (railways) Rijwielshop and Amstel Stalling are the cheapest but their bicycles can be a bit run down. They are cheaper still if you go to a ticket counter on arrival at the station, show your train ticket and buy a *huurfiets-dagkaart* (rental-bicycle day card) which costs a mere f6; a *huurfiets-weekkaart* for one week costs f24 but you must have travelled at least 25km by train. This excellent system applies to 80 train stations around the country – worth remembering for excursions.

Prices are for standard, 'coaster-brake' bikes (one gear, brake in the rear hub operated by pedalling backwards); gears and hand brakes cost more:

Amstel Stalling, Amstelstation (☎ 692 35 84) – f8/32 a day/week, f100 deposit

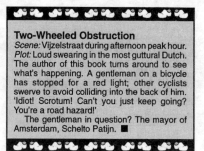

Two-Wheeled Obstruction
Scene: Vijzelstraat during afternoon peak hour. *Plot:* Loud swearing in the most guttural Dutch. The author of this book turns around to see what's happening. A gentleman on a bicycle has stopped for a red light; other cyclists swerve to avoid colliding into the back of him. 'Idiot! Scrotum! Can't you just keep going? You're a road hazard!'

The gentleman in question? The mayor of Amsterdam, Schelto Patijn. ■

Bike City, Bloemgracht 68-70 in the Jordaan opposite the Anne Frankhuis (Map 12; ☎ & fax 626 37 21) – f10/50 a day/week, f50 deposit

Damstraat Rent-a-Bike, Pieter Jacobsdwarsstraat 7-11 near Dam square (Map 13; ☎ 625 50 29) – f10/50 a day/week, f50 deposit

Holland Rent-a-Bike, Damrak 247 in the Beurs van Berlage (Map 13; ☎ 622 32 07) – f12.50/50 a day/week, f50 deposit with a passport or f200 without

MacBike, Houtkopersburgwal 16 at Nieuwe Uilenburgerstraat near Gassan Diamond factory (Map 13; ☎ 620 09 85) – f10/55 a day/week, f50 deposit or a credit-card imprint, passport required. Other MacBike outlets are at Marnixstraat 220 (Map 12; ☎ 626 69 64) next to the Europarking complex, and at the Arena Budget Hotel (Map 17) at 's-Gravesandestraat 49 (☎ 693 21 04)

Rijwielshop, Stationsplein 12 (Map 13; ☎ 624 83 91) – access from the outer side of the railway station at the far east end of the building near the city bus stops; f8 a day, f32 a week, f200 deposit

Moped Rental

Moped Rental Service (Map 12; ☎ 420 19 00; fax 422 21 52), Marnixstraat 208, rents neat little mopeds at f12.50 an hour, f35 a half day, f60 a full day including insurance and a full tank of petrol – a fun way to get out of Amsterdam for a spin. You don't have to wear a helmet on this type of moped and you don't need a licence. The place is open daily 9 am to 8 pm in summer, to 6 pm in winter.

WALKING

The cliché 'Venice of the north' is apt: like Venice, Amsterdam is a joy to discover on foot, and most of the sights are within walking distance in the compact city centre. You can also get lost as in Venice, but never as comprehensively. There's a lot of irregular brick or cobblestone paving, so avoid high heels – and watch out for dog-shit.

Accident statistics show that the Netherlands are the safest country in Europe for pedestrians, who are more than twice as likely to be killed by a car in Britain. Beware of bicycles, though: they have traffic rights separate to those of a pedestrian. A lot of them zig-zag through Amsterdam, ignoring road rules in the same way that pedestrians ignore pedestrian lights. Paving that is coloured reddish is reserved for cyclists, who can get quite angry when pedestrians get in the way, which foreigners often do inadvertently (there are very few polite cyclists).

BOAT
Ferries
The free ferry to Amsterdam Noord for pedestrians, bicycles and mopeds, marked 'Buiksloterwegveer' (*veer* means ferry), goes straight across the IJ from the landing between Pier 8 and Pier 9 at the rear of Centraal Station (Map 13) – a round trip would be an interesting way to kill 45 minutes or so while waiting for a train. It operates every five minutes from 6.30 am to 9 pm, then every 10 minutes from 9 pm to 6.30 am daily. The 'Adelaarswegveer' from Pier 8 goes diagonally across the IJ and takes a bit longer. It operates weekdays every seven or 15 minutes from 6.27 am to 8.57 pm, Saturday every 15 minutes, but not Sunday.

Canal Boat, Bus & Bike
For information about regular canal tours, see Canal Tours in the following Organised Tours section.

The Lovers Museum Boat (Map 13; ☎ 622 21 81) leaves every 30 or 45 minutes (the schedules vary) from in front of Centraal Station at Prins Hendrikkade opposite No 26 and stops at all the major museums. A day ticket for unlimited travel costs f22.50 (f15 if you buy it after 1 pm). If you only join for a single stop it costs f7.50, two stops cost f10,

and three or four stops f12.50; a complete circuit (seven stops) costs f15. The day ticket gives 10% to 50% admission discounts to most museums en route. If you're the sort of person who can handle several museums in a day it's not a bad deal because expert commentary is part of the package and you save on a canal tour.

The Canal Bus (☎ 623 98 86) does a circuit of the tourist centres between Centraal Station and the Rijksmuseum between 10.15 am and 6.45 pm. A day pass costs f19.50 (f27.50 including entry to the Rijksmuseum). Canal 'bikes' (☎ 626 55 74) can be hired from kiosks at Leidseplein, Keizersgracht/Leidsestraat, the Anne Frankhuis and the Rijksmuseum, with two/four-seaters costing f25/41 an hour.

Water Taxi
Amsterdam's canals are sadly under-utilised for transport – there's no equivalent of the Venetian *vaporetto*, *traghetto* or *gondola*. The closest you'll get is the overpriced water taxi that operates from 8 am to midnight. If you catch it at the Lovers terminal in front of Centraal Station (Prins Hendrikkade opposite No 26), it costs f60 an hour (maximum eight people), more if you get on elsewhere. Food can be supplied on board, or you can go for an aquatic pub crawl or a running dinner (three courses at three restaurants). Advance bookings are essential on ☎ 622 21 81.

ORGANISED TOURS
The following organisations offer tours that provide a quick overview of the sights:

Holland International, Nieuwezijds Voorburgwal 103, bookings also at Damrak 90 (☎ 625 30 35) – 3½-hour bus tour includes the Rijksmuseum and a diamond factory; daily at 2.30 pm (f45)

Keytours, Dam 19 near Thomas Cook (☎ 623 50 51) – 3½-hour city sightseeing tours in summer: the morning tour at 9.30 am is by bus and boat (f36.50) while the afternoon tour at 2.30 pm is by bus to the Rijksmuseum and a diamond factory (f42.50); slightly different programme in winter

Lindbergh Tours, Damrak 26 (☎ 622 27 66) – 2½-hour city sightseeing tours by bus daily at 10 am and 2.30 pm in summer (f27.50) and at 2.30 pm in winter (f24); one-hour canal boat tour leaving from in front of the office costs f5 extra

On Ascension Day, Whit Sunday and Whit Monday, and Sundays from mid-June to mid-September, the GVB operates a historic 1920s Tourist Tram that leaves from opposite the Victoria Hotel in front of Centraal Station and trundles past the sights in the centre on the hour from noon to 4 pm for f10 (f7.50 for children and seniors). It also operates from 19 to 24 December (mulled wine is served to foster the Christmas spirit) on Monday, Tuesday, Thursday and Friday at 7 and 8 pm, Saturday and Sunday on the hour from noon to 4 pm. Enquire at the VVV or GVB offices in front of Centraal Station; tickets are available at the NZH kiosk opposite the Victoria Hotel.

Canal Tours

It might come as a surprise that many if not most Amsterdammers have never taken a canal tour. Little do they realise they're missing a totally different perspective of the city. A horde of operators leave from in front of Centraal Station, along Damrak and Rokin and near the Rijksmuseum, and charge around f15 for a one-hour cruise. Advance bookings are unnecessary unless you're planning something special. The operators run slightly different routes, so if there's a canal you desperately want to see from the water, ask. There are evening cruises by candlelight, with wine and cheese (or even five-course dinners) to enhance the experience.

You can save money on a regular day tour by going to one of the two official youth hostels (the Stadsdoelen or Vondelpark – see Hostels in the Places to Stay chapter) and buying your ticket from the receptionist. This will get you a 40% discount on the normal price and you don't need to be staying at the hostel or to show a HI or IYHF card to obtain such a ticket.

Other Water Tours

On Sundays and public holidays from mid-April to mid-October, the GVB runs a Tourist Ferry that leaves from behind Centraal Station at Pier 8 and takes you on a two-hour trip of the harbour at noon, 2 and 4 pm – tickets (f9, or f6 for children) are available at the GVB information office (Map 13) in front of Centraal Station. There are trips to other destinations, including the huge North Sea locks at IJmuiden, the historic trading city of Hoorn (which gave Cape Horn its name) on the IJsselmeer north of Amsterdam, and the Amsterdamse Bos recreational area in the south-west of the city.

More ambitious cruises are offered by Rederij Naco (☎ 626 24 66) from Pier 7 behind Centraal Station. From May to mid-September its six-hour cruise to the historic fort of Pampus and the castle at Muiden leaves at 10 am every Thursday and Sunday (f39, children f22.50). Take along some sandwiches to avoid being dependent on the shipboard restaurant (drinks are reasonably priced). In May, June and September there's a Monday cruise from 10 am to 4 pm along the picturesque Vecht river with its historic country mansions south-east of the city.

Bicycle Tours

Several operators offer bike tours from April to October. Yellow Bike Tours (☎ 620 69 40), Nieuwezijds Kolk 29 off Nieuwezijds Voorburgwal, is the largest of its kind and offers three-hour bicycle tours around town for f29, or longer, 6½-hour tours to the IJsselmeer town of Marken for f42.50. Amsterdam Travel & Tours (☎ 627 62 36), Dam 10 next to the Nieuwe Kerk, has two-hour bicycle tours at f35 including bicycle.

Cycletours (☎ 627 40 98; fax 627 90 32), Keizersgracht 181, 1016 DR Amsterdam, offers a variety of overnight tours around Holland by bicycle and motor boat sleeping 20 to 30 people. They cater mostly to people who have booked in advance from abroad, so it's best to write ahead for a brochure. A one-week tour from Saturday to Saturday costs f940 in the high season or f880 in the shoulder seasons; there are also four or five-day tours from f465.

Things to See & Do

Amsterdam is one of those places where you never get bored just going for a walk. It's full of hidden gems and unexpected delights. The attractions described in this chapter are the more 'important' ones, but visitors as well as residents keep finding interesting things that don't make it into guidebooks or tourist publications. No doubt you'll find some of your own, and begin to understand what keeps drawing people back to the city.

HIGHLIGHTS
According to the VVV, the most visited attractions in Amsterdam are (in order):

1. Canal tour
2. Artis zoo
3. Rijksmuseum
4. Diamond factory visit
5. Van Gogh Museum
6. Holland Casino Amsterdam
7. Concertgebouw
8. Anne Frankhuis
9. Stedelijk Museum
10. Seksmuseum De Venustempel

This ranking includes Dutch as well as foreign visitors. A subjective listing on behalf of foreigners might read as follows:

1. Canal tour
2. Rijksmuseum
3. A few 'brown cafés'
4. Nederlands Scheepvaartmuseum (maritime history)
5. Stedelijk Museum
6. Aimless wandering within the canal belt
7. Albert Cuyp market
8. Begijnhof
9. People-watching at Leidseplein
10. A free summer concert in the Vondelpark

THINGS TO AVOID
Some of the popular sights are overrated, such as Madame Tussaud Scenerama on Dam square (the one in London is better) or the casino off Leidseplein (why come to Amsterdam for a casino?) and even the Anne Frankhuis (a pilgrimage to this place is ruined by the queues – visit the Joods Historisch Museum instead). Other things to avoid include:

- A canal cruise with a bunch of school kids screaming through the commentary
- The Kalverstraat and Nieuwendijk shopping streets on Saturday – far too busy then, and a domain of pickpockets
- Taxis – rude drivers and very expensive
- Driving a car within the canal belt – you'll get stuck behind a truck unloading beer barrels and you won't be able to park without blowing the budget; if you do park, the car will get broken into
- Brightly coloured hire bikes with embarrassing rent-a-bike signs – Amsterdammers consider them a traffic hazard (not that Amsterdammers themselves stick to road rules but at least they know when they're breaking them); ask for something less obvious if you have a choice
- Paying by credit card – many proprietors refuse cards, or charge a hefty 'administration fee'
- Taking photos of prostitutes or loiterers in the red-light district
- Buying drugs on the street

AMSTERDAM FOR FREE
It's easy to spend a fortune in Amsterdam but some of the most enjoyable things cost nothing. The following free activities and sights are described in this chapter in the following order:

- Catch a ferry across the IJ
- Wander through the red-light district and try to admire the architecture
- Visit the Zuiderkerk
- See the NAP display in the Stopera
- Enjoy peace and quiet in the Begijnhof
- Stroll through the Civic Guard Gallery
- Visit the Geelvinck Hinlopen Huis
- Admire the view at the intersection of Keizersgracht and Reguliersgracht
- Wander through the Rijksmuseum garden
- Go to an open-air concert in the Vondelpark in summer
- Watch horses being trained indoors at the Hollandse Manege
- Catch a free lunchtime concert in the Concertgebouw or the Stopera
- Hear a carillon recital while walking along a canal (the VVV has up-to-date schedules)

Central Amsterdam

The city within the canal belt is referred to as Amsterdam Centrum. The Damrak, Dam square and Rokin, which run down the middle of its old medieval core, used to form the final stretch of the Amstel river – the city arose around the dam built across the Amstel at what is now Dam square. The east bank was called Oude Zijde (Old Side), the west bank was the Nieuwe Zijde (New Side).

The marshy surroundings required drainage canals to create reasonably solid land. Eventually the Oude Zijde was bordered by the Kloveniersburgwal and Geldersekade, and the Nieuwe Zijde by the Singel (Moat), which marked the extents of the medieval city. In the late 1400s and early 1500s this modest area received a city wall, with fortified gates at strategic points.

A century later the feudal wall that cost so much to build was torn down again as the city spilled into the surrounding marshes; some of the old fortified gates remain today. Towards the end of the 16th century, habitable islands were built to the east. These form the current Nieuwmarkt neighbourhood, which lies east of the square of the same name.

Finally, in the 17th century an enormous urban construction project resulted in the semicircular canal belt, enclosed by the Lijnbaansgracht and the zigzag Buitensingel (outer moat) now known as the Singelgracht.

DAMRAK, DAM & ROKIN (Map 13)

Most visitors arrive at **Centraal Station** (1889), a Dutch Renaissance edifice with Gothic additions built to a design by Pierre Cuypers, who was also responsible for the Rijksmuseum, and AL van Gendt, who designed the Concertgebouw. Its structure – a central section flanked by square towers

with wings on either side – is indeed similar to Cuypers' Rijksmuseum. It influenced the designers of Tokyo's central station. Note the intricate gilded façade.

The site was hotly debated at the time. Most council members favoured a station at Leidseplein or in the rapidly expanding southern suburbs, but the national government held the purse strings and went for the current site, on three artificial islands in the IJ. This cut the city off from its historical harbour, though the focus of the harbour had already shifted eastwards and would later move well to the west.

You could leave Centraal Station at the rear harbour side, hop on one of the free passenger ferries to Amsterdam Noord and experience the expanse of the IJ. It's quiet now, but in the 17th and 18th centuries this was the busiest harbour in the world.

Leaving the station from the front, city side, the cupola and twin towers of the neo-baroque **St Nicolaaskerk** (1887) are to your left. Designed by AC Bleijs, it is the city's main Catholic church but is under threat of closure. The interior (wooden vaulting with square pillars of black marble) contains many paintings and a high altar with the crown of Holy Roman Emperor Maximilian I, but don't bother if you're pressed for time.

Damrak

The Damrak ('Dam Reach') stretches out in front of you towards Dam square. This used to be the original harbour but soon became unsuitable for larger ships that tied up to palisades along what is now Centraal Station and unloaded onto lighters. Today the Damrak is an agonising stretch of gaudy souvenir shops, exchange bureaus and claustrophobic hotels. At No 18 is **Seksmuseum De Venustempel**, open daily from 10 am to 11.30 pm and well worth the f3.95 admission fee for its bizarre collection of pornographic material. Welcome to Amsterdam!

In the late 19th century the southern half of the Damrak was filled in for the new exchange building, the **Beurs van Berlage** (1903), named after the architect HP Berlage who was still designing it after work began. The functional lines and stark, square clock

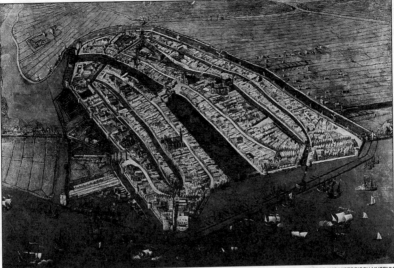

AMSTERDAMS HISTORISCH MUSEUM

Bird's-eye view of Amsterdam, painted in 1538 by Cornelis Anthonisz, looking southwards. This is the oldest surviving 'map' of the city.

tower contrast with the more exuberant designs of the age, but it is considered one of the most important landmarks of Dutch city architecture. You'll understand why when you look more closely at the clever details inside and out. The large central hall, with its steel and glass roof, was the commodities exchange where coffee, tobacco, sugar, wine and colonial merchandise were traded. The traders eventually deserted the building in favour of the neoclassical **Effectenbeurs** (Stock Exchange), built in 1913 by Centraal Station's Pierre Cuypers on the east side of Beursplein.

In the 1970s the foundations of Berlage's bourse were sinking and it was slated for demolition, but it was saved by popular outcry. It is now a cultural centre (home to the Netherlands Philharmonic Orchestra) with concert performances and changing exhibitions, such as Dalí's sculptures and Karel Appel's works that are too large for regular museums. The public entrance is on

the Damrak side, next to the bicycle shop. It's open Tuesday to Sunday from 10 am to 4 pm and entry costs f6 (f4 with discounts). Climb the clock tower for the view (hot soup is served there in winter). In summer there's a café on the Beursplein side – walk inside and see the central hall for free.

Dam Square

The Damrak ends in Dam square (usually referred to simply as the Dam) where the original dam was built across the Amstel, giving the city its name. It was the central market square where everything happened. It used to be much smaller than today, reaching its current size only after buildings on all sides were gradually demolished. It seems empty now, inhabited by thousands of cheeky pigeons and the occasional fun fair.

The original dam was at the eastern end of the current square, with a sluice alongside so ships could pass through. From 1611 they had to lower their masts to pass under the new stock exchange built over the sluice, which was filled in for good in 1672.

The stock exchange itself was demolished in 1838 and the eastern end of the square is now dominated by a phallic obelisk, the **Nationaal Monument**. This was built in 1956 in memory of those who died during WWII and who are still honoured every year on 4 May. In the late 1960s the monument was a camping spot for hippies until angry marines chased them away. It has been weakened by rain and frost and is in danger of falling apart; repairs will be carried out by... a German firm. The statues symbolise war (the four male figures), peace (woman with child) and resistance (men with dogs); the 12 urns at the rear contain earth from the 11 provinces and the Dutch East Indies.

The imposing hulk at the western end of the Dam is the **Royal Palace**, or Koninklijk Paleis (completed 1665, in use since 1655), which started life as the grand new city hall of republican Amsterdam. It replaced the old city hall on the same spot which conveniently burned down. No costs were spared by the architect, Jacob van Campen, for this display of Amsterdam's wealth that rivalled the grandest European buildings of the day. A century-and-a-half later it became the palace of Napoleon's brother king, who contributed one of the world's richest collections of Empire furniture but had the historic Weigh House in front of the building demolished because it spoiled his view.

The building then passed to the House of Orange who stayed here occasionally. In 1935 the national government bought and restored it for state functions (officially Queen Beatrix lives here and pays fl a year rent, though she really lives in The Hague). The stunning interior, particularly the richly decorated Civic Hall, is much more lavish than the stark exterior suggests and is well worth visiting. The limited opening times vary throughout the year and depend on official functions. You might be lucky between 12.30 and 5 pm, but ring ☎ 624 86 98 to check. Admission costs f5 (f3 with discounts).

Next to the Royal Palace is the **Nieuwe Kerk** (New Church; early 15th century), the coronation church of Dutch royalty. This late-Gothic basilica is only 'new' in relation to the Oude Kerk (Old Church), with which it competed to be the grandest church in the city. It was gutted by fire several times, and the planned, exceptionally high tower was never completed because funds were diverted to the city hall. Of interest are the magnificently carved oak chancel, the bronze choir screen, the massive organ, the stained-glass windows, and the mausoleum of the city's greatest naval hero, Admiral Michiel de Ruijter, who died in 1676 fighting the French at Messina. Several other famous Amsterdammers are buried here, including the poets Joost van den Vondel and Pieter Cornelisz Hooft. The building is used for exhibitions (including the premiere of the

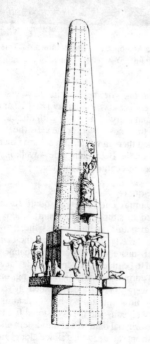

Nationaal Monument

annual World Press Photo exhibition in May) and for organ concerts, no longer as a church. It's open daily from 10 am to 5 pm and entry costs f3.

Rokin

Beyond the Dam, the Damrak becomes the Rokin (a corruption of *rak-in*, 'inner reach'), most of which was filled in the 19th century. It is considerably more up-market than the Damrak, with office buildings (the modern Options Exchange at No 61), prestigious shops (the wood-panelled tobacconist Hajenius at No 92) and art dealers (Sotheby Mak van Waay at No 102). A **column** on the sidewalk at Wijde Kapelsteeg commemorates the Miracle of Amsterdam that made the city a place of pilgrimage in medieval times (see Early Trade in the History section of the Facts about Amsterdam chapter). The chapel built on the spot where the miracle of the incombustible Host took place has been demolished, but it occupied this small block between Wijde and Enge Kapelsteeg.

At Grimburgwal, where the water begins again, the bank opposite the Rokin is called Oude Turfmarkt. Near the Grimburgwal corner, at Oude Turfmarkt 127, is the University of Amsterdam's **Allard Pierson Museum** (☎ 525 25 56), with the world's richest university collection of archaeological material. It's not in the same league as the country's largest collection of antiquities in Leiden, let alone the British Museum or the Louvre, but the exhibits (Egyptian, Mesopotamian, Roman and Greek, among others) are far less overwhelming and provide a good insight into daily life in ancient times. The museum is open Tuesday to Friday from 10 am to 5 pm, weekends from 1 pm; entry costs f7.50 (f4.50 for students and seniors).

The Rokin terminates at Muntplein, a busy intersection dominated by the **Munttoren** (Mint Tower). This was part of the 15th century Regulierspoort, a city gate that burned down in 1619. On what was left of the gate, the architect and tower-specialist Hendrick de Keyser built the tower that received its current name in 1672-73, when the French occupied much of the republic

and the national mint was transferred here from Dordrecht for safe-keeping.

OUDE ZIJDE (Map 13)

East of the Damrak-Rokin axis is the Oude Zijde (Old Side) of the medieval city. The name is misleading because the Nieuwe Zijde (New Side) to the west is actually older – see the following Nieuwe Zijde section.

In the 1380s the Oude Zijde began to expand eastwards towards the Oudezijds Voorburgwal ('front fortified embankment') and soon further towards to the Oudezijds Achterburgwal ('rear fortified embankment').

Originally the city didn't extend further south than Grimburgwal, where the filled-in part of the Rokin ends today. In the 1420s, however, the newly dug Geldersekade and Kloveniersburgwal added more space for the growing population.

Warmoesstraat

One of the original dykes along the Amstel – and thus one of the oldest streets in town – is Warmoesstraat, which runs parallel to Damrak behind the warehouses that used to line the east bank of the river (the southern extension beyond the Dam is called Nes). The city's wealthiest merchants , and anyone else who could afford to, lived here. Today it's a run-down strip of restaurants, cheap hotels and sex shops, with the busiest police station in town (No 44-50). **Geels & Co** (☎ 624 06 83) at No 67 is a tea and coffee shop with an interesting little museum upstairs (free admission). The shop is open normal hours but you can only visit the museum on Tuesday, Friday and Saturday between 2 and 4 pm (4.30 pm Saturday).

Oude Kerk

A few paces east of here, through Enge Kerksteeg, is the mighty Oude Kerk, the Gothic Old Church built early in the 14th century in honour of the city's patron saint, St Nicholas – the 'water-saint', protector of ships' crews and marsh inhabitants. It's the oldest surviving building in town, sadly demeaned by the red-light district that now surrounds it. The original basilica was replaced in 1340 by an intricately vaulted triple-hall church of massive proportions that was miraculously undamaged by the great fire of 1452.

Further extensions ground to a halt as funds were diverted to the Nieuwe Kerk, and a century later Calvinist iconoclasts smashed and looted many of the priceless paintings, statues and altars. The newly Calvinist authorities kicked out the hawkers and vagabonds who had made the church their home, and changed the official name from St Nicolaaskerk to Oude Kerk (as it was commonly known). In the mid-17th century the Nieuwe Kerk took over as the city's main church.

Note the stunning Müller organ (1724), the gilded oak vaults (with remains of paintings above the southern aisle) and the stained-glass windows (1555). Check the lively 15th century carvings on the choir stalls – some of them are outright rude. As in the Nieuwe Kerk, many famous and not so famous Amsterdammers lie buried here under worn tombstones, including Rembrandt's first wife, Saskia van Uylenburgh (died 1642). The church is open daily from 11 am to 5 pm, Sunday from 1 pm, and admission costs f5 (f3.50 with discounts). A Dutch Reformed service is held Sundays at 11 am.

The church's **tower** (1565) is arguably the most beautiful in Amsterdam and is well worth climbing for the magnificent view. The 47-bell carillon, installed by the carillon master François Hemony in 1658, is considered one of the finest in the country. The bell in the top of the tower dates from 1450 and is the city's oldest.

The tower is open between June and September, Wednesday to Saturday from 2 to 4 pm, and admission costs f3 – you might have to wait for the guide to come back down with the previous group.

Red-Light District

The city's (in)famous red-light district is bordered by Warmoesstraat in the west, Zeedijk/Nieuwmarkt/Kloveniersburgwal in the east and Damstraat/Oude Doelenstraat/Oude Hoogstraat in the south. The area, known colloquially as the *wallen* or *walletjes* for the canals that run down the middle, has been sending sailors broke since the 14th century with houses of ill repute and countless distilleries. The distilleries have gone but prostitutes now display themselves in windows under red neon lights, touts at sex theatres lure passers-by with 'live show fucky-fucky podium', and sex-shop displays leave nothing to the imagination. Several years ago three men took up places behind windows in a sociological experiment; there was intense media interest and not a single woman dared enter. One of the prostitutes declared the experiment 'filthy'.

The ambience is laid-back and far less threatening than in red-light districts elsewhere. Crowds of sightseers both foreign and local mingle with would-be pimps, drunks, weirdos, drug dealers and Salvation Army soldiers; police patrolling on foot chat with prostitutes. Streetwalking is illegal, so female sightseers are not automatically assumed to be soliciting and tend to be left alone if they exercise big-city street sense. Advice to all: don't take photos of prostitutes or loiterers, and don't enter into conversation with a drug dealer.

The mainly self-employed prostitutes are taxed on their earnings, undergo mandatory health checks and have a vocal union. Beneath the well-regulated veneer, however, is a world of exploitation, drug addiction and misery – for every happy hooker there's an unhappy one, perhaps a young Eastern European without the right papers, sucked into a vicious circle of high hopes and extortion.

The *wallen*, actually a very pretty part of town, are well worth a stroll for the architecture, if you need that sort of excuse. For a scenic view, face north on the bridge across Oudezijds Voorburgwal linking Lange Niezel and Korte Niezel.

Immediately to your left from here, at

Oudezijds Voorburgwal 40, is the **Museum Amstelkring** (☎ 624 66 04), home to **Ons' Lieve Heer op Solder** (Our Dear Lord in the Attic), one of several 'clandestine' Catholic churches established after the Calvinist coup in 1578. Church property was confiscated and Catholics were only allowed to worship in privately owned real estate so long as it wasn't recognisable as a church and the entrance was hidden. The wealthy hosier Jan Hartman had the house built in 1663, complete with a small church in the attic dedicated to St Nicholas. It remained in use until 1887, when the large St Nicolaaskerk on Prins Hendrikkade diagonally opposite Centraal Station opened its doors.

The following year it became a museum, although occasional services, weddings and organ concerts are still held here. The museum is worth visiting for the 17th century living quarters, including the Dutch Classical *Sael* or reception hall (note the matching rectangular patterns on the floor, walls and ceiling), and of course for the church in the attic – one of the few 'clandestine' churches that has remained intact. The museum is open daily from 10 am to 5 pm, Sunday from 1 pm, and admission is f7.50 (f5 with discounts).

Other places worth considering in the red-light district include the **Hash & Marihuana Museum** (☎ 623 59 61), Oudezijds Achterburgwal 148; and the renowned **Tattoo Museum** (☎ 625 15 65), Oudezijds Achterburgwal 130. The **Erotic Museum** (☎ 624 73 03), Oudezijds Achterburgwal 54, is a waste of time: Seksmuseum De Venustempel on Damrak (see the earlier Damrak, Dam & Rokin section) is far more entertaining.

Zeedijk

North of the red-light district is the Zeedijk, the original sea dyke that curved from the mouth of the Amstel to Nieuwmarkt square and continued from there along what are now St Anthoniesbreestraat, Jodenbreestraat and Muiderstraat. The house at **Zeedijk 1** dates from the mid-1500s and is one of the two timber-fronted houses still left in the city (another, older one is in the Begijnhof).

The Zeedijk used to be (and to some extent still is) a street of wine, women and song, the first port of call for sailors after their long voyages. In the 1950s, wine and song predominated and many of the world's great jazz musicians played in pubs such as the Casablanca at No 26. In the 1970s the street's dubious reputation hit rock-bottom when it became the centre of Amsterdam's heroin trade. A massive police campaign in the mid-1980s restored some of the old merriment and legitimate business is beginning to pick up again, but so too is the heroin trade at the Nieuwmarkt end of the street.

East of the Zeedijk is the Geldersekade, and at the tip of this canal is a small brick tower, dating from around 1480, that used to form part of the city fortifications. It's the oldest such tower still standing and is called the **Schreierstoren** from an old Dutch word for 'sharp', a reference to this sharp corner that jutted out into the IJ. Tourist literature calls it the 'wailing tower' (from *schreien*, to weep or wail) and claims that sailors' wives stood here and cried their lungs out when ships set off for distant lands, which makes a far more interesting story. The women even have a plaque dedicated to them.

The tower seems to attract plaques; another one explains that the English captain Henry Hudson set sail from here in 1609 in his ship the *Halve Maen* (Half Moon). The United East India Company had enlisted him to find a northern passage to the East Indies, but instead he discovered Manhattan and the river that still bears his name. On the return voyage his ship was seized in England and he was ordered never again to sail for a foreign nation. His reports, however, made it back to base, and in 1614 the Dutch established a fort on Manhattan that developed into a settlement called New Amsterdam.

In 1664 the West India Company's local governor, the fanatically Calvinist Pieter Stuyvesant, surrendered the town to the British who promptly renamed it New York. Stuyvesant retired to the market garden called Bouwerij (Agriculture), which is now known as the Bowery section of New York City.

Nieuwmarkt Square

In the 17th century, ships used to sail from the IJ down Geldersekade to the Nieuwmarkt (New Market) to take on board new anchors or load and unload produce. (Nobody then or now adds the world *plein* or 'square' to the name, which is confusing because the whole neighbourhood to the east and south-east is also known as Nieuwmarkt.)

The Nieuwmarkt's imposing **Waag** (Weigh House) dates from 1488, when it was known as St Anthoniespoort (St Anthony's Gate) and formed part of the city fortifications. A century later the city had expanded further east and the gate lost its original function. A section of Kloveniersburgwal was filled in to create the St Anthoniesmarkt (now the Nieuwmarkt). The central courtyard of the gate was covered and it became the city weigh house – the one on the Dam had become too small. Guilds occupied the upper floor, including the surgeons' guild who commissioned Rembrandt to paint *The Anatomy Lesson of Dr Tulp* (displayed in the Mauritshuis in The Hague) and added the octagonal central tower in 1691 to house their new Anatomical Theatre, which has recently been restored and opened to the public.

Public executions took place at the Waag from the early 19th century, after Louis Napoleon decreed that his palace on Dam square was no longer a suitable spot for such gory displays. In later years it served other purposes – fire station, vault for the city archives, home to the Amsterdams Historical Museum and the Jewish Historical Museum. Today it houses a bar-restaurant illuminated by huge candle-wheels for medieval effect, and combines the medieval with the future as the Centre for Old & New Media (see Digital Media in the Facts for the Visitor chapter for more about this interesting initiative).

The area east and south-east of Nieuwmarkt square was the centre of Jewish Amsterdam, which was virtually wiped out during the German occupation. Jews were assembled in front of the Waag for deportation.

South of Nieuwmarkt Square

Just south of the Nieuwmarkt, on the east side of Kloveniersburgwal at No 29, is the **Trippenhuis**. It was built in 1660-64 to house the wealthy Trip brothers, Lodewijk and Hendrik, who made their fortune in metals, artillery and ammunition. The greystone mansion with Corinthian pilasters consists of two separate houses with false middle windows, and the chimneys are shaped like mortars to indicate their owners' trade. Note the narrow house across the canal at No 26 (see the boxed story, Narrow & Wide Houses).

On the west side of Kloveniersburgwal beyond the intersection with Oude Hoogstraat (an extension of Damstraat) is the **Oostindisch Huis**, the former head office of the mighty VOC, the United East India Company. You'd walk straight past if you didn't know it was here – there's no sign or plaque to indicate its presence. The complex of buildings, attributed to Hendrick de Keyser, was built between 1551 and 1643. It was rented to the VOC in 1603 and now belongs to the University of Amsterdam. Enter the courtyard through the small gate at Oude Hoogstraat 24. Even here nothing indicates the historical significance of the place except for the small VOC emblem above the door ahead of you across the courtyard. Along the Kloveniersburgwal frontage, note the gables that defy convention by tilting backwards, which makes them seem higher.

Oude Zijde, Southern Section

The Oude Zijde south of Damstraat/Oude Doelenstraat/Oude Hoogstraat is distinctly

Façade detail of the Oostindisch Huis.

Narrow & Wide Houses

Canal-boat commentators and other tourist guides like to point out the narrowest house in Amsterdam, and account for the phenomenon by explaining that property taxes were levied on frontage – the narrower the house the lower the tax, regardless of the height. Though there is some truth in this, it seems as if each guide has a different 'narrowest' house. So, which house holds the record?

The house at Oude Hoogstraat 22 east of Dam square is 2.02 metres wide and six metres deep. Occupying a mere 12 square metres it is probably the least space-consuming, self-contained house in Europe (though it's a few storeys high). The house at Singel 7 is narrower still, consisting of just a door and a slim, 1st-floor window, but canal-boat commentators fail to point out that it's actually the rear entrance of a house of normal proportions. Further along and on the other side of Singel at No 144 is a house that measures only 1.8 metres across the front; it widens to five metres at the rear and experts with nothing better to do will argue whether this counts.

The Kleine Trippenhuis (Small Trippenhouse) at Kloveniersburgwal 26 is 2.44 metres wide. It's opposite the 22-metre-wide house of the Trip brothers at No 29, one of the widest private residences in the city. The story goes that their coachman exclaimed, 'If only I could have a house as wide as my master's door!' and that his wish was granted. ■

Narrow house at Oude Hoogstraat 22.

residential and the red-light district seems miles away. The southern end of Oudezijds Voorburgwal used to be known as the 'velvet canal' for the wealthy people who lived here. Both the Oudezijds canals end at Grimburgwal and the junction is one of the strongholds of the University of Amsterdam, as evidenced by the chaotic jumble of parked bicycles.

The former municipal university (not to be confused with the orthodox-Protestant Free University in the southern suburbs) has no central campus as such; its buildings are spread throughout the city but there's a large concentration of them here.

At the south end of Oudezijds Voorburgwal, at No 231, is the **Universiteitsmuseum De Agnietenkapel** (☎ 525 33 39), with changing exhibitions on the history of the university, open weekdays from 9 am to 5 pm (ring the door bell; admission f2.50). The complex started life as a convent of St Agnes in 1397 and the beautiful Gothic chapel was added in 1470. When the Calvinists took over it was used as an admiralty warehouse. In 1632 it also became home to the city library (moved from the Nieuwe Kerk) and

the Athenaeum Illustre, the Illustrious Athenaeum, an offshoot of the University of Leiden. Classes (history and philosophy, later also law, medicine and theology, and finally physics and chemistry) were conducted in Latin to prepare students for higher education elsewhere. In 1864 the Athenaeum moved to Singel 421 (part of the present university library) and in 1877 it became the fully fledged Municipal University of Amsterdam – a long gestation for the university of such an eminent city.

Just south of the Agnietenkapel, where the three 'fortified embankments' *(burgwallen)* meet, is the **Huis aan de Drie Grachten** (House on the Three Canals), a beautiful building dating from 1609 that was owned by a succession of prominent Amsterdam families. It's now a bookshop catering for students, with books on linguistics and literature.

Across Oudezijds Achterburgwal, just before the corner with Grimburgwal, is a small, arched gateway called the **Oudemanhuispoort** (Old Man's House Gate) leading to a passage of the same name that extends to Kloveniersburgwal. Note the spectacles above the gateway: an almshouse for elderly men and women was built here in 1601 from the proceeds of a public lottery. It was rebuilt in the mid-18th century and in 1879 it became the seat of the university. The administration has since moved to other premises but the buildings here, referred to simply as 'de Poort', can lay claim to being the heart of the university.

A market has operated in the passage since the mid-1700s, specialising in gold, silver, books and knick-knacks but now devoted entirely to second-hand books – well worth a browse. Halfway along, an entrance leads to a lovely 18th century courtyard dominated by a bust of Minerva (originally there was a bust of Rembrandt but the Roman goddess of wisdom was considered more apt). The university lecture rooms surrounding the courtyard are closed to the public – nobody will pull you up for going inside but they hold little of general interest.

A few steps south of the Oudemanhuis-poort, at the end of Grimburgwal, another gateway leads to the former inner-city hospital, the **Binnengasthuis**, dating from 1582. In 1981 the university took over and the area is now a mini campus, with university buildings, living quarters, a large refectory *(mensa)* and an information centre (see Universities in the Facts for the Visitor chapter).

NIEUWE ZIJDE (Maps 12 & 13)

West of the Damrak-Rokin axis is the Nieuwe Zijde (New Side) of the medieval city. It was actually settled slightly earlier than the Oude Zijde – the names date from the construction of the Nieuwe Kerk and the division of the city into two parishes.

In the early 14th century the western boundary was formed by a watercourse running along Nieuwezijds Voorburgwal (filled in 1884), but this was soon extended westwards to the Nieuwezijds Achter-

burgwal (now also filled and known as Spuistraat). Around 1450 the Singel (Moat) was cut. This linked up with the Gelderse-kade and Kloveniersburgwal in the east to complete the moat around the medieval city, which received proper walls with fortified gates some 50 years later.

Nieuwendijk

The very first houses in Amsterdam probably stood on a strip of raised land, no more than 25 metres wide, on the western bank of the Amstel between the Dam and Oudebrug-steeg. This, the oldest dyke in the city, parallel to the current Damrak, later acquired the name of its northern extension, Nieuwen-dijk. It used to link up with the road to Haarlem, and its shops and other businesses became adept at fleecing unwary travellers on their way to Amsterdam's market on Dam square. Today this pedestrianised shopping street still suffers from a distinctly down-market image, though some of the narrow streets leading to the west can be as picturesquely medieval as it gets.

Singel, Northern Section

The top section of Nieuwendijk, between Martelaarsgracht and Singel, is sometimes referred to as Korte Nieuwendijk (Short Nieuwendijk). Head south from here along the east (odd-numbered) side of Singel, where the former city wall used to run, and you'll pass a house at No 7 (next to the Liberty Hotel) that's no wider than its door – except that this is actually the rear entrance of a house of normal proportions.

The domed church further along is the **Ronde Lutherse Kerk** (Round Lutheran Church), built in 1668-71 to replace the old Lutheran church on Spui square. It's the only round Protestant church in the country and is pure 17th century baroque, though the white interior is suitably sober. The church was rebuilt after a disastrous fire in 1822 but falling attendances forced its closure in 1936 (ironically the old church on Spui square is still in use by Lutherans). It now serves as a conference centre for the nearby Renaissance Hotel, and is open to the public during free chamber-music performances on Sunday morning.

Across the canal, tied up at No 40, is the **Poezenboot** (Cat Boat) owned by an eccentric woman who looks after several hundred stray moggies. They seem endearingly content with life on the water, and visitors are welcome to stroke a few in return for a donation towards cat food.

Further along Singel is **Torensluis**, one of the widest bridges in the city. Here used to stand a tower that formed part of the city fortifications; the bridge was later built around it. The tower was demolished in 1829, leaving a 42-metre-wide esplanade. The view northwards is camera material.

The ghastly statue that dominates the bridge represents Multatuli (Latin for 'I have suffered greatly'), the pen name of the brilliant 19th century author Eduard Douwes Dekker, who would indeed suffer greatly if he stood here now.

A local captain's son who served in the East Indies colonial administration, Multatuli exposed colonial narrow-mindedness in a novel about a coffee merchant. After being sacked he wrote letters and essays. The nearby **Multatuli Museum** (☎ 638 19 38), Korsjespoortsteeg 20, is free but only open Tuesday from 10 am to 5 pm and weekends from noon.

Magna Plaza

Back towards Dam square at Nieuwezijds Voorburgwal 182, facing the Royal Palace, is the imposing orange-and-white façade of Magna Plaza. This was the former GPO, built in 1895-99 by the government architect CH Peters, a pupil of Pierre Cuypers. It used to be one of the grandest post offices in Europe but has now been converted into a luxurious shopping centre dominated by clothing boutiques. By all means pop inside to admire the grand hall. There's an interesting shop selling musical boxes on the top level, and an extensive Virgin Megastore in the basement. Several decades ago the Nieuwezijds Voorburgwal itself was the country's 'Fleet Street' where many newspapers had their head offices.

Kalverstraat

South of Dam square is Kalverstraat, the extension of Nieuwendijk. This was one of the original dykes along the Amstel – together with Nieuwendijk, Warmoesstraat and Nes – which makes it one of the oldest streets in the city. The name (Calves Street) presumably refers to the cattle that were led to market on Dam square. (In the 15th century there was a cattle market in the southern section of Kalverstraat beyond Spui square but the name is older.)

Like Nieuwendijk, pedestrianised Kalverstraat has traditionally been a shopping street, albeit a more up-market one that's well worth visiting on weekdays (it's too busy on Saturdays). The southern tip between Kalverstraat and Singel near Muntplein is being transformed into a shopping and apartment complex called the Vendex Triangle – Vendex is the company name of the Vroom & Dreesmann department store financing the project.

South along Kalverstraat from Dam square, about two-thirds of the way to Spui square, is a gateway to the right at No 92 that leads to the **Amsterdams Historisch Museum** (on the opposite side of Kalverstraat used to be the chapel commemorating the Miracle of Amsterdam). This is a surprisingly interesting museum with attractive displays about the history of the city, housed in the former civic orphanage that existed here till 1960. The restaurant (free entry) serves delicious pancakes. The museum (☎ 523 18 22) is open weekdays from 10 am to 5 pm, weekends from 11 am; admission is f8, or f4 for children and seniors (no student discount). Ask for the English-language booklet.

Even if you want to give this a miss, it's still worth walking into the courtyard (note the cupboards in which the orphans stored their possessions) and from there to the Begijnhof through the **Civic Guard Gallery** (free, open same hours as the museum). The huge group portraits of civic guards displayed here will help you appreciate Rembrandt's ground-breaking interpretation of the genre in *The Nightwatch*, which is displayed in the Rijksmuseum. The gallery used to be a ditch separating the boys' and girls' sections of the orphanage.

Begijnhof

Hidden behind the intersection of Spui and Nieuwezijds Voorburgwal is the enclosed Begijnhof (also spelled Bagijnhof), a former convent dating from the early 14th century – the Nieuwezijds Voorburgwal curved westwards to include it in the city boundary. It's a surreal oasis of peace, with tiny houses grouped around a well-kept courtyard. Amsterdam has many such enclosed *hofjes* (literally 'little courtyards'), or almshouses (old people's homes run by charities), but this is the only one where the public is still welcome. It's open during the day but not for tour groups or camera crews.

Linger a while to recover from the hustle and bustle of the city. Note the house at **No 34**: it dates from around 1465, making it the oldest maintained wooden house in the country. There's a collection of biblical wall tablets on the blind wall to the left.

The Beguines were a Catholic order of unmarried or widowed women from wealthy families who cared for the elderly and lived a religious life without taking monastic vows; the last true Beguines died in the 1970s. They owned their houses, so these could not be confiscated after the Calvinist coup. Their **Gothic church** at the southern end of the courtyard, however, was taken away from them and they were forced to worship in the **'clandestine' church** opposite (note the dogleg entrance), where paintings and stained-glass windows commemorate the Miracle of Amsterdam. The Gothic church was eventually rented out to the local community of English and Scottish Presbyterian refugees – the Pilgrim Fathers worshipped here – and still serves as the city's Presbyterian church. Some of the pulpit panels were designed by a young Piet Mondriaan.

Spui Square

Until 1882, the elongated Spui square (usually referred to simply as the Spui) used to be water. In the 14th century it marked the southern end of the city, together with Grimburgwal, its north-eastern extension across Rokin. The name means 'sluice', or rather the area within a sluice, and it connected the Amstel with the watercourse running along Nieuwezijds Voorburgwal, the western side of the city, and later with the Singel.

A book market is held Fridays on the section of the square in front of the Begijnhof entrance, where the Beguines used to have an outer garden, but the heart of the square is its western part where Nieuwezijds Voorburgwal and Spuistraat meet. The statuette in the middle is an endearing rendition of an Amsterdam street-brat called the *Lieverdje* (Little Darling). It was donated by a cigarette company and became the focal point for Provo 'happenings' in the mid-1960s. The area is now a meeting point for the city's intelligentsia, who congregate in the pubs at the western end of the square and in the surrounding bookshops, including the landmark Athenaeum bookshop and newsagency.

The classicist building between Voetboogstraat and Handboogstraat is the **Maagdenhuis**, the Virgins' House built in 1787 as a Catholic orphanage for girls and now the administrative seat of the university. In 1969 it was occupied by students, a watershed in the development of students' rights in the country. Police cordoned off the building but the occupiers held out for five days, with supplies ferried across a bridge that supportive workers built over the alley. The handsome **Lutheran Church** next door, on the corner of Singel, was built in 1633. It is still used as a church but also by the university for ceremonies such as doctoral promotions, which benefit from its excellent acoustics.

Singel, Southern Section

Around the corner, in the row of buildings at Singel 421-425, is the current **University Library**. Citizen's militias used to meet here: the 'hand-bow' militia in No 421 and the 'foot-bow' militia in No 425 (the latter also served as headquarters for the West India Company and is now obliterated by the modern façade). Their firing ranges at the rear reached to Kalverstraat – the current Handboogstraat and Voetboogstraat are named after the militias. The building at No 423 was constructed by Hendrick de Keyser in 1606 as the city arsenal and was later used as royal stables.

On the opposite side of the canal are the soaring turrets of the neo-Gothic **Krijtberg** ('chalk mountain') church, officially known as the St Franciscus Xaveriuskerk, completed in 1883 to a design by Alfred Tepe. It replaced a 'clandestine' Jesuit chapel on the same site. One of the houses that stood here belonged to a chalk merchant, hence the common name.

You could turn left here to go back to Kalverstraat along the **Heiligeweg**, the Holy Way travelled by pilgrims on their annual procession to the chapel of the Miracle of Amsterdam. The route used to extend all the way from the village of Sloten, south-west of the city, along what is now the Overtoom (once a canal for tow-boats carrying produce) and through the current Leidsestraat, but only this final section has retained the original name. A procession still takes place every year on the Sunday closest to 15 March and attracts Catholics from Holland and abroad.

Halfway to Kalverstraat is a gateway on your right, dating from the early 17th century and attributed to Hendrick de Keyser. This used to give access to the Rasphuis, a model penitentiary where beggars and delinquents were put to work to ease their return to society. One of their back-breaking jobs was to rasp brazil wood for the dyeing industry – hence the name, Rasp House. Later it became a normal prison and in 1896 a public swimming pool; now it is part of the new Vendex Triangle complex.

Back along Singel, the opposite side of the canal towards Muntplein is occupied by the floating **Bloemenmarkt** (Flower Market), open Monday to Saturday from 9 am to 5 pm. Amsterdam has had many flower markets since the first tulip mania in the 17th century,

when the price for a single bulb of this Turkish import reached an unbelievable f5000 for the legendary *Semper augustus* – enough to buy a modest canal house with a garden. The market here dates from the 1860s and specialises in flowers, bulbs, pots, vases and some plants. It's a very pretty sight and the place is packed with tourists and pickpockets. Prices are steep by Amsterdam standards but the quality is good.

WESTERN CANAL BELT
(Maps 11, 12 & 13)

Towards the end of the 16th century, the city burst out of its medieval walls with a flood of Jewish refugees from Portugal and Spain and Protestant refugees from Antwerp. In the 1580s, after the Calvinists took power and reassessed the city's needs, new land was reclaimed from the IJ and Amstel in the east (see Nieuwmarkt Neighbourhood later in this chapter), while in the west the Singel became a residential canal with the addition of a new moat that was to become Herengracht.

In 1613 the authorities embarked on an ambitious expansion project that more than tripled the city's area. Based on a plan drawn up by the city carpenter, Hendrick Jacobsz Staets, Amsterdam received a belt of parallel canals from the IJ to the IJ, one after the other like layers of an onion around the medieval city core. These canals with their many bridges and connecting roads (intended as shopping streets) were all built in one huge effort. Parcels of land were sold along the way to finance the project and buildings arose gradually. The whole city was enclosed by a new outer moat, the zigzag Buitensingel (outer moat), now known as the Singelgracht. The moat's outer quays became the current Nassaukade, Stadhouderskade and Mauritskade.

Work began at the north-western end adjoining the new harbour works and headed south from the radial Brouwersgracht. By 1625 the western canal belt was completed down to the radial Leidsegracht when money ran out. The project was picked up again later but at a much slower pace, and by the end of the 17th century it petered out just short of its original goal (see the Southern Canal Belt section later in this chapter).

These new canals clearly segregated society into haves and have-nots. Until then, merchants lived more or less in their warehouses, mingling with their labourers and suppliers in the thick of the city's activities. Now the wealthiest among them escaped the sweat and the stench by building residential mansions along the delectable Herengracht (named after the Heeren XVII, the '17 Gentlemen' of the United East India Company). The Keizersgracht (the 'emperor's canal' in honour of Maximilian) was similarly up-market, though the houses along its later extension beyond Leidsegracht were a bit more pedestrian. Businesses that could be annoying or offensive were banned, and bridges were fixed to exclude large vessels – though this didn't prevent barges from unloading and loading goods at the warehouses that were built even along these canals.

The Prinsengracht (so named to keep the House of Orange happy) was a 'cheaper' canal with smaller residences, warehouses and workshops. It acted as a barrier against the down-market Jordaan that lay beyond – a low-cost housing estate for the city's many labourers, including those employed in this massive extension project.

Westelijke Eilanden (Map 11)

The wharves and warehouses of the Western Islands, built into the IJ north of the western canal belt, were a focus of the harbour in the first half of the 17th century. The wealthy Bicker brothers, mayors of Amsterdam, even built their very own **Bickerseiland** to cater for their ships.

The area has a character all its own and is well worth a wander. Many warehouses have been converted to residences, and the ones that haven't had much done to them are in demand as studios for sculptors and painters. The **Prinseneiland** and **Realeneiland** (named after the 17th century merchant Reynier Reael) are the prettiest of the islands – the narrow bridge linking the two, the Drieharingenbrug (Three Herrings Bridge), is a modern replacement for the pontoon that used to be pulled aside to let ships through.

Length, Width & Height

Amsterdam has always had a shortage of land suitable for building purposes. When the authorities embarked on their expensive canal-belt project, they drew up detailed regulations to ensure that this scarce commodity would return maximum revenue. Parcels of land had to be large enough to attract top guilder, but small enough to maximise the number of sales flowing to the municipal coffers rather than to speculators.

On the outer bank of Herengracht, for instance, plots were limited to a width of 30 feet and a depth of 190 feet (these were pre-metric days). There were no limits to the height of buildings over the first 110 feet, but anything erected on the remaining 80 feet had to be less than 10 feet high to ensure the unprecedented luxury of large gardens (even today, the gardens behind many Herengracht houses are magnificent). Buyers also had to pay for the brick quayside in front of their plots but the city paid for the street. Subdivisions were prohibited in order to keep these properties desirable and maintain their value.

So much for the theory. In practice, the very wealthiest Amsterdammers got dispensation, as can be seen in the immense palaces along the 'Golden Bend' of Herengracht between Leidsestraat and Vijzelstraat. Elsewhere, regulations were interpreted creatively – for instance, by buying two adjacent plots and building one house with two fronts; or by building one house with two entrances, subdividing the building into upstairs and downstairs and selling the two separately. ■

By all means visit the photogenic **Zandhoek**, the 17th century sand market on the eastern waterfront of Realeneiland. The Zandhoek escaped demolition this century thanks to Jan Mens's 1940 novel, *De Gouden Reael*, named after the bar-restaurant at No 14. Galgenstraat (Gallows Street), which runs across Prinseneiland to Bickerseiland, used to provide a view over the IJ to the gallows at Volewyck, the uninhabited tip of what was to become Amsterdam Noord, where bodies of criminals executed on Dam square were propped up and left to the mercy of crows and dogs.

Haarlemmerbuurt (Maps 11 & 13)

The Haarlem Quarter between the Western Islands and Brouwersgracht gets few visitors, which is just as well because it offers a glimpse of life in central Amsterdam without tourists. **Haarlemmerstraat** and its western extension, **Haarlemmerdijk**, were part of the original sea dyke along the IJ, from the Zeedijk in the east all the way to the western extremities of the IJ north of Haarlem. They have become a lot quieter now that the road artery to/from Haarlem runs north of here; pedestrians have flocked back, mainly local residents lured by a wide range of shops, pubs and restaurants.

Halfway along Haarlemmerstraat is the **Herenmarkt**, which leads to Brouwersgracht at the head of Herengracht. This was planned as a market in the 1613 canal-belt project but it never took off. Now it's a quiet oasis and a prestigious Amsterdam address. The building at the north end of the square used to be a meat hall before it became the **Westindisch Huis** in 1623, head office of the West India Company. In 1628 Admiral Piet Heyn captured the Spanish silver fleet off Cuba and the booty was stored here in the cellars. Every Dutch person knows the nursery rhyme celebrating Heyn's small name and big deeds, sung by soccer supporters at international matches as a warning not to underestimate this small country.

Walk through the east entrance into the courtyard with its statue of Pieter Stuyvesant, the unpopular governor of New Netherlands, which included the Hudson Valley, Delaware (captured from the Swedes) and several Caribbean islands. Today the building houses the John Adams Institute, a Dutch-US friendship society (see Cultural Centres in the Facts for the Visitor chapter). In 1654 the WIC moved premises to its quayside warehouse on the corner of Oude Schans and Prins Hendrikkade (west of the current IJ-Tunnel entrance), and from there to Singel 425 (the current University Library).

The busy road to Haarlem led through the **Haarlemmerpoort** on Haarlemmerplein, where travellers heading into town had to leave their horses and carts. The current structure dates from 1840 and was built as a tax office and a gateway for King William II to pass through on his coronation. It's officially known as the Willemspoort but Amsterdammers never liked the building and still refuse to call it that, even now that it has been converted to housing. It replaced the most monumental of all the city gates, built by Hendrick de Keyser in 1615 but demolished some 200 years later.

In the 17th century a canal was dug from here to Haarlem to transport passengers on horse-drawn barges; in the 19th century the railways took over, but the original canalside road, Haarlemmerweg, is still a major road (which, for obvious reasons, no longer passes through the gate itself). Earlier gateways to Haarlem stood at the Herenmarkt and at the intersection of Nieuwezijds Voorburgwal and Nieuwendijk.

Beyond Haarlemmerbuurt It's worth going across the traffic bridge next to the gateway and turning right, past the statue of Ferdinand Domela Nieuwenhuis (1846-1919) – a Frisian minister who converted to socialism and then to anarchism and played a leading role in the militant 19th century workers' movement – and under the railway bridge. Turn immediately left and follow Zaanstraat for a few minutes until you come to the intersection with Oostzaanstraat, where you'll find a housing estate known as **het**

Schip (the Ship), one of the highlights of Amsterdam School architecture.

This triangular block, loosely resembling a ship, was completed in 1920 to a design by Michel de Klerk for a housing corporation of railway employees. The post office at the 'bow' of the 'ship', with its parabolic window, still has the original interior. The pointed tower at the short side of the block has no purpose whatsoever, apart from aesthetically linking the two wings of the complex – and serving as the symbol of the Amsterdam School. There are several other Amsterdam School-designed housing blocks in this area.

Brouwersgracht (Map 11)

The Brewers' Canal, named after the breweries that used to operate here, was an industrious canal full of warehouses, workshops and factories banned from the residential canal belt. Apart from smelly breweries there were distilleries, tanneries, potash works, whale-oil and sugar refineries, and warehouses for spices, coffee and grain.

The buildings were solidly constructed and many were converted to apartments in the 1970s and 1980s. Note the almost uninterrupted row of former warehouses from No 172 to 212. House boats add to the lazy, residential character of this picturesque canal.

Herengracht (Map 12)

The first section of Herengracht, south from Brouwersgracht, shows a mixture of expensive 17th and 18th century residences interspersed with warehouses – note the 18th century warehouses at Nos 37 and 39, and the early 17th century warehouses at Nos 43 and 45. On the opposite side of the canal, beyond the pretty Leliegracht and just before the first bend, is the White House at No 168 and the adjacent Bartolotti House at No 170-172.

The White House, named for its sandstone façade, was built in 1620 and modified in 1638 to a design by Philips Vingboons. It now houses the **Theatermuseum** (☎ 623 51 04), open Tuesday to Friday from 11 am to 5 pm (admission f5, or f3 with discounts – though this could change when it reopens in mid-1997 after extensive renovations). Even if you're not interested in the history of Dutch theatre, it's well worth visiting for the stunning interior which was completely restyled in the 1730s, with intricate plasterwork and extensive wall and ceiling paintings by Jacob de Wit and Isaac de Moucheron; a magnificent spiral staircase was added then too.

The museum spills over into the **Bartolotti House**, which has one of the most stunning façades in the city – a red-brick, Dutch Renaissance job that follows the bend of the canal. It was built in 1615 by Hendrick de Keyser and his son Pieter by order of the wealthy brewer Willem van den Heuvel, who later assumed the name of his Bolognese father-in-law so he could inherit his bank and develop it into a trading empire. The house was later split down the middle (the Theatermuseum occupies No 170) and both residences were inhabited by prominent Amsterdam families.

Just beyond these houses, Herengracht is crossed by **Raadhuisstraat**, a 'spoke road' built in 1894-96 to link the Jordaan with the Dam. Note the shopping arcade on the far side, which follows the S-bend of Raadhuisstraat towards Keizersgracht. It was designed by AL van Gendt (the Concertgebouw architect) for an insurance company, with sculptures of vicious animals to stress the dangers of life without insurance. Smoke bombs greeted Princess Beatrix's wedding coach as it passed this arcade in 1966.

Continuing along Herengracht, the even-numbered side between Huidenstraat and Leidsegracht shows an interesting mix of architectural styles. The quartet of sandstone neck gables at No 364-370 is known as the Cromhouthuizen, designed in 1662 by Philips Vingboons for Jacob Cromhout. They now house the **Bijbels Museum** (☎ 624 24 36), open Tuesday to Saturday from 10 am to 5 pm, Sunday from 1 pm (admission f5, discounts f3.50), which even atheists might consider visiting for the beautiful 18th century ceiling paintings by Jacob de Wit. The museum focuses on biblical archaeology from the Middle East and Egypt, models of temples, and a collection of Dutch bibles including the *Delft Bible* printed in 1477.

The house at **No 380-382** is unique in that it's designed like a French chateau in early French Renaissance style (a fairly faithful copy of the chateau at Blois) instead of following Dutch Renaissance lines. It was built in the 1880s for Jacob Nienhuys, who made his fortune as a tobacco planter and wanted to live in the most luxurious canal house that money could buy. It was the first house in Amsterdam with electric lighting and had its own generator room. His neighbours took a dim view of such bright displays and spread the rumour that the authorities had prohibited him placing a solid gold gate in front of the house.

Keizersgracht (Map 12)

The three **Greenland warehouses** with their step gables at Keizersgracht 40-44 belonged to the Greenland (or Nordic) Company, which dominated Arctic whaling from the early 17th century when Amsterdam's whalers edged out the Basques. Whalers from Zaandam proved more competitive after the company's monopoly was lifted in 1642, though Amsterdam continued its whaling activities till the early 1800s.

The company established a settlement on an island off Spitsbergen where harpooned whales were dragged ashore for processing. Whale oil was much sought after for a variety of uses (soap, oil lamps, paint), as was whalebone or baleen (corsets, cutlery). Oil-storage wells in these Keizersgracht warehouses (there were five in a row – the ones at No 36 and 38 have been demolished) held 100,000 litres of the precious stuff, and more barrels sat alongside the whalebone on the top floors. The authorities moved the storage facilities to the Western Islands in 1685 to maintain the up-market character of the canal belt. Many houses at this end of Keizersgracht used to belong to whaling executives and still bear decorations related to their trade.

Further south on the opposite side of the canal, halfway between Herenstraat and Leliegracht, is the **House with the Heads** at No 123, one of the finest examples of Dutch Renaissance architecture. The beautiful step gable, with its six heads at door level representing the classical deities, is reminiscent of Hendrick de Keyser's Bartolotti House on Herengracht. This is not surprising: the original owner, Nicolaas Sohier, was related to the Bartolottis and commissioned De Keyser to design the house, though the architect died in 1621 and the job was presumably completed by his son Pieter a year later. Folklore has it that the heads represent six burglars, decapitated in quick succession by an axe-wielding maid of Sohier's as they tried to break into the cellar.

The tall **Greenpeace Building** at No 174-176, which houses the organisation's international headquarters as well as its Dutch branch, is one of the rare examples of Art Nouveau architecture in Amsterdam (The Hague has a much richer collection). It was built in 1905 for a life insurance company – the façade's huge tile tableau shows a guardian angel apparently peddling an insurance policy. On the same side of the canal, note the pink granite triangles of the **Homomonument** at Westermarkt just before you get to Raadhuisstraat. It commemorates those who were persecuted for their homosexuality by the Nazis – homosexuals had to wear a pink triangle, while Jews wore the Star of David. See Gay & Lesbian Travellers in the Facts for the Visitor chapter for more about this monument.

Beyond Raadhuisstraat and still on the same side of the canal, the row of houses from No 242 to 252 became famous as a squatters' fortress known as the **Groote Keyser**. Squatters occupied the empty buildings in November 1978 and couldn't be served with eviction notices until the authorities found out their full names. Notices were served a year later, but the squatters stayed put as they could count on a well-organised support network to meet force with force. They fortified the buildings and set up a pirate radio station, the Vrije Keyser (Free

Keyser), which scanned the police frequencies and broadcast instructions to their supporters – the station played a key role in the massive riots that accompanied Queen Beatrix's coronation on 30 April 1980. Eventually the owners and authorities gave up: in October 1980 the council bought the buildings, legalised the squatters and renovated the houses on their behalf.

A bit further along Keizersgracht, just beyond Berenstraat, is the **Felix Meritis building** at No 324. It was built in 1787 by Jacob Otten Husly for an organisation called Felix Meritis (Latin for 'Happy through Merit'), a society of wealthy residents who promoted the ideals of the Enlightenment through the study of science, arts and commerce. It became the city's main cultural centre in the 19th century. The colonnaded façade served as a model for that of the Concertgebouw, and its oval concert hall (where Brahms, Grieg and Saint Saëns performed) was copied as the Concertgebouw's Kleine Zaal (Small Hall) for chamber music.

The building later passed to a printing company and was gutted by fire in 1932. After WWII it became the headquarters of the Dutch Communist Party (and the offices of the party newspaper), and from 1968 to 1989 the Shaffy Theatre Company staged its avant-garde productions here. Today, the reconstituted Felix Meritis Foundation promotes European performing arts in the building.

Opposite Felix Meritis, at No 317, is the residence where Tsar **Peter the Great** of Russia surprised his host, Christoffel Brants, by sailing right up to the house in the passenger barge from Utrecht to pay his respects. The Brants family used to live in Russia where they shared Peter's interest in ships. In 1697 the young tsar had already paid an incognito visit to the world centre of shipbuilding to serve a stint as an apprentice shipwright; this time, in 1716-17, his visit was official. The city dignitaries greeted him with compliments in cultured French; he answered in earthy Dutch expletives, drank beer straight from the jug at the evening banquet and spent the night on the floor

beside his bed. The next day he moved to the Russian ambassador's house at Herengracht 527 and trashed the place with bouts of drunken revelry over the following months. A similar lot befell Brants' country mansion (called 'Petersburg') along the Vecht river, though Brants received handsome financial recompense and a title.

Prinsengracht (Map 12)

Prinsengracht, named for William the Silent, Prince of Orange and forefather of the royal family, is the least up-market of the main canals and also the liveliest. Instead of stately offices and banks, there are shops and cafés where you can sit outside in summer. The houses are smaller and narrower than along the other canals, and apartments are still relatively affordable by canal standards; house boats line the quays. Together with the adjoining Jordaan neighbourhood (see the following section), this is an area where anyone can feel comfortable.

The **Noorderkerk** at Noordermarkt, near the northern end of the canal, was completed in 1623 to a design by Hendrick de Keyser as a Calvinist church for the 'common' people in the Jordaan (the upper classes attended De Keyser's Westerkerk further south). It was built in the shape of a broad Greek cross (four arms of equal length) around a central pulpit, giving the whole congregation unimpeded access to the word of God in suitably sober surroundings. This design, unusual at the time, would become quite common for Protestant churches throughout the country. A sculpture near the entrance commemorates the bloody Jordaan riots of July 1934, when five people died protesting the government's austerity measures, including a 12% reduction of already pitiful unemployment benefits.

The **Noordermarkt** has been a market square since the early 1600s. It now hosts a lively flea market on Monday morning where you can find some wonderful bargains. Early on Saturday morning there's a bird market (caged birds, rabbits etc – a holdover from the former livestock market), followed till early afternoon by a 'farmer's market' *(boerenmarkt)* with organic produce, herbs etc.

On the opposite side of Prinsengracht, between Prinsenstraat and Leliegracht, is a row of former **warehouses** stretching from No 187 to 217.

At No 263 is the **Anne Frankhuis**, probably the most famous canal house in Amsterdam with half a million visitors a year. Interest focuses on the *achterhuis*, the 'rear house' or annexe where the Jewish Frank family went into hiding to try to escape deportation.

Otto Frank was a manufacturer of pectin (a gelling agent used in jam) who had the foresight to emigrate with his family from Frankfurt to Amsterdam in 1933. In December 1940 he bought this house and moved his business from the Singel to here. By then the German occupiers had already tightened the noose around the city's Jewish inhabitants, and despite signing the business over to his non-Jewish partner, Otto was forced in July 1942 to go into hiding with his family – his wife and daughters Anne (aged 13) and Margot (16). They moved into the specially prepared rear of the building, along with the Van Daan couple and their son Peter, and were joined later by Mr van Dussel. The entrance hid behind a revolving bookcase, and the windows of the annexe were blacked

out to prevent suspicion among people who might see it from surrounding houses (blackouts were common policy to thwart night-time bombing sorties by the Allies).

Here they survived until they were betrayed to the Gestapo in August 1944. The Franks were among the last Jews to be deported and Anne died in Bergen-Belsen concentration camp in March 1945, only weeks before it was liberated. Otto was the only member of the family to survive, and after the war he published Anne's diary which was found among the litter in the annexe (the furniture was carted away by the Nazis). Addressed to the fictitious Kitty, the diary – written in Dutch but translated into 55 languages since – traces the young teenager's development through puberty and displays all the signs of a gifted writer in the making.

In 1957 the then owner donated the house to the Anne Frank Foundation, who turned it into a museum displaying the persecution of Jews in WWII and the dangers of present-day racism and anti-semitism. The museum (☎ 556 71 00) is open Monday to Saturday from 9 am to 5 pm, Sunday from 10 am (to 7 pm daily from June to August). Admission costs f10, or f5 with discounts. The queues can be exasperating though they shouldn't be too bad if you arrive just before opening time.

Anne probably couldn't see but she could certainly hear the carillon in the tower of the **Westerkerk**, at 85 metres the highest church tower in the city. It's topped by the imperial crown that Habsburg emperor Maximilian I bestowed to the city's coat of arms in 1489. The tower, the tourist logo of Amsterdam today, affords a tremendous view over the city, including the differing layouts of the canal belt and the streets in the Jordaan. The climb is strenuous.

The church is the main gathering place for Amsterdam's Dutch Reformed community. It was built as a showcase Protestant church for the rich to a 1620 design by Hendrick de Keyser, who copied his design of the Zuiderkerk but increased the scale. De Keyser died in 1621 and the church was completed by

Anne Frank

The square tower of the Westerkerk.

Jacob van Campen in 1630. The square tower dates from 1638 – De Keyser would have made it hexagonal or octagonal. The nave, 29 metres wide and 28 metres high, is the largest of any Dutch Protestant church and is covered by a wooden barrel vault (the marshy ground precluded the use of heavy stone).

The huge main organ dates from 1686, with panels decorated with biblical scenes and instruments by Gerard de Lairesse. The secondary organ is used for Bach cantatas. Rembrandt, who died bankrupt at nearby Rozengracht, was buried in the church on 8 October 1669 but no-one knows exactly where – perhaps near the grave of his son Titus. The church (☎ 624 77 66) is open Monday to Saturday from 10 am to 4 pm; the tower is open during the same times from April to September.

The church stands on **Westermarkt**. Until 1857 the eastern part of the square was dominated by the monumental Westerhal, with a meat hall at ground level and the headquarters of the city watch upstairs. In 1634 the French philosopher **René Descartes** resided in the house at No 6 on the quiet, northern side of the square. He was one of many foreign intellectuals who found the freedom to develop and express their ideas in Amsterdam (others included Locke, Comenius, Voltaire and Marx), or who had their works published here. As Voltaire saw it, the residents were so preoccupied with profit that they would never notice him even if he spent his entire life here.

Further south along Prinsengracht is the **Pulitzer Hotel**, which started business in 1971 and now occupies the 17 adjoining canal houses between Nos 299 and 331, all connected with internal staircases and passages. The gables have been meticulously restored, along with some of the interior features. A free classical concert is held from barges in the canal at the end of August.

If you continue south along the same (eastern) side of the canal you might notice a number of very narrow **alleyways** between Berenstraat and Leidsegracht, closed off with gates. They were officially intended as side entrances for servants' quarters at the rear but in actual fact such quarters were rented out as accommodation and workshops to the city's poor. These hidden slums, in damp cellars and clustered around dark courtyards, violated the municipal codes of the canal belt but nobody took much notice, probably because they were opposite the southern reaches of the Jordaan; had they been on Herengracht or even Keizersgracht it might have been a different story.

Jordaan (Map 12)

The Jordaan neighbourhood was planned

ROB VAN DRIESUM

RICHARD NEBESKY

ROB VAN DRIESUM

RICHARD NEBESKY

Top Left: The Oude Kerk, with its beautiful tower and fine Hemony carillon
Top Right: The Krijtberg church on Singel
Bottom Left: Groenburgwal, with the tower of the Westerkerk in the background
Bottom Right: The Scheepvaarthuis, an early example of Amsterdam School architecture

RICHARD NEBESKY

ROB VAN DRIESUM

RICHARD NEBESKY

Top: Façade of the Tuschinskitheater - see the interior too!
Middle: The Waag (Weigh House) on Nieuwmarkt
Bottom: Façade detail of the Royal Palace

and built as a working-class district during the canal-belt project in the early 17th century. Here the canal-diggers and bridge-builders, carpenters and stonemasons settled with their families. Here too came the tanneries, breweries, sugar refineries, smithies, cooperages and other smelly or noisy industries banned from the up-market canal belt, along with the residences of the artisans and labourers who worked in them.

The name Jordaan wasn't used until a century later and its origin is unclear. The most popular theory is that it's a corruption of the French *jardin* (garden). After all, many French Huguenots settled here in what used to be the market gardens beyond the city walls – the street pattern follows the original grid of ditches and footpaths, and many streets carry names of flowers. Some historians contend that the name had biblical connotations and referred to the Jordan River.

For centuries, the Jordaan remained a thoroughly working-class area, and for the authorities it was the unruly heart of the city. It was the first precinct where tarred roads replaced brick paving because the latter was often turned into barricades and police-smashing projectiles during riots. Early this century one in seven Amsterdammers lived in the Jordaan, 1000 people packed to the hectare (100m by 100m) in squalid conditions.

New housing estates in Amsterdam's northern, western and southern suburbs brought some relief after WWI, and in the 1960s and 1970s many Jordanese moved to the outlying 'garden suburbs' and the polders of Flevoland. Their places were taken by students, artists and tertiary-sector professionals who began to transform the Jordaan into a trendy area, though there are still enough working-class and elderly people for it to retain some of its original flavour.

Popular conceptions of the Jordaan linger: it is the 'heart and soul' of the 'real' Amsterdam epitomised in schmaltzy oompah ballads, where life happens on the streets or in the corner pub (rather than in the over-crowded houses) and where common folk

still share their experiences; where houses are tiny but tidy, with laced curtains and flowers in window boxes, behind which auntie Greet eyes the street and her front door with the help of a *spionnetje* ('little spy' mirror) attached to the windowsill; and where living, working, shopping, schooling and entertainment are integrated in the one neighbourhood.

Such popular conceptions still hold true, as you will discover when you wander through the Jordaan and soak up the real-life atmosphere of people going about their daily business. Take your time and don't worry if you get lost (which you will): there are plenty of inviting pubs and restaurants, offbeat shops and weird little art galleries to grab your attention. The Jordaan is over-endowed with lively **markets**, such as:

Noordermarkt – see the earlier Prinsengracht section
Lindengracht – general market on Saturday, very much a local affair
Westermarkt on Westerstraat – busy general market from Monday to Saturday
De Looier at Elandsgracht 109 – bargain antiques and bric-a-brac at indoor stalls most days from 11 am to 5 pm, Thursday to 9 pm, closed Friday
Indoor flea market at Looiersgracht 38 – closed Friday

In the late 19th and early 20th centuries many of the Jordaan's ditches and narrow canals were filled in, mainly for sanitary reasons, though their names remain: Palmgracht, Lindengracht, Rozengracht (now a busy thoroughfare), Elandsgracht. The **Bloemgracht** was the most up-market of the canals (the 'Herengracht of the Jordaan') and, for that reason, was never filled in: here wealthy artisans built smaller versions of patrician canal houses. Note the row of three step gables at No 87-91, owned by the Hendrick de Keyser Foundation and known as the Three Hendricks, though they were built in 1645, long after the famous sculptor/architect had died.

The southern tip of the Jordaan beyond Rozengracht is quieter than the area to the north and perhaps less interesting for an aimless wander. It was (and to some extent still is) an area of workshops and artists' studios.

The Jordaan also has a high concentration of **hofjes**, almshouses consisting of a courtyard surrounded by houses built by wealthy benefactors to house elderly people and widows – a noble act in the days before social security. Some hofjes are real gems, with beautifully restored houses and lovingly maintained gardens. The entrances are usually unobtrusive and hidden behind doors. Hofjes became such a popular tourist attraction in recent years that residents complained and in theory they are now closed to the public (the one exception being the famous Begijnhof, discussed in the earlier Nieuwe Zijde section). If the entrance is unlocked, however, and if there are only one or two of you and you exercise the necessary discretion, most residents probably won't mind if you take a quick peek. Try the following:

Lindenhofje, Lindengracht 94-112 – dating from 1614, the oldest surviving hofje
Suyckerhofje, Lindengracht 149-163 – a charming hofje founded in 1670
Karthuizerhofje, Karthuizersstraat 89-171 – a hofje for widows, dating from 1650 and on the site of a former Carthusian monastery
Claes Claeszhofje, Eerste Egelantiersdwarsstraat 3 – also known as Anslo's Hofje; three courtyards dating from around 1630; inhabited by music students
St Andrieshofje, Egelantiersgracht 107-141 – the second-oldest surviving hofje (finished in 1617), founded by the cattle farmer Jeff Gerritzoon
Venetiae, Elandsstraat 106-136 – founded in the mid-1600s by a trader with Venice; very pretty garden

SOUTHERN CANAL BELT (Maps 15 & 16)

The canal project stopped at the radial Leidsegracht in 1625 through lack of funds and was only picked up again later. Even then, work on the southern section progressed much more slowly: it had taken a mere 12 years to construct the canals down

from Brouwersgracht, along with their interconnecting roads and the adjoining Jordaan area, but it took another 40 years to complete the southern canal belt towards the Amstel and beyond the opposite bank. Interest then fizzled out and the only canal that ever made it to the eastern IJ was the (Nieuwe) Herengracht.

The corner of Herengracht and Leidsegracht is a tranquil spot, surrounded by 17th and 18th century houses. You may notice that the buildings along Leidsegracht, as well as those along the southern canal belt, are almost entirely residential – there are very few of the warehouses or combined warehouses and residences found in the western section. The façades are also more restrained and stately, less boisterously decorated.

Herengracht (Map 16)

Along the southern section of Herengracht more than anywhere else, the buildings are larger than in the western section. By now (mid-17th century) some of Amsterdam's merchants and shipping magnates had amassed stupendous fortunes and they saw to it that the authorities (often these same merchants and magnates) relaxed their restrictions on the size of canalside plots.

The Herengracht between Leidsestraat and Vijzelstraat, known as the **Golden Bend**, was the site of some of the largest private mansions in the city. Most of them now belong to financial and other institutions. Dutch architectural themes are still evident but the dominant styles are Louis XIV, XV and XVI – French culture was all the rage among the city's wealthy class.

You can look at the interior of one of these houses by visiting the **Goethe Institut** at No 470 (see Cultural Centres in the Facts for the Visitor chapter). When this house was built in 1669 it was much larger and included No 468 next door.

Another Golden Bend house open to the public is the **Kattenkabinet** (Cats' Cabinet, ☎ 626 53 78) across the canal at No 497. This museum, devoted to the feline presence in art, was founded by a wealthy financier in memory of his red tomcat, John Piermont

The Great Art Fraud

Herengracht 470, which currently houses the Goethe Institut, used to include No 468 next door. The house was later split, and during WWII a German art dealer 'acquired' No 468. The Amsterdam painter Han van Meegeren sold him a painting by the 17th century Delft master Jan Vermeer that the German passed on to Nazi ringleader Hermann Göring in return for f2 million-worth of paintings plundered elsewhere.

When Van Meegeren was accused of collaboration after the war, he declared that he had painted the Vermeer himself and in fact had painted the other Vermeers that had appeared out of nowhere in recent years. To prove his case he painted another 'Vermeer' under supervision.

His work completely fooled the art historians of the day, including the prestigious Boymans-van Beuningen Museum in Rotterdam that bought one of the paintings before the war and gave it top billing. It was the greatest art fraud in Dutch history, all the more remarkable for the fact that Vermeer only produced 35 known paintings. Out of respect for Van Meegeren's talent the judge sentenced him to a lenient one year in prison. ■

Morgan III. It's only open during special exhibitions. Cat fanciers will go ga-ga over the displays but it's also worth visiting for the magnificent interior and views of the garden.

Back on the even side of Herengracht, the corner with Vijzelstraat is dominated by the colossal (some would say monstrous) **ABN-AMRO bank building** that continues all the way to Keizersgracht. It was completed in 1923 as head office for the Netherlands Trading Society, a Dutch overseas bank (successor to the United East India Company and West India Company) that became the ABN Bank in the mid-1960s and merged with the AMRO Bank in 1991. The ABN-AMRO is the largest bank in the country and the largest foreign bank in the USA. It ranks only 16th in the world but has one of the widest international networks (the combination of finance and trade has always been a Dutch speciality).

Beyond Vijzelstraat, past the mayor's residence at No 502, is the **Geelvinck Hinlopen Huis** (☎ 622 10 10) at No 518, a 17th century house with stylish rooms, a formal garden and art in the coach house. Though not as impressive as Museum Willet-Holthuysen a bit further along the canal (see below) or the Museum Van Loon (see the following section on Keizersgracht), it's worth a look and best of all it's free. The limited opening times are Thursday to Saturday from noon to 5 pm.

A few steps past this house is the start of the radial **Reguliersgracht**, the beautiful 'canal of the seven bridges' cut in 1664. You can just about count them all when you stand on the Herengracht bridge. Canal tour boats halt here for photos because it's easier from the water, especially at night when the bridges are lit up and their graceful curves are reflected in the water. This canal was almost filled at the turn of the century to accommodate a tram line.

Walk down Reguliersgracht to take in its serenity and lively mix of architectural styles. Sights include:

The house at No 34 with its massive eagle gable commemorating the original owner, Arent van den Bergh (*arend* is one of the Dutch words for eagle), and its unusual twin entrance against the side walls for the upstairs and downstairs dwellings

The superb scene back towards Herengracht from the east-west bridge at Keizersgracht, and the photogenic lean of the two houses on the corner (not to mention the 15 bridges visible from here)

The Dutch/German woodwork fantasy at No 57-59 reminiscent of the city's medieval wooden houses, built in 1879 for a carpentry firm (the same architect, Isaac Gosschalk, designed No 63)

The Amstelveld with the white, wooden Amstelkerk at Prinsengracht (see the following Prinsengracht section)

The statuette of a stork set into the corner house at No 92 (storks were a protected species; canal-boat operators fantasise that a midwife lived here)

The extension of Reguliersgracht across Herengracht towards the centre of town used to be water but is now **Thorbeckeplein**, with a statue of Jan Rudolf Thorbecke, the Liberal politician who created the Dutch parliamentary system in 1848. He faces outwards and wouldn't like the look of his square, though the second-rate night clubs have all but disappeared and the banning of cars has made it more pleasant than it used to be. An art market (mostly modern pictorial) is held here Sundays from 10.30 am to 6 pm between mid-March and mid-October.

Beyond Thorbeckeplein is **Rembrandtplein**, originally called Reguliersplein and then Botermarkt because the butter market was held here. The proud statue of the painter, gazing pensively towards the Jewish quarter where he lived until circumstances forced him to the Jordaan, was unveiled in 1852 and the square was renamed in 1876. It's lined with pubs, grand cafés and restaurants, and seems to attract outer suburbanites in search of a noisy good time.

The street running west from Rembrandtplein to the Munt is Reguliersbreestraat. (Before the construction of the canal belt, the nuns of the Regulier, or 'Regular', order had a monastery outside the city walls roughly where Utrechtsestraat now crosses Keizersgracht, which explains the frequent use of the name in this area.) About one third of the way along on the left is the **Tuschinskitheater** (Map 13; ☎ 626 26 33) at No 26-28, established in 1921 and still the most glorious cinema in the country. The blend of Art Deco and Amsterdam School architecture with almost camp interior decorations is a visual feast, even before you've seen a film on one of its screens. There used to be guided tours during summer which could well be reintroduced, but why not go for the whole experience by watching a film in the main auditorium, Tuschinski 1?

Back at the Herengracht bridge over Reguliersgracht, continue eastwards across **Utrechtsestraat**, a sedate shopping street that's becoming a lively haunt with interesting shops, restaurants and cafés – worth a wander (turn right).

At Herengracht 605 is **Museum Willet-Holthuysen** (☎ 523 18 70), named after Abraham Willet's widow who bequeathed this beautiful house with its sumptuous interior to the city 100 years ago. Dating from 1687, it has been remodelled several times since and it underwent extensive renovations recently. Some furnishings and artefacts come from other bequests which helps explain the uncoordinated mix of 18th and 19th century styles. It's open weekdays from 10 am to 5 pm, weekends from 11 am, and costs f5 (f2.50 with discounts). It's all very impressive but a bit unnatural – the Museum Van Loon (see the following Keizersgracht section) gives a better idea of the real thing. You can see the formal French garden with its sundial for free through the iron fence at the Amstelstraat end.

Keizersgracht (Map 15 & 16)

The intersection of Keizersgracht and Leidsestraat has a couple of remarkable buildings. The **Metz department store** at Keizersgracht 455 was built in 1891 to house the New York Life Insurance Company (hence the exterior and interior eagles) but soon passed to the purveyor of luxury furnishings. The functionalist designer and architect Gerrit Rietveld added the gallery on the top floor where you can have lunch with a view.

Across the canal at No 508 is the former **PC Hooft store**, built for a cigar manufacturer in 1881 by AC Bleijs (the architect of the St Nicolaaskerk near Centraal Station). The name refers to poet, playwright, historian and all-round national icon Pieter Cornelisz Hooft, whose 300th birthday was commemorated in this Dutch-Renaissance throwback with Germanic tower. Note the playful reliefs depicting the various stages of tobacco preparation.

Further along on this side of the canal, beyond Leidsestraat, is the solid yet elegant **Keizersgrachtkerk** at No 566. It dates from 1888 and was built to house the orthodox-Calvinist Gereformeerd community who left the Dutch Reformed Church two years before (see Religion in the Facts about Amsterdam chapter).

The next side street is **Nieuwe Spiegelstraat**, lined with shops selling luxury antiques and other collectables. Even if you don't have the inclination (or the money!) to buy anything, at least have a look at the goods on offer. The extension of this street, the pretty Spiegelgracht with more antique shops and especially art galleries, leads to the Rijksmuseum.

Further along Keizersgracht, across windswept Vijzelstraat, is the **Museum Van Loon** (☎ 624 52 55) at No 672, built in 1672 (along with the house next door, No 674) for a wealthy arms dealer. The portraitist Ferdinand Bol, a faithful student of Rembrandt, rented the place for a while. In the late 1800s it was acquired by the Van Loons, one of the most prominent patrician families, who lived in a style befitting their status; their stables across the canal at No 607 now house an art gallery. The house, with its period rooms and family portraits, provides a good impression of canalside living when money was no object, and the rococo rose garden is typical of the greenery Amsterdammers aspired to in the 18th century. The museum is only open Monday and Tuesday from 11 am to 5 pm, and Sunday from 1 pm. Entry costs f7.50 (f5 with discounts).

Note the austere, two-storey **Amstelhof** on the opposite side of the river where Keizersgracht meets the Amstel. It was built in 1683 as an almshouse and is still in use today for Dutch Reformed elderly women (and men, in the basement). It illustrates how the canal project ran out of steam by the time it reached the Amstel. Much of the land beyond was given over to charities or turned into recreational area: the wealthy already bought their plots and had built their mansions, and the Dutch Republic went into consolidation mode against the British and French, which meant there was little new wealth (only increased wealth for those who already had money).

Prinsengracht (Maps 15 & 16)

The odd and even house numbers along Prinsengracht are more out of step than along the other canals (where they follow one another fairly closely) due to the many Jordaan streets that lead off it. This is exacerbated by additional streets beyond Leidsegracht, and the result is that house number 1133 sits opposite 868 when Prinsengracht reaches the Amstel.

Near the corner with Leidsegracht is the **Paleis van Justitie** (Court of Appeal) at No 436, a huge, neoclassical edifice modified in 1829 by the city architect Jan de Greef. It started life in 1666 as the city orphanage and was designed for 800 orphans, but by the early 19th century more than half the city's 4300 orphans were crammed in here. A royal decree in 1822 relocated orphans over the age of six to other towns, much to the chagrin of the local authorities who were powerless to act against the 'theft of children'.

A hundred metres or so down Leidsestraat is **Leidseplein**, one of the liveliest squares in the city and the undisputed centre of nightlife. It has always been busy: in the 17th century it was the gateway to Leiden and other points south-west, and travellers had to leave their carts and horses here when heading into town.

The **Stadsschouwburg** (City Theatre) with its balcony arcade at Leidseplein 25 dates from 1894. People criticised the building – as they criticised every city theatre before or since – and the funds for the exterior decorations never materialised. The architect, Jan Springer, couldn't handle this and retired. The theatre is used for large-scale plays and operettas. South across Marnixstraat, the **American Hotel** is an Art Nouveau landmark from 1902 foreshadowing the Amsterdam School's use of brick. No visit to Amsterdam is complete without a coffee in its stylish Café Americain.

The sidewalk cafés at the north end of the square are perfect for watching interesting street artists and eccentric passers-by. There are countless pubs and clubs in the area that continue till daylight, and a smorgasbord of restaurants in the surrounding streets. There are cinemas and other entertainment venues, and even a casino built in the shape of a roulette table. Everybody finds something to enjoy at Leidseplein.

Back at Prinsengracht, eastwards on the far side of the canal, the ebullient neo-Renaissance façade is all that remains of the former **milk factory** at No 739-741, built in 1876 to a design by Eduard Cuypers. Until then, milk was brought into town from the surrounding countryside in wooden barrels and sold on the streets from open buckets – not very hygienic.

Further east, beyond the intersection of Prinsengracht and Reguliersgracht, is the Amstelveld with the wooden **Amstelkerk**. The city planners had envisaged four new Protestant churches in the southern canal belt, linked to one another by the Kerkstraat, but the only one they actually built was the Oosterkerk, way out on Wittenburgergracht near the IJ (Map 14; see the later Eastern Islands section). The Amstelkerk was a temporary structure, erected in 1670 so the congregation had somewhere to congregate while the permanent church arose next to it, but the funds remained elusive and the 'temporary' church still conducts services today. Gothic alterations were made to the interior in the 1840s.

The authorities never completely dropped their plans for a permanent church and kept the **Amstelveld** free of buildings. In 1876 the Monday market moved here from Rembrandtplein. This lively 'free market' had vendors from out of town peddling a wide range of goods (it still operates in the summer months, focusing on plants and flowers). A small statue next to the Amstelkerk commemorates Professor Kokadorus, aka Meijer Linnewiel (1867-1934), the most colourful market vendor Amsterdam has known. People would buy anything from spoons to suspenders ('to hang up your mother-in-law') just to watch his performances interlaced with satirical comments about the politics of the day. The annihilation of the Jewish community in WWII put an end to the city's rich tradition of creative vending.

In summer the Amstelveld is a pleasant space where children play soccer, dogs run around, and patrons laze in the sun at Café Kort against the south side of the Amstelkerk. The Catholic church across the canal at Prinsengracht 756, **de Duif** (the Dove), was first built in 1796, shortly after the French-installed government proclaimed freedom of religion. It was the first Catholic church with a public entrance for over two centuries, and was rebuilt to its current design in the mid-1800s. In the 1970s the Church authorities wanted to sell the building but the priest and other staff continued to hold services in defiance and saved the church.

Continue to the Amstel, and a couple of interesting sights. To your right are the **Amstelsluizen**, which cross the river to Theater Carré (built as a circus in 1868, rebuilt in brick in 1887 and now mainly used as a theatre). These impressive sluices date from 1674 and allowed the canals to be flushed with fresh water from the Amstel rather than salt water from the IJ, which made the city far more livable (see Ecology & Environment in the Facts about Amsterdam chapter). They were still operated by hand until recently.

To your left is the **Magere Brug** (Skinny Bridge), without doubt the most photographed drawbridge in the city. It links Kerkstraat with Nieuwe Kerkstraat and dates from the 1670s, when it was a very narrow pedestrian bridge. Rebuilt and widened several times, it was finally torn down in 1929 to make way for a modern bridge, only to be rebuilt again in wood in its original style. It makes a very pretty sight during the day as well as at night when it's lit up. Stand in the middle and feel it seesaw under the passing traffic.

NIEUWMARKT NEIGHBOURHOOD (Maps 13 & 14)

East of Nieuwmarkt square is the Nieuwmarkt neighbourhood, enclosed by the Geldersekade and Kloveniers-burgwal in the west, the Amstel in the south, the Valkenburgerstraat (the feeder road of the current IJ-Tunnel) in the east and the IJ in the north. It was the birthplace in

1975 of the organised squatter movement in response to the metro line. The planned line snaked through much of the neighbourhood and required the demolition of many houses that were derelict or still quite habitable – often depending on one's point of view (see the History section in the Facts about Amsterdam chapter).

New, subsidised housing estates arose after completion of the line and today the west and south of the neighbourhood are dominated by modern inner-city architecture, some of it interesting and some less than successful.

Unfortunately the heroin scene also seems to have set up shop here, especially along St Anthoniesbreestraat, after having been cleared off the Zeedijk.

Until WWII the area was the focal point of Amsterdam's Jews, a thriving community who enjoyed more freedom here than elsewhere in Europe and made the city a centre for diamonds, tobacco, printing and clothing. They also gave Amsterdam an exceptional variety of lively markets, some of which still exist as sad reminders (eg the flea market on Waterlooplein).

Lastage

The Nieuwmarkt neighbourhood grew haphazardly. Immediately east of Nieuwmarkt square was an area known as the Lastage, a jumble of wharves, docks, rope yards and warehouses that lay beyond the medieval city wall and the protective sea dyke that ran along the current Zeedijk, St Anthoniesbreestraat, Jodenbreestraat and Muiderstraat. In the 1510s, after an attack by troops from Gelderland, the Lastage was fortified by means of the wide **Oude Schans** canal and guarded by a gun turret, the **Montelbaanstoren** – its octagonal tower was added in 1606, presumably to a design by Hendrick de Keyser. Today the spot offers panoramic views over wide expanses of water.

North-west of here, across Waalseilandsgracht on the corner of Binnenkant and Prins Hendrikkade, is the **Scheepvaarthuis**, the Shipping House completed in 1916 to a design by Johan van der Mey. Note the many façade sculptures. This remarkable building, which utilises the street layout to resemble a ship's bow, was the first building in Amsterdam School style and is still one of the finest examples of this architectural movement. It used to house a consortium of shipping companies but is now home to the municipal transport company.

Nieuwmarkt Islands (Map 13)

In the 1580s, the sudden influx of Sephardic Jews from Spain and Portugal prompted the newly Calvinist authorities to reclaim land from the IJ in the form of several rectangular islands east of Oude Schans, one of which, **Uilenburg**, is still recognisable as an island today. Shipyards that operated here soon moved out to the new Eastern Islands (see the following Eastern Islands section), making way for another wave of Jewish refugees: Ashkenazim from Central and Eastern Europe.

On Uilenburg, the vast Gassan diamond factory (☎ 622 53 33), abutting a synagogue at Nieuwe Uilenburgerstraat 173-175, was the first to use steam power in the 1880s. The factory was recommissioned in 1989 after thorough renovations. See Diamonds in the Shopping chapter for more about diamonds and free guided tours offered by diamond factories.

Southern Nieuwmarkt Neighbourhood (Map 13)

South of here, inside the sea dyke, the 16th century authorities reclaimed land from the Amstel: the island of Vlooienburg (the current Waterlooplein), with canals and transverse streets that would become the heart of the Jewish quarter. This was not enough, however, to satisfy the needs of the rapidly growing city and two decades later the authorities gave the go-ahead for the ambitious canal-belt project.

The street that runs from Nieuwmarkt square in the direction of Waterlooplein is St Anthoniesbreestraat, once a busy street that lost its old buildings during the construction of the metro line – the new houses incorporate rubber blocks in the foundations to absorb vibrations caused by the metro. One exception is the **Pintohuis** at No 69 which used to belong to a wealthy Sephardi, Isaac de Pinto, who had it remodelled with Italianate pilasters in the 1680s. In the 1970s a freeway to Centraal Station required the demolition of this building but the controversy stopped the freeway instead. It's now a library annexe – pop inside to admire the ceilings.

Jewish Amsterdam

The Nazis lost the war but they did achieve one of their most gruesome aims: the almost complete annihilation of Amsterdam's Jewish community. Before WWII there were about 140,000 Jews in the Netherlands of whom about 90,000 lived in Amsterdam, where they formed 13% of the population. (Before the 1930s this proportion was about 10% but it increased with Jews fleeing the Nazi regime in Germany.) Only some 5500 of these Amsterdammers survived the war, barely one in 16.

Hanukah lamp

They played an important role in the city over the centuries. In medieval times few Jews lived here but their expulsion from Spain and Portugal in the 1580s brought a flood of Sephardic refugees. More arrived when the Spaniards retook Antwerp in 1585. They settled on the newly reclaimed islands in the current Nieuwmarkt neighbourhood where land was cheap.

The monopolistic guilds kept most trades firmly closed to these newcomers but some of the Sephardim were diamond-cutters, for which there was no guild. Other Sephardic Jews introduced printing and tobacco processing, or worked in similarly unrestricted trades such as retail on the streets, banking and medicine. The majority, however, eked out a meagre living as labourers and small-time traders on the margins of society, and lived in houses they could afford in the Nieuwmarkt area, which developed into the Jewish quarter. Still, they weren't confined to a ghetto and, with some restrictions, could buy property and exercise their religion – freedoms unheard of elsewhere in Europe.

The 17th century saw another influx of Jewish refugees, this time Ashkenazim fleeing pogroms in Central and Eastern Europe. Thus the two wings of the diaspora were reunited in Amsterdam but they didn't always get on well. Sephardim resented the increased competition posed by Ashkenazic newcomers, who soon outnumbered them and were generally much poorer, and the two groups established separate synagogues. Perhaps thanks to this antagonism, Amsterdam became a major Jewish centre in Europe.

The guilds and all remaining restrictions on Jews were abolished during the French occupation, and the Jewish community thrived in the 19th century. There was still considerable poverty and the Jewish quarter included some of the worst slums in the city; but the economic, social and political emancipation of the Jews also helped their burgeoning middle class, who moved out into the Plantage area and later into the suburbs south of the city.

The Holocaust left the Jewish quarter empty, a sinister reminder of its once bustling life. Many of the houses, looted by Germans and local collaborators and deprived of their wooden fixtures for fuel in the final, desperate months of the war, stood derelict until they were demolished in the 1970s.

Some estimates put the current Jewish population of Amsterdam at 30,000, but many are so integrated into Dutch society that they don't consider themselves distinctly Jewish. Amsterdam slang incorporates many terms of Hebrew or Yiddish origin, such as the alternative name for Amsterdam, Mokum (from *makom aleph*, the best city of all); the cheery goodbye, *de mazzel* (good luck), or *joetje* (f10, from the 10th letter of the Hebrew alphabet); and the ultimate put-down, *kapsones maken* (to make unnecessary fuss, from *kapsjones*, self-importance). ∎

A passageway in the modern housing estate across St Anthoniesbreestraat leads to the **Zuiderkerk**, the Southern Church built by Hendrick de Keyser in 1603-11. His tower, one metre out of plumb, dates from 1614. This was the first custom-built Protestant church in Amsterdam – still a Catholic design but without the choir – and served as a blueprint for De Keyser's Westerkerk. The final church service was held here in 1929 and at the end of WWII it served as a morgue.

Now it houses the Municipal Centre for Physical Planning and Public Housing (☎ 622 29 62) with a very interesting exhibit on all aspects of urban planning, open Moday to Friday from noon to 5 pm, Thursday to 8 pm (free admission). A large, computerised laser map answers questions about the city in English. From June to mid-October you can climb the tower for a great view over the city (Wednesday from 2 to 5 pm, Thursday and Friday from 11 am to 2 pm, and Saturday from 11 am to 4 pm).

The former cemetery east of the church adjoins Theo Bosch's community housing project, the **Pentagon**, completed in 1983, with an arty waterfall along the wall. You'll either love it or hate it but you can't ignore it. Visiting architects come to look at the complex.

South of here, across the beautiful **Raamgracht** that city planners wanted to fill in the 1950s, is the narrow **Verversstraat** with a mix of old and new architecture typical of this area. The name, Painters' Street, refers to the polluting paint factories that were limited to this street (originally a canal) beyond the city walls.

The covered walkway over the street used to link sections of the Leeuwenburg sewing-machine factory, slated for demolition but saved by squatters who now live here legally and quite happily (it's an impressive building viewed from the Zwanenburgwal end). At the end of Verversstraat, turn right to the steel drawbridge over the pretty **Groenburgwal**, which affords a good photo opportunity back towards the Zuiderkerk. Note the slight tilt in its tower.

Jodenbreestraat St Anthoniesbreestraat opens on to the wide Jodenbreestraat, a remnant of the freeway-to-be. The grey concrete block along the left-hand side, beyond the picturesque lock-keeper's house, has been called Amsterdam's ugliest building. It's also one of the emptiest: built as a university complex in the late 1960s, it soon became dangerously unstable and will now be demolished.

Across the road, at Jodenbreestraat 4-6, is **Museum Het Rembrandthuis** (☎ 624 94 86), a beautiful house dating from 1606 where Rembrandt lived (downstairs) and worked (upstairs). He bought the house in 1639 for a fortune thanks to his wealthy wife, Saskia van Uylenburgh, but chronic debt got the better of him and he had to bail out and move to the Jordaan in 1658. The years spent in this house were the highlight of his career, when he was regarded as a star and ran the largest painting studio in Holland, though he ruined it all by making enemies and squandering his earnings.

The museum is well worth visiting for the almost complete collection of Rembrandt's etchings (250 of the 280 he is known to have made). There are also several drawings and paintings by his pupils as well as his teacher, Pieter Lastman, and an etching by Albrecht Dürer. It's open Monday to Saturday from 10 am to 5 pm, Sunday from 1 pm, and admission costs f7.50 (f6 or f5 with discounts).

Behind the Rembrandthuis is **Holland Experience** (☎ 422 22 33), Waterlooplein 17. This multimedia hype-fest tries to cram all the little land's big attractions into an overpriced mish-mash of sights, sounds and smells. A plotless half-hour film lurches from tulips to windmills to threatened dykes, without narration or explanation, but with artless extras parading as cutting-edge entertainment. Cheap perfume is puffed into the auditorium while the tulips are on screen. When an on-screen dyke crumbles, room temperature plummets, the audience is sprinkled with water, and a Sony-augmented thunderstorm rages. A plaster ballerina wobbles on rails running in front of a filmed rehearsal of *Swan Lake*. Holland Experience is a superlative example of what can happen with many machines and few ideas, and as entertainment it is very lame. It's open daily from 10 am to 10 pm and costs f17.50 (gulp).

Waterlooplein South of this is Waterlooplein, once known as Vlooienburg and the heart of the Jewish quarter. It's now dominated by the gleaming gold front tooth in the canal belt, the **Stopera**, an oversized city hall and music theatre that opened in 1986 after endless controversy. It was designed by the Austrian architect Wilhelm Holzbauer and his Dutch colleage, Cees Dam, who won a competition back in 1968 with a submission that, in the words of one critic, 'has all the charms of an Ikea chair'. You might wish to attend a music performance in the theatre, or at least a free lunchtime concert on Tuesday, but in any case it's worth having a look at the display in the arcade between city hall and theatre that shows the country's water levels. For more about this subject, see Sea Level & NAP under Geography in the Facts about Amsterdam chapter.

The original Waterlooplein covered the eastern portion of Vlooienburg and was created in 1882 by filling a couple of canals. This was the site of the major Jewish **flea market** where anything was available. The market itself survived the war and is now held north of the Stopera from Monday to Saturday, with a wide range of goods. It's a popular market, not least among tourists. Prices are a bit higher than at other markets but it's definitely worth a wander; beware of pickpockets.

The neoclassical **Mozes en Aäronkerk**, a Catholic church built in 1841 on the northeastern corner of Waterlooplein, shows that this wasn't an exclusively Jewish area. It is still used as a church and also as a centre for social and cultural organisations. It replaced the 'clandestine' Catholic church that occupied two houses named Mozes and Aäron at what is now the rear of the church along Jodenbreestraat.

One of the buildings demolished to make way for the new church was home to the Jewish philosopher Baruch de Spinoza

Baruch de Spinoza

(1632-77), who was born in Amsterdam but spent much of his life making lenses in The Hague after the rabbis proclaimed him a heretic. He is best known for his work *Ethics*, which proposes that the concept of God possesses an infinite number of attributes. 'Polytheism!' cried rabbis and Protestant ministers alike – their approach to religion was, after all, similar in many respects.

Jewish Centres The busy roundabout east of the church is Mr Visserplein ('Mr' stands for *meester*, or 'master', the Dutch lawyer's title). LE Visser was a Jewish president of the supreme court who was dismissed by the Germans. He refused to wear the Star of David and spoke out against the Jewish Council for helping the occupiers carry out their anti-Jewish policies. He died before the Germans could wreak revenge.

On the east side of the square at No 3 is the majestic **Portuguese-Israelite Synagogue**, built between 1671 and 1675 by the Sephardic community. It was the largest synagogue in Europe at the time and is still impressive. The architect, Elias Bouman, was inspired by the Temple of Solomon but the building's classicist lines are fairly typical of Amsterdam. It was restored after the war and is still in use today. The large library of the Ets Haim seminary is one of the most important Jewish libraries in Europe and contains many priceless works. In summer, the synagogue is open Sunday to Friday from 10 am to 12.30 pm and 1 to 4 pm; the same times apply in winter except that Sunday hours are 10 am to noon only. Admission costs f5 (f2.50 with discounts).

South of the synagogue is the triangular Jonas Daniël Meijerplein, named after the country's first Jewish lawyer (actual name Joune Rintel), who did much to ensure full emancipation of the Jews in the Napoleonic period.

On the square, Mari Andriessen's statue of the **Dockworker** (1952) commemorates the general strike that began among dock-workers on 25 February 1941 to protest the treatment of Jews. The first deportation round-up had occurred here a few days earlier. The anniversary of the strike is still an occasion for wreath-laying but has become a low-key affair with the demise of the Communist Party.

On the south side of the square at JD Meijerplein 2-4, across busy Weesperstraat, is the **Joods Historisch Museum** (☎ 626 99 45), the Jewish Historical Museum, in a beautifully restored complex of four Ash-kenazic synagogues linked by glass-covered walkways. These are the Grote Sjoel (Great Synagogue, 1671), the first public syna-gogue in Western Europe; the Obbene Sjoel (Upstairs Synagogue, 1686); the Dritt Sjoel (Third Synagogue, 1700 with a 19th century façade); and the Neie Sjoel (New Syna-gogue, 1752), the largest in the complex, but still dwarfed by the Portuguese Synagogue across the square.

The Great Synagogue contains religious objects as well as displays showing the rise of Jewish enterprise and its role in the Dutch economy. The New Synagogue focuses on different aspects of Jewish identity and the history of Jews in the Netherlands. There's also a kosher coffee shop serving Jewish

specialities. The complex is open daily (except Yom Kippur and Rosh Hashanah) from 11 am to 5 pm and costs f7 (f3.50 with discounts); entry fees might be a bit higher during special exhibitions. It's a very inter-esting and impressive museum.

The area south-east of here, the 'new' canals (Nieuwe Herengracht, Nieuwe Keizersgracht and Nieuwe Prinsengracht) intersected by the busy Weesperstraat traffic artery, was where the canal-belt project petered out around 1700. The canals on the far side of the Amstel were less in demand among the city's wealthy residents and went to charities or were settled by well-off Jews from the nearby Jewish quarter.

PLANTAGE (Map 14)

In the 19th century, the discovery of dia-monds in South Africa led to a revival of Amsterdam's diamond industry and the Jewish elite began to move into the Plantage (Planta-

tion), where they built imposing town villas. Until then the Plantage had been a district of parks and gardens east of the Jewish quarter and north of the 'new' canals.

In the 18th century, wealthy residents rented parcels of land here to use as gardens, and the area developed into a weekend getaway with tea houses, variety theatres and other establishments where the upper class relaxed and enjoyed themselves in green sur-roundings.

The University of Amsterdam's **Hortus Botanicus** (Botanical Garden, ☎ 625 84 11), Plantage Middenlaan 2A, was estab-lished in 1638 as a herb garden for the city's doctors and moved to the south-west corner of the Plantage in 1682. It became a reposi-tory for tropical seeds and plants, ornamental or otherwise, brought to Amsterdam by the West and East India companies' ships. Com-mercially exploitable plants such as coffee, pineapple, cinnamon and oil palm were dis-tributed from here throughout the world, while the herb garden itself, the so-called Hortus Medicus, won world renown for its research into cures for tropical diseases.

The garden is a must-see for anyone with an interest in botany, not just for its historical significance. The wonderful mixture of colonial and modern structures includes the restored, octagonal seed house; a hypermodern, three-climate glasshouse (1993) with subtropical, tropical and desert plants; a monumental palm house with a 400-year-old cycad, the world's oldest plant in a pot; an orangery with a very pleasant terrace; and of course the Hortus Medicus, the medicinal herb garden that attracts students from around the globe. The garden is open weekdays from 9 am to 5 pm, weekends from 11 am, in winter to 4 pm. Admission costs f7.50 (children f4.50); guided tours on Sunday at 2 pm cost f1.

The complex of buildings in front of the garden includes the Association for Nature & Environmental Education (☎ 622 81 15, Plantage Middenlaan 2C), which organises guided walks and other educational activities; the Nature & Environmental Education Centre (☎ 622 54 04, Plantage Middenlaan 2E), an information centre for environmental and nature education; and MilieuBoek (☎ 624 49 89, Plantage Middenlaan 2H), a fascinating bookshop devoted entirely to nature and the environment.

Several buildings in the area serve as reminders of its Jewish past. The **Nationaal Vakbondsmuseum** (National Trade Union Museum, ☎ 624 11 66) at Henri Polaklaan 9 used to house the powerful General Netherlands Diamond Workers' Union, one of the pioneers of the Dutch labour movement under the chairmanship of Henri Polak. The displays probably won't be of great interest to foreigners but the grandiose building itself is definitely worth a look. The architect HP Berlage designed it as the union's headquarters in 1900 and it soon became known as the 'Burcht van Berlage', Berlage's Fortress – a play on Beurs van Berlage, the bourse along Damrak by the same architect.

Berlage considered it his most successful work and it's easy to see why, from the diamond-shaped pinnacle and the magnificent hall with its brick arches and decorated staircase, to the murals, ceramics and leadlight windows by famous artists of the day. The museum is open Tuesday to Friday from 11 am to 5 pm, weekends from 1 pm, but is closed on public holidays; admission costs f5 (f3 with discounts and for union members).

The **Hollandsche Schouwburg** (Holland Theatre, ☎ 626 99 45) at Plantage Middenlaan 24 played a tragic role during WWII. Originally it was the house of the director of Artis zoo across the road; it became the Artis Schouwburg in 1892 and was soon one of the centres of Dutch theatrical life. In WWII, however, the Germans turned it into a theatre by and for Jews, and from 1942 they made it a detention centre for Jews awaiting deportation. Some 60,000 of them passed through here on their way to Westerbork transit camp in the east of the country and from there to the death camps.

After the war no-one felt like reviving the theatre. In 1961 it was demolished except for the façade and the area immediately behind it. A 10-metre-high pylon in the former auditorium commemorates the country's Jews who were killed by the Germans. There's a memorial room and an exhibition room with videos and documents that display the building's tragic history. It's open daily from 11 am to 4 pm and admission is free.

Diagonally across the road, at Plantage Middenlaan 33, is the brightly coloured **Moederhuis** (Mothers' House), a refuge for young, single women awaiting childbirth. It was completed in 1981 to a design by Aldo van Eyck and incorporates the original 19th century building to the right.

Nearby at Plantage Kerklaan 38-40 is the entrance to **Artis zoo** (Maps 14 & 17; ☎ 623 18 36), founded by an association called Natura Artis Magistra (Latin for 'Nature is the Teacher of Art') back in 1838, which makes it the oldest zoo on the European continent. Famous biologists have studied and worked here among the rich collection of mammals, birds, reptiles, amphibians, insects, fish, trees and plants. Unfortunately some of the cramped enclosures hardly seem to have progressed since the 19th century, but the zoo's layout – with ponds, statues and winding pathways through lush surroundings (remnants of some of the former Plantage gardens) – is very pleasant. Concerts and art exhibitions are also held here to observe the original aim of the association, which was to link nature and art.

A highlight of the zoo is the fascinating aquarium, the oldest in the country (1882) with some 2000 fish; its many exhibits include a cross-section of an Amsterdam canal. There's also a planetarium (Dutch commentary with a summary in English), and zoological and geological museums. The zoo is open daily from 9 am to 5 pm and entry costs f21 (children aged between 4 and 11 pay f13.50). Groups of 20 people or more receive a f2.50 discount but that's it. The fee includes the museums (the hourly shows at the planetarium cost extra). Lower prices are charged in September.

East of the Plantage (Map 7 & 17)
At the eastern end of Plantage Middenlaan, past the Artis aquarium and across the canal, is Alexanderplein with the **Muiderpoort** (Map 17), a grim, Doric city gate dating from 1771. Just north of here, along Sarphatistraat, is the 250-metre façade of the **Oranje-Nassau Kazerne**, barracks built to house the French garrison but only finished in 1814, a year after the French left. They've now been converted to homes, offices and studios. The former drill yard along Singelgracht accommodates a remarkable row of six modern apartment blocks, each designed by an architect from a different country (from the Muiderpoort end: Japan, Greece, France, USA, Denmark, UK).

Just north of here, on Funenkade, stands an 18th century grain mill known as **De Gooyer**, the sole survivor of five windmills that once stood in this part of the city. Originally it stood south-west of here but was moved to its current spot in 1814 when the Oranje-Nassau barracks stopped the wind. In 1985 the former public baths alongside, at Funenkade 7, were converted into **Bier-brouwerij 't IJ** (☎ 622 83 25), a small brewery producing 10 different beers, some seasonal, that can be tasted in the windmill Wednesday to Sunday from 3 to 7.45 pm. There's a tour of the brewery on Fridays at 4 pm.

North-East of the Plantage (Map 14)
When the Plantage was constructed in the 1680s, the original sea dyke was moved north to what are now the Hoogte Kadijk and Laagte Kadijk (the 'high section' and 'low section' of the 'quay dyke'). The stretch of water between the Plantage and this new sea dyke is the **Entrepotdok**, established in the 1820s as a storage zone for goods in transit. The 500-m-long row of warehouses, once the largest storage depot in Europe, has been converted to desirable apartments and studios.

On the outer side of the dyke, at Hoogte Kadijk 147, is **Museumwerf 't Kromhout** (☎ 627 67 77), an 18th century wharf that still repairs boats in its western hall. The eastern hall is now a museum devoted to shipbuilding and the early marine engines that were designed and built here. Anyone with an interest in marine engineering will love the place, others will probably want to move on. It's open Monday to Friday from 10 am to 4 pm and costs f3.50.

EASTERN ISLANDS (Maps 7 & 14)
The rapid expansion of seaborne trade led to the construction of new islands in the east of the harbour in the 1650s: the islands of Kattenburg, Wittenburg and Oostenburg.

The United East India Company set up shop on the eastern island of **Oostenburg**, where it established warehouses, rope yards, workshops and docks for the maintenance of its fleet. Private shipyards and dockworkers' homes dominated the central island of **Wittenburg** – the city architect Daniël Stalpaert's **Oosterkerk** (1671) on Wittenburgergracht was the last, and the least monumental, of the four 'compass churches' (the others were the Noorderkerk, Westerkerk and Zuiderkerk).

Admiralty offices and buildings arose on the western island of **Kattenburg**, and warships were fitted out in the adjoining naval dockyards that are still in use today.

The Republic's naval arsenal was housed in an imposing building at Kattenburgerplein 1, completed in 1656 to a design by Daniël Stalpaert. The admiralty vacated the building in 1973 and since 1981 it has housed the **Nederlands Scheepvaartmuseum** (Netherlands Shipping Museum, ☎ 523 23 11) with one of the most extensive collections of maritime memorabilia in the world.

The museum traces the history of Dutch seafaring from the ancient past to the present. Maritime trade, naval combat, fishing and whaling are all explained in interesting displays, including an engaging audiovisual re-enactment of a trip to the East Indies. Less inviting is the jar with bits of skin and flesh belonging to Lieutenant Jan van Speyk, who chose to blow up his ship rather than surrender to Belgian freedom fighters in the port of Antwerp in 1831. There are some 500 models of boats and ships, as well as a stunning collection of charts and navigational material.

The full-scale replica of the East Indiaman moored alongside the museum was a makework project for the chronically unemployed and was completed in 1991. It represents the United East India Company's 700-tonne *Amsterdam*, one of the largest ships of the fleet, that set sail on its maiden voyage in the winter of 1748-49 with 336 people on board but got stuck off the English coast near Hastings; there it became a famous shipwreck that has been much researched in recent years. Actors in 18th century costume do their best to re-create shipboard life.

If you only visit two or three museums in Amsterdam, make this one of them. It's open Tuesday to Saturday from 10 am to 5 pm, Sunday from noon, and costs f12.50 (f10, f8 or f6.50 with discounts). Admission to the *Amsterdam* is included in the entry fee.

West of this museum, the structure resembling a ship's bow on top of the IJ-Tunnel entrance is the **Impuls Dutch Science Center**, designed by the Italian architect Renzo Piano who also worked on the Centre Pompidou in Paris.

Due to open in the summer of 1997, the centre will house the Technologie Museum NINT, which has grown out of its building in the Pijp district south-east of the canal belt. The NINT is already an interesting museum, and a delight for both children and adults with its many interactive displays, but the Impuls Center promises to be bigger and better still. The terrace should afford a great view over the city centre.

Eastern Docklands

There's a lot of building activity in the eastern docklands north of the Eastern Islands – and a lot of to-ing and fro-ing between urban planners, financiers and council politicians over how to reconcile affordable housing with grandiose projects. North of Kattenburg is the **Oostelijke Handelskade**, where the passenger terminal caters for cruise ships. A bridge will link this area to the **Java Eiland** further north, where new housing estates will enclose sheltered parks.

The eastern third of this island is known as the **KNSM Eiland**, named after the Royal Netherlands Steamship Company that based its ships here in the late-colonial period. It has now been transformed by an enormous housing project with pleasant, hyper-modern and overpriced apartment blocks that charm visiting architects. Opinions are divided but everybody seems to form one – it's worth a look. Some interesting cafés have opened up here too.

The **Open Haven Museum** (Open Harbour Museum, ☎ 620 55 22) at KNSM-laan 311 portrays the history of the harbour with creative use of material from the KNSM collection, and is mainly of interest to people interested in maritime trade and harbours. It's open Wednesday to Friday from 1 to 5 pm, and admission costs f5, or f3.50 with discounts).

19th Century Districts

The canal belt was a far-sighted project that sufficed for two-and-a-half centuries. There was no real pressure to expand beyond the canals until the 1860s, when the industrial revolution began to attract workers back to the city. In 1830 there were 200,000 inhabitants – 20,000 less than in the 18th century, due to Napoleon's disastrous Continental System; in 1860 this had increased to 245,000, in 1880 to 320,000, and in 1900 to over 500,000.

This time the city's expansion was uncoordinated. None of the several grand plans got beyond the proposal stage: private initiative and speculation reigned supreme. De Pijp, between the Amstel and Hobbemakade, was the first area to be added in the 1860s, full of dreary and shoddily built tenement blocks for the city's labourers. Further west came the Vondelpark in the 1860s and 1870s, surrounded by up-market housing. The last two decades of the 19th century were a free-for-all as investors grabbed other land beyond the canal belt and built new residential areas, often with very few restrictions. Oud West around Kinkerstraat is a good example, though you'll have to be quick to see the worst buildings here before they're demolished to make way for modern social housing.

OUD ZUID (OLD SOUTH)

This wedge-shaped district is roughly bordered by the Vondelpark in the west and Hobbemakade in the east. Some people call it the Museum Quarter, Concertgebouw area or Vondelpark area, depending on which of these landmarks is closest. Fortunately it escaped the late 19th century free-for-all. Wealthy investors wanted an up-market area for themselves and saw to it that tenement blocks or businesses were prohibited here – a suitable spot for a grand national museum (the Rijksmuseum) and an equally grand new concert hall (the Concertgebouw).

In a re-run of the canal-belt scenario, the park and cultural centres were financed by the sale of plots of land to the highest bidders, who proceeded to build private mansions close to these attractive landmarks. It wasn't until the early decades of this century, however, that the wealthy class deserted its mansions along Herengracht and Keizersgracht altogether.

In the 1920s, plots further south that remained empty were filled with Amsterdam School-designed apartments commissioned by subsidised housing corporations. Good examples can be seen along **JM Coenenstraat** (Map 15; architect: JF Staal) and in the adjoining **Harmoniehof** (Map 9), featuring the robust designs of JC van Epen.

Museum Quarter (Map 15)

Rijksmuseum The Museum Quarter's gateway – literally, with its pedestrian and bicycle underpass – is the Pierre Cuypers-designed Rijksmuseum (1885). It bears a striking resemblance to Centraal Station, which was designed by the same architect and completed four years later. The style is a mixture of neo-Gothic and Dutch Renaissance. Aspects of the former (towers, stained-glass windows) elicited criticism from Protestants including the king, who dubbed the building 'the archbishop's palace' (Cuypers was Catholic, and proudly so in his approach to architecture).

The Rijksmuseum was conceived as a repository for several national collections, including the royal art collection that was first housed in the palace on Dam square and then in the Trippenhuis on Kloveniersburgwal. It became the country's premier art museum and one that no self-respecting visitor to Amsterdam should miss.

There are some 5000 paintings in 200 rooms, and many other works of art, so it pays to be selective if you don't want to spend days here. Grab the free floor plan when you buy your ticket and home in on the areas that interest you most – there are five major collections but you'll need the floor plan to find your way around them. The museum shop on the 1st floor sells guidebooks that describe the collections in more detail.

The most important collection, Paintings, consists of Dutch and/or Flemish masters from the 15th to 19th centuries, with emphasis on the 17th century Golden Age. Pride of place is taken by Rembrandt's huge *Nightwatch* (1650) in room 224 on the 1st floor, showing the militia led by Frans Banningh Cocq, a future mayor of the city – the painting only acquired this name in later years because it had become dark with grime (it's nice and clean now). Room 211 shows earlier (and more colourful) works by Rembrandt. Other 17th century Dutch masters on this floor include Jan Vermeer *(The Kitchen Maid*, also known as *The Milkmaid*, and *Woman in Blue Reading a Letter)*, Frans Hals *(The Merry Drinker)* and Jan Steen *(The Merry Family)*.

The other collections are Sculpture & Applied Art (delftware, beautiful doll's houses, porcelain, furniture), Dutch History (the Amsterdams Historisch Museum and Nederlands Scheepvaartmuseum do this better), Asiatic Art (including the famous 12th century *Dancing Shiva*), and finally the Print Room, with changing exhibitions that can be surprisingly interesting depending on which of the 800,000 prints and drawings are on display when you visit.

The museum (☎ 673 21 21) is open daily from 10 am to 5 pm and costs f12.50 (f7.50 or f5 with discounts, no student discounts). The main entrance faces the city centre at Stadhouderskade 42. The **garden** at the back (free entry) has flowerbeds, fountains and an amazing, chaotic repository of stone memorabilia: statues, pillars and fragments of demolished buildings and monuments collected from all over the country. It's open Tuesday to Saturday from 10 am to 5 pm, Sunday from 1 pm.

Street musicians perform in the pedestrian and bicycle underpass beneath the museum, their sounds echoing off the cavernous walls.

This passage leads to the large, exposed **Museumplein**, which hosted the World Exhibition in 1883 and has never been given a clear purpose since. Drivers floor their accelerators here and cyclists always seem to battle headwinds. The name is somewhat misleading because none of the museums actually face the square.

Van Gogh Museum The next museum down, with its main entrance at Paulus Potterstraat 7, is the Van Gogh Museum (☎ 570 52 00) designed by Gerrit Rietveld. It opened in 1973 to house the collection of Vincent's younger brother Theo, which consists of about 200 paintings and 500 drawings by Vincent and his friends or contemporaries, such as Gauguin, Toulouse-Lautrec, Monet and Bernard.

Van Gogh (pronounced 'khokh', rhymes with Scottish 'loch') was born in 1853 and had a short but very productive life. He didn't begin painting until 1881 and produced most of his works in the four years he spent in France, where he committed suicide to escape mental illness in 1890 (he had already cut off his own ear after an argument with Gauguin). Famous works on display include *The Potato Eaters* (1885), a prime example of his sombre Dutch period, and *The Yellow House in Arles* (1888), *The Bedroom at Arles* (1888) and several self-portraits, sunflowers and other blossoms that show his vivid use of colour in the intense Mediterranean light. One of his last paintings, *Wheatfield with Crows* (1890), is an ominous work foreshadowing his suicide.

His paintings are on the 1st floor; the other floors display his drawings and Japanese prints as well as works by friends and contemporaries, some of which are shown in rotation. The museum is open daily from 10 am to 5 pm and costs f12.50 (f6.25 or f5 with discounts). The library, with a wealth of reference material for serious study, is open Monday to Friday from 10 am to 12.30 pm and 1.15 to 5 pm.

Stedelijk Museum Next to the Van Gogh Museum is the Stedelijk Museum at Paulus

AMSTERDAMS HISTORISCH MUSEUM

Foeliedwarsstraat, an average sort of street in the Jewish quarter, painted by Alexander Hilverdink in 1889.

ROB VAN DRIESUM

RICHARD NEBESKY

RICHARD NEBESKY

TONY WHEELER

Top Left: Main entrance to the Oostindisch Huis
Top Right: Corner tower on the Scheepvaarthuis
Bottom Left: Façade of Magna Plaza
Bottom Right: Begijnhof 34 - the oldest maintained wooden house in the country (1465)

TONY WHEELER

RICHARD NEBESKY

RICHARD NEBESKY

DOEKES LULOFS

DOEKES LULOFS

DOEKES LULOFS

A	B
C	D
E	F

A: Step gable in the medieval centre
B: Row of gables along Damrak
C: Top-floor detail of the Scheepvaarthuis

D: The 'Gnome House'
E: Brickwork in 'The Ship'
F: Bridge decoration, Amsterdam School-style

ROB VAN DRIESUM

ROB VAN DRIESUM

RICHARD NEBESKY

RICHARD NEBESKY

Top Left: Hand touching a breast in the pavement in front of the Oude Kerk
Top Right: Eagle gable on Reguliersgracht 34
Bottom Left: One of the Begijnhof gates
Bottom Right: Old and new along the Rokin

Potterstraat 13, the City Museum that focuses on modern art – paintings, sculptures, photography and anything else that qualifies – from 1850 to the present. It's one of the world's leading museums of modern art, though this wasn't always the case: when the Dutch-Renaissance building opened its doors in 1895 it housed the private collection of art patroness Sophia de Bruijn, mainly bric-a-brac that was thrown out in subsequent years. Before WWII it evolved into the national museum of modern art, and under the driving force of its postwar curator, Willem Sandberg, it amassed the eclectic collection you can enjoy today. The glass wing on Van Baerlestraat was added in 1954.

There are works by Monet, Van Gogh, Cézanne, Matisse, Picasso, Kirchner and Chagall as well as other modern 'classics', including a unique collection of some 50 works by the Russian artist Malevich. There are abstract works by Mondriaan, Van Doesburg and Kandinsky, and a large, post-WWII selection of creations by Appel, De Kooning, Newman, Ryman, Judd, Warhol, Dibbets, Gilbert & George, Baselitz, Dubuffet, Lichtenstein, Polke, Rietveld's furniture, and not to forget Kienholz's *The Beanery* in the basement, a reconstruction of a Los Angeles bar. Sculptures, some of which are displayed in the sculpture garden overlooked by the pleasant café-restaurant, include works by Rodin, Renoir, Moore, Laurens and Visser.

The museum (☎ 573 29 11) displays most of its permanent collection in the summer months; at other times of the year many of the works make way for changing exhibitions. It's open daily from 11 am to 5 pm (to 7 pm in summer) and costs f8 (f4 with discounts); special exhibitions might cost extra. Phone for lectures and art-history courses.

Concertgebouw (Map 15)

The Concert Building at the end of Museumplein, at Concertgebouwplein 2-6, was completed in 1888 to a neo-Renaissance design by AL van Gendt. In spite of his limited musical knowledge, he managed to give the Grote Zaal (Great Hall) near-perfect acoustics that are still the envy of concert-hall designers worldwide.

The Concertgebouw attracts some 800,000 visitors a year, making it the busiest concert hall in the world. The best conductors and soloists consider it an honour to perform here – a far cry from the 1870s, when Brahms tried to knock the musicians in the Felix Meritis building into shape and had to admit they were lovely people but lousy musicians. Under the 50-year guidance of composer and conductor Willem Mengelberg (1871-1951), the Concertgebouw Orchestra (with the epithet 'Royal' since 1988) developed into one of the world's finest orchestras.

In the 1980s the Concertgebouw threatened to collapse because its 2000 wooden piles were rotting. Thanks to new technology the piles made way for a concrete foundation, and the building was thoroughly restored to mark its 100th anniversary. The architect Pi de Bruin added a glass foyer along the south side that most people hate though everyone agrees it's effective.

The Grote Zaal seats 2000 people and is used for concerts. Recitals take place in the 19x15 metre Kleine Zaal (Small Hall), a replica of the hall in the Felix Meritis building. Tickets are available on ☎ 671 83 45 daily between 10 am and 5 pm, or at the door till 7 pm (after 7 pm you can only get tickets for that evening's performance). The VVV and Amsterdam Uitburo (see Tourist Offices in the Facts for the Visitor chapter) also sell tickets. For free lunchtime concerts, turn up Wednesdays at 12.30 pm.

Vondelpark & Surroundings (Maps 8 & 15)

This English-style park, with ponds, lawns, thickets and winding footpaths, is about 1.5km long and 300 metres wide. Laid out on marshland beyond the canal belt in the 1860s and 1870s as a park for the bourgeoisie when the existing city park, the Plantage, became residential, it was soon surrounded by up-market housing. It's named after the poet and playwright Joost van den Vondel

(1587-1679), the 'Shakespeare' of the Netherlands.

In the late 1960s and early 1970s the authorities turned the park into an open-air dormitory to alleviate the lack of accommodation for hordes of hippies who descended on Amsterdam. The sleeping bags have long since gone and it's now illegal to sleep in the park, but there's still plenty of evidence of Italian, French and Eastern European tourists stuck in the '70s.

The park is now used by joggers, children chasing ducks or flying kites, couples in love, families with prams, acrobats practising or performing, teenagers playing soccer – in short, by anybody who enjoys very pleasant, green surroundings. It can get crowded on weekends but never annoyingly so. In summer the park hosts free concerts in its **open-air theatre** (☎ 523 77 90 for information), an experience not to be missed, and there are always people performing music throughout the park. The functionalist **Round Blue Teahouse** (1936) serves coffee with cake.

At Vondelpark 3, close to Constantijn Huygensstraat, is the former Vondelpark Pavilion (1881), now home to the **Nederlands Filmmuseum** (☎ 589 14 00). The museum has a large collection of memorabilia and a priceless archive of films that are screened in two theatres, often with live music and other accompaniments. One theatre contains the Art Deco interior of Cinema Parisien, an early Amsterdam cinema. The museum is open daily from 10 am to 5 pm and entry is free though there's a charge for film screenings. The museum's charming *Café Vertigo* (☎ 612 30 21) is a popular meeting place, and an ideal spot to spend a couple of hours watching the goings-on in the park; on summer evenings there are films on the outdoor terrace.

The impressive library and study centre adjoining the museum at Vondelstraat 69-71 is open Tuesday to Friday from 10 am to 5 pm, Saturday from 11 am. In 1980, the house at Vondelstraat 72, along with the intersection with Constantijn Huygensstraat, were the scene of one of the most dramatic episodes in the history of the squatter movement – see History in the Facts about Amsterdam chapter.

Also in Vondelstraat near the Filmmuseum is the **Vondelkerk** (1880), built to a design by Pierre Cuypers, which now accommodates offices. A few steps down the road at Vondelstraat 140 is the neoclassical **Hollandse Manege** (1882) designed by AL van Gendt, an indoor riding school inspired by the famous Spanish Riding School in Vienna. The building was fully restored in the 1980s, and it's worth walking through the passage to the door at the rear and up the stairs to the café, where you can sip a cheap beer or coffee while enjoying the beautiful interior and watching the instructor put the horses through their paces. The school should be open daily but times vary – ring ☎ 618 09 42 to avoid disappointment.

Beyond the opposite side of the park is narrow, 19th century **PC Hooftstraat**, a shopping street for the cream of society and the nouveau riche (as the parked Ferraris and Daimlers will verify).

Beyond the south-eastern extremities of the park, at Amstelveenseweg just north of the Olympic Stadium, is the former Haarlemmermeer Station. Between this station and Station Amstelveen, the **Tram Museum Amsterdam** (☎ 673 75 38), Amstelveenseweg 264, runs historic trams sourced from all over Europe – a great outing for kids and adults. A return trip (f5, or f2.50 with discounts) takes about an hour and skirts the large Amsterdamse Bos recreational area. Services operate between April and October – contact the museum for a schedule.

DE PIJP (Maps 9 & 16)

This district is enclosed by the Amstel in the east, Stadhouderskade in the north, Hobbemakade in the west and the Amstelkanaal in the south – it's actually a large island connected to the rest

of the city by 16 bridges. The district's name, 'the Pipe' (originally the 'YY neighbourhood'), presumably reflects its straight, narrow streets that are said to resemble the stems of old clay pipes, but nobody really knows. There are a surprising number of attractions for an area that has so often been derided as the city's first 19th century slum.

Its shoddy tenement blocks, some of which collapsed even as they were being built in the 1860s, provided cheap housing not just for newly arrived workers drawn by the city's industrial revolution, but also for students, artists, writers and other poverty-stricken individuals. In the 1960s and 1970s, as many of the working-class inhabitants left for greener pastures, the government started refurbishing the tenement blocks that began to attract a new wave of immigrants from Morocco, Turkey, the Netherlands Antilles and Suriname. In the past as now, the Pijp has often been called the 'Quartier Latin' of Amsterdam thanks to its lively mix of people – labourers, intellectuals, new immigrants and prostitutes (in the city's alternative and very depressing red-light district along Ruysdaelkade opposite Hobbemakade).

This interesting array is best viewed at the **Albert Cuyp market**, Amsterdam's largest and busiest market, Monday to Saturday along Albert Cuypstraat. The emphasis is on food of every description and nationality but clothes and other general goods are on sale too, often cheaper than anywhere else. If you want to experience the 'real' Amsterdam at its multicultural best, this market is not to be missed. As always at busy markets, beware of pickpockets.

The surrounding streets hide a large number of neighbourhood cafés, along with small (and usually very cheap) restaurants that offer a wide range of cuisines.

Many tourists head for the **Heineken Museum** (☎ 523 94 36) at Stadhouderskade 78, still commonly known as the Heineken Brewery. Tours of the former brewery complex are offered at 9.30 and 11 am weekdays all year, and in mid-summer extra tours are laid on at 1 and 2 pm. A token f2 donation to charity is collected at the door. The visit

Taste it at the Heineken Museum.

ends with a beer 'tasting' session at which up to six glasses per person may be consumed (they aren't stingy), and the green Heineken baseball caps sold at the exit for f7.50 make great souvenirs.

The brewery closed in 1986 due to inner-city congestion and since then the building has been used only for the tours and administration (the company's head office is still here). Heineken beer is presently brewed at a larger plant in 's-Hertogenbosch (Den Bosch) in the south of the country that opened in 1950. In 1975 the company also constructed what it claims is the largest brewery in Europe at Zoeterwoude near Leiden. The Heineken tours are a great favourite among beer-swilling backpackers who often come several times during their stay. If you can prove it's your birthday you get a free beer mug.

South of Albert Cuypstraat is the **Sarphatipark**, an English-style park named after the energetic 19th century Jewish doctor and chemist Samuel Sarphati (1813-66). His diverse projects (a waste-disposal service, a slaughterhouse, a factory for cheap bread, trades and business schools, the

Amstel Hotel, a mortgage bank) exasperated the dour city council, though many of them still operate to this day.

The street along the south side of the park is Ceintuurbaan, a traffic artery that holds little of interest except the so-called **Kabouterhuis** (Gnome House), near the Amstel at No 251-255. Its whimsical woodwork façade incorporates a couple of gnomes playing ball, a reference to the surname of the original owner, Van Ballegooijen ('of ball-throwing').

South of here, at Amsteldijk 67, is the neo-Renaissance **Gemeentearchief** (☎ 572 02 02), the Municipal Archives housed in the former town hall of Nieuwer Amstel, a town annexed by Amsterdam during the late 19th century expansion. Anyone interested in their family history or the history of the city can peruse the archives free of charge, and occasionally there are surprisingly interesting exhibitions. Nearby, at Tolstraat 129, is the Technologie Museum NINT, which has probably moved to the Impuls Dutch Science Center atop the IJ-Tunnel entrance by the time you read this (see the earlier Eastern Islands section).

South of Ceintuurbaan, the Pijp has some of the most interesting examples of early 20th century housing estates built in Amsterdam School style.

The imposing **Cooperatiehof**, surrounded by Burgemeester Tellegenstraat, was designed for the socialist housing corporation De Dageraad (The Dawn) by one of the main Amsterdam School architects, Piet Kramer. Another leading architect, Michel de Klerk, designed the idiosyncratic housing estates at Henriëtte Ronnerplein and Thérèse Schwartzeplein. As with other architecture of this school, the eccentric details are worth noting: vertically laid bricks, letterboxes as works of art, asymmetric windows, oddly shaped doorways, funny chimneys, creative solutions for corners etc.

OOSTERPARK DISTRICT (Map 17)

This south-eastern district, named after the lush, English-style park at its centre, was built in the 1880s. At the time, the city's diamond

workers suddenly found themselves with money to spare thanks to the discovery of diamonds in South Africa. About a third of Jewish families worked in the diamond industry in one way or another, and many of these could finally afford to leave the Jewish quarter for this new district beyond the Plantage (the delectable parklands where only the wealthiest could afford to live). Signs of this district's lower middle-class heritage have long since disappeared and now it's depressingly similar to the other 19th century slums that arose around the canal belt.

The only exception, apart from the park, is the **Tropenmuseum** (☎ 568 82 00) at Linnaeusstraat 2, an impressive complex completed in 1926 to house the Royal Institute of the Tropics, still one of the world's leading research institutes for tropical hygiene and agriculture. Part of the building became a museum for the institute's collection of colonial artefacts, but this was overhauled in the 1970s to create the culturally aware and imaginatively presented displays you see today.

A huge central hall with galleries over three floors offers reconstructions of daily life in several tropical countries (a north African street, Javanese house, Indian village, African market etc). Separate exhibitions focus on music, theatre, religion, crafts, world trade and ecology, and there are special exhibitions throughout the year. Expert guides introduce children to tropical cultures in the separate children's section (☎ 568 83 00) reserved for six to 12-year-olds – book ahead, especially if you want your kids entertained in English. There's an extensive library, a shop selling books and gifts, a pleasant café, a restaurant serving Third World cuisine, and the Soeterijntheater, a theatre that screens films but also hosts music, dance, plays and other performances by visiting artists.

The museum itself is open Monday to Friday from 10 am to 5 pm, weekends from noon, and costs f10 (f5 or f2.50 with discounts). It's a good place to spend a lazy Monday when most of the other museums are closed. There's a useful notice board for travellers, with lift shares, people looking for travel partners etc. The theatre has a separate entrance – ring ☎ 568 85 00 for information and bookings (Monday to Friday between 10 am and 4 pm). The library (☎ 568 82 54) is open Monday to Friday from 10 am to 4.30 pm, Sunday from noon.

Greater Amsterdam

The city's population stabilised at around 700,000 by 1920, which is still the figure today. Of course, the authorities didn't foresee this at the time and cautiously expected 950,000 by the year 2000. Despite a slight pause during the Depression and WWII, the city kept gobbling up one outlying town after another as increased mobility fuelled urban sprawl.

NIEUW ZUID (NEW SOUTH)
(Maps 8 & 9)

The Housing Act of 1901 set minimum standards for new houses and enabled the compulsory purchase and demolition of old houses that didn't meet these standards. It also forced municipal authorities to come up with proper blueprints for city expansion. One such plan was the Plan Zuid of 1917 for the south of the city, drawn up by the progressive architect Berlage and instigated by the labour party alderman FM Wibaut.

The result was Nieuw Zuid, between the Amstel and what was to become the Olympic Stadium. Not since the canal-belt project had urban planners, architects and municipal authorities worked together so closely, successfully integrating solid housing and wide boulevards that enclosed quiet neighbourhoods with cosy squares. There was even a canal linking the Amstel in the east with the Schinkel in the west: the Amstelkanaal that split in two about halfway along and rejoined again behind the Olympic Stadium. Subsidised housing corporations provided funding for innovative designs by architects of the Amsterdam School; many of these architects worked for the city housing department, and the council preferred their designs to the functionalist designs of Berlage himself.

Funding cutbacks in the 1930s meant that these architects couldn't be as creative as they had been in their earlier designs, but even today the area is as elegant as it was then. Streets such as Churchillaan, Apollolaan and Stadionweg are 'good' addresses. The area's main shopping street, Beethovenstraat, is lined with expensive shops and other establishments for elderly women in fur coats.

Among the first residents were Jewish refugees from Germany and Austria, many of them writers and artists, who settled around Beethovenstraat. The Frank family lived at Merwedeplein further to the east, where Churchillaan and Rooseveltlaan merge around the **'Skyscraper'** (1930), a 12-storey building with spacious luxury apartments designed by JF Staal.

Nearby, in a former synagogue at Lekstraat 63, the **Verzetsmuseum** (Resistance Museum, ☎ 644 97 97) provides an excellent insight into the difficulties faced by those who fought the German occupation on the home front. A booklet in English helps with the exhibits, many of them interactive, that explain such issues as active and passive resistance, how the illegal press operated, how 300,000 people were kept in hiding, and how such activities were funded (a less glamorous but vital detail). The museum shows in no uncertain terms how much courage it takes to actively resist an adversary so ruthless that you can't trust neighbours, friends or even family. It's open Tuesday to Friday from 10 am to 5 pm, weekends from 1 pm, and costs f5 (f2.50 with discounts). There's also a library.

South-west of here is the **RAI** exhibition and conference centre (☎ 549 12 12; fax 646 44 69) at Europaplein 8, the largest such complex in the country. It opened in the early 1960s and new halls are still being added. There's always some sort of exhibition or trade fair going on: cars, two-wheelers, boats, camping gear – ring to find out. The name comes from the regular exhibitions hosted earlier this century by the Rijwiel & Automobiel Industrie (Bicycle & Car Industry).

AMSTELVEEN (Maps 8 & 9)

This suburb south of Amsterdam has a long history. In the 12th century it was a moor drained by the Amstel (*veen* means peat). Local farmers built canals to drain the land for agriculture, thus turning the Amstel into a clearly defined river. As the soil along the Amstel compacted, the farming community moved further west, which is why the west bank of the Amstel at this latitude is relatively uninhabited today. There's not much to draw you to Amstelveen, but a couple of attractions are worth considering.

First there's the **Amsteldamse Bos** (Amsterdam Woods), a large recreational area built as a work-creation project in the 1930s. Amsterdammers flock here on weekends but it's so huge (940 hectares) that it never gets too crowded. It's open 24 hours a day free of charge, and its only drawback is that it's close to Schiphol and there can be a lot of noise from low-flying aircraft. A bus (No 70) does a circuit through the area.

The visitor's centre (☎ 643 14 14) is at Nieuwe Kalfjeslaan 4 and is open daily from 10 am to 5 pm. There are lakes, wooded areas and meadows, an animal enclosure with bison, a goat farm, paths for walking, cycling

and horse-riding (ask the visitor's centre about hiring bikes and horses), a rowing course (the Bosbaan, with several water craft for hire), an open-air theatre (☎ 638 38 47) with plays in summer, a sport park, a pancake house, a forestry museum (☎ 645 45 75, open daily from 10 am to 5 pm, free admission; displays about the construction and flora & fauna of the area) and much more. You can get here by historic tram from the Haarlemmermeer Station (see the earlier Vondelpark & Surroundings section) or with bus No 170, 171 or 172 from Centraal Station.

The other main attraction is the **CoBrA Museum** (☎ 547 50 50), Sandbergplein 1-3 just north of the A9 freeway's Amstelveen exit (bus No 170, 171 or 172 from Centraal Station). The CoBrA artistic movement was formed in the postwar years by artists (mainly painters) from Denmark, Belgium and the Netherlands – the name consists of the first letters of their respective capital cities. Members included Asger Jorn, Corneille, Constant and the great Karel Appel. The Stedelijk Museum has a good collection of their work but this museum in Amstelveen is the treasure trove. It's open Tuesday to Sunday from 11 am to 5 pm and costs f5 (f3.50 or f2.50 with discounts). From Centraal Station, take bus No 170, 171 or 172, or tram No 5 or 51; from the Bijlmer, it's bus No 174.

AMSTERDAM NOORD (Map 6)

In the dim, dark past, the area across the IJ now known as Amsterdam North was marshland with shifting contours. Roman sentries may have stared at it and glimpsed the barbarians outside their empire. Several hundred years ago its tip was known as Volewyck, a place where executed criminals were left to be devoured by crows and dogs. Few people actually lived here.

As ships became larger and the sandbanks in the IJ posed more of a problem, engineers built an 80-km canal, the Noordhollands Kanaal (North Holland Canal), from Volewyck right up to Den Helder in the northern tip of Holland. It opened in 1824 but by 1876 was replaced by the more efficient Noordzeekanaal (North Sea Canal) west to IJmuiden. The area wasn't properly colonised until the turn of this century, and the opening of the IJ-Tunnel in 1968 finally established a fixed connection.

These days Amsterdam Noord is a predominantly working-class area offering glimpses of authentic Dutch life away from the tourists in the old town. Forget about it if you're pressed for time, but otherwise it's worth spending half a day exploring the older parts of the area.

Take the free pedestrian ferry marked 'Buiksloterwegveer' (between Pier 8 and Pier 9) from behind Centraal Station across the IJ to the Shell Oil installations at Buiksloterweg, where you'll disembark next to the **Noordhollands Kanaal**. Climb up onto the first lock, the Willemsluis near the ferry wharf, for the view. Return to the main street and walk north 10 minutes on Van der Pekstraat. Ahead you'll eventually see the massive **Galaxy Hotel**, formerly Amsterdam Noord's general hospital. Today it's used mostly by European tourists on bus tours. The hotel's gift shop (open daily from 7 to 10.30 am and 5.30 to 10 pm) has a good selection of cheap souvenirs and the latest British and American newspapers.

A passageway to the right of the hotel leads into **Mosveld** where a large public market is held on Wednesday, Friday and Saturday (the best days to do this walk). The market is used almost exclusively by local residents and seldom sees any tourists. Facing the war memorial on the market square is *Café de Bult* (☎ 637 10 08), a pleasant place for a coffee or a beer and the food is good too; Saturday afternoons around 6 pm there's live music and locals in their late 20s and 30s come to dance and have fun. Next door is *Grillroom Max*, which has coffee for f1 till 4 pm – unless you ask first

they'll say this price only applies on certain days and charge you f2. In the underpass next to Max is a snack bar serving quite good Flemish fries.

The best place to eat in these parts, however, is the *Tong Chow Chinees Indonesisch Restaurant* (☎ 636 08 54), Kamperfoelieweg 7, on the left about a block and a half straight ahead beyond a supermarket called Super. Be aware that the menu posted in the window outside is the take-away menu and the regular restaurant menu is slightly more expensive, although two people can still eat here with drinks for around f35 (at least a third less than the same meal would cost in central Amsterdam).

To return to central Amsterdam, catch bus No 34 or 35 from the stop next to the large **Egyptian Coptic Church** (the only one in Holland) on Mosplein, diagonally opposite Super. These buses go through the IJ-Tunnel straight back to Centraal Station.

If you have a bit more time, take any street east to the Noordhollands Kanaal, which you follow north through **Florapark**. You'll pass a public swimming pool and reach a small bridge which crosses another lock on the canal. The old road on both sides of this bridge is lined with picturesque little Dutch cottages. Don't cross the canal but continue north along its west bank and you'll come to a large windmill, the **Krijtmolen**, originally used to grind chalk, with a children's animal park alongside (free). Just north of here is Amsterdam Noord's massive new public hospital where you can catch bus No 34 back to town. This interesting walk could easily fill a morning or afternoon.

'GARDEN CITIES'

The outer suburbs west of Amsterdam – **Geuzenveld**, **Bos en Lommer**, **Slotermeer**, **Osdorp** and **Slotervaart** – were planned in the 1930s as part of the city's grand General Extension Plan and were

fully established after WWII to meet the continued demand for housing, made ever more acute by the demographic shift away from extended families. These spacious new estates, known as 'garden cities' *(tuinsteden)*, with carefully planned traffic systems, lakes, sporting fields, greenery and abundant natural light, represented the latest thinking in suburban living but they seem rather dreary and windswept today.

Similar concepts dominated the massive Bijlmermeer housing project south-east of the city, now simply called the **Bijlmer**. The huge apartment blocks, laid out in a honeycomb pattern around artificial parks, were considered most progressive when the foundations were laid in the mid-1960s. By the time they were finished in the early 1970s, however, most people with a choice in the matter avoided such an environment and the area was doomed to become an instant slum, inhabited by Creole immigrants from the Netherlands Antilles, black immigrants from newly independent Suriname, and anyone else who didn't have the money to live elsewhere.

In October 1992 the Bijlmer made world headlines when an El Al freighter jumbo crashed into one of the apartment complexes after take-off from Schiphol, just as the residents were settling in to their evening dinner. Officially 45 people died in the inferno but the figure was probably higher, despite the subsequent amnesty on illegal immigrants.

Walking Tours

Amsterdam is tailor-made for walking. You could simply follow your nose or, if a particular area takes your fancy, you could explore it following the text in this chapter.

Alternatively, you could follow one or more of the official VVV walks designed by the ANWB (the Dutch automobile association) that are indicated on the maps in the back of this book and on occasional public maps at points en route. They take you through the most interesting parts of the city, though by necessity they do bypass some of the sights (make your own detours). Obviously they can be walked in either direction and you can combine them or jump from one to the other:

Red route – probably gives the best overview of some of the most attractive areas. Starts at Centraal Station and goes along Nieuwendijk, the Dam, Kalverstraat, Spui square (Begijnhof), Leidsestraat, Leidseplein, and finally Museumplein, ending at the Concertgebouw. You could return via the Grey route

Blue route – a bit of a west-east marathon. Starts at the Westerkerk (Anne Frankhuis) and heads into the city along Raadhuisstraat; passes Dam square and continues east through the red-light district; on to Jodenbreestraat and the Jewish quarter; up towards the old harbour area north-east of the Plantage and on to the Tropenmuseum

Green route – shorter alternative to the Blue route. Starts at Centraal Station and follows the Zeedijk to Nieuwmarkt square (detour for the red-light district), through the Jewish quarter and then the Plantage before ending at the Tropenmuseum. In reverse order, it could be tacked on to the Blue route to make a full day trip

Grey route – combines the old medieval centre with glimpses of authentic daily life just south of the canal belt; starts at Centraal Station and goes down Damrak and Rokin to Rembrandtplein; along beautiful Reguliersgracht; then past the Heineken Museum to the Albert Cuyp market (multicultural Amsterdam at its best); and on to the Concertgebouw (detour southwards to Harmoniehof for Amsterdam School architecture); could return via the Red route

Purple route – starts at either the ship-passenger terminal or Centraal Station and goes past the IJ-Tunnel entrance (Impuls Dutch Science Center) to Waterlooplein; then on to Rembrandtplein and Muntplein, and through Nieuwe Spiegelstraat (antiques) to Leidseplein; return via the Brown route or latch on to the Red route

Brown route – goes past and through the Jordaan area (make your own detours), starting at Centraal Station and ending at Leidseplein

Activities

Soccer, ice skating, cycling, tennis, swimming and sailing are just a few activities that keep the locals fit – and of course jogging, of which there's a lot in the Vondelpark and other parks. The Amsterdamse Bos has several walking and jogging trails for serious exercise. Het Twiske, near Landsmeer north of Amsterdam (bus No 91 or 92 from Centraal Station), is another recreational area with nature trails, cycle routes, rentals of water craft, beaches and a children's swimming pool and playground; for information, ring Info-centrum Het Twiske on ☎ 075-684 43 38.

The whole coast of Holland, from the Hook of Holland right up to Den Helder, is one long beach, backed by often picturesque dunes that are ideal for walks. The closest seaside resort is Zandvoort (see the Excursions chapter) which can get packed in summer (forget about parking then – take the train), but more pleasant resorts can be found further north, such as Castricum north of IJmuiden, or Egmond and Bergen a bit further north near Alkmaar.

For information about sport and leisure activities and venues, visit the city hall information centre (☎ 624 11 11) at Amstel 1 in the arcade between the Stopera and the city hall, or ring the Amsterdam Sport Council on ☎ 552 24 90. Local community centres (consult the phone book under *Buurtcentrum*) organise fitness courses.

See Spectator Sports in the Entertainment chapter for details about soccer, field hockey or the Dutch sport of korfball.

FITNESS CENTRES

These are listed in the pink pages of the phone book under *Fitnesscentra*. To pump iron, head for *Barry's Health Centre* (☎ 626 10 36), Utrechtsedwarsstraat 25, though the loud disco music might not be to everyone's taste. A day card is f17.50 and a monthly pass is f95. For aerobics and feel-good activities, including sauna, massage, physiotherapy and dietary advice, try *The Garden Gym* (☎ 626 87 72), Jodenbreestraat 158. A one-day pass ranges from f15 to f22.50, a monthly pass costs f115.

New Age

Oibibio (Map 13; ☎ 553 93 55) at Prins Hendrikkade 20-21, near Centraal Station opposite Hotel Ibis, is a New-Age activities centre offering esoteric reflection in a high-tech mould. Downstairs is a grand café, tea garden, specialist bookstore and ditto supermarket, upstairs are several therapeutic centres (yoga etc), and on the top floor is a sauna. There's also a vegetarian restaurant overlooking the café. The Oibibio Passage leads into the same complex from Nieuwendijk 25. It's definitely worth a visit, even if you don't consider yourself a New-Age type.

Sauna

Saunas are mixed and there's no prudish swimsuit nonsense, though they do cater for people who have a problem with this – ask.

Deco (Map 12; ☎ 623 82 15), Herengracht 115, is a respectable, elegant sauna with good facilities including a snack bar. The building itself is an early creation of the architect HP Berlage and its Art-Deco furnishings used to grace a Parisian department store. It's open Monday to Saturday from 11 am to 11 pm, Sunday from 1 to 6 pm. There's a reduced admission of f17.50 weekdays from 11 am to 2 pm, at other times it's f25. You can also have massages and beauty therapies.

In the *Oibibio* complex (see New Age above), the top-floor sauna (☎ 553 93 11) costs f22 to use before 5 pm, f25 thereafter. The rickety, antique elevator is an experience in itself. After your sauna, relax in a hammock on the huge roof terrace and enjoy the splendid view.

The *Eastern Bath House/Hammam* (☎ 681 48 18), Zaanstraat 88 in the northwest beyond the Haarlemmerpoort, is a Turkish bath house for women only.

Gay *Mandate* (Map 15; ☎ 625 41 00), Prinsengracht 715, is a beautiful 18th century canal house with a very modern, gay-only sport school and sauna; it's open weekdays from 11 am to 10 pm, Saturday from noon to 6 pm and Sunday from 2 to 6 pm. The large *Thermos Day Sauna* (Maps 12 & 15; ☎ 623 91 58), Raamstraat 33, is a popular place for sexual contacts, with porn movies and private (or not so private) areas; it's open weekdays from noon to 11 pm, weekends to 6 pm, and admission costs f25. The *Thermos Night Sauna* (Map 15; ☎ 623 49 36), Kerkstraat 58-60, is similar to the day sauna except there's no restaurant; admission also costs f25 and it's open from 11 pm to 8 am.

SWIMMING POOLS

There are indoor pools and, only in summer, outdoor pools. Admission at municipal pools is f4.25 for adults, f3.75 for children. Within the next few years these pools will be privatised, probably resulting in admissions being increased and hours reduced. This will save the city money (the system is presently highly subsidised) but there will be a social price to pay.

It's always best to ring ahead to ensure the pool is open to the general public (English is almost always spoken) because some pools have restricted sessions – nude, Muslim, children, seniors, clubs, swimming lengths etc. Of course that might just be what you're after, but bear in mind that schedules for these sorts of sessions change constantly.

Flevoparkbad, Zeeburgerdijk 630 east of the city centre (Map 7; ☎ 692 50 30) – outdoor pool only; open May to September from 10 am to 5.30 pm

Zuiderbad, Hobbemakade 26 near the Rijksmuseum (Map 15; ☎ 671 02 87) – indoor pool only; worth going for a swim just to admire the beautiful early 20th century architecture; open weekdays from 7 am to 10 pm, Saturday from 10.30 am to 4 pm, Sunday from 10.30 am to 2 pm; definitely ring ahead to avoid (or catch) the restricted sessions

Brediusbad, Spaarndammerdijk 306, north-west of the city centre (☎ 682 91 16) – outdoor pool only; open May to September from 10 am to 5 pm

Marnixbad, Marnixplein 5-9 at the western end of Westerstraat (Map 12; ☎ 625 48 43) – indoor pool only, closed in July and August

Jan van Galenbad, Jan van Galenstraat 315 west of the city centre (☎ 612 80 01) – outdoor pool only, open mid-May to August

Sloterparkbad, Slotermeerlaan 2 in the western suburbs next to the terminus of tram No 14 (☎ 613 37 00) – in an attractive recreational area with yacht harbour etc; both indoor and outdoor pools (on cold, rainy days in summer the indoor pool will also be open); outdoor pools can get overcrowded but there's a less frequented nudist

island reached by walking straight back past the pools and across a causeway

De Mirandabad, De Mirandalaan 9 south of the city centre (Map 9; ☎ 644 66 37) – tropical 'aquatic centre' complete with beach and wave machine; indoor and outdoor pools, though many of the outdoor facilities will disappear after renovations in 1997; open all year

Bijlmersportcentrum, Bijlmerpark 76, Bijlmer (☎ 697 31 44) – indoor and outdoor pools; open all year except public holidays

Floraparkbad, Sneeuwbalweg 5, Amsterdam Noord (☎ 636 81 21, recording in Dutch) – indoor and outdoor pools; open all year

SAILING

The Dutch are avid sailors – windsurfing in particular is a national sport. *Watersportschool De Duikelaar* at Jachthaven Sloterplas (☎ 613 88 55), Noordzijde 41 at the Sloterplas in the western suburb of Slotervaart (*plas* is one of the words for lake), rents sailboards for f17.50 per hour. You can rent other water craft or go swimming in the above-mentioned Sloterparkbad.

On the weekends a fleet of restored flat-bottomed boats, called the 'brown fleet' because of their (reddish) brown sails, crisscross the watery expanse of the IJsselmeer. Some are privately owned but many are rented, and sailing one is an unforgettable experience. The cheapest options are *botters*, former fishing boats with long, narrow leeboards and sleeping space (usually for a maximum of eight people) below deck. Larger groups could rent a converted freight barge known as a *tjalk*, originally with jib and spritsail rig though modern designs are made of steel and have diesel motors. Other vessels include anything from ancient pilot boats to massive clippers.

Costs are quite reasonable if you can muster a group of fellow enthusiasts. The usual weekend arrangement is that you arrive at the boat Friday at 8 pm, sleep on board, sail out early the next morning, and visit several places around the IJsselmeer before returning on Sunday between 4 and 6 pm. Food is not included in the packages, nor is cancellation insurance (trips are cancelled if wind is stronger than 7 Beaufort).

A botter in all its glory.

Contact the following companies to find the deal that suits you best:

Hollands Glorie Amsterdam, Oostelijke Handelskade 1 east of Centraal Station (☎ 694 94 93; fax 693 49 23) – weekend trips from 8 pm Friday to 4 pm Sunday; in the high season (May to September) a botter costs f1400 (maximum eight people), a tjalk f1800 (maximum 14 people), and a clipper for a large group of people f4700; there are also weekly arrangements, eg a tjalk from Monday to Sunday from f3000; in March, April and October prices are discounted by 10%

Zeilcharter Volendam, Oude Draaipad 3, Volendam (☎ & fax 0299-36 97 40) – a botter costs f600 per day (10 am to 6 pm, maximum 12 people), f1100 per weekend (Friday 8 pm to Sunday 5 pm, maximum eight people), f1000 for two weekdays, or f2500 for five days; there are also more expensive boats

Holland Zeilcharters, Monnickendam (☎ 0299-65 23 51; fax 0299-65 36 18) – similar deals to Zeilcharter Volendam

Stichting Zeilvloot Muiden, Herengracht 49, Muiden (☎ 0294-26 39 27; fax 26 23 07) – similar deals to Zeilcharter Volendam

Muiden Jacht Charter Station (☎ 0294-26 14 12; fax 26 10 04) – has four botters costing from f550 per day (10 am to 6 pm, maximum 10 people); a weekend costs f1250 (maximum eight people)

ICE SKATING

When the canals freeze over in winter (which doesn't happen often enough) the whole city goes for a skate. Lakes and waterways in the countryside also fill up with colourfully clad skaters making trips tens of kilometres long. It's a wonderful experience, though a bit painful on the ankles and butt if you're only just learning to skate.

Keep in mind that people drown under ice every year. Don't take to a patch of ice unless you see large groups of people, and be very careful at the edges and areas under bridges (the latter usually don't freeze properly).

You can only rent skates at a skating rink. A pair of simple hockey skates costs upwards of about f100 at a department store (sports shops might have a wider selection but tend to be more expensive). Hockey skates are probably the best choice for learners: figure skates (with short, curved blades) are difficult to master, and speed skates (with long, flat blades) put a lot of strain on the ankles. Check for second-hand skates on notice boards at supermarkets or at the Centrale Bibliotheek (Central Library), Prinsengracht 587. Old wood-framed skates that you tie under your shoes can be picked up cheaply at antique and bric-a-brac shops. Don't dismiss them: they're among the fastest skates around if they're freshly sharpened and make great souvenirs.

The *Jaap Edenbaan* (Map 10; ☎ 694 98 94), Radioweg 64 in the eastern suburb of Watergraafsmeer (tram No 9), has an indoor and outdoor rink.

TENNIS & SQUASH

The huge *Borchland Sportcentrum* (☎ 696 14 41 or 696 14 44), Borchlandweg 8-12, next to the Arena stadium in the Bijlmer (metro: Strandvliet, or the Ouderkerk aan de Amstel exit of the A2/E35 freeway towards Utrecht), has tennis, squash and badminton courts, bowling alleys and other facilities including a restaurant.

Tenniscentrum Amstelpark (Map 9; ☎ 644 54 36), Karel Lotsylaan 8, has 36 open and covered courts and runs the country's biggest tennis school. It's conveniently close to the

World Trade Center and RAI exhibition buildings.

Squash City (☎ 626 78 83), Ketelmakerstraat 6 at the railway line at Bickerseiland (west of Centraal Station), charges f35 (f45 in the evenings) for two people to use a squash court, the gym and the sauna.

More courts are listed under *Tennisbanen* and *Squashbanen* in the pink pages of the phone book.

CHESS
The *Max Euwe Centrum* (Map 15; ☎ 625 70 17), Max Euweplein 30A1 off Leidseplein, has a permanent exhibition devoted to the history of chess and to the country's one and only world chess champion, for whom the centre is named. You can play against live or digital opponents. Admission is free and it's open from 10.30 am to 4 pm Tuesday to Friday plus the first Saturday of the month. At other times, chess enthusiasts can be found in *Schaakcafé 't Hok* (☎ 624 31 33), Lange Leidsedwarsstraat 134.

GOLF
The main problem with golf in this country is lack of space and the consequent lack of affordable golf courses. It was long derided as a sport for the elite but has become increasingly popular in recent years.

Golfcenter Amstelborgh (☎ 697 50 00), Borchlandweg 6 adjoining the Borchland Sportcentrum (see the earlier Tennis & Squash section), has nine holes and charges f20; club rental is f15 for half a set. It's open daily all year (closed 1 January and 25 December). *Openbare Golfbaan Sloten* (☎ 614 24 02), Sloterweg 1045 on the southwest side of town (bus No 142), also has nine holes and charges f20 weekdays or f25 weekends (play as many rounds as you like); club rental is f12.50 for half a set. It's open weekdays all year and in summer on weekends too.

Look under *Golfbanen* in the pink pages of the phone book for several other options.

BUNGY JUMPING
Bungy Jump Holland (Map 14; ☎ 419 60 05), Oostelijke Handelskade 1 at the waterfront half a km east of Centraal Station, offers jumps from a mobile crane suspended 75 metres above the water. It's expensive (f100 for the first jump, f75 for the second or f400 for 10) but if you can keep your nerves under control you'll never forget the view.

Courses

The Foreign Student Service is a support agency for foreign students that supplies information about study programmes and intensive language courses. For more details about this organisation, or about study at academic level, see Universities in the Facts for the Visitor chapter.

LANGUAGE COURSES
Dutch is a close relative of English but that doesn't make it an easy language to learn. 'Normal' courses take months and intensive courses last several weeks. Plan ahead and make enquiries well in advance.

The Volksuniversiteit Amsterdam (☎ 626 16 26), Rapenburgerstraat 73, 1011 VK Amsterdam, offers a range of day and evening courses that are well regarded and don't cost a fortune. The British Language Training Centre (☎ 622 36 34), Nieuwezijds Voorburgwal 328E, 1012 RW Amsterdam, tends to be more expensive but has a good reputation. The same applies to Language Solution (☎ 422 31 22), Vinkenstraat 79, 1013 JM Amsterdam.

OTHER COURSES
The above-mentioned Volksuniversiteit offers a range of courses, some in English. The Amsterdam Summer University (☎ 620 02 25), Keizersgracht 324, 1016 EZ Amsterdam, conducts all its courses and workshops in English. Subjects focus on arts and sciences, as befits the traditions of the Felix Meritis building that houses it.

Also enquire at museums: the Stedelijk Museum, for instance, conducts courses in art history.

For courses in yoga, relaxation massage, acupuncture, herbalism and so forth, contact the Oibibio centre (Map 13; ☎ 553 93 55), Prins Hendrikkade 20-21 diagonally opposite Centraal Station.

The city hall information centre (☎ 624 11 11), Amstel 1 in the arcade between the Stopera and the city hall, has lots of information about informal courses and workshops (cooking, pottery, needlework, car repairs, stamp-collecting – you name it). Most or all of these are in Dutch but that shouldn't be an insurmountable problem. For similar activities in your neighbourhood, contact the nearest community centre listed under *Buurtcentrum* in the phone book.

Places to Stay

Amsterdam attracts many tourists throughout the year – book ahead if you want a 'good' place to stay. Even camping grounds can be filled to capacity in summer. It's worth paying a bit extra for something reasonably central so you can enjoy the nightlife without having to rely on night buses or the most expensive taxis in Europe. This doesn't mean having to stay within the canal belt: accommodation in the Museum Quarter or around the Vondelpark, for instance, is still well within walking distance of the lively Leidseplein area.

Theft is not uncommon at camping grounds or in dormitories (bring your own padlock for the locker) but is rare in 'normal' hotel rooms. It's always wise to deposit valuables for safe keeping at the reception desk. Some hotels have safety deposit boxes in the rooms which may be coin-operated (f1 per usage).

Ask about parking if travelling by car. In almost all cases parking is a major problem and the most you'll get is a (payable) parking permit out on the street – with all the attendant headaches and security risks – or a referral to the nearest parking garage (at up to f60 a day) that may be a fair distance away. The top-end hotels have their own expensive parking arrangements but like to be warned in advance.

CAMPING GROUNDS

There are several camping grounds in and around Amsterdam, but the four listed here seem to be the most popular and accessible. The Vliegenbos and Zeeburg sites attract crowds of young people, the other two sites are more suited to older campers and families. At the time of research none of these camping grounds had finalised their rates for the coming season, so expect prices to be slightly higher than quoted here. The Vliegenbos, Zeeburg and Amsterdamse Bos sites also rent out cabins with different bed configurations that can work out as cheaply as f15-20 per person – ideal for families.

Camping Vliegenbos (Map 7; ☎ 636 88 55; fax 632 27 23), Meeuwenlaan 138, Amsterdam Noord, is open from April to September and is probably the most convenient camping ground for people without a car. Tent campers under 30 years of age pay f9 per person, older campers f10.50, tent spot included. From Centraal Station, take bus No 32 or night bus No 72. Alternatively, hop aboard the free 'Adelaarswegveer', the ferry from Pier 8 behind Centraal Station (bicycles and mopeds are also carried free). From the other side, it's a 20-minute walk or five-minute ride by bicycle. When this ferry doesn't operate (see Boat, Ferries in the Getting Around chapter), take the larger, 24-hour 'Buiksloterwegveer' (between Pier 8 and Pier 9) straight across the IJ and walk across the locks of the Noordhollands Kanaal, which adds five minutes to the trip on foot.

Camping Zeeburg (☎ 694 44 30; fax 694 62 38), Zuiderzeeweg 29, is in an industrial area on an artificial island east of the city, near a huge bridge over the IJ (bus No 37 from Amstelstation). It's not as bad as it sounds: the nearby Flevopark has walking trails, a swimming pool and sporting facilities. Camping costs f6.50 per person, f3.50 per tent, and parking is f6. It's open from March to December.

Camping Het Amsterdamse Bos (☎ 641 68 68; fax 640 23 78), Kleine Noorddijk 1, Bovenkerk, Amstelveen, is open from April to October. It's a long way south-west of town in the southern extremities of the Amsterdamse Bos, but bus No 171 from Centraal Station provides a painless connection, and the terminus of night bus No 67 is a short stroll away. The noise from nearby Schiphol airport can be annoying but the recreational facilities in the Amsterdamse Bos are great. It costs f8 per person, f5 per tent and f4 per car.

Gaaspercamping (☎ 696 73 26; fax 696 93 69), Loosdrechtdreef 7, Gaasperdam, is in a large park-cum-recreational area in the south-eastern suburbs (metro to Gaasperplas, then a short walk). It costs f5.75 per person, f5 per tent and f5 per car, and is open from mid-March to December. This place is also a good bet for backpackers, but requires a longer, more expensive ride by public transport.

HOSTELS
Official Youth Hostels
The head office of the Netherlands Youth Hostel Association (NJHC; Map 17; ☎ 551 31 33; fax 623 49 86) is at Professor Tulpplein 4, 1018 GX Amsterdam (in front of the Amstel Inter-Continental Hotel, the most luxurious hotel in the country). The association uses the Hostelling International logo for the benefit of foreigners but has kept the 'youth hostel' name. For information about youth hostels, ☎ 551 31 55.

A youth-hostel card (or rather, an International Guest Card) costs f28 at this office or at the hostels; alternatively, nonmembers pay f5 a night more for a bed and after six nights they're a member. HI or NJHC members can get discounts on international travel (eg 10% discount on Eurolines tickets) and don't pay commission on money exchange at the GWK (official exchange) offices. Members and nonmembers have the same rights at the hostels and there are no age limits.

Bookings are strongly advised in summer – a phone call to the hostel is enough. Apart from the usual dormitories there are rooms for two, four, six and eight people that are often used by families (single rooms are normally reserved for bus drivers). These should be booked well ahead in busy periods (spring, summer and autumn holidays) and rates vary considerably – enquire at the hostel.

The *Stadsdoelen Youth Hostel* (Map 13; ☎ 624 68 32), Kloveniersburgwal 97 near the red-light district in the old town, is very central and charges f26 for members. There's a midnight curfew, though the door is opened on the hour to let people in and out. The

Vondelpark Youth Hostel (Map 15; ☎ 683 17 44), Zandpad 5 (more or less in the Vondelpark), is probably the most pleasant of the two HI hostels and is certainly the busiest, with 300,000 guests a year. Members pay f28, with discounts during renovations in 1997. There's a 2 am curfew.

The *Haarlem Youth Hostel* (☎ 023-37 37 93), Jan Gijzenpad 3 in Haarlem, charges f25. It's open from March to September though after renovations it should be open all year from 1998. Rules include 10 pm silence and midnight curfew – front door key supplied for a f10 deposit. It's a 10-minute walk from Santpoort Zuid train station and is a good alternative for anyone with a rail pass; trains direct to Amsterdam pass about every half hour taking 24 minutes to cover the 24 km.

Other Hostels
The *Arena Budget Hotel* (Map 17; ☎ 694 74 44; fax 663 26 49), 's-Gravesandestraat 51 near the Tropenmuseum, is a huge complex (600 beds) in the lush Oosterpark. It was originally a monastery, then a hospital, and not so long ago it was known as the Sleep-In. It's popular – in mid-summer every place will be taken. Dorm beds are f22.50 in summer, f20 in winter, breakfast not included; double rooms, all with own shower and toilet, cost f105 in summer, f95 in winter. There's wheelchair access throughout. Parking costs f5 whenever you leave the parking area, which is great value if you take the tram or rent a bike – MacBike has a rental outlet here. There's no age limit or curfew but you have to vacate the large dorms from 11 am to 3 pm, the small dorms from 11.30 am to 2 pm. Attractions include a café, live music in the bar, weekend dance nights (discounts for hotel guests), and a concert hall with rock bands Thursday, Friday and Saturday nights.

Christian backpackers will feel right at home in *Christian Youth Hostel Eben Haëzer* (Map 12; ☎ 624 47 17; fax 627 61 37), Bloemstraat 179 in the Jordaan. A bed costs f20 including breakfast, there's a 1 am curfew, and the age limit is 36. A similar setup is *Christian Youth Hostel 'The Shelter'* (Map 13; ☎ 625 32 30), Barndesteeg 21 in the red-light area. A bed here is f18 including breakfast, the age limit is 35, and curfew is at midnight (1 am on Saturday and Sunday).

Bob's Youth Hostel (Map 13; ☎ 623 00 63; fax 675 64 46), Nieuwezijds Voorburgwal 92 (four blocks from Centraal Station), is devoid of Christian leanings and has a very relaxed policy on dope. A bed is f22 including breakfast, there's no age limit, and the curfew is at 3 am. It's a basic and convenient place to crash if you roll into Amsterdam exhausted and don't wish to search further, but with a little effort you'll do better.

HOTELS
Ratings & Facilities
The star-rating system for hotels goes up to five stars; accommodation rating less than one star can call itself a pension or guesthouse but not a hotel. The ratings are not very helpful because they have more to do with the amenities – lifts, phones in the rooms, mini bar etc – and the number of rooms than with the quality of the rooms themselves.

Many hotels (like many of the houses) have steep and narrow stairs but no lifts (elevators), which make them inaccessible for people with mobility problems. Check when you make enquiries. Of course the top-end hotels have lifts, and some mid-range ones do too.

Rooms usually come with TV, though in the cheaper places you might have to feed coins into a timer to help pay for the cable subscription that delivers all those foreign channels. Then again, there might be no room TV even in some expensive hotels, so if this means a lot to you, check when making enquiries.

Hotels tend to be small – any hotel with more than 20 rooms is 'large' – so if you book a room with shower or toilet in the corridor you won't have to share it with too many other guests. If you book a room with private shower, this will usually include a toilet but not always. Hotels in the top price bracket have bathrooms with real baths attached to the rooms; cheaper hotels tend to

have showers only but they might have a few rooms with baths for the same price – ask.

Bookings
The VVV offices in front of and inside CS, or the GWK (money exchange office) inside, have hotel-booking services that can save you a lot of hunting around during busy periods. The VVV offices charge f5 commission plus a f10 deposit on the price of the room; the GWK office charges f5 commission and you pay the full room charge in advance. The Netherlands Reservation Centre (☎ +31-70-320 25 00; fax 320 26 11), Postbus 404, 2260 AK Leidschendam, accepts hotel bookings from abroad.

Hotels tend to charge a bit more if you come to them through these services – you can save money by booking directly with the hotel. Many of them won't accept credit-card details over the phone (if they accept cards at all) and may insist on a down payment by cheque or money order before they'll confirm the booking.

When booking for two people, make it clear whether you want a twin (two single beds) or double (a bed for two). It should make no difference to the price, but the wrong bed configuration could be impossible to fix on the spot when rooms are fully booked in summer.

Prices
Generally you get what you pay for and you don't get much. Hotels in the lowest price bracket (below f125 for a double) can be run-down and invariably seem to suffer from mouldy smells due to the damp climate, coupled with the Dutch aversion to decent ventilation. Still, they can be good value, especially if they've just been renovated. Hotels above this price bracket are more pleasant, and they may even have doubles for less than f125 depending on the season and whether or not you want breakfast or a shower in the room. Breakfast in the hotel might be a good idea because few food establishments open early (see the Places to Eat chapter).

Single rooms cost about two-thirds of the

RICHARD NEBESKY

RICHARD NEBESKY

RICHARD NEBESKY

Café terraces: great places to sit and watch people

RICHARD NEBESKY

RICHARD NEBESKY

RICHARD NEBESKY

Top & Left: If you like café society, you've come to the right place
Right: The never-dull Rembrandtplein

rates quoted here for doubles; add a third to a half for triples. Hotels that accept children (many of them don't) often have special rates for families. Prices drop a bit in the low season (roughly October to April excluding Christmas/New Year and Easter) but it's always worth asking for 'special' rates, especially if you're staying a few nights.

Hotels – bottom end (doubles under f125)

These places are popular with backpackers, and some have lounges filled with happy smokers who would be in jail if this weren't Amsterdam. Some hotels, however, are very strict about this sort of thing and lighting a joint could lead to instant expulsion.

Inside the Canal Belt *Hotel Continental* (Map 13; ☎ 622 33 63; no fax), Damrak 40-41 near Centraal Station, has small rooms but is clean and bright. Doubles with shower and breakfast range from f95 in the off season to f125 on a weekend night at the height of summer; a single with shower in the corridor costs f60. The owner is a member of the respectable (some would say 'yuppie') Harley Owners Group and likes to talk 'real' bikes.

Frisco Inn (Map 13; ☎ 620 16 10; no fax), Beursstraat 5 off Damrak, is a youth hotel with doubles for f75 without shower, f85 with, breakfast not included; triples/quads with bunk beds cost f35 a head. There's a bar downstairs. Next door, *Hotel Beursstraat* (Map 13; ☎ 626 37 01), Beursstraat 7, has doubles without shower for f75, or f95 with, breakfast not included. The sign outside advertises double rooms from f55 and f60, but these only apply to rooms without shower in the low season. The place is slightly more respectable than others in this area.

Hotel Centrum (Map 13; ☎ 624 35 35; no fax), Warmoesstraat 15 near Centraal Station, charges f90 for a double with shared shower, f115 with private shower, f135 with shower and toilet. All rooms have TV and there's a bar downstairs.

Hotel Kabul (Map 13; ☎ 623 71 58; fax 620 08 69), Warmoesstraat 42 next to the red-light district's police station, is popular and really packs the customers in. A dorm bed costs f32 and a double room f92, both including breakfast. Local rock bands play in the bar from 10 pm onwards so it's not what you'd call a quiet place. *Hotel Winston* (Map 13; ☎ 625 39 12 or 626 80 45; fax 639 23 08), Warmoesstraat 123 a block from the Dam, is also a multimedia centre with a good-value restaurant. Brightly coloured doubles with facilities in the corridor cost f95, or f116 with toilet and shower; breakfast is f7 per person extra.

Hotel Crown (Map 13; ☎ 626 96 64; fax 420 64 73), Oudezijds Voorburgwal 21 in the red-light area, has tidy doubles with shared shower for f75-100 depending on the season, or f90-120 with private shower – good value for the location, even though breakfast costs extra. The dorm beds for f25-35 are a worthwhile alternative to those offered in the more 'institutional' hostels. There's a 24-hour bar downstairs.

Hotel Brian (Map 13; ☎ 624 46 61; no fax), Singel 69 near Centraal Station, is somewhat shabby but friendly enough, and it's hard to argue with a canalside location charging f80 for a double with shower in the corridor, breakfast included.

Hotel Groenendael (Map 13; ☎ & fax 624 48 22), Nieuwendijk 15 near Centraal Station, has doubles with/without shower for f95/85, breakfast included. It's one of the better kept hotels in this bargain-basement price category.

Around the corner, back towards the station, *Hotel BA (Budget Amsterdam)* (Map 13; ☎ 638 71 19; fax 638 88 03), Martelaarsgracht 18, has doubles with shared shower for f75-120 depending on the season, including breakfast, and dorm beds start at f25. The old section at No 12 is a bit of a dive but the new section at No 18, with the restaurant downstairs, is fine.

Keizersgracht Hotel (Map 13; ☎ 625 13 64; fax 620 73 47), Keizersgracht 15, has doubles with shower (but shared toilet) for f105, and breakfast is f8 per person extra. Formerly this was the International Student Center, now it's a regular tourist hotel with one star. Rooms on the canal side are quite OK for this price.

Bill's Residence (Map 12; ☎ 622 31 09; no fax), Leliegracht 18, is in a beautiful location on a quiet canal. You wouldn't know it was there – no hoardings etc, only a small name tag at the bottom bell. A double without shower costs f75. As the name indicates, this really is Bill's residence; it feels more like a B&B and the rooms are a bit run-down. Bill is quite a character.

Near the Westerkerk, the red-brick, curving building along the S-bend of Raadhuisstraat has a few hotels worth checking, all of them up steep flights of stairs. It's a busy street with noisy trams, so a room at the back would be preferable. *Hotel De Westertoren* (Map 12; ☎ 624 46 39; fax 618 74 17), Raadhuisstraat 35, has doubles without/with shower for f95/110, breakfast included. *Hotel Pax* (Map 12; ☎ 624 97 35), Raadhuisstraat 37, has doubles without shower or toilet for f85, breakfast excluded. *Hotel Clemens* (Map 12; ☎ 624 60 89; fax 626 96 58), Raadhuisstraat 39, has doubles without shower for f90 including breakfast; it's full all summer though it's no better than the other hotels in this row.

Budget Hotel Bonaire (Map 12; ☎ & fax 620 15 50), Raadhuisstraat 51-53, opened in late 1996. The rooms are a bit smaller than at the neighbours but are newly furnished and all come with shower and toilet. Costs are f60 (single), f120 (double) or f160 (triple), without breakfast. The front rooms have a balcony. Part of the hotel faces Keizersgracht – ask for a room overlooking the canal.

The *International Budget Hotel* (Map 12 & 15; ☎ 624 27 84; fax 626 18 39), Leidsegracht 76, is a popular backpacker hangout in an attractive old canal house. A double with shower will set you back f110 (f100 without shower); a bed in a four-bed dorm costs f35 in the high season (f32.50 low); breakfast is not included.

There is a string of hotels in this price category along Leidsekade, close to the many entertainment options around Leidseplein. They're all pretty similar, ie slightly run-down and musty, but offer reasonable value. *Hotel Impala* (Map 15; ☎ 623 47 06; fax 638 92 74) at No 77 has doubles without shower for f100, with shower for f115, and with toilet and shower for f125. At No 82, *Hotel Kooyk* (Map 15; ☎ 623 02 95; fax 638 83 37) has doubles without shower for f95-110 depending on the season, breakfast included, and four-bed family rooms for f150 (f175-200 for a 'family' of grown-ups). *Hotel King* (Map 15; ☎ 627 61 01; fax 620 72 77) at No 86 has doubles without shower for f95-115, depending on the season, breakfast included, and is probably the cleanest and most attractive of the lot.

The Veteran (Map 16; ☎ 620 26 73; fax 625 35 06), Herengracht 561 at Thorbeckeplein, has doubles with/without shower for f120/100, breakfast included. It's a bit run-down, and not everyone will appreciate the exotic fumes from the coffee shop next door. If you want to stay in this area, you're better off at the *City Hotel* (Map 16; ☎ 627 23 23; fax 638 47 93), Utrechtsestraat 2 off Rembrandtplein (above the Old Bell pub). A double without shower goes for f95-110 depending on the season, or f125-140 with shower (some rooms with bath) and toilet, breakfast included. It's clean and good value in this price category, certainly considering the location.

Euphemia Budget Hotel (Map 16; ☎ & fax 622 90 45; e-mail euphjm@pi.net for 10% discounts), Fokke Simonszstraat 1, is on a quiet street just off busy Vijzelgracht. It's a former monastery – the institutional layout still attests to that. Doubles without shower cost f75-120 depending on the season, with shower f90-150; breakfast from the menu is up to f7.50 per person extra.

Hotel Sphinx (Map 16; ☎ & fax 627 36 80), Weteringschans 82, charges f85 for doubles without shower, f115 with shower and toilet, or f125 with bath and toilet, breakfast included. It faces a noisy tram line so you might want a room at the back.

In the north-eastern corner of the canal belt, *Hotel Pension Hortus* (Map 14; ☎ 625 99 96), Plantage Parklaan 8, faces the Botanical Garden. Small doubles with or without shower (luck of the draw) are f80 including breakfast. A bed in a quad dorm costs f40 including breakfast. It's a relaxed place on a quiet sidestreet and the clientele is youngish.

Hotel Pension Kitty (Maps 14 &17; ☎ 622 68 19), Plantage Middenlaan 40, has doubles with shared shower for f100 including breakfast.

Outside the Canal Belt *Hotel PC Hooft* (Map 15; ☎ 662 71 07; fax 675 89 61), PC Hooftstraat 63 south of Leidseplein, is an OK place but you get what you pay for (which isn't much). A double costs f95 without shower or f105 with (toilets in the corridor), breakfast included. It's above a sidewalk café near the museums.

Hotel Museumzicht (Map 15; ☎ 671 29 54; fax 671 35 97), Jan Luijkenstraat 22 next to the Rijksmuseum, has doubles without/ with shower for f105/f140, breakfast included. It faces a noisy tram line but is well kept.

Hotel Bema (Map 15; ☎ 679 13 96; fax 662 36 88), Concertgebouwplein 19B, has spacious doubles without shower for f85-95, or f110-125 with, breakfast in bed included. It's a friendly place but faces a noisy tram line. On a quiet street nearby is *Hotel Peters* (Map 15; ☎ 673 34 54; fax 623 68 62), Nicolaas Maesstraat 72. It's a private home where they've done little to create a hotel 'feel', which could be a plus or a minus depending on your preferences. A double without shower is f90, with shower is f110, and with shower and toilet is f125, breakfast included; all rooms have a fridge.

Hotels – lower middle (f125 to f175)

Hotels in this price range are pleasant enough for most people, though not all rooms will be worth the money compared with some of the better rooms in the previous category.

Inside the Canal Belt The *Amstel Botel* (Map 14; ☎ 626 42 47; fax 639 19 52) at Oosterdokskade 2-4 is a floating hotel alongside the district post office, a few minutes walk east of Centraal Station. Doubles cost f139 on the land side, f149 on the water side. All rooms have shower, toilet, TV and

phone; breakfast is f10 per person extra. This is a safe choice.

Hotel Belga (Map 12; ☎ 624 90 80; fax 623 68 62), Hartenstraat 8, charges f160 for a double with shower, toilet and TV, or f125 without, breakfast included. The rooms could use a bit of maintenance but they're decent enough and you pay for the location.

Hotel van Onna (Map 12; ☎ 626 58 01; no fax), Bloemgracht 104, consists of 39 rooms in three houses along a beautiful, quiet canal in the Jordaan. Clean, well-kept, modern doubles cost f140 with shower and toilet, or f110 without, breakfast included. Ask for a room on the canal side (no mark-up in price). The movie *Twice a Woman* starring Anthony Perkins was filmed here in 1979. Owner Loek van Onna is very helpful and the place is friendly and relaxed. Book ahead because it's often full.

Hotel Agora (Map 12; ☎ 627 22 00; fax 627 22 02), Singel 462 off Koningsplein near the Flower Market, has doubles without shower for f110-135, or f160-200 with, breakfast included. It's a comfortable hotel in an old building with a large, stylish lobby and breakfast area.

Hotel Hans Brinker (Map 15; ☎ 622 06 87; fax 638 20 60), Kerkstraat 136, is a large, slick place with an institutional feel – excited groups of preteens mingle with middle-aged Irishmen worried about where to park the car. The hotel has built an advertising campaign around its spartan rooms and lack of facilities or service ('Our luxurious bridal suite... with towels!'; 'Our parking facilities' – scene of a bicycle rack; 'Our wake-up call' – scene of a drunken house guest careening into one room door after another), but it's not that bad and is often filled to capacity. Small, clean doubles with shower and toilet cost f141-146 depending on the number of nights, including breakfast; dorm beds are considerably cheaper.

Hotel Titus (Map 15; ☎ 626 57 58; fax 638 58 70) at Leidsekade 74 charges f140 for a double with shower and TV including breakfast, which seems a bit overpriced compared with other hotels along this quay near Leidseplein.

Hotel Nes (Map 13; ☎ 624 47 73; fax 620 98 42), Kloveniersburgwal 137-139, has doubles with bath for f160 during the week, f195 on weekends, or f140 any time with shower. It looks fancy from the outside but some of the rooms are below average for that sort of money – check before you commit yourself.

Hotel Eureka (Map 13; ☎ 624 66 07; fax 624 13 46), 's-Gravelandseveer 3-4 around the corner from Hotel Nes, has doubles with shower for f120-180 depending on the season, breakfast included. The rooms aren't magnificent but the view over the Amstel is. Small, dark doubles at the back of the building (no view) cost f100-160 depending on the season, and for that sort of money you can do better.

Hotel De Admiraal (Map 16; ☎ 626 21 50; fax 623 46 25), Herengracht 563 at Thorbeckeplein, has doubles without shower for f105-115, with shower for f135, and with toilet and shower for f145-165; breakfast is f7.50 per person extra. It's not a bad choice in this area.

Just down the canal, the *Seven Bridges* (Map 16; ☎ 623 13 29; no fax), Reguliersgracht 31, has doubles without shower from f125, with shower from f185, room breakfast on fine china included. The well-kept, beautiful rooms are tastefully decorated with expensive furniture. It's a lovely hotel on one of the loveliest canals, but many people know this and you're unlikely to get in if you haven't booked well ahead.

Hotel Prinsenhof (Map 16; ☎ 623 17 72; fax 638 33 68), Prinsengracht 810 near Utrechtsestraat, is a beautiful old canal house with an electric hoist through the central staircase for luggage. As is often the case in canal houses, every room is different – the two attic rooms with their diagonal beams are the most popular (mind your head!). Doubles without shower cost f125, with shower f175, breakfast in the pleasant breakfast room included. It's one of the better choices in this price range.

Hotel de Munck (Map 16; ☎ 623 62 83; fax 620 66 47), Achtergracht 3 off Frederiksplein, is an equally good choice. Well-kept,

clean doubles without shower or toilet start at f125, or f135 with both; triples and quads start at f55 per person. Prices include breakfast.

Hotel Adolesce (Map 16; ☎ 626 39 59; fax 627 42 49), Nieuwe Keizersgracht 26, is in a quiet location just off the Amstel. It charges f120 for a double without shower or f140 with shower and toilet, breakfast in the sunny patio included. You could ask for a room at the front overlooking the canal but one of the two rooms behind the patio would be just as pleasant. *Hotel Fantasia* (Map 16; ☎ 623 82 59), a few doors along at Nieuwe Keizersgracht 16, has similar prices. Both hotels are closed from November to mid-March.

In the Plantage area near the Botanical Garden and Artis zoo, try *Hotel Rembrandt* (Map 14; ☎ 627 27 14; fax 638 02 93) at Plantage Middenlaan 17. Smallish doubles without shower cost f105, larger doubles with bath or shower are f150. This includes breakfast in the stunning, wood-panelled breakfast room with 17th century paintings on the linen wall coverings, which alone makes this hotel worth staying at. It faces a noisy tram line, so ask for a room at the back.

Outside the Canal Belt *Hotel Smit* (Map 15; ☎ 676 63 43; fax 662 91 61), PC Hooftstraat 24, has doubles with bath and toilet for f130-160 depending on the season, including breakfast. It's clean, reasonably new and well kept, and there's even a lift. It's not a bad choice, close to Leidseplein and the museums.

Hotel Acro (Map 15; ☎ 662 05 26; fax 675 08 11), Jan Luijkenstraat 44, has clean doubles with shower and toilet for f140, breakfast included, which is good value at this quiet location near the museums. *Hotel Acca International* (Map 15; ☎ 662 52 62; fax 679 93 61), Van der Veldestraat 3A near the Van Gogh and Stedelijk museums, has doubles with shower (or bath) and toilet for f150 during the week, f175 on weekends; breakfast costs extra. All rooms are similar so you won't have any nasty surprises – a safe choice (though the same sort of room could be had elsewhere for f20 less).

Hotel Parkzicht (Map 15; ☎ 618 19 54; fax 618 08 97), Roemer Visscherstraat 33 adjoining the Vondelpark, is OK, with doubles for f120-150 including shower, toilet and breakfast; the *Hotel Sipermann* (Map 15; ☎ 616 18 66; fax 683 51 14) next door at No 35 is similar.

Hotel De Filosoof (☎ 683 30 13; fax 685 37 50), Anna van den Vondelstraat 6, is a stately hotel in a quiet street next to the Vondelpark. Rooms are decorated to different philosophical themes – a Nietzsche room, a Wittgenstein room, a Humanism room etc – and there's a 'philosophical café' downstairs that hosts philosophical lectures (in Dutch) on Thursday evenings. A double with bath and TV costs f155 in the low season, f175 in the high season, including breakfast.

Hotel Van Bonga (Map 9; ☎ 662 52 18; fax 679 08 43), Holbeinstraat 1 off Stadionweg south-west of the city centre, has doubles with bath for f140 including breakfast – worth considering by an exhibitor needing a place near the RAI.

Hotels – upper middle (f175 to f250)

Hotels in this category are comfortable without being formal, and, with the exception of Hotel Ibis, are small enough to offer personal attention. All of the following are within the canal belt.

Hotel Ibis Amsterdam Centre (Map 13; ☎ 638 30 80; fax 620 01 56), Stationsplein 49, is an 11-storey high-rise attached to Centraal Station, convenient for business travellers. A double with bath costs f210, breakfast included.

RHO Hotel (Map 13; ☎ 620 73 71; fax 620 78 26), Nes 11-23 just off the Dam, has doubles with bath for f195 including breakfast. For this sort of money you could do better if you had the time to hunt around, but the rooms are OK and you can't beat the location.

The *Canal House Hotel* (Map 12; ☎ 622 51 82; fax 624 13 17), Keizersgracht 148, is an olde worlde sort of place spread over three grand canal houses. It's the pick of the bunch in this price category, though some of the

rooms already fall in the next category. All rooms are different and have been kept as original as possible with antique furniture and no TVs (though there are computer sockets for e-mail etc). A double with bath costs f225-270, breakfast included.

Hotel Toren (Map 12; ☎ 622 60 33; fax 626 97 05), Keizersgracht 164 near the Westerkerk, has doubles with shower from f175 and luxury rooms up to f275, breakfast included. Some rooms are fairly small – ask to see a few before committing yourself.

The *Waterfront Hotel* (Map 12; ☎ 623 97 75; fax 620 74 91), Singel 458 near Koningsplein, has water beds and private showers in all rooms. A double costs f175-190, depending on whether there's a view of the canal. The place is a bit too ragged to charge that sort of money but the rooms are decent enough.

Hotels – top end (doubles f250 to f400)

Hotels in this category constantly change their rates to meet the competition, and calling around to ask if they have any 'specials' going could save a few hundred guilders on a stay of several nights; if they think you're in town on business and the company is paying you may be charged more. All rooms have bathrooms with proper bath, shower and toilet.

Inside the Canal Belt *Hotel Estheréa* (Map 12; ☎ 624 51 46; fax 623 90 01), Singel 305-307, occupies three canal houses. It has doubles for f220-315 depending on the season, breakfast included. The rooms are fine but the staff are a bit officious – a more relaxed approach would fit this price category better.

The *Ambassade Hotel* (Map 12; ☎ 626 23 33; fax 624 53 21), Herengracht 341, is a stylish place spread over nine canal houses. All rooms are different and tastefully appointed with beautiful furniture. Check the antique clock (1750) in the lounge, with its rocking ships and mermaids. Doubles cost f295/305 in the low/high season, including breakfast. There are also suites with two bedrooms for f475, and apartments with kitchen for f450.

Outside the Canal Belt The *Garden Hotel* (Map 9; ☎ 664 21 21; fax 679 93 56), across from the Hilton Hotel at Dijsselhofplantsoen 7, south-west of the centre, has doubles with jacuzzi from f275, breakfast not included. It's a relatively small hotel in a low-rise building.

The *Galaxy Hotel* (Map 6; ☎ 634 43 66; fax 636 03 45), Distelkade 21 in Amsterdam Noord, has doubles for f250 including breakfast. It's a former hospital and rooms are a bit soulless, but it's popular with Europeans on bus tours and there's plenty of parking space.

Hotels – over the top
Hotels in this category have all the facilities that the international jet-setter would expect – fitness centres, conference rooms, business centres (or at least 'desks') – and they'll probably be able to park your car, which is saying something in Amsterdam. Breakfast, too mundane to be included in the price, will cost another f25-40. They often have weekend deals – something to keep in mind for that special occasion.

Hotels with the most 'character' are the Krasnapolsky, Pulitzer, Grand Amsterdam, De l'Europe, American and the undisputed king, the Amstel Hotel.

Inside the Canal Belt The *Victoria Hotel* (Map 13; ☎ 627 11 66; fax 627 42 59), in the imposing building opposite Centraal Station at Damrak 1-5 (entrance along Prins Hendrikkade), has modern doubles with bath from f395 to f425 (extra bed f60, breakfast f27.50), and all the mod cons including swimming pool and business centre.

The *Golden Tulip Barbizon Palace* (Map 13; ☎ 556 45 64; fax 624 33 53) at Prins Hendrikkade 59-72 to your left opposite Centraal Station is a sterile, six-storey building with a Splash Palace Fitness Club on the premises. Doubles cost f390-510, or f300 on the weekend with breakfast. Call ahead to

enquire about 'specials', and check elsewhere at the same time.

The *Grand Hotel Krasnapolsky* (Map 13; ☎ 554 91 11; fax 622 68 07), Dam 9 behind the national monument, is an elegant, historic hotel on Amsterdam's main square. It's a bit of a monument itself and charges accordingly: doubles are f405-575. The 'winter garden' with its steel and glass roof is renowned.

The *Pulitzer Hotel* (Map 12; ☎ 523 52 35; fax 627 67 53), Prinsengracht 315-331, occupies a row of 17th century canal houses with beautifully restored façades and some original (restored) interiors. Doubles start at f455.

The Grand Amsterdam (Map 13; ☎ 555 31 11; fax 555 32 22), Oudezijds Voorburgwal 197, is housed in the former admiralty building that served as city hall until the late 1980s. Queen Beatrix's civil wedding took place here in 1966. The listed monument has been restored to its former grandeur and charges f645 for doubles. Weekend deals go for f430, or f530 including an excellent dinner in one of the eight banquet chambers. There are all the usual five-star accoutrements including indoor swimming pool.

Hotel De l'Europe (Map 13; ☎ 623 48 36; fax 624 29 62), Nieuwe Doelenstraat 2-8, has doubles for f575-650. It's an impressive redbrick building near Muntplein. The attached Excelsior Restaurant is very good.

The Art Deco *American Hotel* (Map 15; ☎ 624 53 22; fax 625 32 36), Leidsekade 97 just off Leidseplein, is a listed monument built in 1902. Doubles cost f425-600, and breakfast in the stylish Café Americain is another f29.50. Cheaper deals are available when booked in conjunction with a KLM flight to Amsterdam.

The *Amstel Inter-Continental Hotel* (Map 16; ☎ 622 60 60; fax 622 58 08), Professor Tulpplein 1, has an imposing location overlooking the Amstel. It was extensively renovated in 1992 and is probably the finest hotel in the country. A double with bath on the river side costs f550 on weekend days (f500 on the less interesting land side) but on weekdays you're looking at f850 (f800 on the land side). Breakfast is another f38.50 per person. Rooms go right up to f4400 for the royal suite. The hotel has all the facilities you could imagine, including limousine service, health club and swimming pool. It also boasts La Rive, Amsterdam's first (and so far only) restaurant with two Michelin stars.

Outside the Canal Belt
The *Golden Tulip Barbizon Centre* (Map 15; ☎ 685 13 51; fax 685 16 11), Stadhouderskade 7 at Leidseplein, has doubles for f390-485. It's a fine hotel with nothing in particular to recommend it apart from the location. The same applies to the slightly more luxurious *Marriott Hotel* (Map 15; ☎ 607 55 55; fax 607 55 11), Stadhouderskade 21 off Leidseplein, which has doubles for f490.

The *Hilton Amsterdam* (Map 9; ☎ 678 07 80; fax 662 66 88), Apollolaan 138-140, south-west of the city centre, has doubles for f445-515. It's your standard Hilton in a 10-storey building, although it does boast a marina with 'authentic traditional' boats for hire. In the late 1960s it became famous when John Lennon and Yoko Ono stayed in bed here for world peace, waving at screaming fans out on the street.

The *Okura Hotel* (Map 9; ☎ 678 71 11; fax 671 23 44), Ferdinand Bolstraat 333, has doubles for f420-520. It's a 22-storey hotel next to the Amstelkanaal, not far from the RAI exhibition centre. It might be a good choice for an exhibitor who wanted to be near the RAI and wasn't overly concerned about room prices.

Gay & Lesbian Hotels
Most hotels are pretty relaxed about same-sex couples (and would be breaking the law if they refused them) but some are more welcoming than others.

The *Arena Budget Hotel* (see the earlier Hostels section) is particularly friendly towards gays and lesbians. So too is the mid-priced *Waterfront Hotel*, also described earlier.

The *Aerohotel* (Map 15; ☎ 622 77 28; fax 638 85 31), in the middle of the gay action

at Kerkstraat 49, is a popular gay hotel that charges f100-165 for a double. Another favourite is *Hotel Orfeo* (Map 15; ☎ 623 13 47; reception ☎ 622 81 80), Leidsekruisstraat 14, which charges f100 for a double. The *Stablemaster Hotel* (Map 13; ☎ 625 01 48; fax 624 87 47), Warmoesstraat 23, caters for the leather crowd and has doubles for f160.

The sole women-only establishment in town is *Liliane's Home* (Map 17; ☎ 627 40 06), Sarphatistraat 119, which has singles, doubles, triples and quads from f50 per person.

The *Hotel Quentin* (Map 15; ☎ 626 21 87; fax 622 01 21), Leidsekade 89, is popular with lesbians, though heteros and gays also stay here; a double costs f125-130 with private shower, f97.50 without.

LONG-TERM RENTALS
Rental accommodation costing less than f1047.91 a month unfurnished is subject to a housing permit. This is only issued to legal residents who are bound to the region through work or study, and the price and size of the dwelling must match their income and needs. This means that as a foreigner you'll usually pay more – say, f1500 a month for a smallish, two-bedroom flat in the Vondelpark area – and you might not like what you get.

Apartments tend to be small so sharing is rare. Housing permits are not required in Amsterdam Zuidoost (south-east) but that's because it's a rather unattractive area.

Residents usually procure accommodation through housing corporations. Others have more luck through property ads in the daily newspapers *De Telegraaf* (especially Wednesdays) and *De Volkskrant* or *Het Parool* (especially Saturdays – look under *Te Huur*, For Rent), or through the classifieds paper *Via Via* (published Thursdays). The national organisation of real-estate agents lists properties at www.nvm.nl. on the Internet.

Speaking English can work against you in a variety of ways when apartment-hunting, so get a Dutch friend to help, and act swiftly because it's very much a seller's market. The owner will probably want a deposit of a month's rent, and the previous tenant may demand key money disguised as take-over costs for furnishings or recent handiwork.

Official information on renting is supplied by the Information Centre for Physical Planning and Housing in the Zuiderkerk (☎ 622 29 62), Zuiderkerkhof 72, Monday to Friday from noon to 5 pm (Thursday to 8 pm). The central information telephone line for those seeking housing (☎ 665 91 71) operates Monday to Thursday from 8.30 am to 3 pm, Friday to noon. They might not be too helpful if you're not a resident. Try the following agents:

LDA Housing Services, Den Texstraat 30 (☎ 624 83 01; fax 623 38 44) – furnished apartments from f1800 a month, minimum six months (sometimes shorter in summer)

Goudsmit Estate Agents, AJ Ernststraat 735 (☎ 644 19 71; fax 644 23 76) – furnished apartments from f2000 a month, minimum rental one year

Riverside Apartments, Weteringschans 187E (☎ 627 97 97; fax 627 98 58) – specialises in 'exclusive executive accommodation in central Amsterdam'; rates start at f1000 a week or f1500 a month

Intercity Room Service, Van Ostadestraat 348 (☎ & fax 675 00 64) – only if you're desperate: single rooms from f350 a month, also for shorter periods, occasionally apartments too; commission two weeks' rent (one month for apartments longer than six months). Agencies operating in this price bracket need a municipal permit, which this one has.

Places to Eat

FOOD

Dutch cuisine is not exactly world famous but you'll find virtually every other cuisine under the sun. Prices are reasonable by European standards and servings are generous.

Smoking is still an entrenched habit in restaurants. A few places have non-smoking sections but even the most self-righteous vegetarian establishments have trouble banning smokers altogether.

When & Where

The main meal of the day is dinner, from around 6 to 9.30 pm. The types of people who live in Amsterdam (young professionals, students, artists, business people etc) like to eat out, and the more popular places fill up by 6.30 pm (the Dutch eat early). Book ahead or arrive early, or be prepared to wait at the bar. Alternatively, arrive late: films, concerts and other performances usually start at 8.30 or 9.30 pm and tables may become available then, but keep in mind that many kitchens close at 10 pm (though the restaurants stay open longer). Vegetarian restaurants tend to close earlier.

Lunch is more modest, with sandwich and salad menus, though you'll find places that serve full meals if you really want one.

Don't overlook the many *eetcafés*, pubs that also serve meals – see Cafés (Pubs) in the Entertainment chapter: most of them could just as well be listed here as places to eat and many are excellent, though they don't always take reservations. They're affordable and lively, and if you enjoy the atmosphere you can hang around for drinks afterwards. The grand cafés in particular are good places for lunch.

The streets around Leidseplein (Lange Leidsedwarsstraat and Korte Leidsedwarsstraat) are packed with restaurants, a culinary United Nations. They cater for tourists and most of them are OK, though few stand out. Walk along and pick whatever takes your fancy.

There's a high staff turnover in cafés and restaurants, and some of the places mentioned here may have declined in quality. Don't despair: there's plenty to choose from, and for every place that has gone bad there will be a new one doing its best to attract customers.

Breakfast

Dutch hotel breakfasts typically consist of a selection of breads and toast with butter, cheese and meats (ham, roast beef, salami), jam, and coffee or tea. A soft-boiled egg is sometimes part of the package, and Anglo-American eggs and bacon might be available on request. The Dutch version of fried eggs and meat, the *uitsmijter* served in snack bars and some pubs (see Fast Food), is not commonly eaten for breakfast. You might have trouble finding places other than hotels that serve breakfast before 9 or even 10 am.

Cuisines

Cuisines such as Italian, Spanish, Mexican, Thai, Chinese, Indian and Turkish will be similar to what you're used to, though they might be adapted a bit to suit the Dutch palate and ingredients available locally.

Dutch The standard Dutch meal consists of potatoes, meat and vegetables in large portions (though meat is expensive, so don't expect plate-filling steaks). Not many restaurants serve exclusively Dutch cuisine but many places have a few standard Dutch dishes on the menu, especially in winter, that are filling and good value for money:

stamppot ('mashed pot') – potatoes mashed with vegetables (usually kale or endive) and served with smoked sausage or strips of pork

hutspot ('hotchpotch') – similar to stamppot, but with carrots, onions and braised meat

erwtensoep – thick pea soup (a spoon stuck upright in the pot should fall over slowly) with smoked sausage and bacon *asperges* – asparagus (always white, very popular in spring) served with ham and butter

kroketten – croquettes: dough-ragout with meat (sometimes fish or shrimp) that's crumbed and deep-fried; often in the form of small balls called *bitterballen* served with mustard, a popular pub snack

mosselen – mussels, popular (and best eaten) in the months that contain an 'R' also in Dutch, ie September to April; cooked with white wine, chopped leeks and onions, and served in a bowl or cooking pot with a side dish of French fries (*frites* or *patat*); use an empty shell as a pincer to pluck out the bodies; don't eat mussels that haven't opened properly as they can be poisonous

Seafood doesn't feature as prominently as one might expect in a seafaring nation, though there's plenty of it. Popular fish include *schol* (plaice), *tong* (sole), *kabeljauw* (cod), and freshwater *forel* (trout). *Garnalen* (shrimps, prawns) are also found on many menus, often large species known by their Italian name of *scampi*. *Haring* (herring) is a national institution, eaten lightly salted or occasionally pickled but never fried or cooked; *paling* (eel) is usually smoked. Don't dismiss herring or eel until you've tried them – see the Fast Food section later in this chapter.

Typical Dutch desserts are fruit pie (apple, cherry or other fruit), *vla* (custard) or pancakes.

Indonesian This is a tasty legacy of Dutch colonial history. Some dishes, such as the famous *rijsttafel* ('rice table' – white rice with heaps of side dishes, take your time), are colonial concoctions rather than traditional Indonesian, but that doesn't make them less appealing.

One slight problem, however, is that most places serving Indonesian food are Chinese-Indonesian, run by Chinese (some with Indonesian backgrounds) who have perfected bland dishes to suit Dutch palates. The food is fine and usually great value, but if you want the real thing, avoid places that call themselves *Chinees-Indonesisch* (or order Chinese dishes there instead).

Even at 'genuine' Indonesian restaurants,

rijsttafel can be a bit of a rip-off and the ingredients don't always taste authentic – once you've had a really good one you'll know the difference. A few good rijsttafel places are mentioned in this chapter, but it's an expensive dish and if you eat elsewhere you're better off ordering *nasi rames* (literally: boiled rice), a plate of rice covered in several accompaniments that would be served in separate bowls in a rijsttafel.

Gado-gado (lightly steamed vegetables and hard-boiled egg, served with peanut sauce and rice) feels good in all respects. *Saté* or *sateh* (satay) is marinated, barbecued beef, chicken or pork on small skewers; unfortunately it's often cooked electrically and smothered in peanut sauce. Other standbys are *nasi goreng* (fried rice with onions, pork, shrimp and spices, often topped with a fried egg or shredded omelette) and *bami goreng* (the same thing but with noodles).

Indonesian food is usually served mild for sensitive western palates. If you want it hot (*pedis*, pronounced 'p-DIS'), say so but be prepared for the ride of a lifetime. Better to play it safe by asking for *sambal* (chilli paste), if it isn't already on the table, and helping yourself. Usually it's *sambal oelek*, which is red and hot; the dark-brown *sambal badjak* is based on onions and is mild and sweet. If you overdo it, a spoonful of plain rice will quench the flames; drinking distributes the oily sambal and only makes things worse.

Indonesian food should be eaten with a spoon and fork (chopsticks are Chinese) and the drink of choice is beer or water.

'International' Many restaurants fall into this category, which mixes cuisines from different parts of the world, often depending on the skill or preference of the cook. Dishes might represent a genuine mixture, eg Italian fettuccine topped with Provençale ratatouille and meat stir-fried in soy sauce, or Dutch braised beef served with North African couscous, but more often the menu will simply list an international range of dishes. These are variations on the potatoes-meat-vegetables theme but might include dishes such as an indeterminate curry, a spaghetti bolognese, a beef stroganoff, a plate of Mexican corn chips (nachos) or a bowl of mussels. Main dishes usually come with salads that can be quite imaginative.

Surinamese Food from this former South American colony is similar to Caribbean food – a unique African/Indian hybrid – with Indonesian influences contributed by indentured labourers from Java. Chicken features strongly, along with curries (chicken, lamb or beef), potatoes and rice, and delicious *roti* (unleavened bread pancakes). Steer clear of this type of food if you can't handle hot and spicy, but it's always wholesome and good value.

Costs

The prices quoted in this chapter are probably the minimum you'll end up spending; add something to drink and one or two other dishes and you could spend twice as much. Drinks other than draught beer *(pils)* will pad out the bill, and wine can be a blatant rip-off, with bottles that cost f10 in the shops going for anything up to f45. 'House wines' are no different: a half-litre carafe of acidic house red will cost at least f15, though some restaurants do serve drinkable stuff.

Many places list a *dagschotel* (dish of the day) or *dagmenu* that will be good value, but don't expect an exciting culinary adventure.

Service is included in the bill and tipping is at your discretion, though most people leave small change (5% or so) if the service hasn't been bad enough to warrant customer revenge. The protocol is to say how much you're paying in total as you settle the bill.

DRINKS
Nonalcoholic

Amsterdam tap water is fine but it does have a slight chemical taste, so mineral and soda waters are popular. Dairy drinks include chocolate milk, Fristi (a yoghurt drink), *karnemelk* (buttermilk) and of course milk itself, which is of high quality and relatively cheap. A wide selection of fruit juices and all the international soft drinks are available too.

Tea & Coffee For a city with such a rich tradition in the tea and coffee trade, tea is a bit of a disappointment. It's usually served as a cup of hot water with a tea bag, though many places do offer a wide choice of bags from a special box. If you want milk, ask *met melk, graag* ('with milk, please'), though locals prefer to add a slice of lemon instead.

The hot drink of choice is coffee, which should be strong and can be excellent if it's freshly made or horrendous if it has been simmering in the jug for a couple of hours. If you simply order *koffie* you'll get a sizable cup of the black stuff with a separate jug (or small airline container) of *koffiemelk*, a slightly sour-tasting cream similar to unsweetened condensed milk that enhances the flavour. *Koffie verkeerd* (coffee 'wrong') comes in a bigger cup or mug with plenty of real milk. If you order *espresso* or *cappuccino* you'll be lucky to get a decent Italian version; most cappuccinos are just covered in watery froth, though the blandness may be disguised somewhat by a sprinkle of cinnamon.

Alcoholic

Beer is the staple, served cool and topped by a two-finger-thick head of froth – supposedly to trap the flavour. Requests of 'no head please' will meet with a steely response. Popular brands include Heineken, Amstel, Grolsch, Oranjeboom, Dommelsch, Bavaria and the cheap Brouwersbier put out by the Albert Heijn supermarket chain. They contain 5% alcohol by volume in the bottle and close to 5% on tap, so a few of those seemingly small glasses can pack quite a wallop. Tasty and stronger Belgian beers, such as Duvel and Westmalle Triple, have become very popular and are reasonably priced. *Witbier* is a somewhat murky, crisp beer drunk in summer with a slice of lemon; the dark, sweet *bokbier* is available in autumn.

Dutch gin *(genever)* is made from juniper berries and is drunk chilled from small glasses. Most people prefer *jonge* (young) genever, which is smooth and relatively easy to drink; *oude* (old) genever has a strong juniper flavour and can be an acquired taste. A common combination, known as a *kopstoot* (head butt), is a glass of genever with a beer chaser – few people can handle more than two or three of those. Brandy is known as *vieux* or *brandewijn*. There are plenty of indigenous liqueurs, including *advocaat* (a kind of eggnog) and the herb-based *Beerenburg*, a Frisian schnapps.

Wines in all varieties have become very popular. This has everything to do with European unity which has given French vintners and their overpriced products a run for their money. The average Amsterdam supermarket stocks a host of wines from every corner of Europe (with excellent value from Spain and Bulgaria) and many countries further afield, such as Chile, South Africa and Australia. The most expensive bottle in a supermarket rarely costs more than f12.50 and will be good to excellent. Australians may discover that a so-so wine at home commands top guilder here for its snob appeal.

AMERICAN (NORTH & LATIN)

Amsterdam's very own *Planet Hollywood* (Map 13; ☎ 427 78 27), Reguliersbreestraat 35, opened with Arnie Schwarzenegger doing the honours in late 1996. It's housed in a former cinema and has its own real cinema screen – few (if any) of the other branches around the world can claim such appropriate surroundings. It serves expensive hamburgers, Mexican dishes and bad pasta, and the wine comes from Gerard Départieu's own vineyard. The toilets offer an assortment of aftershaves, colognes, lotions, nail polish and tampons that would make a drugstore jealous.

Rose's Cantina (Maps 13 & 16; ☎ 625 97 97), Reguliersdwarsstraat 38, was one of the first Mexican restaurants in town and is still as busy as ever. Big main portions à la Dutch go for around f25, and litre pitchers of margarita for f45. You can't reserve but it's worth waiting for a table. Food is served from 5.30 to 11 pm daily (the bar stays open until 1 or 2 am).

ASSYRIAN

Eufraat (Map 16; ☎ 672 05 79), Eerste van der Helststraat 72 just off the Sarphatipark, serves Middle Eastern food, but the speciality, as the name almost suggests, is Assyrian. The service is friendly and the food excellent and good value, with mains around f20, three courses for under f30.

CHINESE

For 'real' Chinese, with the freshest ingredients at affordable prices, visit the strip of Chinese restaurants along the Zeedijk near Nieuwmarkt square. Don't worry about reservations – if a place is full, the one next door will have space.

Oriental City (Map 13; ☎ 626 83 52), Oudezijds Voorburgwal 177-179 on the corner of Oude Doelenstraat (the extension of Damstraat), is a large, efficient Chinese restaurant serving tasty main dishes from f17.50 to f45. Many Chinese eat here. *Si-Chuan Kitchen* (☎ 420 78 33), next to Hotel Centrum (Map 13) at Warmoesstraat 17-19, is a cut above the average Chinese restaurant, with spicy Sechuanese main dishes at around f17.50.

DUTCH

De Blauwe Hollander (Map 15; ☎ 623 30 14), Leidsekruisstraat 28, is a cosy little place that serves the types of dishes you might get in a Dutch home, daily from 5 to 10 pm. All plates are under f25 – good value in this part of town, which helps to explain why it's always full.

De Roode Leeuw (Map 13; ☎ 624 96 83), Damrak 93, used to be a place where Dutch tourists stopped for a meal on their way home via Centraal Station. It attracts a wider clientele these days but the food is still well prepared, with main dishes under f30.

d'Vijff Vlieghen Restaurant (Map 12; ☎ 624 83 69), Spuistraat 294-302, is a large restaurant spread out over several canal houses, catering for splurging foreigners keen to sample Dutch food in authentic surroundings (the food and surroundings are good indeed). Mains start at f39.50 and there are four-course menus for f72.50. Book ahead.

Dorrius (Map 13; ☎ 420 22 24), Nieuwezijds Voorburgwal 5, serves a wide range of Dutch dishes in olde worlde surroundings that were transferred whole when the business moved premises a few years ago. It's fairly up-market but is trying hard to re-establish itself as the premier venue for Dutch cuisine, and the prices (many main dishes under f40) are worth it.

At *Hollands Glorie* (Map 16; ☎ 624 47 64), Kerkstraat 220-222 off Vijzelstraat, the 'authentic' 17th century interior puts you in the right mood to enjoy the well-prepared dishes (most main plates under f30) – a good choice. *Haesje Claes* (Map 12; ☎ 624 99 98), Nieuwezijds Voorburgwal 320, is similarly priced, with dark wooden panelling to enhance the experience. It's open daily from noon to 10 pm and reservations are recommended.

For cheaper fare, try the *Koffiehuis van den Volksbond* (Map 14; ☎ 622 12 09), Kadijksplein 4 south of the Scheepvaartmuseum. It started life as a charitable coffee house for dockers and still offers good value, with mains around f17.50 served to a youngish clientele. Even cheaper is the *Keuken van 1870* (Map 13; ☎ 624 89 65), Spuistraat 4 not far from Centraal Station, a former soup kitchen still serving dirt-cheap meals from an old-fashioned open kitchen in a spacious locale. Nothing is over f16.50, and the set menu weekdays is f11. It's open weekdays from 12.30 to 8 pm, weekends from 4 to 9 pm.

Moeder's Pot Eethuisje (Map 11; ☎ 623 76 43), Vinkenstraat 119 near the Haarlemmerpoort, is mentioned in many budget guidebooks for its solid, inexpensive meals. It's a small place full of kitsch, with wooden chairs and only a few small tables, open Monday to Saturday from 5 to 9.30 pm. The focus is the open kitchen (singles can eat at the counter). The proprietor might seem gruff but he's been doing the food and the gruff comments for over 25 years. You could try reserving but you might not survive the response – it's best to turn up early.

FRENCH

Tout Court (Map 12; ☎ 625 86 37), Runstraat 13, is a somewhat pretentious place with tasty mains around f42.50 and menus from f49.50. For a worthwhile splurge in quieter surroundings, try *Zuidlande* (Map 16; ☎ 620 73 93), Utrechtsedwarsstraat 141. The cook, who served his apprenticeship with Paul Bocuse, prepares creative French and Mediterranean food with an excellent balance of flavours. Main dishes (generous servings) are under f40.

Jean Jean (Map 12; ☎ 627 71 53), Eerste Anjeliersdwarsstraat 12 in the Jordaan, has meat and fish dishes for under f30, as well as crêpes, soups and salads. It's open daily from 5.30 to 10.30 pm. The *Lawenda* chocolate shop across the road at No 17 makes delicious bonbons but is only open during normal shop hours.

The very best French food in town is served in the small restaurant in *Maison Descartes* (Map 16; ☎ 622 19 13 for reservations), Vijzelgracht 2A, open Monday to Friday from 11 am to 2.30 pm and 5 to 11 pm. The building also houses the French cultural centre and consulate, and is closed weekends for security reasons. The restaurant area is authentic 17th century Dutch (covered in Delft tiles because it used to be a huge kitchen) and looks out over an equally authentic garden. The current kitchen is small and serves different dishes daily. A satisfying three-course dinner should cost f50-70, but lunches (salads etc) are cheaper. Book days ahead.

INDIAN

There are a few Indian restaurants in town, and one of the best is *Memories of India* (Map 16; ☎ 623 57 10), Reguliersdwarsstraat 88. This clone from London has great vegetarian menus for f30, non-vegetarian for f35, and main dishes around f27. It's a bit more expensive than the average Indian restaurant but worth the money.

INDONESIAN

Indonesia (Map 15; ☎ 623 20 35), Korte Leidsedwarsstraat 18, is one of the few places that does a really good rijsttafel, including properly marinated and barbecued satay that isn't smothered in peanut sauce. Prices start at f37.50 for the small rijsttafel nasi kuning (yellow rice) which is large enough to fill most stomachs. Book ahead, and be prepared for over-eager service.

Nearby, *Bojo* (Map 15; ☎ 622 74 34), Lange Leidsedwarsstraat 51, is open daily from 5 pm to 2 am (4 am on weekends) and is an institution among late eaters. The quality is uneven but it's surprisingly cheap for the Leidseplein area.

Restaurant Speciaal (Map 12; ☎ 624 97 06), Nieuwe Leliestraat 142, does good Indonesian food though this too can vary – perhaps it depends on the cook on duty. *Cilubang* (Map 12; ☎ 626 97 55), Runstraat 10, has a reasonable, filling rijsttafel for f36. At *Sukasari* (Map 13; ☎ 624 00 92), Damstraat 26 near the Dam, most dishes are under f20 (the nasi rames 'Sukasari' makes a good mini-rijsttafel for f18.50). It has seen better days before it was discovered by tourists but is still not a bad choice. The lunch specials won't disappoint.

Tempo Doeloe (Map 16; ☎ 625 67 18), Utrechtsestraat 75, is always good and charges accordingly. Book ahead.

'INTERNATIONAL'

Behind Centraal Station, *Pier 10* (Map 6; ☎ 624 82 76), at the end of a pier on the IJ at De Ruijterkade Steiger 10, offers a great view of the harbour as you dine by candlelight – freight barges pass right by your window. Its French/Dutch/Italian dishes are on the pricey side (mains around f35) but worth the money. The delicious plunger coffee for f6 fills three cups and comes with a huge plate of sweets. When booking, ask for a table in the rotunda at the tip of the pier (watch the sun set over the North Sea Canal).

De Belhamel (Map 13; ☎ 622 10 95), Brouwersgracht 60 (entrance around the corner in Binnen Wieringerstraat), is worth visiting for its Art Nouveau interior alone but the food is good too and quite affordable, with most mains under f30.

De Bolhoed (Map 12; ☎ 626 18 03),

Prinsengracht 60-62, serves organic food in arty surroundings. It's open daily from noon to 10 pm (dinner menu after 5 pm) and has a three-course dagmenu for f27.50. Lunch is soup and salad, dinner a choice of casserole, Mexican dishes and fish.

La Strada (Map 13; ☎ 625 02 76), Nieuwezijds Voorburgwal 93-95, has a mixed lesbian, gay and hetero clientele. There's a good atmosphere with a reasonable kitchen and very friendly service. Three-course menus start at f25, mains à la carte are under f30 (avoid the dagschotel or dagmenu). *Spanjer en van Twist* (Map 12; ☎ 639 01 09), Leliegracht 60, is a gayish place (after closing time you'll find most of the staff in Reguliersdwarsstraat) with romantic canalside tables in summer that are hard to beat. It serves sandwiches for lunch, and a main meal at night will set you back about f20.

If cheese fondue is your thing, try *Café Bern* (Map 13; ☎ 622 00 34), Nieuwmarkt 9; book ahead. *Eetcafé Gerrit van Beeren* (Map 13; ☎ 622 23 29), nearby at Koningsstraat 54, is an old-fashioned eetcafé serving fish and steaks daily from 4 pm to 1 am (kitchen closes at 10 pm). All dishes are under f30. Also in this area is *Hemelse Modder* (Map 13; ☎ 624 32 03), Oude Waal 9, a popular, slightly up-market restaurant serving international dishes at less than up-market prices (most mains under f30).

Szmulewicz (pronounced 'smoolerwitch'; Map 13; ☎ 620 28 22), Bakkersstraat 12 off Rembrandtplein, has a filling dish of the day for f16.50; other dishes are around f22. The food is very worthwhile (other places would charge more) and the ambience is lively; book ahead. Not far from here, *Sluizer* (Map 16; ☎ 622 63 76), Utrechtsestraat 43-45, does meat as well as fish (see the Seafood section). One of its famous specialities is spare ribs at f22.75; other mains cost around f29. Definitely book ahead.

Françoise Coffee Gallery (Map 15; ☎ 624 01 45), Kerkstraat 176, is a cosy, 'women-friendly' place serving snacks, salads and meals with classical music in the background. Works by women artists enliven the walls. The food is good and relatively cheap.

ITALIAN

Toscanini Caffè (Map 11; ☎ 623 28 13), Lindengracht 75 in the Jordaan, is a convivial place in a former courtyard, with mains under f30 and three-course menus for f55. It's always busy, so book ahead. Also in the Jordaan, *Burger's Patio* (Map 12; ☎ 623 68 54), Tweede Tuindwarsstraat 12, serves trendy Italian food in the evenings only. Despite the name, hamburgers are not the speciality.

Piccolino (Map 15; ☎ 623 14 95), Lange Leidsedwarsstraat 63, is one of the top Italian places in the Leidseplein area, open daily from noon to midnight. It's more than affordable and always packed – bookings are essential. Try the pizza calzone.

Deep Pan Pizza (Map 16; ☎ 622 31 60), Rembrandtplein 8-10, usually has space daily from noon to midnight. It's nothing special but serves all the pizza and pasta you can eat for f11, though you'd be better to order from the menu unless you're starved.

Panini (Map 16; ☎ 626 49 39), Vijzelgracht 3-5, serves delicious focaccias for lunch and equally tasty meals in the evenings (mains under f25); book ahead.

PANCAKES

The Dutch know how to make delicious, filling pancakes (savoury or sweet) and one of the best places to try them is *The Pancake Bakery* (Map 12; ☎ 625 13 33), Prinsengracht 191, in the basement of a restored old warehouse near Prinsenstraat. It has literally dozens of kinds of pancakes for f8 to f19, as well as omelettes, soups and desserts. The kitchen is open daily from noon to 9.30 pm.

SEAFOOD

Albatros (Map 12; ☎ 627 99 32), Westerstraat 264 in the Jordaan, is a good fish restaurant with a somewhat camp décor and a smoke-free section (totally smoke-free on the third Tuesday of the month). Main courses cost f28.50, three-course menus are f45, and the kitchen is open from 6 to 11 pm (closed Wednesday).

Sluizer (Map 16; ☎ 622 63 76), Utrechtsestraat 43-45, consists of two restaurants: a renowned fish restaurant at No 45 and a 'meat' restaurant at No 43, though both menus are offered in either, including the upstairs 'spillover' area. It's an Amsterdam institution along what is becoming a street of interesting little restaurants. The place is lively and always busy, so book ahead.

De Visscher (Map 13; ☎ 623 73 37), Kalverstraat 122, is a fast-food chain serving inexpensive, good seafood, open from 10 am to 7 pm (Sunday from noon).

SPANISH

Try *El Barco* (Map 16; ☎ 679 50 92), Daniël Stalpertstraat 93-95 near the Albert Cuyp market, and don't be put off by the silly boat-shaped bar and somewhat down-market interior. Excellent main dishes go for around f27.

SURINAMESE

Surinamese restaurants are small and specialise in takeaway food, though there might be a few tables and chairs. They close early and some are only open during the day (eg for lunch). Stroll around the backstreets near the Albert Cuyp market (Map 16), or try *Albert Cuyp 67* (☎ 671 13 96) at Albert Cuypstraat 67, or *Albina* (☎ 675 51 35) next door at No 69.

For Surinamese Indian and ditto Indonesian cuisine, head for *Riaz* (Map 6; ☎ 683 64 53), Bilderdijkstraat 193, a totally unpretentious local eatery with sterile décor. It's a bit out of the way but is worth seeking out: the food is surprisingly good and three courses will come to less than f25. Apart from meat dishes you can also have Surinamese and Indian vegetarian (the Surinamese dishes are larger). The place is halal and there's no pork or alcohol. Arrive early: it closes at 9 pm and all day Saturday.

THAI

Pathum Thai (Map 6; ☎ 624 49 36), Willemsstraat 16 in the northern Jordaan, is good, busy and cheap, with mains around f20.

THIRD WORLD

The *Soeterijn Café-Restaurant* (☎ 568 83 92), Linnaeusstraat 2, belongs to the Tropenmuseum (Tropics Museum; Map 7). People often have dinner here before attending a performance in the adjacent theatre and the specials of the week coincide with the performers' country of origin. It's open Monday to Saturday from 5 to 8.30 pm (also for lunch Tuesday to Friday) and you're advised to reserve.

TURKISH

Kilim (Map 11; ☎ 639 31 67), Lindengracht 248 in the Jordaan, is a Turkish eetcafé with wonderfully kitsch interior trimmings found in old-fashioned Jordaan cafés. The food isn't bad either.

VEGETARIAN

Vegetarianism is popular and almost all restaurants have one or two vegetarian dishes on the menu. If you prefer vegetarian surroundings, try the following:

The smoke-free vegetarian restaurant (☎ 553 93 22) in the *Oibibio* complex (Map 13; see Activities in the Things to See & Do chapter), Prins Hendrikkade 21, serves excellent food, though snacks and meals in the café downstairs are cheaper.

Vegetarisch Eethuis 'Sisters' (Map 13; ☎ 626 39 70), Nes 102 (the street parallel to Rokin), serves good-value food (special for f13) daily from 5 to 9.30 pm.

De Vliegende Schotel (Map 12; ☎ 625 20 41), Nieuwe Leliestraat 162 in the Jordaan, is a popular, homey little place with a blackboard menu. Meals are inexpensive (under f15) and are served daily from 5.30 to 10.15 pm.

Shizen (Map 15; ☎ 622 86 27), Kerkstraat 148 at Nieuwe Spiegelstraat, serves macrobiotic Japanese cuisine in an authentic Japanese décor, open Tuesday to Sunday from 5.30 to 10 pm.

Deshima Proeflokaal (Map 15; ☎ 625 75 13), Weteringschans 65 near the Rijksmuseum, is part of the macrobiotic Kushi Institute and provides a pseudo-intellectual scene while you consume a New Age lunch,

open weekdays from noon to 2 pm. The shop downstairs is open weekdays from 10 am to 6 pm, Saturday to 5 pm. The place could be closed for holidays in July.

A bit further east, *De Vrolijke Abrikoos* (Map 16; ☎ 624 46 72), Weteringschans 76, isn't fully vegetarian (it also serves meat and fish) but all ingredients are organic or at least environmentally kosher. Dishes are under f30, and it's open Wednesday to Sunday from 5.30 to 9.30 pm.

Harvest (Map 16; ☎ 676 99 95), Govert Flinckstraat 251, is fully vegetarian and purchases the ingredients at the nearby Albert Cuyp market. Dagschotels are under f20, and there's a terrace out the back. It's open Tuesday to Saturday from 5.30 to 11.30 pm (kitchen closes at 9.30 pm).

SELF-SERVICE CAFETERIAS

At Centraal Station, the *2nd-Class Restaurant* (☎ 627 33 06) along track 2A is a self-serve affair that does reasonable dagschotels for f12.50 and dagmenus for f18. The *Hema department store* (Map 13; ☎ 623 41 76), Nieuwendijk 174 a couple of blocks south of Centraal Station, has a good, inexpensive self-service cafeteria upstairs, open Monday to Friday from 11 am to 5.15 pm, Thursday to 8.15 pm, Saturday to 4.45 pm, Sunday from noon to 4.15 pm. It's also good for coffee and ice cream. Other department stores (*Vroom & Dreesmann, Bijenkorf*) also have worthwhile cafeterias.

The *Atrium* (Map 13; ☎ 525 39 99) is a student refectory (mensa) in the Binnen-gasthuis university complex, off the southern end of Oudezijds Achterburgwal. A student magazine rated the food a 4½ out of 10 but where else can you eat for f5.85 (with an Amsterdam university card) or f6.90 (without)? It's open weekdays from noon to 2 pm and 5 to 7 pm.

FAST FOOD

There are any number of sandwich shops (*broodjeszaken*) or snack bars to still your immediate hunger. The latter serve greasy junk food (French fries etc) but the former do a reasonable job with buns rather than sandwiches. If you're in a particularly healthy

RICHARD NEBESKY

ROB VAN DRIESUM

RICHARD NEBESKY

ROB VAN DRIESUM

Top Left: Amsterdam is full of interesting boutiques
Top Right: Souvenir T-shirts
Bottom Left: Cheese shop, Haarlemmerstraat
Bottom Right: Shop-window of a gay video shop in Kerkstraat

DAVID STANLEY

LIVE PORNO SHOW

LIVE PORNO SHOW THEATRE

RICHARD NEBESKY

RICHARD NEBESKY

Top: Water-borne revelry during Koninginnedag
Left: Red-light district
Right: Street performer

mood, ask for a *bruin broodje gezond* (brown bun healthy), with salad filling.

Vlaamse frites (Flemish fries) are French fries made from whole potatoes rather than the potato pulp you'll get if the sign only says 'frites'. They're supposed to be smothered in mayonnaise (though you can ask for ketchup or *pindasaus*, peanut sauce) and will fill your stomach for around f3. One of the best places to try them is at the Vlaams Friteshuis (Map 13), Voetboogstraat 31 off Spui square, Monday to Saturday from 11 am to 6 pm, Sunday from noon to 5.30 pm.

An *uitsmijter* (literally: 'bouncer') is fried eggs – sunny, often gluggy, side up – with cheese or meat (usually ham, sometimes beef) and garnish. Many cafés and snack bars serve this and it makes a filling breakfast or inexpensive lunch for less than f10.

Also try seafood at one of the seafood stalls around town. Raw, slightly salted herring (about f3.50, cut into bite-sized bits and served with optional onion and gherkin) might not sound appealing, but you could very well think differently once you've tried it. The same applies to smoked eel, which, like herring, is very filling, especially if taken in a bun. If you still can't bear the thought, go for shrimps or *gerookte makreel* (smoked mackerel).

Israeli or Lebanese snack bars specialise in *shoarma*, a pitta bread filled with sliced lamb from a vertical spit, salad and a choice of sauces, which makes a filling snack. In some parts of the world it's known as a *gyros* or *döner kebab*. Such places also do mean *felafel* (spiced chickpea patties, deep-fried).

Poffertjes are miniature pancakes, heaped on a plate and topped with butter and sprinkled with caster sugar – absolutely delicious. They're not a dessert but a snack served at special stalls or parlours using supposedly secret recipes.

SELF CATERING

Albert Heijn (AH), the country's dominant supermarket chain, seems pretty much to have sewn up the centre of Amsterdam, with branches at Koningsplein 6 (near Leidsestraat), Vijzelstraat 117, Haarlemmerdijk 1, PC Hooftstraat 129, Nieuwmarkt 18, Jodenbreestraat (new building, no number yet), Westerstraat 79-87 and Van Woustraat 148-150, among others. They've driven many neighbourhood shops and other supermarkets out of business, and the lack of competition shows in their occasional shabbiness and disinterested service. Still, they're cheap and open long hours – to 8 pm Monday to Saturday (to 9 pm Thursday) and some on Sunday afternoon. The AH at Koningsplein is open all week from 10 am to 10 pm (to 6 pm Sunday).

As you're paying at a supermarket the clerk may ask, *Wilt u zegels?* (Do you want stamps?). Say *nee* (no) because the stamps cost money and are only a nuisance. Beer bottles, crates and plastic soft-drink containers are returnable for a deposit (added to the purchase price when you buy them).

Other food shops include:

Hema, Nieuwendijk 174 (Map 13; ☎ 623 41 76) – good food section at the back of this department store

Bakkerij Paul Annee, Runstraat 25 (Map 12; ☎ 623 53 22) – a healthy organic bakery, weekdays from 8.45 am to 6 pm, Saturday from 9 am to 3 pm

Dirk van den Broek, behind the Heineken Museum at Eerste van der Helststraat 25 with another entrance at Marie Heinekenplein 25 (Map 16; ☎ 673 93 93) – one of the country's least expensive supermarket chains; open weekdays from 9 am to 7.30 pm (Monday from 11 am, Thursday to 9 pm, Friday from 8.30 am), Saturday to 6.30 pm); beats AH on price

Aldi Supermarket, Nieuwe Weteringstraat 28 near Vijzelgracht (Map 16) – cheaper than any of the above (though pretty depressing); open to 5.30 pm weekdays, to 4 pm Saturday

Entertainment

Amsterdam is many things to many people but no-one in their right mind would call it boring. It's one of the entertainment capitals of Europe, with wonderful pubs; music, theatre and film programmes to suit all tastes; and frantic nightlife that arouses even the most jaded party animals.

CAFÉS (PUBS)

When locals say *café* they mean a pub, also known as a *kroeg*, and there are over 1000 of them in the city. Proprietors prefer the term *café* (yes, they serve coffee as well, but very much as a sideline). See Drinks in the Places to Eat chapter for a summary of popular drinks.

Many cafés have outside seating on a *terras* (terrace) that may be covered and heated in winter. These are great places to relax and watch passers-by, soak up the sun, read a paper or write postcards for a few hours. Once you've ordered a drink you'll be left alone but you might be expected to order the occasional top-up. If all tables are occupied, don't be shy about asking if a seat is taken and sharing a table.

A good tradition in many cafés is the indoor reading table with the day's papers and news magazines, including one or two in English.

The price for a standard beer varies from around f2.50 in the outer suburbs to f4.25 in the popular Leidseplein and Rembrandtplein areas. If you occupy a table or sit at the bar, it's common to put drinks on a tab and to pay when you leave. If things are busy or you sit outside you'll probably have to pay per service.

Types of Cafés

Once upon a time cafés only served a few perfunctory snacks but many these days have proper menus. Those that take their food seriously (or would like their customers to think they do) call themselves *eetcafé* and

their food can be very good indeed. Many cafés in the following categories serve food.

The most famous type is the **brown café** (*bruin café*). The true specimen has been in business for a while, is stained by smoke (recent aspirants simply slap on the brown paint), has sand on the wooden floor, and provides an atmosphere conducive to deep and meaningful conversation. There might be Persian rugs on the tables to soak up spilled beer.

Grand cafés are spacious with comfortable furniture. They're all the rage, and any pub that installs a few solid tables and comfortable chairs will call itself a grand café. Some are grand indeed, and when they open at 10 am they're perfect for a lazy brunch with relaxing chamber music tinkling away in the background.

Theatre cafés attract performing artists and other types who do a lot of drinking. There are also a few **tasting houses** (*proeflokalen*) attached to distilleries, where you can try dozens of *genevers* and liqueurs (a holdover from the 17th century when many small distilleries operated around town) but no food.

Some cafés straddle these categories and others don't really fit in, such as the relatively new phenomenon of Irish pubs.

Opening hours depend on whether the café has opted to be a 'day business' (7 am to 1 am, weekends to 3 am), an 'evening business' (8 pm to 3 am, weekends to 4 am) or a 'night business' (10 pm to 4 am, weekends to 5 am). Cafés are free to adjust their hours within these limits and very few open before 9 am.

Brown Cafés

Medieval Centre There are more brown cafés in this part of town than elsewhere but many are newcomers that pander to tourists. *De Meester* (Map 13; no phone), Zeedijk 30, does no pandering whatsoever and has been going for about a century. Singing groups sometimes practise or perform here (Amsterdam ballads, klezmer) and if you stumble across such an occasion it's one of the most memorable pubs in town.

Not far from here on Nieuwmarkt square is *Lokaal 't Loosje* (Map 13; ☎ 627 26 35), Nieuwmarkt 32-34, an old café with beautiful tile tableaus on the walls. It's a student pub in the evening with mixed Nieuwmarkt clientele during the day.

Further south, *De Engelbewaarder* (Map 13; ☎ 625 37 72), Kloveniersburgwal 59, is a one-time literary café that's having its ups and downs.

Near Spui square are a few more brown cafés worth seeking out. The *Pilsener Club*, popularly known as the Engelse Reet (Map 13; ☎ 623 17 77), Begijnesteeg 4, is small, narrow and ramshackle. You can't do anything here but drink and talk, which is what a 'real' brown café is all about. It only started in 1893 but has hardly changed since then. Beer comes straight from the vat behind the draughting alcove and connoisseurs say they can taste the difference (most places have vats in a cellar or side room with long hoses to the bar). *De Schutter* (Map 13; ☎ 622 46 08), Voetboogstraat 13-15, is a student eetcafé open daily from 11 am but the kitchen operates from 5.45 to 10 pm; inexpensive dagschotels start at f14.50 and mains go up to f17.50. Several small bars on this street are lively.

On Spui square itself, visit *Hoppe* (Map 12; ☎ 623 78 49), Spui 18, one of the best known cafés in the city. It has been enticing drinkers behind its thick curtain for more than 300 years – the entrance is to the right of the pub-with-terrace of the same name. The crowd spills over onto the pavement in summer and helps Hoppe achieve one of the highest beer turnovers in the city; they wear blazers and twin-sets and coexist peacefully with left-wing journalists and writers at *Café De Zwart* (☎ 624 65 11) across the alley.

Within the Canal Belt The Jordaan area and adjoining Prinsengracht are packed with wonderful cafés. *Het Papeneiland* (Map 11; ☎ 624 19 89), Prinsengracht 2 on the corner

of Brouwersgracht, is a 17th century gem with its Delft-blue tiles and central stove. The name, Papists' Island, goes back to the Reformation when there was a clandestine Catholic church across the canal, allegedly linked to the other side by a secret tunnel. You won't be the only tourist visiting this café, and with good reason.

Nearby is *De II Prinsen* (Map 12; ☎ 624 97 22), Prinsenstraat 27 on the corner of Prinsengracht. Its large windows, mosaic floor and big terrace on Prinsengracht create a pleasant setting. Diagonally across the canal, *De 2 Zwaantjes* (Map 12; ☎ 625 27 29), Prinsengracht 114, is an authentic Jordaan café where Uncle Ben and Auntie Lena meet friends to play cards. On Friday, Saturday and Sunday it's sing-along Dutch ballads. The imposing leadlight awning over the bar (backlit for effect) is unique. Almost next door, *De Prins* (Map 12; ☎ 624 93 82), Prinsengracht 124, is a pleasant, unassuming brown café popular among locals, with good lunchtime sandwiches.

In the Jordaan itself, *Café Nol* (Map 12; ☎ 624 53 80), Westerstraat 109, is the epitome of the Jordaan café, a place where the original Jordanese (ie before students, artists and professionals moved in) still sing oompah ballads with drunken abandon. The kitsch interior is so over-the-top that it's a must-see. *De Tuin* (Map 12; ☎ 624 45 59), Tweede Tuindwarsstraat 13, has a youngish clientele, and is a good place to start the evening. *De Reiger* (Map 12; ☎ 624 74 26), Nieuwe Leliestraat 34, was one of the first brown cafés to serve food. It's narrow at the front but the noisy dining section at the back is more spacious.

A bit further south on Prinsengracht is *Van Puffelen* (Map 12; ☎ 624 62 70), Prinsengracht 377, a café-restaurant popular among students and other intellectual types. The restaurant area, with food prices marked on blackboards, is quieter than the pub (in most places it's the other way round). It's open weekdays from 3 pm, weekends from noon, and the kitchen from 6 pm. *De Doffer* (Map 12; ☎ 622 66 86), Runstraat 12-14, is another popular student café with affordable food.

De Pieper (Maps 12 & 15; ☎ 626 47 75), Prinsengracht 424, is small and unassuming but unmistakably old (from 1664), and is considered by some to be the king of the brown cafés. There's a replica at the Hilton Hotel, the *Hilton Yacht Club*.

On Leidseplein, venerable *Reynders* (Map 15; ☎ 623 44 19), Leidseplein 6, has a pleasant terrace (heated in winter) and is a good place for people-watching. *Eylders* (Map 15; ☎ 624 27 04), Korte Leidsedwarsstraat 47 a few buildings up from Reynders, is an artists' café with exhibits and attractive leadlights. During WWII it was a meeting-place for artists who refused to toe the cultural line imposed by the Nazis.

In the southern corner of the canal belt is *De Fles* (Map 16; ☎ 624 96 44), Vijzelstraat 137 (entrance down the stairs on Prinsengracht). It's a somewhat forgotten but proud café, with an open kitchen that served meals long before it became fashionable for pubs to do so. You'll eat well for less than f25, but they really should fix that kitchen ventilation.

Not far from here, *Oosterling* (Map 16; ☎ 623 41 40), Utrechtsestraat 140, is as authentic as it gets and steeped in history (it started in the early 1700s as a tea and coffee outlet for the United East India Company). Things get pretty busy at the end of the working day, when employees from the Nederlandsche Bank (Central Bank of the Netherlands) come across the road to swap bills for drinks. It's one of the few cafés with a bottle-shop permit (highly unusual).

Outside the Canal Belt

Koffiehuis Dusart (Map 9; ☎ 671 28 18), Dusartstraat 53, is a typical Pijp eetcafé with kitsch interior, frequented by taxi drivers and other locals. There's a large menu with mains for around f19 (try the spare ribs).

Grand Cafés

The *Oibibio* centre (Map 13; ☎ 553 93 22, see Activities in the Things to See & Do chapter), diagonally opposite Centraal Station at Prins Hendrikkade 20-21, includes a spacious, thoughtfully designed grand café

and tea garden. Out towards the west is *Dulac* (Map 11; ☎ 624 42 65), Haarlemmerstraat 118. This former bank building has been beautifully decorated in a mixture of styles and is definitely worth a visit, but forget about the food. It's open from 4 pm to 1 am (to 2 am weekends).

Café de Jaren (Map 13; ☎ 625 57 71), Nieuwe Doelenstraat 20, is a large, bright grand café overlooking the Amstel from its balcony and water terraces. People here are in their 20s and 30s, slightly yuppish. Service can be indifferent but it's a pleasant place to have brunch on a Sunday. The great reading table has some foreign publications. Nearby, *Café-Restaurant Dantzig* (Map 13; ☎ 620 90 39), Zwanenburgwal 15 in the Stopera on the Amstel, has a great riverside terrace in summer with a good view over the water – just the place to unwind after shopping at Waterlooplein market.

The pearl of the grand cafés is *Mediacafé De Kroon* (Map 13; ☎ 625 20 11), Rembrandtplein 17-1, which attracts people of all ages. Walk through the recessed entrance and up the stairs to the 1st floor or take the lift. It has an appealing, neocolonial design with a biological bent (ancient microscope on the counter, cabinets with pinned butterflies and skeletons), and a beautiful covered balcony terrace with a good view over Rembrandtplein. The food in the restaurant section (mains around f30) is worth trying. The rest of the building houses radio and TV studios.

On Spui square, stop at *Luxembourg* (Map 12; ☎ 620 62 64), Spui 22-24, a brown café on a grand scale with an interesting mix of people. Watch the goings-on in the square from the terrace. The menu includes tasty breakfasts, great sandwiches and other lunchtime surprises. Check the reading table or buy a paper at Athenaeum newsagency and read it in the morning sun.

The oldest and by far the most stylish grand café is *Café Americain* (Map 15; ☎ 624 53 22), in the American Hotel at Leidsekade 97 just off Leidseplein (entrance on the Leidseplein side). This Art Deco monument opened in 1902 and was extensively renovated in 1993. Anyone who thinks they are anybody can be found here at some stage. Prices are stiff but it's worth visiting at least once for a coffee, beer or snack; meals are fine but will cost a bit. The reading table is a serious affair, and there's a non-smoking section.

Irish, English & American Pubs

Mulligans (Map 13; ☎ 622 13 30), Amstel 100 near Rembrandtplein, is probably the most 'authentic' of Amsterdam's crop of Irish bars, at least music-wise. There's live Irish music and dancing most nights at 9 pm (no cover charge), Guinness on tap, and a friendly, congenial atmosphere. *O'Donnell's* (Map 16; ☎ 676 77 86), Ferdinand Bolstraat 5 at Marie Heinekenplein (just south of the Heineken Museum), is a large Irish pub with a few snugs (great if you can grab one). In the red-light district, try *Durty Nelly's* (Map 13; ☎ 638 01 25), Warmoesstraat 117 (also a rear entrance at Sint Annendwarsstraat), which attracts many foreign visitors from the cheap hotels in the area. Irish breakfasts are served from 9 am.

Nearby is the *Last Waterhole* (Map 13; ☎ 624 48 14), Oudezijds Armsteeg 12, a popular place for young, mainly English-speaking travellers. It has three pool tables, a giant video screen, jam sessions Wednesdays at 10 pm, and rock or blues groups Friday and Saturday at 10 pm. There's also a happy hour from 9 to 10 pm and hostel beds for f25.

Homesick English visitors might wish to sample a pint at the *Old Bell* (Map 16; ☎ 624 76 82), Rembrandtplein 46 on the corner of Utrechtsestraat, a comfortable English pub that has barely changed since it began in the 1960s. It's popular among business people and staff from the nearby banks, and of course tourists, but is less appealing on weekends when brazen Dutch youth take over.

At *Harry's American Bar* (Map 12; ☎ 624 43 84), Spuistraat 285 near Spui, you can try 21 different cocktails and a dozen long drinks daily from 5 pm to 1 am (to 2 am Saturday and Sunday).

Tasting Houses

Just off Dam square, *Proeflokaal Wijnand Fockinck* (Map 13; ☎ 622 53 34), Pijlsteeg 37 (through an arcade behind Grand Hotel Krasnapolsky), is a small tasting house without seats or stools, where you can try scores of different genevers and liqueurs – some are quite expensive and all are potent!

Nearby is *De Drie Fleschjes* (Map 13; ☎ 624 84 43), Gravenstraat 18 behind the Nieuwe Kerk. The place dates from 1650, and is dominated by old vats that are rented out to groups whose members can help themselves. It's closed Sunday.

Theatre Cafés

De Smoeshaan (☎ 625 03 68), in Theater Bellevue (Map 15) at Leidsekade 90, gets pretty lively with theatre visitors and artists. There's a good restaurant upstairs.

Another theatre café worth checking is *Blincker* (Map 13; ☎ 627 19 38), in the Frascati theatre complex at Sint Barberenstraat 7-9 (an alley off Nes). It has an attractive modern design in steel and marble with plants and an open mezzanine floor. There's a large collection of wines and the food isn't bad either.

De Brakke Grond (Map 13; ☎ 626 00 44), Nes 43, is part of the Flemish Cultural Centre and does an honest trade in Flemish beer and food.

Women's Cafés

Vrouwencafé Saarein (Map 12; ☎ 623 49 01), Elandsstraat 119 in the south of the Jordaan, has been a women-only café since the late 1970s when it was a focal point of the feminist movement. The venue itself dates from the early 1600s – the stunningly beautiful interior has been kept intact except for the paintwork. The feminist radicalism has dimmed somewhat but it's still a premier meeting place for women of all persuasions.

In the north of the Jordaan, at Lindengracht 95, is *Vandenberg* (Map 11; ☎ 622 27 16), a cosy eetcafé popular among lesbians but men come here too. A good meal will set you back about f15, or you can just have a drink.

Villa Zeezicht (Map 13; ☎ 626 74 33), Torensteeg 7 west of Dam square, is not a women's café as such but the vast majority of the clientele is female, mostly students from the arts faculty around the corner who come for the good cakes and coffee.

Vivelavie (Map 13; ☎ 624 01 14), Amstelstraat 7 off Rembrandtplein, is one of the more popular women's bars in town, though the youngish clientele is by no means exclusively female. It's a lively place, with loud music and large windows so everyone can see out or in.

Other Cafés

In de Wildeman (Map 13; ☎ 638 23 48), Kolksteeg 3 between Nieuwendijk and Nieuwezijds Voorburgwal, is a former distillery tasting house, now transformed into a beautiful 'beer café' with many different beers and a separate smoke-free area (!).

Two alleys south of here is *Eetcafé Het Splintertje* (Map 13; ☎ 627 53 60), a tiny place at Nieuwe Nieuwstraat 28. A sign by the door says 'no drugs sold here' (it's stuck between two coffee shops). Vivacious Sylvia provides a home away from home for the many foreigners who work in budget hotels in the area – ask to see the guest book (she'll show it anyway). The food is so-so (menu of the day with soup, main dish and a big mug of coffee for f19.50), but the toilets (f1 fee for non-customers) are excellent.

Himalaya (Map 13; ☎ 626 08 99), Warmoesstraat 56, is a New Age tearoom, open Monday from 1 to 6 pm, and Tuesday to Saturday from 10 am to 6 pm (Thursday to 8.30 pm) – just the place to put some yin back into your yang.

North of Spui square is *Gollem* (Map 12; ☎ 626 66 45), Raamsteeg 4, the pioneer of Amsterdam's 'beer cafés'. Choose from 200 beers on tap or in the bottle. It's small and never dull.

Maximiliaan (Map 13; ☎ 626 62 80), Kloveniersburgwal 6-8 off Nieuwmarkt square, is a rambling brewery pub with copper kettles. It opened in 1992 on the site of a former monastery brewery and is one of the two breweries that operate in the city (the

other is Bierbrouwerij 't IJ – see East of the Plantage in the Things to See & Do chapter). It has a restaurant, tasting area, tours and beer seminars, and several home-brewed beers on tap (some seasonal). There's usually live music Thursday from 8 pm (first Thursday of the month jazz, second Thursday tango squeezebox).

Café-Restaurant Kapitein Zeppo's (Map 13; ☎ 624 20 57), Gebed Zonder End 5 just off Grimburgwal, has a mixed clientele including many young students, and is one of the livelier pick-up joints in town. There's regular live music, and first Sunday in the month is 'café chantant' where anyone can get up and sing with real big-band backing. The food is mediocre but the atmosphere more than compensates.

Further east is *Vins Petrus* (Map 13; ☎ 625 89 03), Waterlooplein 125 (along on a 1st-floor gallery on Houtkopersdwarsstraat, between Waterlooplein and Jodenbreestraat), a convivial wine bar where the owner is happy to uncork a bottle or two for tasting purposes. Snacks and simple meals are also available but unfortunately it could be closed during the day.

At Rembrandtplein, *Café Schiller* (Map 16; ☎ 624 98 46), Rembrandtplein 26, is worth a visit for its stylish, Art Deco interior with portraits of Dutch actors and cabaret artists from the 1920s and 1930s. It's a small-ish place with a clientele of journalists, artists and students, and does good food with dagschotels from f18.50.

South of here, *Kort* (Map 16; ☎ 626 11 99), Amstelveld 12 along the southern wall of the Amstelkerk, has a wonderful, quiet terrace looking out over Prinsengracht where you can spend peaceful hours in summer. The interior is up-market with art displays and the menu is a bit overpriced.

South-east of the canal belt is *Café De IJsbreker* (Map 17; ☎ 665 30 14), Weesperzijde 23 on the Amstel beyond the Amstel Inter-Continental Hotel (through the pedestrian underpass under Mauritskade). This pleasant café belongs to the IJsbreker centre for contemporary music and has a great riverside terrace in summer where you can mix it with the country's leading experimental musicians.

Out towards the west, in the Westergasfabriek complex beyond the Haarlem Quarter, is *Café West Pacific* (Map 11; ☎ 597 44 58), Haarlemmerweg 8-10. It's a large café with a restaurant and lots of character, and is an 'in' place among the 25 to 35 age group. It's open from 11.30 to 1 am (to 3 am on weekends); after 11 pm from Thursday to Sunday it functions as a disco (1970s and trip-hop music).

CINEMAS

There are only 14 cinemas in Amsterdam but many have several theatres and there's always a good choice of films, including a high proportion of 'art' movies for the discerning viewer. The 'film ladder' – the listing of what's on at cinemas around town – is pinned up at cinemas and in many pubs, or you can check it in the paper on Thursdays, when weekly programmes change. *AL* means *alle leeftijden*, all ages, and 12 or 16 indicate the minimum age for admission.

Films are almost always screened in their original language with Dutch subtitles; the exceptions are children's matinees, where the latest Disney creation may come with Dutch voices.

The mainstream Hollywood cinemas around Leidseplein have half-price matinee tickets for their first screening weekdays, but check beforehand. The following cinemas may be worth seeking out:

Tuschinskitheater, Reguliersbreestraat 26 near Rembrandtplein (Map 13; ☎ 626 26 33) – a monument worth visiting for its sumptuous Art Deco interior; the façade offers only a hint of what's inside

Kriterion, Roetersstraat 170 (Map 17; ☎ 623 17 09) – Amsterdam School/Art Deco building showing cult movies, with occasional 'sneak previews' of not-yet-released films; lively café worth visiting in its own right; popular among students from the university faculties across the road

The Movies, Haarlemmerdijk 161 (Map 11; ☎ 638 60 16) – 'interesting', often highbrow films without intermission (visit the toilet beforehand); there's also a restaurant

De Uitkijk, Prinsengracht 452 just off Leidsestraat (Map 15; ☎ 623 74 60) – the city's oldest surviving cinema, a cosy affair in an old canal house

Desmet, Plantage Middenlaan 4A near Artis zoo (Map 14; ☎ 627 34 34) – art cinema showing avantgarde European films

Nederlands Filmmuseum, Vondelpark 3 (Map 15; ☎ 589 14 00) – films shown daily (admission f10); live jazz in the café Sunday afternoons; has a large terrace overlooking the park (a good place to arrange to meet someone)

Gay & Lesbian

Desmet often has gay cinema on Saturday night, and both Desmet and *De Uitkijk* sometimes show films with a gay or lesbian theme. For other options, enquire at gay venues or ring the Gay & Lesbian Switchboard (☎ 623 65 65).

MUSIC

For a description of the local music scene, see Music in the Facts about Amsterdam chapter. Many of the venues listed below are easy – just turn up at the door and pay to get in. You might want to book ahead, however, for famous acts or highbrow performances – check the *Uitkrant* to see what's happening where. For further information and bookings, contact the venues direct or get in touch with the Amsterdam Uitburo (Map 15; ☎ 621 12 11, seven days a week from 9 am to 9 pm), Leidseplein 26. For bookings from abroad, call the National Reservations Centre on ☎ +31-70-320 25 00.

Classical & Contemporary

A pleasant feature of the Amsterdam music scene is the free lunchtime concerts, usually chamber music, from 12.30 to 1.30 pm (not in June, July or August when everyone goes on holidays). The Muziektheater offers free concerts of 20th century music on Tuesday in the Boekmanzaal; on Wednesday the Concertgebouw has chamber music or classical concerts, sometimes also jazz, but you won't be the only visitor taking advantage of this; and Friday the Bethaniënklooster puts on anything from medieval to contemporary, while the IJsbreker specialises in contemporary music.

Bethaniënklooster, Barndesteeg 6B (Map 13; ☎ 625 00 78) – small former monastery near Nieuwmarkt square; ticket office open half an hour before performances

Beurs van Berlage, Damrak 243 (Map 13; ☎ 627 04 66) – two small concert halls; ticket office open Tuesday to Friday from 12.30 to 6 pm, Saturday to 5 pm, and 75 minutes before performances

Churches – check the Amsterdam Uitburo for performances (not just organ recitals) in the Oude Kerk, Nieuwe Kerk, Engelse Kerk (the English/Scottish Presbyterian church in the Begijnhof), Round Lutheran Church, Waalse Kerk (the Walloon Church at Oudezijds Achterburgwal 157), Amstelkerk etc

Koninklijk Theater Carré, Amstel 115-125 (Map 16; ☎ 622 52 25) – opera, operetta, ballet, musicals, cabaret; ticket office open daily from 10 am to 7 pm (Sunday from 1 pm)

Concertgebouw, Concertgebouwplein 4-6 (Map 15; ☎ 671 83 45, recording in Dutch) – world-famous concert hall with near-perfect acoustics; ticket office open daily from 10 am to 7 pm (telephone only to 5 pm); after 7 pm you can only get tickets for that evening's performance

Muziekcentrum De IJsbreker, Weesperzijde 23 (Map 17; ☎ 693 90 93) – centre for contemporary music; ticket office open daily from 9.30 am to 5.30 pm, and from 7.45 pm on performance nights

Muziektheater, Waterlooplein 22 (☎ 625 54 55) – large-scale ballet and opera in the Stopera (Map 13); ticket office open Monday to Saturday from 10 am to 6 pm, Sunday and public holidays from 11.30 am

Stadsschouwburg, Leidseplein 26 (Map 15; ☎ 624 23 11) – opera and operetta; ticket office open Monday to Saturday from 10 am to start of performances

Rock

Information and tickets are available at the Amsterdam Uitburo or at the venues direct, but when it comes to large pop concerts you can also ring the Postbank ticket service on ☎ 0900-30 01 25.

Arena concert hall, 's-Gravesandestraat 51 in the Arena Budget Hotel complex (Map 17; ☎ 694 74 44) – rock concerts Thursday, Friday and Saturday nights

Arena Stadium in the Bijlmer (☎ 311 13 33 for information) – the ultimate stadium venue (seats 52,000) with shows that are big on lights, screens and production, and performers who are tiny little dots; for the world's top crowd-pullers (Michael Jackson, Tina Turner, Pavarotti, Celine Dion etc)

Bourbon Street Jazz & Blues Club, Leidsekruisstraat 6-8 (Map 15; ☎ 623 34 40) – blues, funk and rock & roll; open weekdays from 10 pm to 4 am, weekends to 5 am

Jaap Eden Hal, Radioweg 64 (☎ 694 98 94, recording in Dutch) – ice hockey rink used two or three times a year for rock concerts; take tram No 9 from Centraal Station

De Koe, Marnixstraat 381 (☎ 625 44 82) – *the* place to check what's happening in the Amsterdam pop scene, with regular band performances on Sunday from 4 pm (free admission)

Korsakoff, Lijnbaansgracht 161 (Map 12; ☎ 625 78 54) – open daily from 10 pm to 4 am; hard rock and alternative music, young clientele; could be difficult to get in

Melkweg (Milky Way), Lijnbaansgracht 234 (Map 15; ☎ 624 17 77) – membership f4 a month, extra admission depending on what's on; cinema, art gallery, café, multimedia entertainment; live music four times a week (often world music, from Aboriginal to Eskimo); the place remains as stoned as ever and the police station across the road doesn't mind

Paradiso, Weteringschans 6 off Leidseplein (Map 15; ☎ 626 45 21 or 623 73 48) – membership f4 a month, extra admission depending on what's on; 'activity centre' housed in a former church; opens at 8 pm when there's a concert, 10 pm when it's a dance; big-name groups have been appearing here since the 1960s (the Stones recorded a video clip recently with a crowd of 'beautiful people' provided by modelling agencies)

Westergasfabriek, Haarlemmerweg 8-10 (Maps 6 & 11) – a former gas factory that hosts two or three rock concerts a year in the old, round gas-holder, as well as the Drum Rhythm Festival, other arts events, raves etc; contact the Amsterdam Uitburo on ☎ 621 12 11, or Café West Pacific (see the earlier pubs section)

Jazz & Blues

Jazz is popular and there's a lot happening in cafés around town; blues thrives less. The world's largest jazz festival is the North Sea Jazz Festival in The Hague in July (see Public Holidays & Special Events in the Facts for the Visitor chapter), and throughout that month many international greats take the opportunity to strut their stuff in Amsterdam venues.

Jazz Café Alto, Korte Leidsedwarsstraat 115 (Map 15; ☎ 626 32 49) – music daily from 10 pm to 2 am

Bamboo Bar, Lange Leidsedwarsstraat 64 (Map 15; ☎ 624 39 93) – open daily from 9 pm, music from 10 pm

Bimhuis, Oude Schans 73-77 (Map 13; ☎ 623 33 73) – Amsterdam's main jazz venue (Dutch and international jazz greats play here); bar open from 8 pm Monday to Saturday, closed Sunday and from July to mid-August; concerts Thursday, Friday and Saturday from 9 pm; might move to a new location due to noise problems as yuppies move into renovated homes in this formerly industrial area

Casablanca, Zeedijk 26 (Map 13; ☎ 625 56 85) – jazz café with an illustrious history since it opened in 1946; its glory days are over, and apart from jam sessions on Tuesday and the occasional jazz and big-band performances on other nights it's mainly a karaoke bar, albeit a fun one with none of the sadness normally attached to such establishments; open from 8 pm daily

Heeren van Aemstel, Thorbeckeplein 5 off Rembandtplein (Map 16; ☎ 620 21 73) – open daily from noon (Friday from 4 pm); office workers and somewhat elitist students; live music begins around 10 pm (jazz throughout the week, covers Friday and Saturday and funk Sunday); convincing grand café interior (it used to be the Moulin Rouge night club); also eetcafé

Maloe Melo, formerly known as De Kroeg, Lijnbaansgracht 163 (Map 12; ☎ 420 45 92) – live blues every night; pub opens at 9 pm, the hall at 10.30 pm, and live music begins at 11 pm

Latin American

The following places are dance-oriented (which goes with the music) and could be a bit too loud to sit and have a quiet chat:

Canecão, Lange Leidsedwarsstraat 70 (Map 15; ☎ 626 15 00) – live Brazilian music; open from 10 pm to 4 am Sunday to Thursday, to 5 am Friday and Saturday

Iboya, Korte Leidsedwarsstraat 29 (Map 15; ☎ 623 78 59) – salsa and rumba; open Thursday to Sunday from 11 pm to 4 am

World Music

This is one of the European centres for music from exotic parts of the world. See Music in the Facts about Amsterdam chapter for information sources, or contact the Amsterdam Uitburo about gigs in the venues listed below, as well as at Paradiso, Melkweg and Latin bars.

Akhnaton, Nieuwezijds Kolk 25-27 (Map 13; ☎ 624 33 96) – bills itself as a 'centre for world culture'; open Friday and Saturday from 11 pm to 4 am, with live music Friday: first Friday of the month

is hip hop, the second is dance parties for 30+ (jazz dance, salsa, raj, souk), the third African and the fourth salsa, but this changes so ring to find out; last Sunday of the month is 'salon de tango' from 4 to 8 pm ; f10 admission, f12.50 if there's a band (no fee after 3 am)

Soeterijntheater, Linnaeusstraat 2 (☎ 568 85 00) – in the Tropenmuseum (Map 17); phone operates weekdays from 10 am to 4 pm; mostly Asian, Indian and African music with admissions varying from f12 to f22; the adjoining restaurant serves food to suit the performances

THEATRE

There are about 50 theatres – the ones listed below are merely a selection. Performances are often in Dutch, sometimes in English (especially in summer) and sometimes it doesn't matter. Check the *Uitkrant* or contact the Amsterdam Uitburo (☎ 621 12 11, also for bookings, seven days a week from 9 am to 9 pm), or call the following theatres direct. For bookings from abroad, call the National Reservations Centre on ☎ +31-70-320 25 00.

Amsterdamse Bos Theatre (☎ 638 38 47) – large, open-air amphitheatre with plays in summer

De Balie, Kleine Gartmanplantsoen 10 (☎ 623 29 04) – international productions for trendy intellectuals (see Cultural Centres in the Facts for the Visitor chapter)

Theater Bellevue, Leidsekade 90 (Map 15; ☎ 624 72 48) – experimental theatre, cabaret and dance

Boom Chicago, Korte Leidsedwarsstraat 12 (Map 15; ☎ 422 17 76) – English-language stand-up comedy throughout the year

De Brakke Grond, Nes 45 (Map 13; ☎ 626 68 66) – Flemish theatre

Koninklijk Theater Carré, Amstel 115-125 (Map 16; ☎ 622 52 25) – the largest theatre in town (1700 seats), with international shows, musicals, cabaret, circuses etc

Felix Meritis, Keizersgracht 324 (Map 12; ☎ 623 13 11) – the former cultural centre of the city, now with experimental theatre and dance

Frascati, Nes 63 (Map 13; ☎ 626 68 66 day, or ☎ 623 57 23 evening) – experimental theatre

De Kleine Komedie, Amstel 56 near Rembrandtplein (☎ 624 05 34) – concerts, dance and cabaret, sometimes in English

Melkweg, Lijnbaansgracht 234A (Map 15; ☎ 624 17 77) – world-renowned cultural centre, with anything from music and film to plays, dance and multimedia productions

Soeterijntheater, Linnaeusstraat 2 (☎ 568 85 00) – theatre of the Tropenmuseum (Map 17), with plays, dance, film and anything else relating to non-Western culture

Stadsschouwburg, Leidseplein 26 (Map 15; ☎ 624 23 11) – the city's most beautiful theatre, home to the stolid Toneelgroep Amsterdam; large-scale productions and operetta; English-language productions in summer

Universiteitstheater, Nieuwe Doelenstraat 16 (☎ 623 01 27) – home to the Institute for Dramatic Art, with some performances in English

Vondelpark Theatre, Vondelpark (☎ 673 14 99) – large (1800-seat) open-air amphitheatre in the middle of the Vondelpark, with a wide range of performing arts in June, July and August

Westergasfabriek, Haarlemmerweg 8-10 (Maps 6 & 11) – former gas factory that hosts a wide range of theatre and music performances, events and festivals; for details contact the Amsterdam Uitburo (☎ 621 12 11)

DISCOS

Not much happens before 10 pm and some places don't start bopping till well after midnight. Many places are *alleen voor leden* (only for members) but you can 'join' at the door if the bouncer likes the look of you and the place isn't packed to capacity. You don't have to tip him (or the rare her) on the way out but f2.50 to f5 might be wise if you want helpful treatment next time. Dress standards are casual and with one or two exceptions you'll be out of place if you dress up, though some people do put effort into looking casual.

The venues listed below close at 4 or 5 am. Pill-poppers head for house parties in different parts of town from 5 or 6 am till noon – keep an eye out for fliers (printed or human) at discos or ask around at closing time. (Only in Amsterdam: a guy called August de Loor, who frequents the house circuits, will check ecstasy pills for purity for a fee of f2.50. Alternatively, contact him at the Adviesburo Drugs, ☎ 623 79 43, Entrepotdok 32A, in which case the test costs f5.)

The following discos could be worth trying:

Arena Budget Hotel (Map 17; see Places to Stay) – disco parties with large crowds

Club 114, Herengracht 114 (Map 12; ☎ 622 76 85) – daily from 11 pm; mainly house and techno music but the programme can vary; formerly this was the legendary Okshoofd, an anything-goes place where students, drug barons and partying rock stars felt at home, but heavy-handed police intervention forced a name and staff change and it's still recovering

Dansen bij Jansen, Handboogstraat 11 off Spui square (Map 13; ☎ 620 17 79) – popular student disco that's been in business for over 20 years; often too busy to dance; happy hour from 11 pm to midnight; *d'Oude Herbergh* bar next door (Map 13) gets lively with fraternity students

Escape, Rembrandtplein 11 (Map 13; ☎ 622 11 11) – commercial disco, the largest in Amsterdam, with popular music (young, house), laser shows and heavy security at the door; open from 10 pm Thursday to Saturday; admission f20

iT, Amstelstraat 24 (Maps 13 & 16; ☎ 625 01 11) – Thursday to Sunday from 11 pm (Friday and Saturday gays only); fancy or semi-nude dress required for admission (check the photos outside); a huge disco with professional dancers, drag queens, go-go girls, fake Madonnas and occasionally the real Grace Jones; a very 'in' place; admission f10 (Thursday free); popular among VIPs; expensive drinks

Mazzo, Rozengracht 114 (Map 12; ☎ 626 75 00) – daily from 11 pm; house and jungle; many young foreigners; admission f10

Odeon, Singel 460 (Map 12; ☎ 624 97 11, recording in Dutch) – disco opens at 11 pm nightly; 'three floors of dancing' with different types of music, mainly jazz dance and hip hop; jazz cellar

Richter, Reguliersdwarsstraat 36 (Map 16; ☎ 626 15 73) – daily from midnight; soul, R&B and jazz dance

RoXY, Singel 465 near Muntplein (Map 13; ☎ 620 03 54) – in a former cinema (note the Art Deco interior); closed Monday and Tuesday; open from 11 pm; house-party trend-setter; Wednesday gay, Thursday soul, Friday glam and Saturday sweat; very difficult to get in on Friday and Saturday

Seymour Likely, Nieuwezijds Voorburgwal 250 (☎ 627 14 27) – dance club for the trendy 'in' crowd; don't arrive before midnight; major record companies often use it for launching new albums

Soul Kitchen, Amstelstraat 32 next to iT disco (Maps 13 & 16; ☎ 620 23 33) – Wednesday to Sunday from 11 pm; soul music and old dance music, popular among 'elderly youngsters' (minimum age for admission 25) who don't feel at home in regular discos

Café West Pacific (Map 11) – see the earlier Cafés (Pubs) section

Hotel Winston (Map 13; see the Places to Stay chapter) – the café has a popular weekend disco with 1970s music

GAY & LESBIAN

Apart from the commercial venues listed below there's an active alternative circuit, for instance there's the *COC* (mixed disco Friday night, women's disco Saturday night) and *De Trut* (Map 6; no phone), a Sunday-night-only disco (mixed lesbian and gay) at Bilderdijkstraat 165E. Unfortunately these clubs are so popular that they're becoming less 'alternative'. Non-commercial venues with names like the Sissy-Club, Clitclub and Dirty Dicks generally don't last long. Ask around or contact the Gay & Lesbian Switchboard to find out about the latest 'in' places.

The following areas are centres for gay entertainment.

Reguliersdwarsstraat (Map 13)

The street for the 'trendy Wendys' (ie those who are well dressed and 'with it'), also known simply as the Straat, has some of Amsterdam's most famous gay establishments. Plan to spend at least a whole evening here in summer and bring plenty of money (you won't get a beer for under f4). During the day, have coffee and cake at *Downtown* (No 31), where they have the best gay reading table in town.

Around 11 pm things begin to pick up. Drink a genever at *Havana* (No 17) and relocate to *April's* (No 37) for the happy hour between midnight and 1 am. Then head for *Exit* (No 42) diagonally across the street. The bar downstairs is very popular, with camp sing-alongs; upstairs is another café and a disco playing the latest music; above that is yet another café, and the darkroom is on the top floor.

Amstel & Rembrandtplein (Map 13)

This is real queen territory where Rembrandt would have gained plenty of inspiration for different versions of his *Nightwatch* – one with moustaches at *Monopole* (Amstel 60), elderly leather boys at *Company* (Amstel 106), or a varied disco crowd at *Montmartre*

(Halve Maansteeg 17). *De Steeg* (Halve Maansteeg 10) is quite an experience, with dancing lamps above the bar when Dutch ballads are played (you'll understand it when you see it) – singing brings people closer together and you'll probably make contact more easily here than elsewhere. And then of course there's *iT* in Amstelstraat (see the earlier Discos listing), one of the most extravagant discos in town.

Warmoesstraat

Kinky Amsterdam congregates in pubs with illustrious names such as *Cockring* (No 96), *Eagle* (No 86) and *Argos* (No 95) – anything from leather, rubber and piercings to slings, darkrooms and, of course, hard-core porn. Patrons are quite clear about what they want.

'COFFEE SHOPS'

Many establishments that call themselves *koffieshop* (as opposed to *koffiehuis*, espresso bar or sandwich shop) are in the cannabis business, though they do serve coffee. There are also a few *hashcafés* serving alcohol that are barely distinguishable from pubs. The ubiquitous hemp leaves have been taken down to appease concerned politicians (see Drugs in the Facts for the Visitor chapter), but it's a safe bet that an establishment showing palm leaves and perhaps Rastafarian colours (red, yellow and green) will have something to do with cannabis – take a look at the clientele and ask at the bar for the list of goods on offer, usually packaged in small bags for f25.

Another concession to politics is that 'space' cakes and cookies are no longer on display and are often unavailable, mainly because tourists had problems. If you're unused to their effects, or the time they take to kick in and run their course, you could indeed be in for a rather involved experience. Many coffee shops sell magic mushrooms, which is quite legal because it's an untreated, natural product (though this could change, with the argument that drying the mushrooms is a treatment, which makes them illegal).

Cannabis products used to be imported but

these days the country has top-notch home produce, so-called *nederwiet* (NAY-der-weet) developed by diligent horticulturalists and grown in greenhouses with up to five harvests a year. Even the police admit it's a superior product, especially the potent 'superskunk' with up to 13% of the active substance THC (Nigerian grass has 5% and Colombian 7%). According to a government-sponsored poll of coffee-shop owners, nederwiet has captured over half the market and hash is in decline even among tourists.

Price and quality are OK – you won't get ripped off in a coffee shop like you would on the street. The most famous chain, frequented by tourists and with prices to match, is *The Bulldog* with five branches around town, the chief one being at Leidseplein 13-17. *Goa* at Kloveniersburgwal 42 is in a pleasant location with outside seating, but more discreet is *Rusland*, nearby at Rusland 16. In the Jordaan, backpacker favourites include *La Tertulia* on the corner of Prinsengracht and Oude Looiersstraat, and the canalside *Pie* on Lauriergracht.

Conscious Dreams (Map 15; ☎ 626 69 07) at Kerkstraat 117 isn't a coffee shop in the Amsterdam sense but a 'normal' shop that sells magic mushrooms and other natural products that enhance whatever might need enhancing. Informative leaflets and enthusiastic staff explain everything.

SPECTATOR SPORTS

See Activities in the Things to See & Do chapter for sports you can engage in as well as watch. If you only want to watch, there are few sporting events particularly worth seeking out apart from soccer (of course), field hockey and the unique Dutch sport of korfball. For general information on sporting events, contact the Amsterdam Sport Council on ☎ 552 24 90.

The Olympic Stadium at Stadionplein is defunct. There are plans to transform it into an athletics stadium by the end of 1998.

Soccer

Local club Ajax is usually at or near the top of the European league. Other Dutch leaders are PSV (the Philips Sport Association) from Eindhoven and Feijenoord from Rotterdam, and if any of these three play against one another it's a big event. Dutch soccer is 'cool' and 'technical', characterised by keep-the-ball and lightning strikes. Local hooligans, however, are every bit as hot-headed as their British counterparts but you should be quite safe if you buy seat tickets (as opposed to standing-room tickets).

Ajax plays in the new Arena Stadium (☎ 311 13 33; metro: Bijlmer), office address Haaksbergweg 59, which seats 52,000 spectators and has an Ajax museum with cups and other paraphernalia. It's a massive and massively expensive, high-tech complex with portable turf and retractable roof, built over a highway. Soccer games usually take place Sundays at 2.30 pm during the playing season, which lasts from early September to early June (with a winter break from just before Christmas to the end of January).

Hockey

Dutch (field) hockey teams compete at world-championship level. In contrast to soccer, which is played by working-class boys in school yards, streets and parks, hockey is still to a large extent an elitist sport played by either sex on expensive club fields. The season is more or less the same as that for soccer. A good contact for information and matches is the Amsterdamse Hockey- en Bandy Club (☎ 640 11 41), Wagener Stadion, Nieuwe Kalfjeslaan 1 in the Amsterdamse Bos.

Korfball

This sport tends to elicit stupid giggles from foreigners who don't understand how appealing it can be. With a vivid local club scene, it's a cross between netball, volleyball and basketball, where mixed-sex teams toss a ball around and try to throw it into the opposing team's hoop 3.5 metres off the ground; players can only mark opponents of the same sex. For information, contact the Amsterdam Sport Council (☎ 552 24 90) or try the Vereniging Amsterdam-Zuid Korfbal (☎ 646 15 15), Kinderdijkstraat 29.

Shopping

With a few exceptions – dope, pornography, flower bulbs, rounds of cheese, obscure types of *genever* (Dutch gin) – there's nothing in Amsterdam that you won't find elsewhere, and fantastic bargains are rare. Where Amsterdam shines is in its speciality shops and markets. You might be able to find a glow-in-the-dark toothbrush or peppermint-flavoured condom back home, but Amsterdam has whole shops devoted to toothbrushes or condoms – or hammocks, mosquito nets and of course clogs, to name just a few of the eccentric goods on offer.

Worth chasing are pictorial art, music, funky clothes, diamonds, pastries/chocolates and collectors' books (but not current English-language books, which are prohibitively expensive). Potheads can purchase smoking paraphernalia at corner tobacco shops, but should keep in mind that flights from Amsterdam attract more than their fair share of attention from customs officials elsewhere.

The most popular shopping streets are lowbrow Nieuwendijk and slightly less lowbrow Kalverstraat, with department stores, clothing boutiques and speciality shops that cater for large crowds on Saturday (a good day to avoid). Leidsestraat is more up-market with less junk, though the goods are still rather mainstream. Pretentious shoppers head for expensive shops and boutiques along PC Hooftstraat, and antique and art buffs check Nieuwe Spiegelstraat and Spiegelgracht. The Jordaan neighbourhood is full of quirky shops and galleries, as are the radial streets in the canal belt, especially in the western section.

Souvenirs are sold everywhere, most of them tacky, but try a small Delft-blue brooch set in silver, or bulbs to plant back home (home legislation permitting). Metz & Co department store has interesting but pricey things.

As for markets, the Albert Cuyp is not to be missed, with its food and other goods from all corners of the globe. The floating flower market along Singel is unique, though photographers will be frustrated by the crowds and the fact that most of the market is in the shade. Waterlooplein flea market specialises in bric-a-brac, army clothes and music; other markets might be cheaper but don't stock as wide a selection.

If you intend to do serious shopping (eg diamonds) and live outside the EU, see Taxes & Refunds under Money in the Facts for the Visitor chapter about reclaiming the 17.5% value-added tax.

ART GALLERIES

Amsterdam is full of art galleries, from tiny operations with one person's work in a small shop to huge, commercial, museum-like complexes. Try the following:

Amsterdams Beeldhouwerskollektief, Zeilmakerstraat 15 in the Western Islands (☎ 625 63 32) – sculpture exhibitions; open Thursday to Sunday from noon to 5 pm

Animation Art, Berenstraat 39 (☎ 627 76 00) – for caricatures and cartoons

Art Works, Herengracht 229-231 (☎ 624 19 80) – a small gallery displaying paintings and sculptures

Arti et Amicitiae, Rokin 112 (☎ 626 08 39) – well-established artists' club displaying contemporary art; open Tuesday to Sunday from noon to 6 pm

Aschenbach Gallery, Bilderdijkstraat 165C (☎ 685 35 80) – large gallery focusing on contemporary figurative tendencies and photography

Barbara Farber, Keizersgracht 265 (☎ 627 63 43) – exhibitions of paintings and drawings; open Tuesday to Saturday from 1 to 6 pm, closed in July and August

Boekie Woekie, Berenstraat 16 (☎ 639 05 07) – books and postcards as objets d'art, made by artists using different techniques; apparently the only other shop like it is in New York

Guido de Spa, Tweede Weteringdwarsstraat 34 (☎ 622 15 28) – ceramic art, paintings, etchings and drawings; open Wednesday to Saturday (and first Sunday of the month) from 2 to 5 pm

Josine Bokhoven, Prinsengracht 154 across the canal from the Anne Frankhuis (☎ 623 65 98) – for contemporary art including young artists; open

Tuesday to Saturday (and first Sunday of the month) from 1 to 6.30 pm

Kunsthaar, Berenstraat 21 (☎ 625 99 12) – contemporary Dutch art; collective exhibitions; open Tuesday to Friday from 10 am to 6 pm, Saturday from 9 am to 4 pm

Nanky de Vreeze, Lange Leidsedwarsstraat 198-200 (☎ 627 38 08) – large, impressive gallery with contemporary art; open Wednesday to Saturday (and the first Sunday of the month) from noon to 6 pm

Open Space, Korte Prinsengracht 14 (☎ 420 09 58) – open Wednesday to Saturday from 3 to 7 pm

Paul Andriesse, Prinsengracht 116 (☎ 623 62 37) – modern art; open weekdays from 10 am to 12.30 pm and 2 to 6.30 pm, Saturday from 2 to 6 pm

Prestige Art Gallery, Reguliersbreestraat 46 near Rembrandtplein (☎ 624 01 04) – specialist in 17th to 20th century oil paintings and bronzes; open Monday to Friday from 10 am to 6 pm, Saturday to 5 pm

Reflex Modern Art Gallery, Weteringschans 79A opposite the Rijksmuseum (☎ 627 28 32) – prominent gallery with contemporary art, aimed at tourists

SAK (Stichting Amsterdamse Kunstenaars – Foundation Amsterdam Artists), Keizersgracht 22 in De Zaaijer 'clandestine' church (☎ 420 31 54) – large, impressive gallery with works by local artists; open all week from 11 am to 6.30 pm

Schoo, Fokke Simonszstraat 10 (☎ 623 15 47) – for contemporary and mostly figurative art by South Asian artists; open Tuesday to Saturday from 1 to 6 pm, and every first Sunday of the month from 2 to 5 pm

Steltman, Spuistraat 330 off Spui square (☎ 622 86 83) – large gallery with unusual surrealist and romantic paintings, figurative modern art and design; open Tuesday to Saturday from 11 am to 6 pm

XY, Tweede Laurierdwarsstraat 42 (☎ 625 02 82) – figurative, contemporary paintings on trendy themes; open Tuesday to Friday from noon to 5 pm, Saturday to 4 pm

BOOKS

Amsterdam is still a major printing centre in Europe. Unfortunately books are expensive whether they're imported or locally produced, and you may wish to steer clear of English-language titles if you're used to US or British prices. However, bibliophiles will delight in the large number of bookshops, both new and antiquarian, with knowledgeable and enthusiastic staff. The following are some of the better known outlets, but keep an eye out for obscure, second-hand shops where you might find some real bargains. See also the following Markets section for dedicated book markets.

English-Language

American Discount Book Center, Kalverstraat 185 (Map 13; ☎ 625 55 37) – 10% discount with a valid student card; good travel-guide section, cheaper than competitors; many US newspapers and magazines (Sunday edition of the *New York Times* for f17.50)

The English Bookshop, Lauriergracht 71 (Map 12; ☎ 626 42 30) – interesting selection of English books; open Tuesday to Friday from 1 to 6 pm, Saturday from 11 am to 5 pm

WH Smith, Kalverstraat 152 (Map 13; ☎ 638 38 21) – specialist in English-language books; strong on travel guidebooks, maps and novels; translated Dutch literature on the 1st floor

Gay & Lesbian

Intermale, Spuistraat 251 (Map 12; ☎ 625 00 09) – gay photo books, magazines and videos

Vrolijk, Paleisstraat 135 (Map 13; ☎ 623 51 42) – most of the major gay and lesbian magazines worldwide

Vrouwen in Druk, Westermarkt 5 (Map 12; ☎ 624 50 03) – new and second-hand women's books (the name means 'Women in Print')

Xantippe, Prinsengracht 290 (Map 12; ☎ 623 58 54) – largest women's bookshop in the country, anything from classical fiction to modern research

Health, Environment & Philosophy

Au Bout du Monde, Singel 313 (Map 12; ☎ 625 13 97) – Eastern and Western philosophy, alternative medicine and other esoteric subject matter

JH&G van Heteren, Keizersgracht 756 (Map 16; ☎ 624 00 66) – health, diet, vegetarianism etc

MilieuBoek, Plantage Middenlaan 2H in front of the Botanical Garden (☎ 624 49 89) – books on nature and the environment

Oibibio bookshop, Prins Hendrikkade 21 (Map 13; ☎ 553 93 44) – large selection of New-Age titles

Travel

Allert de Lange, Damrak 62 (Map 13; ☎ 624 67 44) – one of the leading travel bookshops; also many general titles

Amber, Da Costastraat 77 (Map 13; ☎ 685 11 55) – behind the travel agency is a crammed bookshop that's a veritable Aladdin's Cave, with many hard-to-find (and some pretty obscure) travel guidebooks in Dutch, English, German and French

á la Carte, Utrechtsestraat 110 (Map 16; ☎ 625 06 79) – travel books, maps and globes

Evenaar Literaire Reisboekhandel, Singel 348 (Map 12; ☎ 624 62 89) – travel literature

Pied à Terre, Singel 393 (Map 12; ☎ 627 44 55) – specialist in hiking and cycling guidebooks and maps

Jacob van Wijngaarden, Overtoom 97 (Map 15; ☎ 612 19 01) – geographical bookshop with a large collection of travel guidebooks and maps

Other Bookshops

Antiquariaat Kok, Oude Hoogstraat 14-18 (☎ 623 11 91) – wide range of antiquarian stock (literature, coffee-table books, old prints etc)

Art Unlimited, Keizersgracht 510 (☎ 624 84 19) – thousands of well-catalogued postcards with unusual and unexpected subject matter; beautiful art posters

Athenaeum bookshop & newsagency, Spui 14-16 (☎ 623 39 33) – vast assortment of unusual books for browsers; the separate newsagency has the city's largest selection of international newspapers and magazines

Broekmans & Van Poppel, Van Baerlestraat 92-94 (☎ 662 80 84) – the best address for sheet music (classical)

The Book Exchange, Kloveniersburgwal 58 (☎ 626 62 66) – rabbit warren of second-hand books

The Frisian Embassy, Spuistraat 120 (Map 13; ☎ 422 27 41) – not an embassy (though the name hasn't done it any harm) but a tiny bookshop and information centre for Friesland (more Frisians live in Amsterdam than anywhere else outside the province of Friesland); also provides information on the Frisian language, the closest linguistic relative of English; worth visiting for maps etc if you plan to head up that way

Lambiek, Kerkstraat 78 (Map 15; ☎ 626 75 43) – for serious collectors of comic books; doubles as an informal museum

Scheltema Holkema Vermeulen, Koningsplein 20 (Map 12; ☎ 523 14 11) – the largest bookshop in town, a true department store with many foreign titles

De Slegte, Kalverstraat 48 (Map 13; ☎ 622 59 33) – specialist in second-hand or remaindered titles; a lot of dirt-cheap rubbish on the ground floor but some gems upstairs

Stadsboekwinkel, Voormalige Stadstimmertuin 4-6 near Theater Carré (☎ 551 17 16) – bookshop run by the city printer; books and other publications about Amsterdam, some in English

CAMPING & OUTDOOR

The Dutch enjoy outdoor pursuits and don't mind spending on the right gear. Quality and prices tend to be high.

Bever Zwerfsport, Stadhouderskade 4 (Map 15; ☎ 689 46 39) near Leidseplein – large range of camping and other outdoor gear

Carl Denig, Weteringschans 115 near the Rijksmuseum (☎ 626 24 36) – probably Amsterdam's best in its field, though you pay for the quality; good selection of packs, tents and hiking/camping accessories

Perry Sport, Overtoom 2 (Map 15; ☎ 618 91 11) – cheaper than Bever Zwerfsport nearby, but quality could be less; camping goods kept downstairs

CLOTHING

This is not the place to buy extravagant designer clothes. The Calvinist ethos frowns on conspicuous consumption and demands value for money, and as a consequence clothing is bland (or low-key stylish) and very reasonably priced. Amsterdam is in a league of its own, however, in funky and alternative apparel, often second-hand and sold at markets and in countless small boutiques. The choice seems endless – simply go for a walk in the Jordaan or along the radial streets in the canal belt. Otherwise, the following shops may be of interest:

Awareness Winkel, Weteringschans 143 near the Rijksmuseum (Map 15; ☎ 638 10 59) – environmentally friendly clothing; everything from hats to socks made from organically grown cotton

Mail & Female, Prinsengracht 489 (☎ 623 39 16; fax 624 88 35) – erotic lingerie and other arousing products by and for women; does postal orders too

Puck & Hans, Rokin 66 (Map 13; ☎ 625 58 89) – designer clothes for young trendoids

Reflections, Stadhouderskade 23, in the Byzantium complex (Map 15) next to the Vondelpark entrance (☎ 612 61 41) – for the haute-couture crowd with unlimited funds; the complex is worth a wander even if you don't buy anything

DEPARTMENT STORES

With the possible exception of Metz & Co, the department stores stick to safe, mainstream products.

Bijenkorf, Dam 1 (Map 13; ☎ 621 80 80) – the city's most fashionable department store; good clothing, toys, household accessories and books

Hema, Nieuwendijk 174 (Map 13) and Reguliers-breestraat 10, among other locations – the nation's equivalent of Woolworths or K-Mart, with low prices and reliable quality; wide range of products including good-value wines and delicatessen goods

Metz & Co, Keizersgracht 455 at Leidsestraat (Maps 12 & 15; ☎ 624 88 10) – luxury furnishings, up-market souvenirs and gifts; lunch room with a splendid view on the top floor

Vroom & Dreesmann, Kalverstraat 201 (☎ 622 01 71) – large national chain with a wide range of products, slightly more up-market than Hema; popular for clothing and cosmetics; great bread; the restaurant is quite good too

DIAMONDS

Amsterdam has been a major diamond centre since Sephardic Jews introduced the cutting industry in the 1580s (one of the few occupations open to them at the time). The *Cullinan*, the largest diamond ever found (3106 carats), was split into more than 100 stones here in 1908 – the master cutter spent three months recovering from stress. The *Kohinoor* or Mountain of Light was cut here too – a very large, oval diamond (108.8 carats) acquired by Queen Victoria that now forms part of the British crown jewels.

WWII dealt a serious blow to the industry but there are about a dozen diamond factories in the city today, five of which offer guided tours – the Gassan tour is probably the most interesting. The tours are free (the theory being that you'll buy diamonds, though you don't have to) and are usually conducted seven days a week, but ring ahead for details.

Diamonds aren't necessarily cheaper in Amsterdam than elsewhere but prices are fairly competitive. At least you will have seen how they're worked, and when you buy from a factory, you get an extensive description of the purchase so you know exactly what you're buying. The Diamond Stock Exchange (☎ 696 22 51) is in the Bijlmer at Hogehilweg 14, 1101 CD Amsterdam.

Amsterdam Diamond Center, Rokin 1 (☎ 624 57 87)
Coster Diamonds, Paulus Potterstraat 2-6 (Map 15; ☎ 676 22 22)
Gassan Diamonds, Nieuwe Uilenburgerstraat 173-175 (Map 13; ☎ 622 53 33)

Stoeltie Diamonds, Wagenstraat 13-17 (☎ 623 76 01)
Van Moppes & Zoon, Albert Cuypstraat 2-6 (☎ 626 12 42)

FOOD & DRINK

Dutch cuisine is nothing to write home about but some of the following shops are hard to resist:

Drinkland, Spuistraat 116 (☎ 638 65 73) – genevers, liqueurs, wines, beers

Geels & Co, Warmoesstraat 67 (Map 13; ☎ 624 06 83) – tea and coffee merchant; the shop is open normal hours, but have a look at the interesting little museum upstairs if you visit Tuesday, Friday or Saturday between 2 and 4 pm (4.30 pm Saturday)

Lawenda, Eerste Anjeliersdwarsstraat 17 (☎ 420 52 62) – delicious chocolates (closed Monday)

Puccini, Staalstraat 21 near Waterlooplein (☎ 626 54 74) – large, hand-made bonbons with rich chocolate (try the unforgettable spicy bonbon with peppers); many other desserts and cakes made with natural ingredients

Simon Lévelt, Prins Hendrikkade 26 (Map 12; ☎ 622 84 28), Prinsengracht 180 (☎ 624 08 23, opposite the Anne Frankhuis) and Ferdinand Bolstraat 154 (☎ 400 40 60) – old-fashioned tea and coffee merchant

De Waterwinkel, Roelof Hartstraat 10 (☎ 675 59 32) – more than 100 types of bottled water from all parts of the world; try before you buy

Wegewijs Kaas & Delicatessen, Rozengracht 32 (Map 12; ☎ 624 40 93) – dozens of different cheeses

Wijnkoperij Otterman, Keizersgracht 300 (☎ 625 50 88) – French wines with character; also wines without preservatives

Wijnkoperij Woorts, Utrechtsestraat 51 (☎ 623 74 26) – hundreds of different wines

MARKETS

No visit to Amsterdam is complete if you haven't experienced one or more of its lively markets. The following is merely a selection. For more information about some of these markets, see the relevant entries in the Things to See & Do chapter.

Albert Cuypmarkt, Albert Cuypstraat (Map 16) – general market with food, clothing, hardware etc, often very cheap; wide ethnic mix (Amsterdam's melting pot in action); daily except Sunday

Antiques market, Noordermarkt in the Jordaan – antiques, fabrics, second-hand bric-a-brac etc; Monday morning

RICHARD NEBESKY

RICHARD NEBESKY

DOEKES LULOFS

DOEKES LULOFS

RICHARD NEBESKY

DOEKES LULOFS

A	B
C	D
E	F

A: Enkhuizen
B: Hoorn
C: The Vecht river at Vreeland

D: Ransdorp, Waterland
E: Enkhuizen
F: The harbour dyke at Marken

RICHARD NEBESKY

DOEKES LULOFS

RICHARD NEBESKY

ROB VAN DRIESUM

MARK HONAN

MARK HONAN

A	B
C	D
E	F

A: Hoorn harbour
B: Skating near Schermerhorn,
   between Hoorn and Alkmaar
C: Waterland

D: The Ridderzaal, The Hague
E: Clog machine, Zaanse Schans
F: Cheese-tasting centre, Zaanse
   Schans

Antiques market, Nieuwmarkt square – many genuine articles; every Sunday from April to October

Antiques market, Elandsgracht 109 in the Jordaan – indoor stalls in De Looier complex; daily except Friday

Art markets on Thorbeckeplein and Spui square – quiet markets with quality art, mostly modern pictorial, but too modest in scope to yield real finds; every Sunday between March and October from 10.30 am to 6 pm

Bloemenmarkt, along Singel near Muntplein – floating flower market, colourful in the extreme; daily except Sunday

Boerenmarkt (Farmer's Market) on Noordermarkt in the Jordaan and Nieuwmarkt square – homegrown produce, organic foods, herbs etc; only on Saturday

Book market, Oudemanhuispoort (the old arcade between Oudezijds Achterburgwal and Kloveniersburgwal, blink and you'll miss either entrance) – frequented by students from the surrounding university buildings; anything from a 19th century copy of *Das Kapital* to a semantic analysis of Icelandic sagas; weekdays

Book market, Spui square – not very cheap but a good selection; only on Friday

Mosveldmarkt, Mosveld, Amsterdam Noord (bus No 34 or 35 from Centraal Station to the first stop after the IJ-Tunnel) – typical Dutch market not intended for tourists; mostly food and clothing; Wednesday, Friday and Saturday

Plant market, Amstelveld – all sorts of plants, pots and vases; every Monday during summer

Stamp & Coin market, in front of the Nova Hotel at Nieuwezijds Voorburgwal 276 – stamps, coins, medals; Wednesday and Saturday from 10 am to 4 pm

Waterlooplein flea market, Waterlooplein – curios, second-hand clothing, music, electronic stuff slightly on the blink, erotica, hardware etc; daily except Sunday

MUSIC

CD prices are steep, so Amsterdam is not the place to buy popular material. Collector's items are another story, thanks to the wide variety of shops with often interesting (not to say obscure) stock. Also, many shops and markets sell second-hand CDs that can be absolute bargains.

Broekmans & Van Poppel, Van Baerlestraat 92-94 (☎ 675 16 53) – classical music

Concerto, Utrechtsestraat 52-60 (Map 16; ☎ 623 52 28) – rambling shop spread over several buildings; the city's best selection of new and second-

hand CDs and records, from classical, jazz and world music to techno, often cheap and always interesting; great facilities to listen before you buy

FAME Music, Kalverstraat 2-4 at Dam square (Map 13; ☎ 638 25 25) – the largest number of titles in Amsterdam, with good collections of pop, jazz and classical

Get Records, Utrechtsestraat 105 (☎ 622 34 41) – eclectic range of rock, folk and blues

Jazz Inn, Vijzelgracht 7 opposite the French Consulate (Map 16; ☎ 623 56 62) – Amsterdam's best selection of jazz CDs

Musiques du Monde, Singel 281 (Map 12; ☎ 624 13 54) – great source of world-music CDs (some second-hand), though they cost a few guilders more than elsewhere; Indian music and nature sounds are specialities; publishes the quarterly magazine *Wereldmuziek* (in Dutch, free subscription, or f22 outside the country)

Nieuwe Muziekhandel, Leidsestraat 50 (☎ 627 14 00) – good selection of classical and opera

Saul B Groen, Ferdinand Bolstraat 6 (☎ 679 46 34) – chamber music, baroque

Tropenmuseum, Linnaeusstraat 2 (Map 17; ☎ 568 82 00) – this museum has one of the most interesting selections of ethnic-music CDs for sale anywhere

Virgin Megastore, Nieuwzijds Voorburgwal 182 in the basement of the Magna Plaza complex (Map 12; ☎ 622 89 29) – trendy shop, worth visiting for the building

SPECIALITIES

If you're at a loss for souvenirs or gifts, try some of the following shops:

Aurora Kontakt, Vijzelstraat 27 near Muntplein (☎ 623 59 89) – huge assortment of electronic gizmos at competitive prices

Bangla Klamboe Imports, Prinsengracht 232 (Map 12; ☎ 622 94 92) – mosquito nets for a good night's sleep in the tropics, the Arctic summer, or the canal belt in the warmer half of the year

Bell Tree, Spiegelgracht 10 not far from the Rijksmuseum (Map 15; ☎ 625 88 30) – toys for kids of all ages; good selection of technical toys for children aged eight to 14

Computercollectief, Amstel 312 (Map 16; ☎ 638 90 03; www.noord.bart.nl/cc) – one of the best addresses in the country for computer software, books and magazines, at prices higher than in the USA

Condomerie Het Gulden Vlies, Warmoesstraat 141 (Map 13; ☎ 627 41 74) – 1000 different types of condoms; well situated for its trade

Foto Professional, Nieuwendijk 113 (☎ 624 60 24) – photographic gear and repairs, and the country's largest selection of second-hand cameras, lenses etc; you'll probably find what you need here

The Frozen Fountain, Prinsengracht 629 near the main public library (☎ 622 93 75) – progressive furniture and other interior design; expensive but worth a look

Hajenius, Rokin 92 (☎ 623 74 94) – renowned for tobacco products and paraphernalia, including traditional leaf cigars (house brand) and clay pipes

The Headshop, Kloveniersburgwal 39 on the corner of Nieuwe Hoogstraat (☎ 624 90 61) – all kinds of drug devices

3-D Hologrammen, Grimburgwal 2 (☎ 624 72 25) – gallery and shop with an interesting collection of holographic pictures, jewellery, stickers etc

De Klompenboer, Nieuwezijds Voorburgwal 20 (☎ 623 06 32) – clog specialist; also a small museum

Maranón Hangmatten, Singel 488 at the floating flower market (Maps 12 & 13; ☎ 420 71 21) – Europe's largest selection of hammocks

De Witte Tanden Winkel, Runstraat 5 (☎ 623 34 43) – large range of toothbrushes and other dental-hygiene products; free advice

THIRD WORLD & NEW AGE

This is one of the best cities for getting in touch with the Third World, nature and the inner you, often all at once.

Abal Wereldwinkel, Ceintuurbaan 238 (Map 15; ☎ 664 10 83) – shop run by volunteers selling Third-World crafts, clothes, books, toys and food, with the profits going to the producers; some bargains

African Heritage, Zeedijk 59 (Map 13; ☎ 627 27 65) – curios and clothing from Africa

Fair Trade Shop, Huidenstraat 16 (Map 12; ☎ 625 22 45) – charitable shop featuring Third-World products, including clothes, gifts and CDs; more expensive than Abal but worth a look

Greenpeace Infoshop, Leliegracht 51 around the corner from the Greenpeace International head office (Map 12; ☎ 524 95 79) – environmentally friendly T-shirts, books, gifts and other items

Himalaya, Warmoesstraat 56 (Map 13; ☎ 626 08 99) – New-Age CDs and books

Oibibio supermarket, Prins Hendrikkade 21 (☎ 553 93 55) – wide range of ecologically aware products

Excursions

This is a small country, and you can visit many areas on day or overnight excursions from Amsterdam. All the major cities are less than 2½ hours away by train, even distant Maastricht (in the south-eastern province of Limburg) and Groningen (in the north-eastern province of Groningen). Many sights are concentrated in the west of the country, in the provinces of North and South Holland (Amsterdam itself is in the south of North Holland), and are less than an hour's drive or train ride away.

Getting Around The Country

See the earlier Getting There & Away and Getting Around chapters for general information about travelling by car or public transport. There's a dense network of freeways but in most cases the train is your best bet, and there are packages that combine train tickets and admission fees to numerous sights and events (see the following Rail Idee section).

Dutch trains are efficient, fast and comfortable, especially the new double-decker ones. Services along the major routes stop around midnight (often much earlier on minor routes), but there are night trains once an hour in both directions along the route Utrecht-Amsterdam-Schiphol-Leiden-The Hague-Delft-Rotterdam. Tickets for these cost the same as during the day or evening and can be bought at the counter (if it's open) or ticketing machines; alternatively, notify the conductor as you board the train, in which case you'll pay a bit more.

Trains can be a *Stoptrein*, a faster *Sneltrein* (Fast Train, indicated with 'S'), or an even faster Intercity (IC) or Intercity Plus (IC+). EuroCity (EC) trains travel between Amsterdam and Cologne nine times a day during the week, eight times a day on weekends, and only stop in Utrecht and Arnhem; they're quite fast (a 10-minute saving to Arnhem) but you pay a f3 supplement at the counter or f6.50 on board the train. From Amster-

dam, the high-speed *Thalys* only stops at Schiphol (from The Hague it only stops in Rotterdam) and requires a special ticket, available at the international ticket counters in Centraal Station.

The national train timetable book is available for f9.75 from train-station counters and newsagencies, but don't bother unless you're planning numerous trips to small destinations only serviced by local stop-trains. There are frequent trains from Centraal Station to most corners of the country and it's unlikely you'll have to wait long. Make a note of return trains listed on the timetable board at your destination.

All major train stations have luggage lockers and/or depots, and 80 stations throughout the country rent bicycles (with a discount if you show a train ticket – see Bicycle Rental in the Getting Around chapter). You can bring your own bicycle on the train for a small fee so long as the train has a separate luggage wagon (many of them do), but not weekdays between 6.30 and 9 am or 4.30 and 6 pm (no hour restrictions in July and August).

For train and ticketing information, ring the national public-transport number, ☎ 0900-92 92 (f0.50-0.75 a minute) weekdays from 6 am to midnight, weekends and public holidays from 7 am.

Tickets With a valid ticket you can get out anywhere along the direct route; in other words, with a ticket from Amsterdam to Rotterdam you can visit Haarlem, Leiden, The Hague and Delft along the way, but backtracking is not permitted. Return tickets are 10 to 15% cheaper than two one-ways but, like one-way tickets, are only valid on the same day; if you want to return the next day, even on weekends, you have to buy separate one-way tickets.

Children aged under four travel free if they don't take up a seat; those aged between four and 11 pay a so-called *Railrunner* fare of f2.50 if accompanied by an adult or get a 40% discount on the normal fare if travelling alone.

A *Dagkaart* (Day Card) for unlimited train travel throughout the country costs f66 (2nd class) or f99 (1st class), which is the same as you'll pay for a return ticket to any destination more than 200km away. Add f7.50 for a *Stad/Streek-Dagkaart* (City/Region Day Card) and you'll have use of trams, buses and metros as well.

A *Meerman's Kaart* (Multiple-Person Card) provides unlimited train travel for up to six people during the same periods as the *Voordeel-Urenkaart* discussed in the next paragraph; for two people this costs f98 (2nd class) or f148 (1st class). Two children aged between four and 11 count as one person, though the above-mentioned Railrunner is usually cheaper.

If you plan to do a lot of travelling, consider investing f99 in a *Voordeel-Urenkaart* (Advantage Hours Card) valid for one year, which gives 40% discount on train travel weekdays after 9 am, as well as all weekend, on public holidays and throughout July and August; the discount applies to normal tickets as well as special tickets and cards. It also gives access to weekend return tickets (50% cheaper than normal returns) and evening return tickets (65% cheaper). A similar version for those aged 60 and over gives an additional seven days' free travel a year.

In June, July and August you can buy a *Zomertoer* (Summer Tour) ticket that allows three days' unlimited train travel within the country during any 10-day period for f85 (2nd class) or f105 (1st class); two people travelling together pay f115 or f155. If you pay an extra f17 (f25 for two) the ticket becomes a *Zomertoer Plus* which is also valid for all trams, buses and metros during those three days. If you start the ticket on 31 August it can be used until 9 September.

During school holidays in May, summer, autumn and Christmas, those aged under 19 can buy a *TourTime* ticket for f65, which gives unlimited train travel for four days out of 10 within the Netherlands and Belgium (but not on through trains to France and Luxembourg). Proof of age (passport) and a photo are required. For f15 extra it becomes a *TourTime Plus* which is also valid for all trams, buses and metros within the Netherlands during those four days.

A *Waddenbiljet* (Wadden Ticket) combines the train, ferry and bus tickets required for a visit to one of the Wadden Islands in the north of the country (Texel, Vlieland, Terschelling, Ameland or Schiermonnikoog), and you can stay there however long you like. The ticket provides a 20% saving on the train fare and gives discounts on bicycle rental on the island.

Rail Idee The NS offers numerous Rail Idee day trips throughout the country (and even to Antwerp, Brussels, Ghent or Bruges in Belgium, with the possibility to return the next day). These packages include a return 2nd-class ticket plus selected admissions, brochures, bicycle hire and even meals. The price is sometimes less than a return ticket by itself. These trips are not advertised to foreign tourists and the illustrated *Er-op-Uit!* booklet (f5.75) describing the trips is only in Dutch, but of course anyone can sign up. The booklet is available at train-station counters, where you can also book the actual trips.

The NS Reisburo (Travel Bureau, ☎ 622 04 51) in Centraal Station might be able to help you choose the trip, but its main focus is organised tours and other packages offered by more than 30 companies. There's another NS Reisburo (☎ 624 74 54) at Rokin 44.

NORTH OF AMSTERDAM

The finger of land north of Amsterdam used to be known as West Friesland; today it's the northern tip of the province of North Holland, whose capital is Haarlem. Much of it is polder that has been claimed from the water in the past 400 years.

Wadden Islands

The country's five northern isles in the shallow Waddenzee stretch in an arc from Texel to Schiermonnikoog. They are important bird-breeding grounds and provide an escape for stressed southerners who want to touch roots with nature. Ferries connect the islands to the mainland, and there are (mainly summer) hostels on all except Vlieland. Bicycles are a good way to get around and can be hired – usually with discounts if you travel on a Waddenbiljet. Texel belongs to the province of North Holland and the language is Dutch; the other islands are Frisian.

Texel This is the largest and most populated island. Its 24km of beach can seem overrun all summer but even more so in June when the world's largest catamaran race is staged here. The biggest village is Den Burg, where you'll find the VVV (☎ 0222-31 47 41) at Groeneplaats 9. For information on the ecology of the island and the Waddenzee in general, visit **EcoMare** at Ruyslaan 92 – it's also a hospital for sick seals from the sometimes polluted Waddenzee.

You could visit Texel in a day from Amsterdam if you catch an early train but it's best to allow a day or two. Upon arrival, you'll get a good introduction to the island by taking bus No 29 to De Cocksdorp at the north end. Immediately change to bus No 27 from De Cocksdorp to De Koog on the west coast. Hike south along the beach a couple of km, then cut inland to a lovely moor and forest with hiking trails. Follow any of the signs pointing towards Den Burg and you'll find another bus stop eventually (allow a couple of hours for this hike).

For camping in isolation, head to *Loodsmansduin* (☎ 0222-31 92 03) at Rommelpot 19 near Den Hoorn. *De Krim* camping (☎ 0222-31 66 66) at Roogeslootweg 6 in Cocksdorp is open all year. There are two NJHC hostels on opposite sides of Den Burg: the pleasant *Panorama* (☎ 0222-31 54 41) is at Schansweg 7 (bus No 29); *De Eyercoogh* at Pontweg 106 is 10 minutes' walk from town, or get bus No 28 from the ferry.

Hotel De Merel (☎ 0222-31 31 32) at Warmoesstraat 22 has rooms for f55 per person; *'t Koogerend* (☎ 0222-31 33 01) at Kogerstraat 94 charges f81/112 for singles/doubles.

Trains from Amsterdam to Den Helder (1½ hours) are met by a bus that whisks you to the awaiting, hourly car ferry. The ferry trip takes 20 minutes, and costs f11.25/5.75 return for adults/children; cars/bicycles are charged f50/6.50.

Vlieland & Terschelling Both these islands are connected by ferry to the Frisian town of Harlingen. Vlieland is one of the two car-free isles, Terschelling is the group's longest. Vlieland is a popular family island and has one village: Oost-Vlieland; its western sister drowned in the 1700s. The VVV (☎ 0562-45 11 11) is on Havenweg 10.

Terschelling, 30km long, is known as a good-time isle, but it also has some stunning scenery and is great for cycling. Its main village is West-Terschelling, where the VVV (☎ 0562-44 30 00) is at Willem Barentszkade 19 opposite the ferry terminal.

Accommodation on Vlieland includes *De Stortemelk* camping ground (☎ 0562-45 12 25) at Kampweg 1. The 'cheapest' hotel is *De Herbergh van Flieland* (☎ 0562-45 14 00) at Dorpsstraat 105, with doubles for f130.

On Terschelling, *Dellewal* camping ground (☎ 0562-44 26 02) is next to the *NJHC hostel* (☎ 0562-44 31 15) at Burgemeester van Heusdenweg 39. On the same road, *Dellewal Hotel* (☎ 0562-44 23 05) at No 42 charges f55 per person. In the town centre, *Hotel NAP* (☎ 0562-44 32 10) at Torenstraat 50 has impressive singles/doubles from f115/150.

Twice-hourly trains run from Leeuwarden to Harlingen (25 minutes, f8) where three boats a day in summer (two in winter) make the 1¾-hour voyage to Vlieland. A return costs f39.40/19.70/16.70 for adults/children/bicycles. The trip to Terschelling takes the same time and costs the same – cars can be taken but that's expensive. There's also a faster ferry – twice a day to Terschelling and once daily to Vlieland – that costs f7.50 extra each way and takes 45 minutes.

Ameland Ameland has no notable features except for its quaint villages and the number of tourists who explode onto the scene in summer. There are four villages; the main one, Nes, is home to the VVV (☎ 0519-54 20 20) at Rixt van Doniaweg 2.

At Nes, there's *Camping Duinoord* (☎ 0519-54 20 70) at Jan van Eijckweg 4. The *NJHC hostel* (☎ 0519-55 41 33) is at Oranjeweg 59 near the lighthouse at Hollum – take bus No 130 from Nes. *Hotel de Jong* (☎ 0519-54 20 16) across from the VVV in Nes has singles/doubles from f57/120. In the quieter village of Ballum, *Hotel Nobel* (☎ 0519-55 41 57) at Kosterweg 16 has rooms for f70/140.

From Leeuwarden, take bus No 66 to the port at Holwerd; from Groningen it's bus No 34. On weekdays there are six boats a day, weekends four. Returns cost f18.80/9.90/8.90 for adults/children/bicycles, and cars start at f99 (all prices are slightly cheaper in winter). The ferry trip takes 45 minutes.

Schiermonnikoog This is the smallest island (with a most tongue-tying name) and is off limits to cars. In the only village, about three km from the ferry terminus, you'll find the VVV (☎ 0519-53 12 33) at Reeweg 5.

Any bus will drop you at the *NJHC hostel* (☎ 0519-53 12 57) at Knuppeldam 2. There's also *Seedune* camping (☎ 0519-53 13 98) at Seeduneweg 1, or *Hotel Zonneweelde* (☎ 0519-53 11 33) at Langestreek 94, with singles/doubles for f75/150.

There are four ferries on weekdays (fewer on weekends) from the village of Lauwersoog, between Leeuwarden and Groningen. To get there from Leeuwarden, take bus No 50; from Groningen, bus No 63. The voyage takes 45 minutes each way and return tickets cost f18.30/9.90/8.40 for adults/children/bikes (fares are a few guilders cheaper in winter).

The Afsluitdijk

The IJsselmeer (IJssel Lake) north-east of Amsterdam used to be known as the Zuiderzee before it was cut off from the open sea in 1932 by a large dyke, the 30-km Afsluitdijk (Barrier Dyke). This impressive dam (it's not really a dyke because there's

water on either side) connects the provinces of North Holland and Friesland (Fryslân). Driving along the dyke's A7 motorway, you'll pass the **Stevinsluizen**, sluices named after the 17th century engineer Henri Stevin, who first mooted the idea of reclaiming the Zuiderzee.

You can cross the dyke on the hourly bus No 350 from Alkmaar to Leeuwarden, but not by train.

A second dyke from Enkhuizen slices this inland sea in half – the southern portion is officially known as the Markermeer. The original plan was to drain these seas and reclaim the land, as happened in the southeastern portion of the IJsselmeer now known as Flevoland, but these schemes have been shelved for environmental reasons. On a nice day you'll see hundreds of yachts and traditional Zuiderzee fishing and cargo boats (see Sailing under Activities in the Things to See & Do chapter for rental details).

IJsselmeer Towns

Several towns along the IJsselmeer have proud maritime histories and are well worth exploring.

The lively little port of **Hoorn**, which gave its name to Cape Horn at the southern tip of South America, was the capital of West Friesland and a mighty trading city (one of the six founding members of the United East India Company). Many of its 17th century buildings are still intact, and its small harbour full of old wooden fishing boats and barges is as picturesque as they come. The ANWB/VVV office (☎ 0229-21 83 43) is at Veemarkt 4.

North-east of here, **Enkhuizen** was another founding member of the East India Company, and an important fishing and whaling port. There's some interesting architecture but the big attraction is the wonderful Zuiderzee Museum (☎ 0228-31 01 22) at Wierdijk 12-22, especially the outdoor section with the reconstructed village open in summer; the maritime exhibits in the former East India Company buildings are also worth a look. The VVV (☎ 0228-31 31 64) is at Tussen Twee Havens 1.

North-west of Enkhuizen is **Medemblik**, one of the oldest towns along the IJsselmeer, with a history going back to the early Middle Ages. Its cathedral and castle are well worth visiting. The VVV (☎ 0227-54 28 52) is at Dam 2.

Closer to Amsterdam is **Edam**, a pretty town that was once a whaling port but is now known mainly for its cheeses. The cheese market is held Wednesday mornings in summer. The stained-glass windows in the 17th century Grote Kerk are stunning. The VVV (☎ 0299-37 17 27) is at Damplein 1 in the centre of town.

South-east of Edam is **Volendam**, once a former fishing port that reinvented itself as a tourist town when the Afsluitdijk killed the fishing industry. It's picturesque enough but the hordes of tourists spoil the fun – you'll encounter less of them when you explore some of the pretty streets behind the harbour. The VVV (☎ 0299-36 37 47) is at Zeestraat 37.

Monnickendam also attracts tourists and justifiably so: its meticulously restored 17th century houses and old fishing cottages are picture-postcard material, and the whole setup is far less tacky than in Volendam. The tower of the former town hall has a beautiful carillon with mechanical knights. The VVV (☎ 0299-65 19 98) is at Zarken 2.

Marken was an isolated fishing community on an island that was connected to the mainland by a causeway in the 1950s. Tourists flock here in summer to photograph people in costume. The location is impressive and you can easily imagine how harsh it must have been here with frequent Zuiderzee storms. For more information, contact the VVV in Monnickendam or Volendam.

Just north of Amsterdam is **Waterland**, a region of green farmland with dykes, ditches and some unique flora and fauna. It's an important bird-breeding area. The construction of the Noordhollands Kanaal in the 1820s cut the area in two. In the west near Landsmeer is the nature reserve and recreational area Het Twiske (see the introduction to Activities in the Things to See & Do chapter).

The eastern half of Waterland in particular is well worth exploring for its isolated farming communities that seem frozen in time. If you're looking for an interesting cycling trip on a pleasant summer's day, this is it (bring a picnic). From Amsterdam Noord, follow the sea dyke from Schellingwoude via Uitdam to Monnickendam. Backtrack a bit and cut through to Broek in Waterland, with its old wooden houses, and continue westwards to the Noordhollands Kanaal and the bird-breeding areas around Watergang. When you return to Amsterdam you'll suffer from culture shock.

Getting There & Away A fun way to see some of these IJsselmeer towns is on a *Historische Driehoek* (Historic Triangle) train/boat/train package included from April to October in the Rail Idee offerings. This involves a train from Amsterdam to Enkhuizen, a connecting boat to Medemblik, a narrow-gauge steam train from Medemblik to Hoorn, and the train from Hoorn back to Amsterdam. You'll need to get an early start if you want time to look around the Zuiderzee Museum in Enkhuizen before catching the boat. The whole package is f39.75 per person.

Useful NZH buses leaving from the Open Havenfront in front of Centraal Station about every half hour include No 111 to Marken, Nos 110 and 112 to Volendam and Edam, and No 114 to Hoorn. An excellent, inexpensive day excursion would be to take a morning bus from Amsterdam to Marken, which has pleasant trails along the shore. Hike around the island in a couple of leisurely hours, then take an excursion boat from Marken to Volendam (April to September only). Edam is only five minutes from Volendam by bus (No 110, 112, 113 or 116). From Volendam or Edam, catch a bus back to Amsterdam with the possibility of a stop at Monnickendam. If you use a strip ticket this would only cost six strips from Amsterdam to Marken and another seven from Volendam back to Amsterdam. In winter, or whenever the ferry isn't operating, you could backtrack from Marken to Monnickendam on bus No 111, then catch another bus up to Volendam from there. For the money, this is one of the best-value day trips in Europe.

NORTH-WEST & WEST OF AMSTERDAM
Alkmaar

This pleasant town with a picturesque old centre is famous for its **cheese market**, staged in the main market square (Waagplein) at 10 am every Friday in summer. Arrive early if you want to get more than a fleeting glimpse of the famous round cheeses being whisked away on sledges carried by porters with brightly coloured straw hats (the colours denote which guild they belong to). Other attractions include the **Waag** (Weigh House) with its cheese museum, and an interesting **beer museum** across the square. Nearby are the seaside resorts of **Bergen**, **Egmond** and **Castricum**, which require a bit of effort to reach but are far more pleasant than over-developed Zandvoort (see the following Zandvoort section). The VVV (☎ 072-511 42 84) in the Waag at Waagplein 3 provides information on the surrounding areas as well.

There are two trains an hour from Centraal Station (30 minutes) and at the other end it's a 10-minute walk to Waagplein.

Zaanse Schans

Several authentic working **windmills** stand along the Zaan river at Zaanse Schans just north of Zaandam (a bustling city north-west of Amsterdam). There are a few small museums among the old houses of the Zaanse Schans 'tourist village' but it costs nothing to stroll around and several attractions are free, such as the cheesemaker's shop (free samples!) and the wooden shoe factory (with a contraption that copies clogs in a similar way to a locksmith's key machine). A tourist boat does 45-minute cruises on the Zaan several times a day (f7, children half price).

Zaanse Schans is a great picnic spot, so take a lunch and don't forget your camera! Also be sure to visit old **Zaandijk** directly across the Zaan from Zaanse Schans. It's far

less visited by tourists and provides a more authentic appreciation of 'old Holland'.

In **Zaandam** itself, you could pay a quick visit to the small wooden cabin at Krimp 23, where Tsar Peter the Great of Russia stayed incognito for five months in 1697. He worked as a shipwright's apprentice on the nearby wharves, where he learnt much about shipbuilding, drinking and swearing in Dutch. The Zaandam VVV (☎ 075-616 22 21 or ☎ 635 17 47) is at Gedempte Gracht 76.

Getting to Zaanse Schans by bus is only three zones (four strips) but allow an hour for the journey. From Centraal Station, take bus No 92 or 94 to Zaandam and get off at the stop immediately after the large canal in the centre of town. Zaandam's pedestrian shopping mall is directly in front of this stop. Here you change to a northbound bus No 89. Ask the driver to let you out at Zaandijk near the Zaanse Schans open-air museum, which will be across a large bridge to the right. All in all, in good weather it's a great afternoon out.

IJmuiden

The huge **North Sea locks** are one of the main attractions in this town at the mouth of the North Sea Canal – the largest is 400 metres long and 45 metres wide. Few people realise, however, that IJmuiden is also the largest fishing port in Western Europe, home to factory trawlers that stay out in the North Atlantic for weeks at a time. Several **fish restaurants** line the fishing harbour.

The easiest way to get here by public transport is to take a train to Haarlem and catch NZH bus No 70 or 86 (25 minutes, six buses an hour Monday to Saturday, four an hour Sunday). Alternatively, take NZH bus No 82 or 83 from Amsterdam Sloterdijk station (25 minutes, two buses an hour weekdays, one an hour weekends). If you travel by road along the North Sea Canal, you'll have the surreal experience of passing ships that float well above road level.

Haarlem

The capital of the province of North Holland is a small but vibrant city with a beautiful centre similar to Amsterdam's. There are a couple of great museums that can easily be covered in a day if you don't plan to visit the nearby Keukenhof gardens as well (see the following South of Amsterdam section). The VVV (☎ 0900-320 240 43) is at Stationsplein 1, to the right outside the impressive, semi-Art Nouveau **train station** (1908). From here it's a 10-minute walk southwards, straight down Kruisweg, to the city's pleasant central square at Grote Markt.

The **Frans Hals Museum** (☎ 023-516 42 00), another 10 minutes south of Grote Markt at Groot Heiligland 62, features many of the master's group portraits and works by other great artists – a must-see if you're interested in Dutch painting. It's open Monday to Saturday from 11 am to 5 pm, Sunday from 1 pm, and costs f6.50/3 for adults/children. The **Teylers Museum** (☎ 023-531 90 10), just east of Grote Markt at Spaarne 16, is the oldest museum in the country (1778), with a curious collection including drawings by Michelangelo and Raphael. It's open Tuesday to Saturday from 10 am to 5 pm, Sunday from noon, and costs f7.50/3.50 for adults/children.

The impressive Gothic cathedral on Grote Markt, the **St Bavo**, also known as the Grote Kerk, is home to the stunning Müller organ which was played by a young Mozart. You can hear it roar in summer on Tuesday at 8.15 pm and Thursday at 3 pm. The church is normally open to visitors Monday to Saturday from 10 am to 4 pm. Entry is f2.50/1.50.

Intercity trains run every 15 minutes to/from Centraal Station (15 minutes, f6) and Leiden (30 minutes, f8.75).

Zandvoort

The seaside resort of Zandvoort is 10 minutes by train from Haarlem. In summer it seems as if half of Amsterdam deposits itself here, and the only reason you might want to do likewise is that it's easy to get to – trains leave every 30 minutes from Centraal Station and a return trip costs about f15 (do not – repeat, not – try to get here by car on a sunny weekend day in summer). The famous Formula One road-racing track in the dunes still hosts motor-sports events, but lost its (and therefore the country's) round of the world championship in the 1970s when smug residents complained about noise.

A worthwhile day trip involves a return ticket to Zandvoort and stopping off in Haarlem en route. After lunch, continue to Zandvoort and stroll along the beach before returning to Amsterdam.

SOUTH OF AMSTERDAM

The compact Randstad (literally, 'Urban Agglomeration') describes a circle from Amsterdam, incorporating The Hague, Rotterdam and Utrecht, and smaller towns such as Haarlem, Leiden and Delft. It's the country's most densely populated region, with a 'green heart' of farmland and lakes that begin immediately south of Amsterdam. The region's many sights are highlighted by the bulb fields, which explode in intoxicating colours between March and May.

Amstel & Vecht Rivers

A trip along the Amstel is a popular excursion for cyclists, and with good reason. The road southwards along the west bank soon leaves the city behind, and goes upriver through rural moors and polders. The town of **Ouderkerk aan de Amstel** is a few centuries older than Amsterdam and has several pleasant riverside cafés. Continue along the west or east bank to the township of **Nes aan de Amstel**, and then head eastwards along the Oude Waver river back to Ouderkerk along the Waver and Bullewijk rivers. These peat-drainage rivers enclose an empty polder called **De Ronde Hoep** that attracts many birds, impervious to Amsterdam's skyscrapers looming in the distance. On this trip you'll experience the serenity of the flat Dutch landscape, with church steeples and the occasional windmill on the horizon, and you'll understand how Dutch artists learned to paint such dramatic skies.

South-east of Amsterdam, the winding Vecht river is another cyclists' paradise, and a popular touring route to Utrecht. Before the completion of the Amsterdam-Rhine Canal this was an important waterway, but it's peaceful now. The scenery is not as starkly rural as along the Amstel – the small towns, woods and 17th and 18th century country mansions provide plenty of variety. Trivia buffs will be interested to know that Brooklyn was named after the town of Breukelen.

Nieuwkoopse Plassen

The Nieuwkoop Lakes south of Amsterdam and west of the Vecht river are former peat lakes in an old polder area in the Randstad's 'green heart'. You can go windsurfing, sailing, rowing or canoeing, but the lakes are also a nature reserve with the world's largest colony of purple herons. In the town of Nieuwkoop, Tijsterman (☎ 0172-57 17 86), Dorpsstraat 118, rents boats, and the similarly named restaurant next door has a pleasant terrace and good *dagschotels* from f25.

From Centraal Station, take bus No 170 along the Amstel to Uithoorn and change to bus No 147 (50 minutes). By car, take the A2 towards Utrecht, turn off at Vinkeveen and follow the signs to Mijdrecht, De Hoef and Nieuwveen to Nieuwkoop.

Aalsmeer

This town south-west of Amsterdam hosts the world's biggest **flower auction** weekdays in the largest commercial complex in Europe (600,000 sq metres, or 100 football fields). The experience will blow you away. Bidding starts early, so arrive between 7.30 and 9 am to catch the action from the viewing gallery. Selling is by Dutch auction, with a huge clock showing the high starting price dropping until someone takes up the offer. Admission costs f4.50 for anyone aged over 12 (free for those under). Take bus No 172 from Centraal Station.

Keukenhof & Bulb Fields

The Keukenhof is the world's largest flower garden, between the towns of Hillegom and Lisse south of Haarlem. It attracts a staggering 800,000 people for a mere eight weeks every year. Nature's talents are combined with artificial precision to create a garden where millions of tulips and daffodils bloom every year, perfectly in place and exactly on time. It's open from late March to May but dates vary slightly, so check with the Amsterdam VVV or the Keukenhof itself (☎ 0252-46 55 55). Admission costs f16/8 for adults/children. Take bus No 50 or 51 from Haarlem station.

The whole region between Hillegom and Katwijk (west of Leiden) is full of bulb fields – tulips, daffodils and hyacinths – that burst into bloom each spring and carpet the countryside in swathes of bright red, yellow or purple. The middle of April tends to be a good time for viewing, which is most enjoyably done by bicycle along the back roads (smell the scents). The train between Haarlem and Leiden passes through many of these fields as well.

The **Museum voor de Bloembollenstreek** (Museum for the Flower-Bulb District, ☎ 0252-41 79 00), Heereweg 219 in Lisse, displays everything you want to know about bulbs. The Lisse VVV (☎ 0252-41 42 62) is at Grachtweg 53A.

Leiden

Leiden is a cheerful city with an aura of intellect generated by the 20,000 students who make up a sixth of the population. The university, the oldest in the country, was a present from William the Silent for withstanding a long Spanish siege in 1574. A third of the residents starved before the Spaniards retreated on 3 October, now the date of Leiden's biggest festival.

Most of the sights lie within a confusing network of central canals, about a 10-minute walk south-east of the train station. The VVV (☎ 071-514 68 46) is at Stationsplein 210 in front of the station.

The **Rijksmuseum van Oudheden** (National Museum of Antiquities, ☎ 071-516 31 63) at Rapenburg 28 has a world-class collection and tops Leiden's list of 11 museums. Its striking entrance hall contains the Temple of Taffeh, a gift from Egypt for the Netherlands' help in saving ancient monuments from inundation when the Aswan High Dam was built. It's open Tuesday to

Saturday from 10 am to 5 pm, Sunday from noon, and costs f5/4 for adults/children.

The **Hortus Botanicus** (☎ 071-527 35 00), Europe's oldest botanical garden (late 1500s), is at Rapenburg 73. It's open daily from 9 am to 5 pm (Sunday from 10 am) but is closed Saturday in winter. Admission costs f5/2.50 for adults/children.

The 17th century **Lakenhal** (Cloth Hall, ☎ 071-512 08 20), Oude Singel 28, houses an assortment of works by old masters, as well as period rooms and temporary exhibits. It's open weekdays from 10 am to 5 pm, weekends from noon, and costs f5/2.50 for adults/children.

De Valk (The Falcon, ☎ 071-516 53 53), Leiden's landmark windmill at Tweede Binnenvestgracht 1, is a museum that will blow away notions that windmills were a Dutch invention. It's open Tuesday to Saturday from 10 am to 5 pm, Sunday from 1 pm, and costs f5/3 for adults/children.

There are trains every 15 minutes to/from Amsterdam (35 minutes, f12.25).

The Hague

The Hague is the country's seat of government and residence of the royal family, though the capital city is Amsterdam. Officially it's known as 's-Gravenhage (the Count's Domain) because a count built a castle here in the 13th century, but the Dutch call it Den Haag. An interesting bit of trivia is that this third-largest city in the country, the capital of the province of South Holland, never received city rights and is still officially a village – the Dutch cities didn't want their seat of government to upstage them.

It has a refined air, created by the many stately mansions and palatial embassies that line its green boulevards, though much of the city centre has been transformed into a concrete jungle in the last 20 years and the construction-mania shows no signs of abating. There's a lot to see but it's all a bit scattered. There are prestigious art galleries, a huge jazz festival (the biggest in the world) in mid-July, and the miniature town of Madurodam. The poorer side to all this finery lies south of the centre.

Trains stop at Station HS (Hollands Spoor), 20 minutes' walk south of the centre, or CS (Centraal Station), five minutes east of the centre – head straight up Herengracht. The main VVV office (☎ 0900-34 03 50 51) is at Koningin Julianaplein 30 in front of CS; the other is in the seaside suburb of Scheveningen (same phone number), at Gevers Deynootweg 1134. Both are open Monday to Saturday from 9 am to 5.30 pm; in July and August, they're also open Sunday from 10 am to 5 pm.

Things to See & Do The **Mauritshuis** (☎ 070-346 92 44), Korte Vijverberg 8, is a small museum but a great one. It houses the superb royal collection of Dutch and Flemish masterpieces (several famous Vermeers, and a touch of the contemporary with Andy Warhol's *Queen Beatrix*) in an exquisite 17th century mansion, open Tuesday to Saturday from 10 am to 5 pm, Sunday from 11 am; admission costs f10/5 for adults/children.

The parliamentary buildings around the adjoining **Binnenhof** (Inner Court) have long been the heart of Dutch politics, though parliament now meets in a new building just outside the Binnenhof. Tours take in the 13th century Ridderzaal (Knight's Hall) and leave from Binnenhof 8A daily (except Sunday) from 10 am to 3.45 pm (f5.50).

Outside the Binnenhof, the **Gevangenpoort** (Prison Gate, ☎ 070-346 08 61) at Buitenhof 33 has hourly tours showing how justice was dispensed in early times. It's open weekdays from 10 am to 4 pm, in summer also Sunday from 1 pm, and costs f5/3 for adults/children. Nearby, the 1565 **old town hall** on Groenmarkt is a splendid example of Dutch Renaissance architecture, but unfortunately you can only admire it from the outside. The huge **new town hall** on the corner of Grote Marktstraat and Spui is a much-criticised architects' delight that opened in 1996.

Admirers of De Stijl, and in particular of Piet Mondriaan, won't want to miss the Berlage-designed **Gemeentemuseum** (Municipal Museum, ☎ 070-338 11 11) at Stadhouderslaan 41. It has a large collection of works by the neo-plasticist and other artists from the late 19th century onwards, as well as extensive exhibits of applied arts, costumes and musical instruments. It's open Tuesday to Sunday from 11 am to 5 pm, and costs f8/4 for adults/children – take tram No 7 or 10 or bus No 4 or 14. The adjoining **Museon** (☎ 070-338 13 38) displays the world and its people for school kids, and next door is the high-tech **Omniversum** (☎ 070-354 54 54), a planetarium-cum-cinema that shows impressive 180° Omnimax documentaries of the earth and space. If you've never seen an Omnimax film before, grab the opportunity.

Another worthwhile art museum is the **Mesdag Museum** (☎ 070-364 25 63), Zeestraat 65B, with works by the Hague School of artists, including the impressive and recently restored *Panorama Mesdag* (1881), a gigantic, 360° painting of Scheveningen viewed from a dune. It's open Monday to Saturday from 10 am to 5 pm, Sunday from noon.

The **Peace Palace** (☎ 070-302 42 42) at Carnegieplein 2 is the home of the International Court of Justice. It can be visited by guided tours only, which cost f5/3 for adults/children and must be booked – enquire at the palace or the VVV. To get there, take tram No 7 or bus No 4 from CS.

Towards Scheveningen is **Madurodam** (☎ 070-355 39 00), Gevers Deynootweg 61, a miniature town containing everything that's quintessentially Netherlands. It's big with children and adults alike, and is open daily from 9 am to 10 pm (to 5 pm from October to March). Admission is f19.50/14 for adults/children. Take tram Nos 1 or 9, or bus No 22, from CS.

Scheveningen itself is an important fishing port and an over-developed seaside resort. There's plenty of beach, a fun-fair pier, and a casino in the landmark Kurhaus hotel. It gets very crowded on summer weekends.

Saturday is a busy shopping day in The Hague as elsewhere in the country, especially in the morning, which is a good time to visit. The indoor general market south of

Grote Marktstraat gets quite lively. The **Passage**, a glass-covered shopping arcade between Spuistraat, Buitenhof and Hofweg, is a stylish affair.

Getting There & Away Trains to/from Amsterdam (45 minutes, f16), Delft (five minutes, f3.75), Leiden (10 minutes, f7) and Rotterdam (15 minutes, f7) travel via Station HS, though the line that takes in Schiphol airport (40 minutes, f12.25) via Leiden on its way to/from Amsterdam uses CS. Utrecht trains (45 minutes, f16) use CS.

Delft

Historic Delft is well worth visiting for its 17th century buildings and its distinctive blue-and-white pottery – the famous delftware that 17th century artisans copied from Chinese porcelain. Delft is home to the country's largest technical university, which helps explain the high proportion of young males.

The train and neighbouring bus station are a 10-minute stroll south of the central Markt. The VVV (☎ 015-212 61 00) is at Markt 85.

Things to See & Do Most visitors come to buy delftware, and there are three factories where you can watch working artists. The most central and modest outfit is **Atelier de Candelaer** (☎ 015-213 18 48) at Kerkstraat 14. The other two factories sit poles apart outside the town centre. **De Delftse Pauw** (☎ 015-212 49 20) at Delftweg 133 is the smaller, employing 35 painters who work mainly from home (take tram No 1 to Pasgeld, walk up Broekmolenweg to the canal and turn left). It has daily tours but you won't see the painters on weekends. **De Porceleyne Fles** (☎ 015-256 92 14), south at Rotterdamseweg 196, is the only original factory operating since the 1650s, and is slick and pricey. Bus No 63 from the train station stops nearby, or it's a 25-minute walk from the town centre.

The 14th century **Nieuwe Kerk** houses the crypt of the Dutch royal family and the mausoleum of William the Silent. It's open daily except Sunday, and costs f2.50/1 for adults/children. The Gothic **Oude Kerk**, with 140 years' seniority and a two-metre tilt in its tower, is at Heilige Geestkerkhof. A combination ticket to both churches costs f4/1.50 for adults/children.

Opposite the Oude Kerk at St Agathaplein 1 is the **Prinsenhof**, a collection of buildings where William the Silent held court until he was assassinated in 1584 – the bullet hole in the wall has been enlarged by visitors' fingers and is now covered by perspex. The buildings host displays of historical and contemporary art Tuesday to Saturday from 10 am to 5 pm, Sunday from 1 pm; admission is f5/2.75 for adults/children.

Getting There & Away Delft is 10 minutes by train to Rotterdam, less to The Hague. A pleasant alternative to/from The Hague is tram No 1, which leaves every 15 minutes from in front of Delft train station for the 30-minute trip.

Rotterdam

The catastrophic bombardment of the country's second-largest city on 14 May 1940 left it crippled then and somewhat soulless today. Its centre is modern, with mirror-window skyscrapers and some extraordinarily innovative buildings. The city prides itself on this experimental architecture as well as on its port, the largest in the world. The Delta Works in the province of Zeeland south-west of the city, with massive causeways, bridges and mobile dams, were constructed after the disastrous floods of 1953 and represent Dutch water-engineering at its most grandiose.

Searching for a city 'centre' is fruitless: there is none. The sights are scattered over a large area, accessible by determined foot-slogging, metro or tram. The sights lie within a region bordered by the old town of Delfshaven, the Meuse river (Maas in Dutch) and the Blaak district. The VVV (☎ 0900-340 340 65) is at Coolsingel 67.

Things to See & Do The city's major museum is the **Boymans-van Beuningen** (☎ 010-441 94 00), a rich gallery of art from the 14th century to the present (Dutch, Flemish and Italian masters, Kandinsky, surrealists etc), at Museumpark 18-20. It's open Tuesday to Saturday from 10 am to 5 pm, Sunday from 11 am, and costs f6/3 for adults/children.

The 185-metre-high **Euromast** (☎ 010-436 48 11) pricks the skyline at Parkhaven 20, offering stunning views of the city and its harbour; admission is f14.50/9 for adults/children (tram No 6 or 9, or the metro to Dijkzigt). The **Kijk-Kubus**, a series of 'cube houses' with Escher-like design, offer a new angle to modern living. The display house is open daily from 11 am to 5 pm (from November to February it's open Friday to Sunday only). Adults/children pay f3.50/2.50 (metro: Blaak).

Rotterdam's old port (now closed off) is **Delfshaven**, where the Pilgrim Fathers set off for the New World in the *Speedwell*. They joined the *Mayflower* in Southampton but had to return there several times for repairs; eventually they gave the *Speedwell* up as unsafe and crowded on to the *Mayflower*. Before leaving Delfshaven they worshipped in the Oude Kerk at Aelbrechtskolk 20 (metro: Delfshaven).

Spido (☎ 010-413 54 00), Leuvehoofd 1, runs daily, 75-minute harbour cruises which cost f13/6.50 for adults/children, and day trips from f35 to the heart of the modern harbour at Europoort, or through the northern part of the Delta works (f42.50), taking in the windmills at Kinderdijk and the historic fortified town of Willemstad.

Getting There & Away There are trains every 15 minutes to/from Amsterdam (one hour, f21.75), Delft (10 minutes, f4.75), The Hague (15 minutes, f7) and Utrecht (40 minutes, f14). Half-hourly services run to/from Middelburg, the capital of Zeeland (1½ hours, f31) and Hook of Holland (30 minutes, f8).

Utrecht

Utrecht is a historic city, the ecclesiastical centre of the Low Countries from the early Middle Ages. Today it's an antique frame surrounding an increasingly modern interior, lorded over by the tower of the Dom (Cathedral), the country's tallest church tower. The 14th century canals, once-bustling wharves and cellars now brim with chic shops, restaurants and cafés. The student population (Utrecht is home to the country's largest university) adds spice to a once largely church-oriented community.

The most appealing quarter lies between Oudegracht and Nieuwegracht and the streets around the Dom. None of this historic character is evident when arriving at the train station, which lies behind Hoog Catharijne, the Netherlands' largest indoor shopping centre and a modern-day monstrosity. The VVV (☎ 0900-340 340 85) is five minutes east of the station at Vredenburg 90.

Things to See & Do There are excellent views from the **Dom Tower** after you've survived the 465 steps to the top. From April to October, it's open weekdays from 10 am to 5 pm, weekends from noon; at other times of the year it's open only on weekends from noon to 5 pm. Entry costs f4/2 for adults/children.

There are 14 museums, most of them bizarre hideaways for paraphernalia – a laundry museum is one example. The **Grocery Museum** on Hoogt 6 is worth 10 minutes: the one-room collection sits above a sweet shop filled with the popular Dutch *drop* (sweet or salted liquorice). It's open Tuesday to Saturday from 12.30 to 4.30 pm, and entry is free.

The **Nationaal Museum Van Speelklok tot Pierement** (National Museum From Musical Clock to Street Organ, ☎ 030-231 27 89), Buurkerkhof 10, has a colourful collection of musical machines from the 18th century onwards, demonstrated with gusto on hourly tours. It's open Tuesday to Saturday from 10 am to 5 pm, Sunday from 1 pm, and costs f7.50/5/4 for adults/students/children. **Het Catharijneconvent** (☎ 030-231 72 96) winds through a 15th century convent at Nieuwegracht 63 and has the country's largest collection of medieval Dutch art. It's open Tuesday to Friday from 10 am to 5 pm,

weekends from 11 am, and costs f5/3.50 for adults/children.

Getting There & Away Utrecht is the national rail hub, and there are frequent trains to/from Amsterdam (30 minutes, f10.75), Arnhem (40 minutes, f16), Den Bosch (30 minutes, f12.25), Maastricht (two hours, f39), Rotterdam (40 minutes, f14) and The Hague (45 minutes, f16).

EAST OF AMSTERDAM
Muiden
This historic town at the mouth of the Vecht river has a large yacht harbour, where you can rent sailing boats to tour the IJsselmeer (see Activities in the Things to See & Do chapter) or join an organised trip to the derelict fort on the island of Pampus. The VVV (☎ 0294-26 13 89), Kazernestraat 10, has details.

The main attraction in the town itself is **Muiderslot** (Muiden Castle, ☎ 0294-26 13 25), Herengracht 1, a 13th century castle where the popular count of Holland was murdered by jealous colleagues in 1296. In the 17th century the multi-talented PC Hooft entertained his male and female friends here; these gatherings of the century's greatest artists and scientists (including Vondel, Huygens, Grotius, Bredero and probably Descartes) became known as the Muiderkring (Muiden Circle). The period rooms dating from this time can be visited only on guided tours; ring to find out if you can join one in English (worth the effort).

Muiden is a pleasant bicycle trip from Amsterdam if the sun is out and the wind behaves itself. You can also take Midnet bus No 136 from the terminus at Weesperplein metro stop (it travels past the Arena Budget Hotel and Amstelstation). For a pleasant walk on a sunny day, stay on this bus to the beach at Muiderberg (near the bridge to Flevoland polder) and walk back several km along the dyke to Muiderslot.

Naarden
The fortifications and moat in the shape of a 12-pointed star around this little town were

built in the late 17th century, partly in response to the Spaniards' total massacre of the inhabitants a century earlier. The perfectly preserved walls and bastions were still staffed by the army until the 1920s, and can be visited at the **Vestingmuseum** (Fortress Museum, ☎ 035-694 54 59), Westwalstraat 6. The VVV (☎ 035-694 28 36) is at Adriaan Dortsmanplein 1B.

The town has become a bit of a tourist attraction and is well worth exploring for its quaint little houses and impressive **Grote Kerk**, with stunning vault paintings and famous St Matthew Passion performances over Easter. Czechs will be interested to know that the 17th century educational reformer Jan Amos Komensky (Comenius) is buried here – the **Comenius Museum** (☎ 035-694 30 45) is at Kloosterstraat 33.

There are two trains an hour from Centraal Station to the station at Naarden-Bussum (more trains if you change at Weesp), but bus No 136 (see the previous Muiden section) also brings you here.

Hoge Veluwe & Arnhem

The Hoge Veluwe (High Veluwe, pronounced VAY-loo-wer), about an hour's drive east of Amsterdam, is the country's largest national park and home to the prestigious Kröller-Müller museum with its vast collection of Van Goghs and sculptures.

The town of Arnhem is south of here, the site of fierce fighting in 1944 between the Germans and Allied airborne troops during the failed Operation Market Garden. Today it's a peaceful town, the closest base to the park if you're travelling by public transport.

The Arnhem VVV (☎ 0900-320 240 75) is at Stationsplein, to the left out of the train station, but is closed Sunday. Buses to the various sights leave from the right as you exit the station.

Things to See & Do Arnhem is a pleasant town, worth a quick look. Its pedestrianised centre around the well-hidden Korenmarkt is a five-minute walk from the station – head down Utrechtsestraat, cross over Willemsplein and cut through Korenstraat. The

Airborne Museum Hartenstein (☎ 026-333 77 10), Utrechtseweg 232 in the western suburb of Oosterbeek, is housed in the villa where the Allies had their temporary headquarters. It displays the failed Allied operation and is open weekdays from 11 am to 5 pm, Sundays from noon (bus No 1).

The **Open-Air Museum** (☎ 026-357 61 11) at Schelmseweg 89 has a collection of rural buildings including farmhouses, workshops and windmills, and is more attractive than it sounds. It's open from 1 April to 1 November (bus No 3).

The **Hoge Veluwe** park itself, covering nearly 5500 hectares, is a strange mix of forests and woods, shifting sands and heathery moors that provide a sense of isolation found nowhere else on the Dutch mainland. Red deer, wild boar and mouflon (a Mediterranean sheep) roam here. The area is most impressive from mid-August to mid-September when ablaze with heather, or during the red deer's rutting season in September and October, and is best seen on foot or bicycle – 400 white bicycles are available free of charge from the visitor centre inside the park.

There are three entrances, but if you're using public transport the easiest route is with special bus No 12 that leaves from the VVV in Arnhem and goes to the visitor centre. It runs at least three times a day from early April to 31 October and costs f7.35/4.15 return for adults/children. Alternatively, you could catch the hourly bus No 107 from Arnhem bus station to Otterlo. From there, you can either follow the signs to the entrance one km away and then walk the remaining four km to the visitor centre or wait for the hourly bus No 110 to Hoenderloo which will drop you at the visitor centre. The park is open daily from 8 or 9 am to sunset and costs f8/4/8 for adults/children/cars. A Museumcard is not valid.

The **Kröller-Müller Museum** (☎ 0318-59 10 41), Houtkampweg 6, Otterlo, is near the Hoge Veluwe visitor centre. Its 278 Van Goghs are only a start: there are works by Picasso and Mondriaan, and out the back is Europe's largest sculpture garden, with works by Dubuffet, Rodin, Moore, Hepworth and Giacometti, among others. Admission is included in the park fee. It's open Tuesday to Sunday from 10 am to 5 pm.

Getting There & Away Trains to/from

Amsterdam (f25.25, 65 minutes) and Rotterdam (f28.75, 75 minutes) go via Utrecht (f16, 40 minutes).

There are a couple of Rail Idee packages to the Hoge Veluwe but these aren't good value.

Index

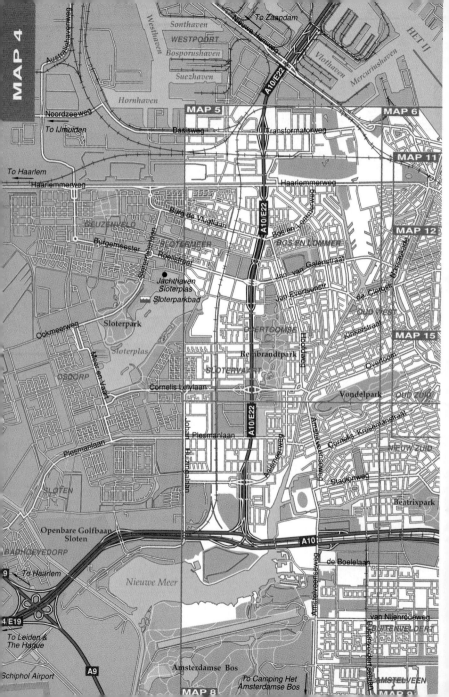

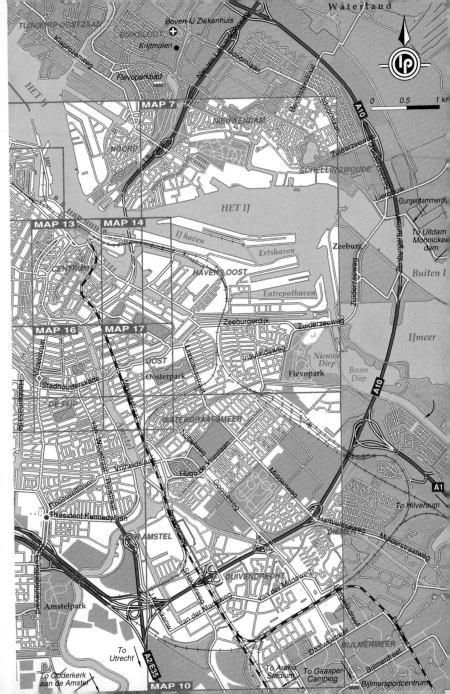

Top: Walkers in the Vondelpark
Left: Tulips for sale, (or flower power)
Right: Details of 'The Ship', a highlight of Amsterdam School architecture

DOEKES LULOFS

TONY WHEELER

DOEKES LULOFS

MAP 6

1 Tong Chow
2 Egyptian Coptic Church
3 Galaxy Hotel
4 Mosveld Market
5 Willemsluis
6 Pier 10
7 De Trut
8 Riaz

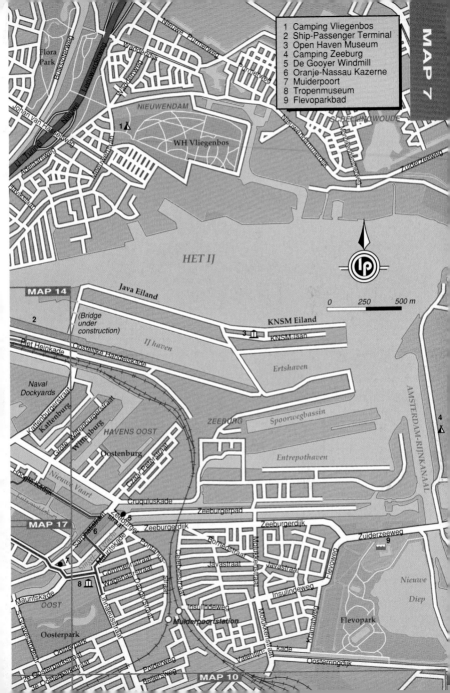

MAP 7

1 Camping Vliegenbos
2 Ship-Passenger Terminal
3 Open Haven Museum
4 Camping Zeeburg
5 De Gooyer Windmill
6 Oranje-Nassau Kazerne
7 Muiderpoort
8 Tropenmuseum
9 Flevoparkbad

Flora Park

Johan van Ha... ...euwen

IJ-Tunnel

NIEUWENDAM

WH Vliegenbos

SCHELLINGWOUDE

HET IJ

MAP 14

Java Eiland

(Bridge under construction)

KNSM Eiland

KNSM-laan

Piet Heinkade

Oostelijke Handelskade

IJ haven

Ertshaven

AMSTERDAM-RIJNKANAAL

Naval Dockyards

Kattenburg

Wittenburg

ZEEBURG

Spoorwegbassin

HAVENS OOST

Oostenburg

Entrepothaven

Nieuwe Vaart

Czaar Peterstraat

Cruquiuskade

MAP 17

Zeeburgerpad

Zeeburgerdijk

Zeeburgerdijk

Zuiderzeeweg

Pontanusstraat

Borneostraat

Molukkenstraat

Javastraat

Javastraat

Flevoweg

Nieuwe Diep

Mauritskade

OOST

Commeliustraat

Insulindeweg

Flevopark

Oosterpark

Waldenlaan

Insulindeweg

Muiderpoortstation

Kramatweg

Oosterringdijk

2e Oosterparkstraat

Polderweg

Oosterringdijk

MAP 10

0   250   500 m

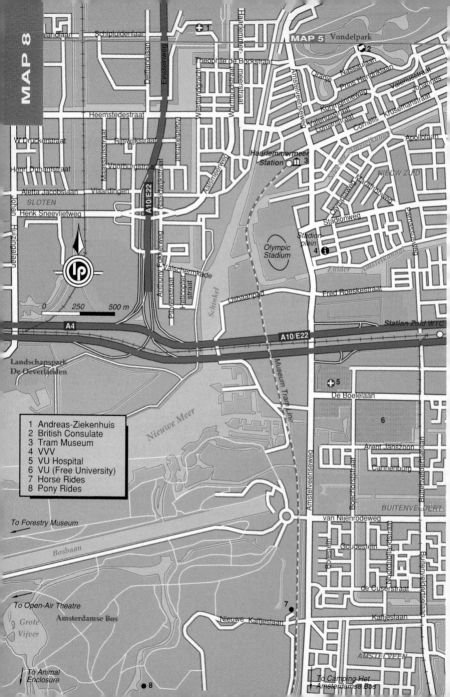

MAP 8

MAP 5 Vondelpark

Ierlandlaan Schipluidenlaan
Einsteinweg
Delflandlaan
Theophile de Bockstraat
Haarlemmermeerstraat
Westlandgracht
Warmondstraat
Amstelveenseweg
Oranje
Nassaulaan
Prins Hendriklaan
Valeriusstraat
Johannes

Heemstedestraat
Koninginneweg
Valeriusstraat
Lomanstraat
Cornelis
Krusemanstraat
Apollolaan

W. Druckerstraat
Rijswijkstraat
Maasstraat
Vlaardingen
NIEUW ZUID

Henri Dunantstraat
Marasstraat
Voorburgstraat
Naaldwijkstraat

Aletta Jacobslaan
Vlaardingen
Haarlemmermeer-
Station
3
Olympiaweg
Marathonweg
Apollolaan

SLOTEN
Henk Sneevlietweg
Aalsmeerweg
Stadionweg

Johan Huizingalaan
Anthony Fokkerweg
Valschermkade
Helikopterstraat
Pilotenstraat
Olympic
Stadium
Stadion-
plein
4
Zuider Amstelkanaal

0 250 500 m

A4
Schinkel
Ringsloot
Fred Roeskestraat

A10/E22
A10/E22
Station Zuid WTC

Landschapspark
De Oeverlanden
Museum Tram Line
5
De Boelelaan

Nieuwe Meer
6
Arent Janszoon
Cannenburg

BUITENVELDERT

1 Andreas-Ziekenhuis
2 British Consulate
3 Tram Museum
4 VVV
5 VU Hospital
6 VU (Free University)
7 Horse Rides
8 Pony Rides

To Forestry Museum
Amstelveenseweg
van Nijenrodeweg

Bosbaan
Boelelaan
Goudestein

To Open-Air Theatre
Amsterdamse Bos
7
Noordhollandstraat
Buitenveldertselaan

Grote
Vijver
Nieuwe Kalfjeslaan
de Cuserstraat
Kalfjeslaan

To Animal
Enclosure
8
AMSTELVEEN

To Camping Het
Amsterdamse Bos

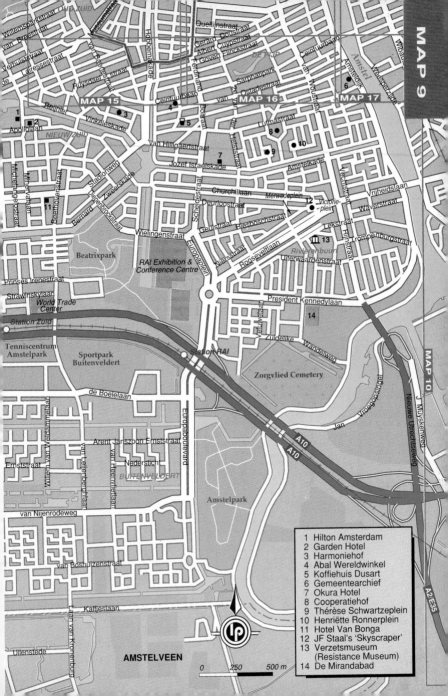

MAP 15
MAP 16
MAP 17
MAP 10

1 Williamsparkstraat
van Breestraat
Vermulststraat
Lairessestraat
Ruysdaelstraat
Apollolaan
NIEUW ZUID
Michelangelostraat
Beethovenstraat
Bernard
Reijnier
Vinkeleskade
Stadionweg
Zuider Amstellaan
Zweerskade
Van Hilligaertstraat
Jozef Israëlskade
Schinkelstraat
Beethovenstraat

OUD ZUID

Quellijnstraat
Gerard Doustraat
Albert Cuypstraat
Ferdinand
Govert Flinckstraat
Hobbemakade
Centuurbaan
Sarphatipark
van Ostadestraat
van der
DE PIJP
Ruysdaelkade
Hemonystraat
Amstel
Ceintuurbaan
Boerhaave
Lutmastraat

Amsteldijk
Weesperzijde
Maasstraat

Amstelkade

Merwedeplein
Churchilllaan
Victorieplein
Deurloostraat
Geulstraat
Biesboschstraat
Waverstraat
Vrijheidslaan
Vechtstraat
Rijnstraat
Lekstraat
Trompenburgstraat

Wielingenstraat
Europaplein
Maasstraat
Rooseveltlaan
Rivierenbuurt
Uiterwaardenstraat

Beatrixpark

RAI Exhibition &
Conference Centre

Prinses Irenestraat
Strawinskylaan
World Trade
Center
Station Zuid

President Kennedylaan
Kennedylaan
Zuidelijke Wandelweg

Tenniscentrum
Amstelpark
Sportpark
Buitenveldert
Station RAI

Zorgvlied Cemetery

de Boelelaan

Arent Janszoon Ernststraat
Nedersticht
BUITENVELDERT
Ernststraat
Willem van Weldammelaan
van Leijenberghlaan
van Nijenrodeweg

Amstelpark

Jan
Vroegopsingel
Nieuwe Utrechtseweg
J. Muyskenweg

A10
A10

van Boshuizenstraat

van Nijenrodeweg

Kalfjeslaan

Laan van Kronenburg
Uilenstede

AMSTELVEEN

A2/E35

0   250   500 m

1 Hilton Amsterdam
2 Garden Hotel
3 Harmoniehof
4 Abal Wereldwinkel
5 Koffiehuis Dusart
6 Gemeentearchief
7 Okura Hotel
8 Cooperatiehof
9 Thérèse Schwartzeplein
10 Henriëtte Ronnerplein
11 Hotel Van Bonga
12 JF Staal's 'Skyscraper'
13 Verzetsmuseum
    (Resistance Museum)
14 De Mirandabad

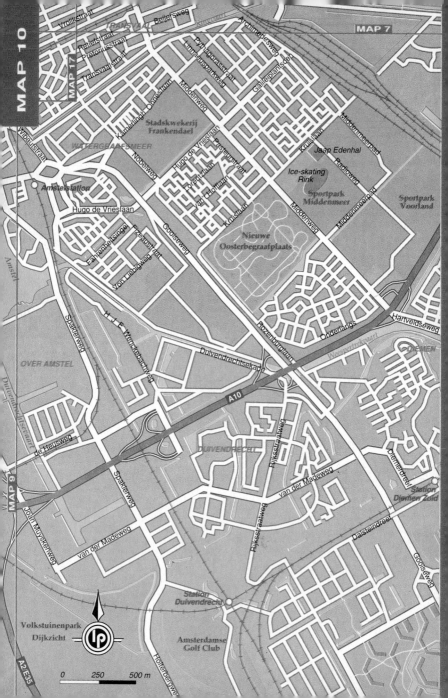

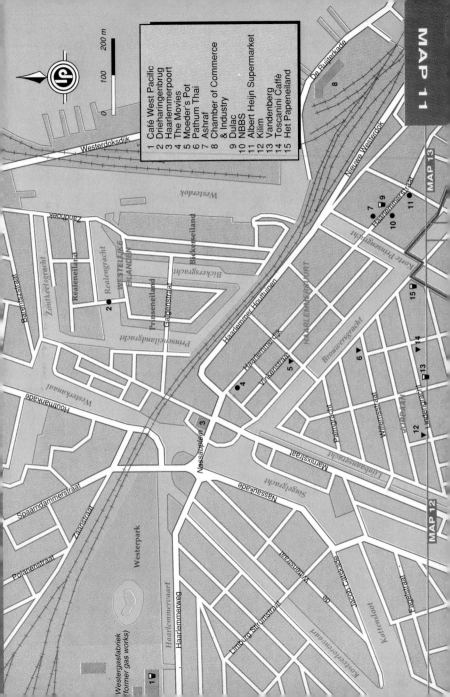

MAP 11

1 Café West Pacific
2 Drieharingenbrug
3 Haarlemmerpoort
4 The Movies
5 Moeder's Pot
6 Pathum Thai
7 Ashraf
8 Chamber of Commerce
  & Industry
9 Dulac
10 NBBS
11 Albert Heijn Supermarket
12 Kilim
13 Vandenberg
14 Toscanini Caffè
15 Het Papeneiland

MAP 12

MAP 11

Lindengracht

Noorder-
markt

1

11

12

Westerstraat

2

3

4

5

8

9

10

Abjelierssstraat

6 7

JORDAAN

Tuinstraat

Egelantiersstraat

17

16

18

19

Egelantiersgracht

13

14

15

21

26

27

23

Nieuwe Lelliestraat

25

28

22

24

29

Bloemgracht

30

Westermarkt

31

32

33

37

36

Bloemstraat

39

40

41

42 43

35

44

34

Rozengracht

45

38

Rozenstraat

52

Laurierstraat

56 57

Reestraat

Hartenstraat

55

Lauriergracht

54

46

58

47

60

50

Elandsstraat

53

63

61 62

48

49

51

Berenstraat

Wolvenstraat

JORDAAN

64

Elandsgracht

75

67 68

71

73

74 76

Runstraat

Huidenstraat

77

69 70

78

Spui

72

79

80

81

65

82

66

83

91

84

85

86

87 Koningspl

90 88

89

0   100   200 m

95

93 94

MAP 15

92

PLACES TO STAY

16 Hotel Toren
17 Canal House Hotel
24 Hotel van Onna
28 Bill's Residence
34 Eben Haëzer
40 Budget Hotel Bonaire
41 Hotel Clemens
42 Hotel Pax
43 Hotel De Westertoren
45 Pulitzer Hotel
57 Hotel Belga
60 Hotel Estheréa
73 Ambassade Hotel
85 Waterfront Hotel
87 Hotel Agora
93 International Budget Hotel

PLACES TO EAT

3 Albatros
5 Jean Jean
6 Burger's Patio
8 De Bolhoed
10 The Pancake Bakery
15 Spanjer en van Twist
22 De Vliegende Schotel
23 Restaurant Speciaal
68 Cilubang
70 Tout Court
74 d'Vijff Vlieghen Restaurant
75 Haesje Claes

CAFÉS

4 Café Nol
7 De Tuin
9 De II Prinsen
13 De 2 Zwaantjes
14 De Prins
21 De Reiger
51 Vrouwencafé Saarein
54 Van Puffelen
62 Gollem
67 De Doffer
76 Harry's American Bar
78 Hoppe
80 Luxembourg
94 De Pieper

OTHER

1 Noorderkerk
2 Marnixbad
11 Greenland Warehouses

12 Euro Business Center
18 House with the Heads
19 Club 114
20 Deco
25 Bike City
26 Anne Frankhuis
27 Greenpeace Headquarters
29 René Descartes Residence
30 Westerkerk
31 Homomonument
32 Theatermuseum
33 Bartolotti House
35 Mazzo
36 Wegewijs Kaas & Delicatessen
37 Simon Lévelt
38 COC Amsterdam
39 Vrouwen in Druk
44 Main Post Office
46 Moped Rental Service
47 MacBike
48 Korsakoff
49 Maloe Melo
50 The English Bookshop
52 Bangla Klamboe Imports
53 Xantippe
55 Groote Keyser
56 Gilde Amsterdam
58 Musiques du Monde
59 Intermale
61 Au Bout du Monde
63 Evenaar Literaire Reisboekhandel
64 Felix Meritis Building
65 Amber Travel Agency
66 Police Headquarters
69 Bakkerij Paul Annee
71 Fair Trade Shop
72 Bijbels Museum
77 Athenaeum Bookshop & Newsagency
79 Pied á Terre
81 Lutheran Church
82 The Mini Office
83 University Library
84 Krijtberg
86 Odeon
88 Albert Heijn Supermarket
89 Maranón Hangmatten
90 Scheltema Holkema Vermeulen
91 Centrale Bibliotheek (Main Public Library)
92 Thermos Day Sauna
95 Metz & Co Department Store

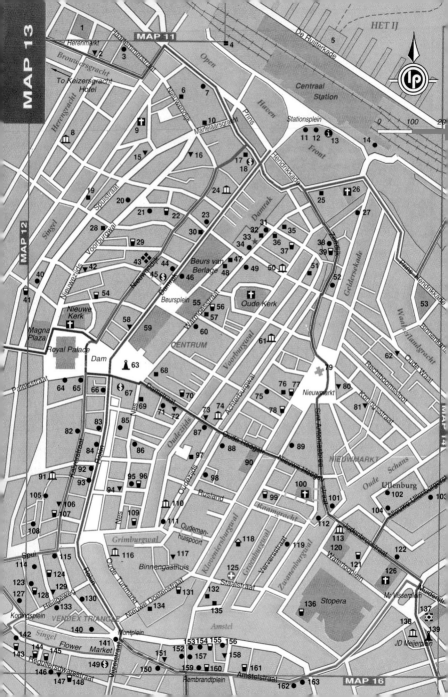

MAP 13

MAP 11

HET IJ

De Ruijterkade

Centraal
Station

MAP 16

MAP 12

continued on next page...

RICHARD NEBESKY

Royal Palace on Dam square

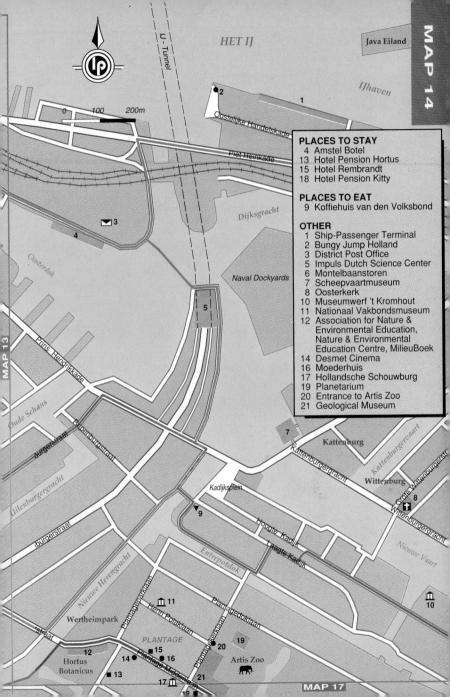

MAP 14

HET IJ

Java Eiland

IJhaven

Oostelijke Handelskade

Piet Heinkade

IJ - Tunnel

0   100   200m

Dijksgracht

Oosterdok

Naval Dockyards

MAP 13

Prins Hendrikade

Oude Schans

Burgerstraat

Rapenburgerstraat

Uilenburgergracht

Iburgerstraat

Kattenburg

Kattenburgergracht

Wittenburg

Kattenburgervaart

Grote Wittenburgerstraat

Wittenburgergracht

Nieuwe Vaart

Kadijksplein

Hoogte - Kadijk

Laagte Kadijk

Entrepotdok

Nieuwe Herengracht

Plantagedoklaan

Henri Polaklaan

Plantage Middenlaan

Plantagedoklaan

Plantage Kerklaan

Wertheimpark

PLANTAGE

Hortus
Botanicus

...straat

Artis Zoo

MAP 17

PLACES TO STAY
4   Amstel Botel
13 Hotel Pension Hortus
15 Hotel Rembrandt
18 Hotel Pension Kitty

PLACES TO EAT
9   Koffiehuis van den Volksbond

OTHER
1   Ship-Passenger Terminal
2   Bungy Jump Holland
3   District Post Office
5   Impuls Dutch Science Center
6   Montelbaanstoren
7   Scheepvaartmuseum
8   Oosterkerk
10 Museumwerf 't Kromhout
11 Nationaal Vakbondsmuseum
12 Association for Nature &
    Environmental Education,
    Nature & Environmental
    Education Centre, MilieuBoek
14 Desmet Cinema
16 Moederhuis
17 Hollandsche Schouwburg
19 Planetarium
20 Entrance to Artis Zoo
21 Geological Museum

MAP 15

OUD WEST

MAP 12

Leidsegracht

Keizersgracht

Marnixstraat

Leidsekade

Nassaukade

Tweede Helmersstraat

Eerste Helmersstraat

Eerste Helmersstraat

Overtoom

Constantijn

Vondelstraat

Roemer Visscher straat

Stadhouderskade

Leidsekade

Korte

Lange

Leidsedwarsstraat

Kerkstraat

Prinsengracht

Leidsestraat

Leidsekruisstraat

Leidsedwarsstraat

Nieuwe Spiegelstraat

Leidseplein

Max Euweplein

Weteringschans

Spiegelgracht

Singelgracht

Stadhouderskade

Lijnbaansgracht

To Vondelkerk

Zandpad

Vossiusstraat

Vondelpark

Huygensstraat

Hobbemastraat

To Round Blue Teahouse

Pieter

Cornelisz Hooftstraat

Jan Luijkenstraat

Van de Veldestraat

Paulus Potterstraat

Teniers straat

Ruysdaelkade

Hobbemakade

Boerenwetering

DE PIJP

OUD ZUID

van Breestraat

Museumstraat

Museumplein

Vermeerstraat

Johannes

Jacob Obrechtstraat

Concertge-bouwplein

van Baerlestraat

de Lairessestraat

Banstraat

Nicolaas Maesstraat

Frans van Mierisstraat

Ruysdaelstraat

JM Coenenstraat

Albert   Cuypstraat

Ceintuurbaan

0   100   200 m

PLACES TO STAY
2 International Budget Hotel
16 Hotel Titus
17 Hotel Impala
18 Hotel Kooyk
19 Hotel King
20 The Hotel Quentin
22 American Hotel
29 Aerohotel
36 Hotel Orfeo
38 Hotel Hans Brinker
50 Golden Tulip Barbizon Centre
51 Marriott Hotel
54 Hotel Sipermann
55 Hotel Parkzicht
56 Vondelpark Youth Hostel
64 Hotel Smit
66 Hotel Museumzicht
67 Hotel PC Hooft
68 Hotel Acro
72 Hotel Acca International
80 Hotel Bema
81 Hotel Peters

PLACES TO EAT
14 Indonesia
35 Bojo
39 Shizen
40 Françoise Coffee Gallery
41 Piccolino
42 De Blauwe Hollander
63 Deshima Proeflokaal

CAFÉS
3 De Pieper
12 Eylders
13 Reynders
23 Café Americain

OTHER
1 Thermos Day Sauna
4 Metz & Co Department Store
5 PC Hooft Store
6 Paleis van Justitie
7 Boom Chicago

8 Iboya
9 Bamboo Bar
10 Canecão
11 Police Station
15 Melkweg
21 Theater Bellevue
24 Stadsschouwburg
25 VVV office
26 De Uitkijk
27 Mandate
28 The Clean Brothers
30 Thermos Night Sauna
31 Lambiek
32 Keizersgrachtkerk
33 Conscious Dreams
34 Milk Factory
37 Bourbon Street Jazz & Blues Club
43 Jazz Café Alto
44 Amsterdam Uitburo
45 Thomas Cook
46 HIV Vereniging & Lesbisch Archief
47 Perry Sport
48 Bever Zwerfsport
49 Albert Heijn Supermarket
52 Jacob van Wijngaarden
53 Nederlands Filmmuseum
57 Byzantium Complex
58 Casino
59 Max Euwe Centrum
60 De Balie
61 Paradiso
62 Bell Tree Toy Shop
65 SAD-Schorerstichting
69 Rijksmuseum
70 Awareness Winkel
71 Coster Diamonds
73 Stedelijk Museum
74 Van Gogh Museum
75 Zuiderbad
76 ANWB Office
77 US Consulate
78 Concertgebouw
79 KLM Office
82 Abal Wereldwinkel

DOEKES LULOFS

Playful reliefs on the former PC Hooft store

MAP 16

MAP 15

MAP 17

MAP 13

1
2
3
4 🏛
5 ▼
6
Rembrandtplein
Amstelstraat
14
15
13 🏛

Reguliersdwarsstraat

Thorbecke-
plein
7
8
9
10
11
12

17
18
Herengracht
19 🏛

Vijzelstraat
Reguliers
gracht

Keizersgracht
20

21 ▼
Utrechtsestraat
Amstel

Nieuwe Herengracht
16

Nieuwe
Keizersgracht

Nieuwe Kerkstraat

Nieuwe
Prinsengracht

27 🏛
28 ▼
29
30
Kerkstraat

26
25
24 ▼
Kerkstraat

Magere
Brug

22
23

Prinsengracht
33
34 ▼
35

31
32
Amstel-
veld

38
39 ▼
37
36 ✝

Amstel-
sluizen

40

41

42
43
44
45
Weteringstr.

Fokke Simonszstraat

Utrechtse
dwarsstraat
Achtergracht

Lijnbaansgracht

46

Falckstraat

Frederiksplein

Sarphatistraat
47

Wetering-
plantsoen
49 ▼ 48

Weteringschans

Singelgracht

Nederlandsche
Bank

Westeinde
Oosteinde

Stadhouderskade
50
Stadhouderskade

Marie
Heineken-
plein
51
Quellijnstraat
52
53 ▼

54 ▼

Amsteldijk

55

Daniel Stalpertstraat
Ferdinand
Bolstraat

Gerard Doustraat
Albert Cuyp Market
Albert Cuypstraat

DE PIJP

Govert Flinckstraat
56 ▼

Sarphatipark

Ceintuurbaan
van

Ceintuurbaan
van der
2e van der Helststraat
Sarphatipark
Ostadestraat

57

Woustraat

0   100   200 m

RICHARD NEBESKY

Statue of the master on Rembrandtplein

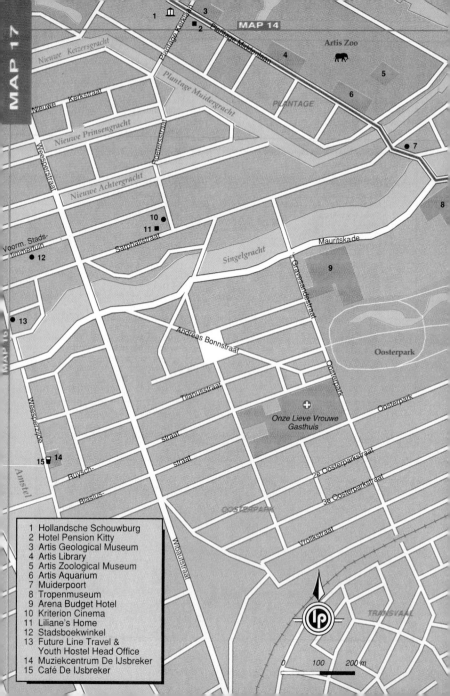

MAP 17

MAP 14

Artis Zoo

Nieuwe Keizersgracht

Plantage Kerklaan

Plantage Middenlaan

PLANTAGE

Plantage Muidergracht

Nieuwe Kerkstraat

Nieuwe Prinsengracht

Nieuwe Achtergracht

Roetersstraat

Weesperstraat

Voorm. Stads-timmertuin

Sarphatistraat

Singelgracht

Mauritskade

Andreas Bonnstraat

'sGravesandestraat

Oosterpark

Oosterpark

Titiausstraat

straat

Onze Lieve Vrouwe Gasthuis

Oosterpark

Weesperzijde

Amstel

Ruysch-

straat

2e Oosterparkstraat

Blasius-

3e Oosterparkstraat

OOSTERPARK

Wibautstraat

Vrolikstraat

TRANSVAAL

1 Hollandsche Schouwburg
2 Hotel Pension Kitty
3 Artis Geological Museum
4 Artis Library
5 Artis Zoological Museum
6 Artis Aquarium
7 Muiderpoort
8 Tropenmuseum
9 Arena Budget Hotel
10 Kriterion Cinema
11 Liliane's Home
12 Stadsboekwinkel
13 Future Line Travel &
   Youth Hostel Head Office
14 Muziekcentrum De IJsbreker
15 Café De IJsbreker

0   100   200 m

MAP LEGEND

ROUTES

Freeway
Highway
Major Road
Minor Road
City Road
City Street
Railway
Metro
Ferry Route

WALKING TOURS

Red Route
Blue Route
Green Route
Grey Route
Purple Route
Brown Route

AREA FEATURES

Park, Gardens
Building
Hotel
Pedestrian Mall
Market
Cemetery
Built-Up Area

BOUNDARIES

International Boundary
Suburb Boundary

HYDROGRAPHIC FEATURES

River, Creek
Intermittent River or Creek
Rapids, Waterfalls
Lake, Intermittent Lake

SYMBOLS

✪ CAPITAL		National Capital
◉ Capital		Regional Capital
CITY		Major City
● City		City
● Town		Town
● Village		Village
■ ▼		Place to Stay, Place to Eat
⚑ ♟		Cafe, Pub or Bar
✉ ☎		Post Office, Telephone
❶ ❸		Tourist Information, Bank
⊜ ℗		Transport, Parking
🏛 ⚐		Museum, Youth Hostel
⚏ ⚘		Caravan Park, Camping Ground
✚ ✚		Church, Cathedral
☾ ✡		Mosque, Synagogue
卍 卐		Buddhist Temple, Hindu Temple
✛ ★		Hospital, Police Station

◔	⛽	Embassy, Petrol Station
✈	✝	Airport, Airfield
▭	❋	Swimming Pool, Gardens
✦	🐘	Shopping Centre, Zoo
⚘	⛰	Winery or Vineyard, Picnic Site
←	A25	One Way Street, Route Number
🏛	▲	Stately Home, Monument
Ⱥ	□	Castle, Tomb
⌂	⛺	Cave, Hut or Chalet
▲	❋	Mountain or Hill, Lookout
⛫	⚓	Lighthouse, Shipwreck
)(	●	Pass, Spring
⚐	⚐	Beach, Surf Beach
	∴	Archaeological Site or Ruins
		Ancient or City Wall
		Cliff or Escarpment, Tunnel
		Railway Station

Note: not all symbols displayed above appear in this book